W9-BQM-726

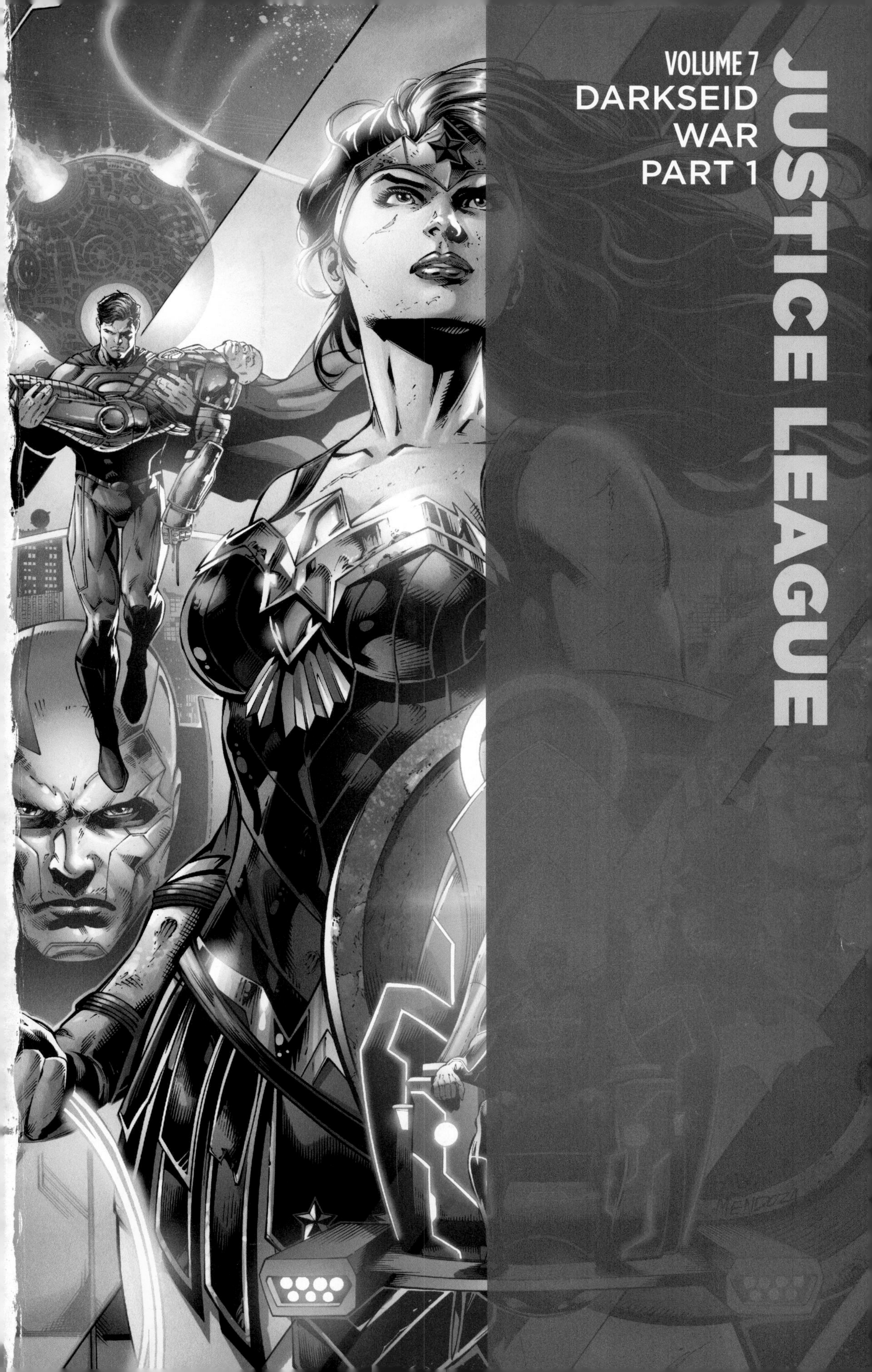

JUSTICE LEAGUE

VOLUME 7
DARKSEID WAR
PART 1

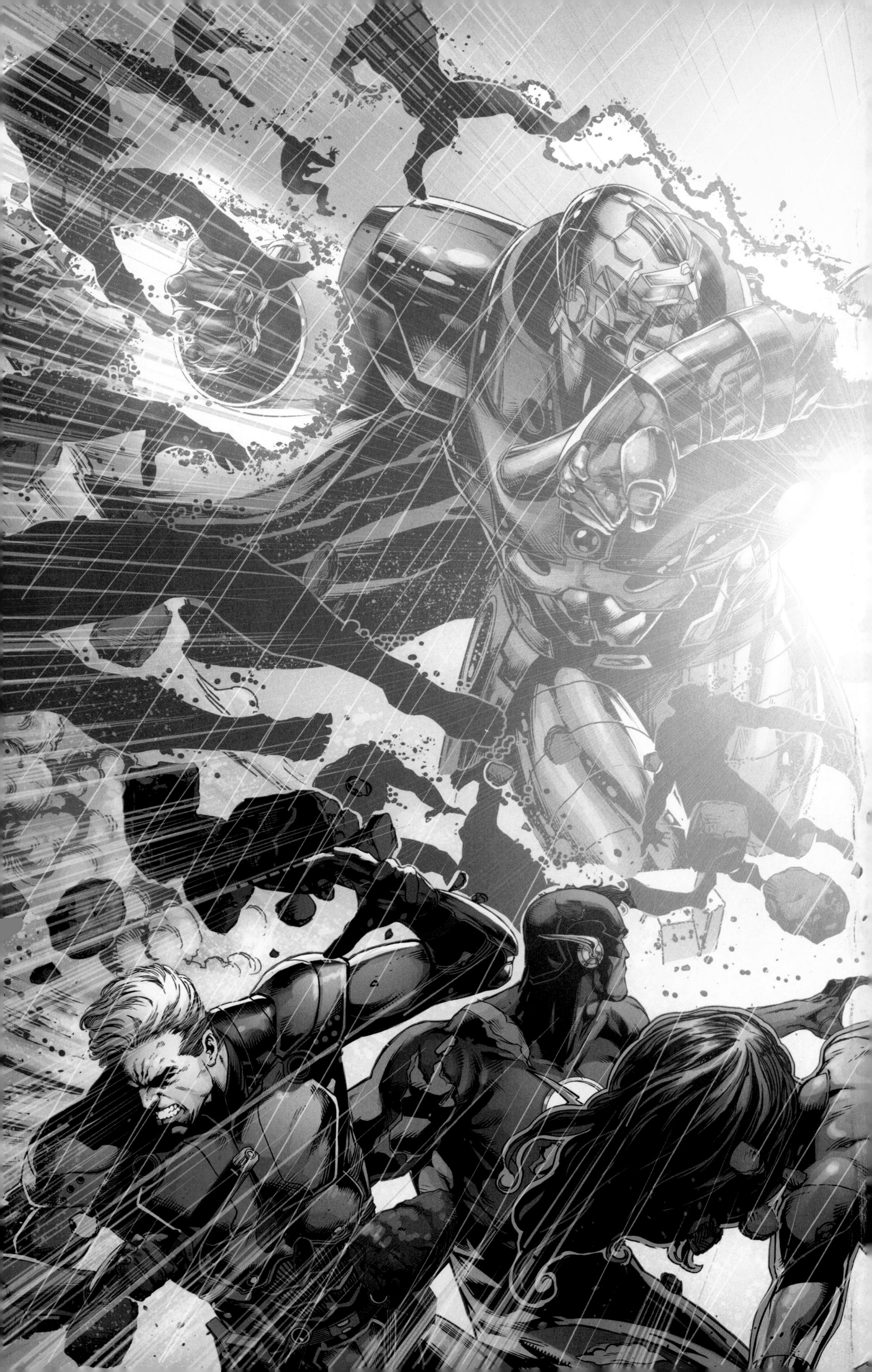

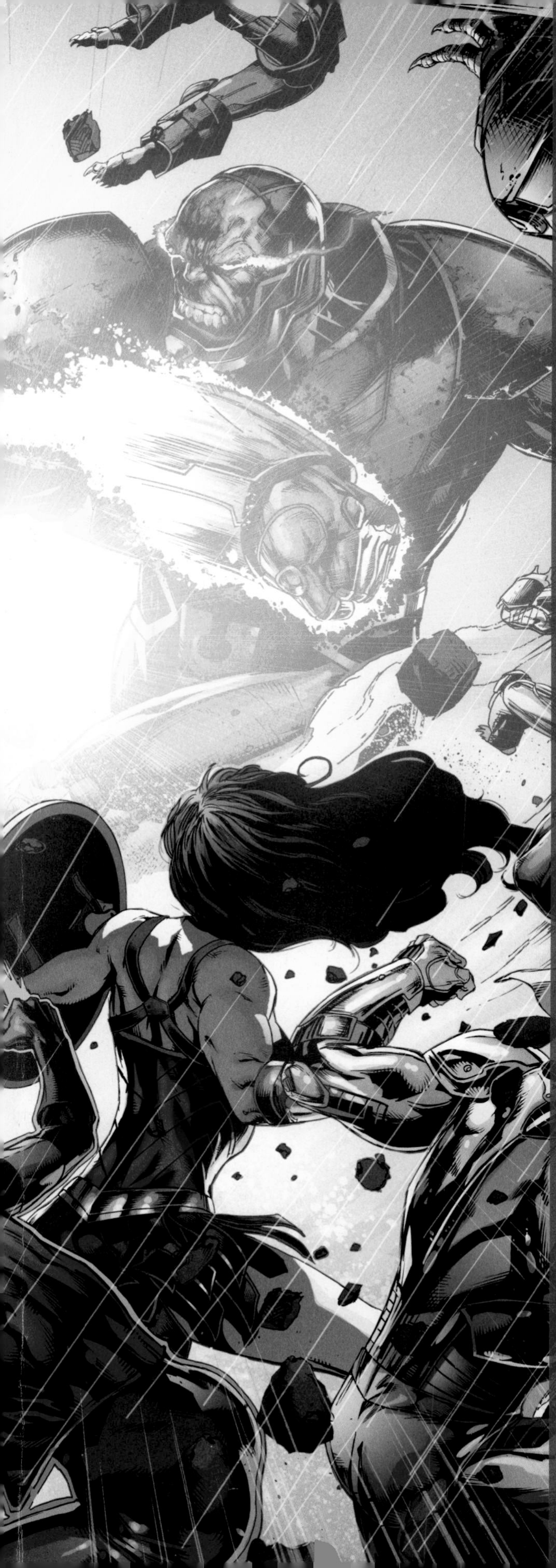

JUSTICE LEAGUE

VOLUME 7
DARKSEID WAR PART 1

WRITTEN BY
GEOFF JOHNS

ART BY
JASON FABOK
KEVIN MAGUIRE
PHIL JIMENEZ
DAN JURGENS
JERRY ORDWAY
SCOTT KOLINS
JIM LEE
SCOTT WILLIAMS

COLOR BY
BRAD ANDERSON
ALEX SINCLAIR

LETTERS BY
ROB LEIGH

COLLECTION COVER ART BY
JASON FABOK &
BRAD ANDERSON

SUPERMAN CREATED BY
JERRY SIEGEL &
JOE SHUSTER
BY SPECIAL ARRANGEMENT
WITH THE JERRY SIEGEL FAMILY

THE NEW GODS CREATED BY
JACK KIRBY

BRIAN CUNNINGHAM Editor – Original Series
AMEDEO TURTURRO Assistant Editor – Original Series
JEB WOODARD Group Editor – Collected Editions
ROBIN WILDMAN Editor – Collected Edition
STEVE COOK Design Director – Books
DAMIAN RYLAND Publication Design

BOB HARRAS Senior VP – Editor-in-Chief, DC Comics

DIANE NELSON President
DAN DIDIO and JIM LEE Co-Publishers
GEOFF JOHNS Chief Creative Officer
AMIT DESAI Senior VP – Marketing & Global Franchise Management
NAIRI GARDINER Senior VP – Finance
SAM ADES VP – Digital Marketing
BOBBIE CHASE VP – Talent Development
MARK CHIARELLO Senior VP – Art, Design & Collected Editions
JOHN CUNNINGHAM VP – Content Strategy
ANNE DEPIES VP – Strategy Planning & Reporting
DON FALLETTI VP – Manufacturing Operations
LAWRENCE GANEM VP – Editorial Administration & Talent Relations
ALISON GILL Senior VP – Manufacturing & Operations
HANK KANALZ Senior VP – Editorial Strategy & Administration
JAY KOGAN VP – Legal Affairs
DEREK MADDALENA Senior VP – Sales & Business Development
JACK MAHAN VP – Business Affairs
DAN MIRON VP – Sales Planning & Trade Development
NICK NAPOLITANO VP – Manufacturing Administration
CAROL ROEDER VP – Marketing
EDDIE SCANNELL VP – Mass Account & Digital Sales
COURTNEY SIMMONS Senior VP – Publicity & Communications
JIM (SKI) SOKOLOWSKI VP – Comic Book Specialty & Newsstand Sales
SANDY YI Senior VP – Global Franchise Management

JUSTICE LEAGUE VOLUME 7: DARKSEID WAR PART 1

DC Comics, 2900 West Alameda Avenue, Burbank, CA 91505
Printed by RR Donnelley, Salem, VA, USA. 2/5/16. First Printing.
ISBN: 978-1-4012-5977-8

Library of Congress Cataloging-in-Publication Data is available.

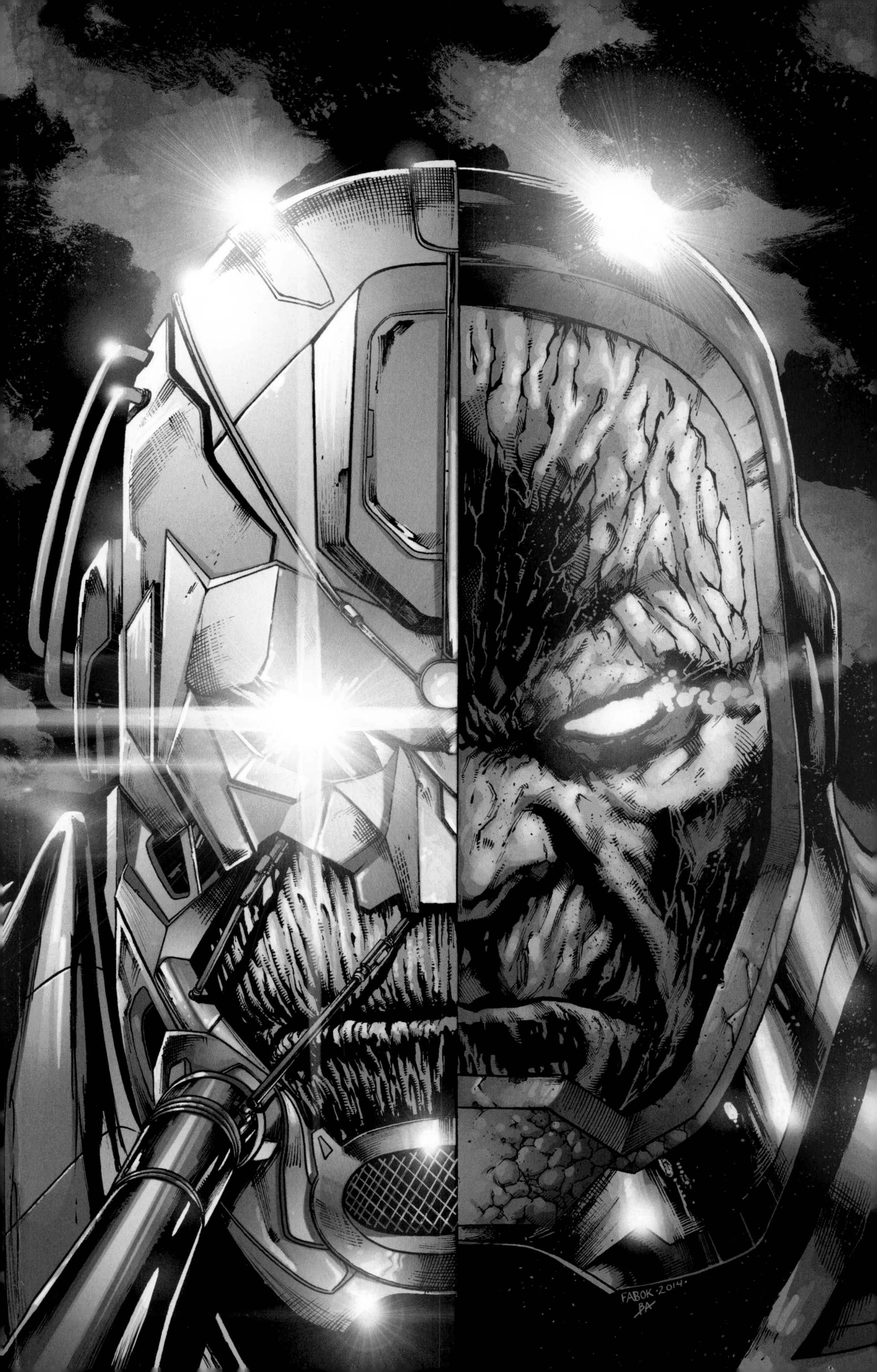
FABOK ·2014·
BA

DARKSEID WAR SNEAK PEEK GEOFF JOHNS writer JASON FABOK artist BRAD ANDERSON colorist ROB LEIGH letterer
DARKSEID WAR PROLOGUE GEOFF JOHNS writer KEVIN MAGUIRE, PHIL JIMENEZ, DAN JURGENS, JERRY ORDWAY, SCOTT KOLINS, JASON FABOK, JIM LEE, SCOTT WILLIAMS artists BRAD ANDERSON, ALEX SINCLAIR colorists ROB LEIGH letterer cover by JASON FABOK & BRAD ANDERSON

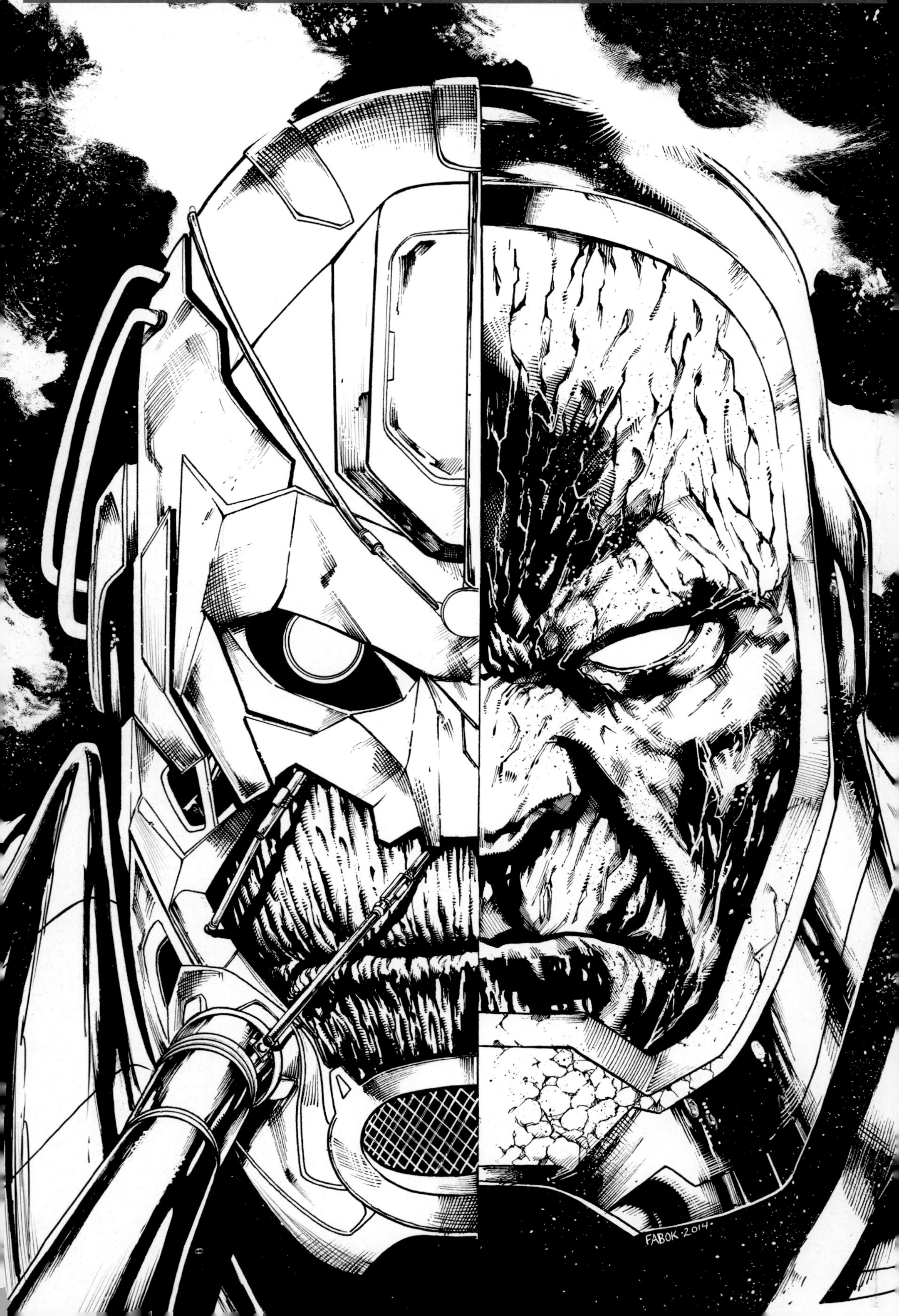
FABOK·2014·

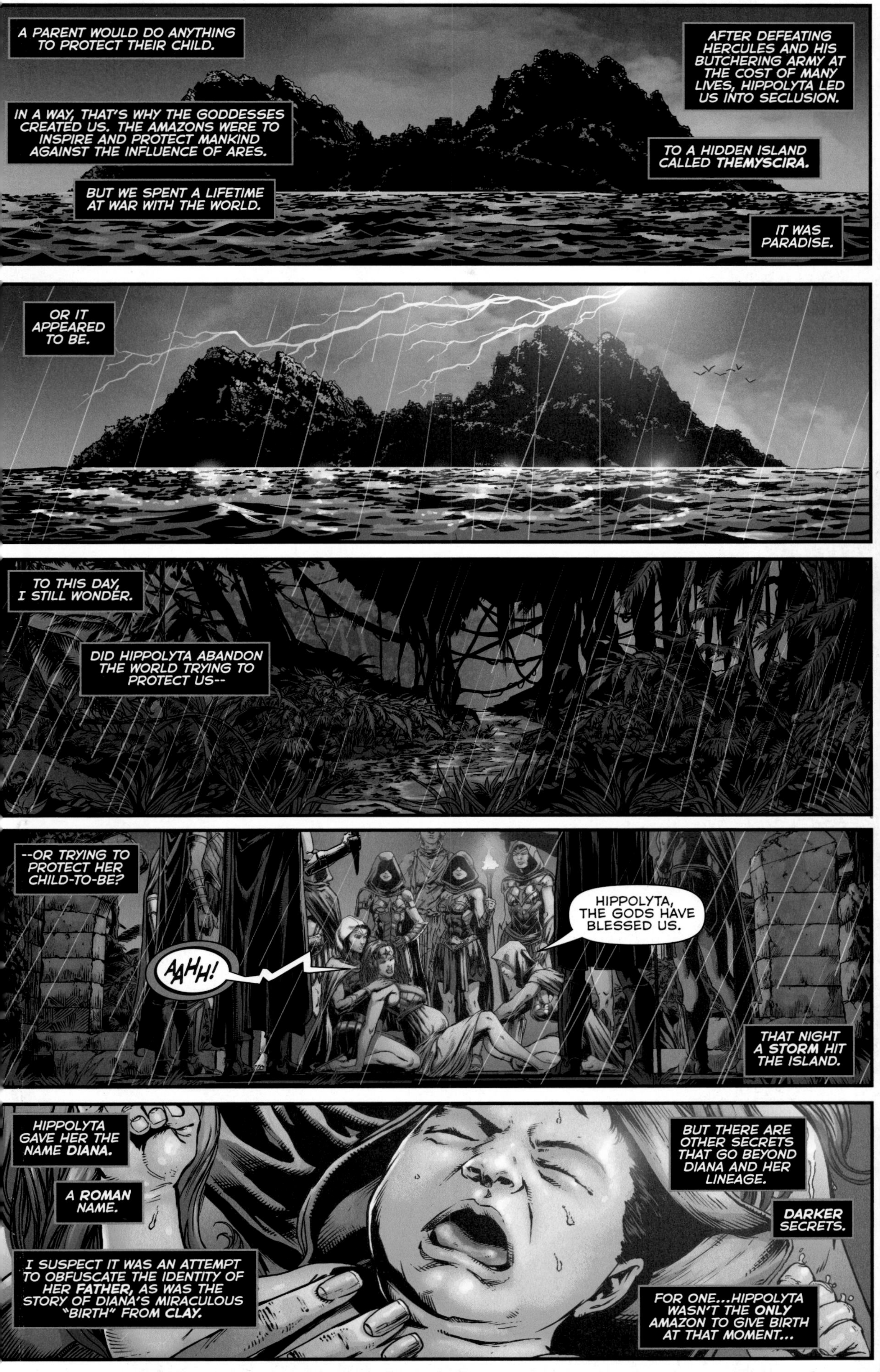
A PARENT WOULD DO ANYTHING TO PROTECT THEIR CHILD.
IN A WAY, THAT'S WHY THE GODDESSES CREATED US. THE AMAZONS WERE TO INSPIRE AND PROTECT MANKIND AGAINST THE INFLUENCE OF ARES.
BUT WE SPENT A LIFETIME AT WAR WITH THE WORLD.
AFTER DEFEATING HERCULES AND HIS BUTCHERING ARMY AT THE COST OF MANY LIVES, HIPPOLYTA LED US INTO SECLUSION.
TO A HIDDEN ISLAND CALLED THEMYSCIRA.
IT WAS PARADISE.
OR IT APPEARED TO BE.
TO THIS DAY, I STILL WONDER.
DID HIPPOLYTA ABANDON THE WORLD TRYING TO PROTECT US--
--OR TRYING TO PROTECT HER CHILD-TO-BE?
AAHH!
HIPPOLYTA, THE GODS HAVE BLESSED US.
THAT NIGHT A STORM HIT THE ISLAND.
HIPPOLYTA GAVE HER THE NAME DIANA.
A ROMAN NAME.
I SUSPECT IT WAS AN ATTEMPT TO OBFUSCATE THE IDENTITY OF HER FATHER, AS WAS THE STORY OF DIANA'S MIRACULOUS "BIRTH" FROM CLAY.
BUT THERE ARE OTHER SECRETS THAT GO BEYOND DIANA AND HER LINEAGE.
DARKER SECRETS.
FOR ONE...HIPPOLYTA WASN'T THE ONLY AMAZON TO GIVE BIRTH AT THAT MOMENT...

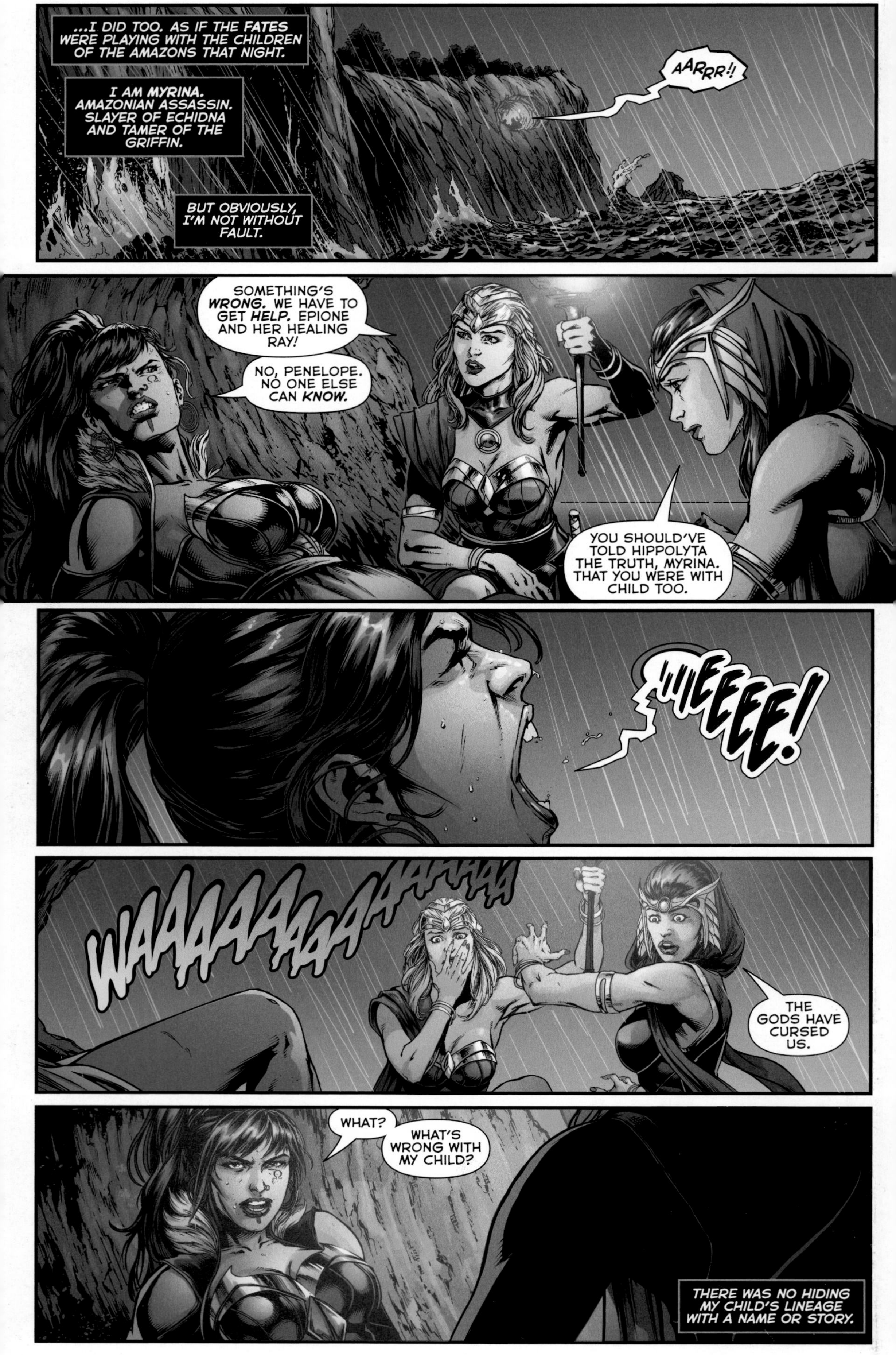
...I DID TOO. AS IF THE FATES WERE PLAYING WITH THE CHILDREN OF THE AMAZONS THAT NIGHT.
I AM MYRINA. AMAZONIAN ASSASSIN. SLAYER OF ECHIDNA AND TAMER OF THE GRIFFIN.
AARRR!!
BUT OBVIOUSLY, I'M NOT WITHOUT FAULT.
SOMETHING'S WRONG. WE HAVE TO GET HELP. EPIONE AND HER HEALING RAY!
NO, PENELOPE. NO ONE ELSE CAN KNOW.
YOU SHOULD'VE TOLD HIPPOLYTA THE TRUTH, MYRINA. THAT YOU WERE WITH CHILD TOO.
EEEE!
WAAAAAAAAAAAAAA
THE GODS HAVE CURSED US.
WHAT?
WHAT'S WRONG WITH MY CHILD?
THERE WAS NO HIDING MY CHILD'S LINEAGE WITH A NAME OR STORY.

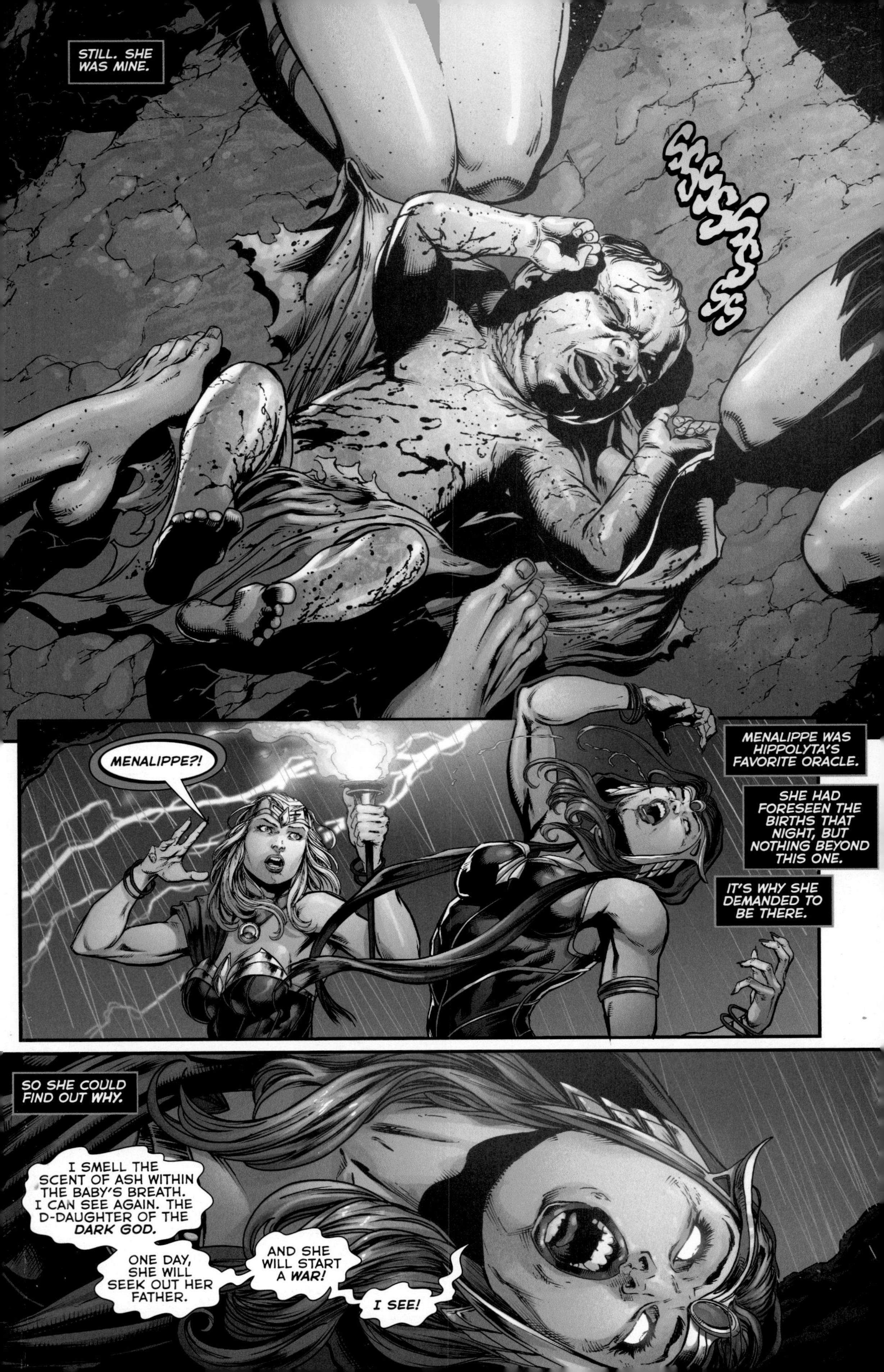
STILL. SHE WAS MINE.
SSSSSSSSS
MENALIPPE?!
MENALIPPE WAS HIPPOLYTA'S FAVORITE ORACLE.
SHE HAD FORESEEN THE BIRTHS THAT NIGHT, BUT NOTHING BEYOND THIS ONE.
IT'S WHY SHE DEMANDED TO BE THERE.
SO SHE COULD FIND OUT WHY.
I SMELL THE SCENT OF ASH WITHIN THE BABY'S BREATH. I CAN SEE AGAIN. THE D-DAUGHTER OF THE DARK GOD.
ONE DAY, SHE WILL SEEK OUT HER FATHER.
AND SHE WILL START A WAR!
I SEE!

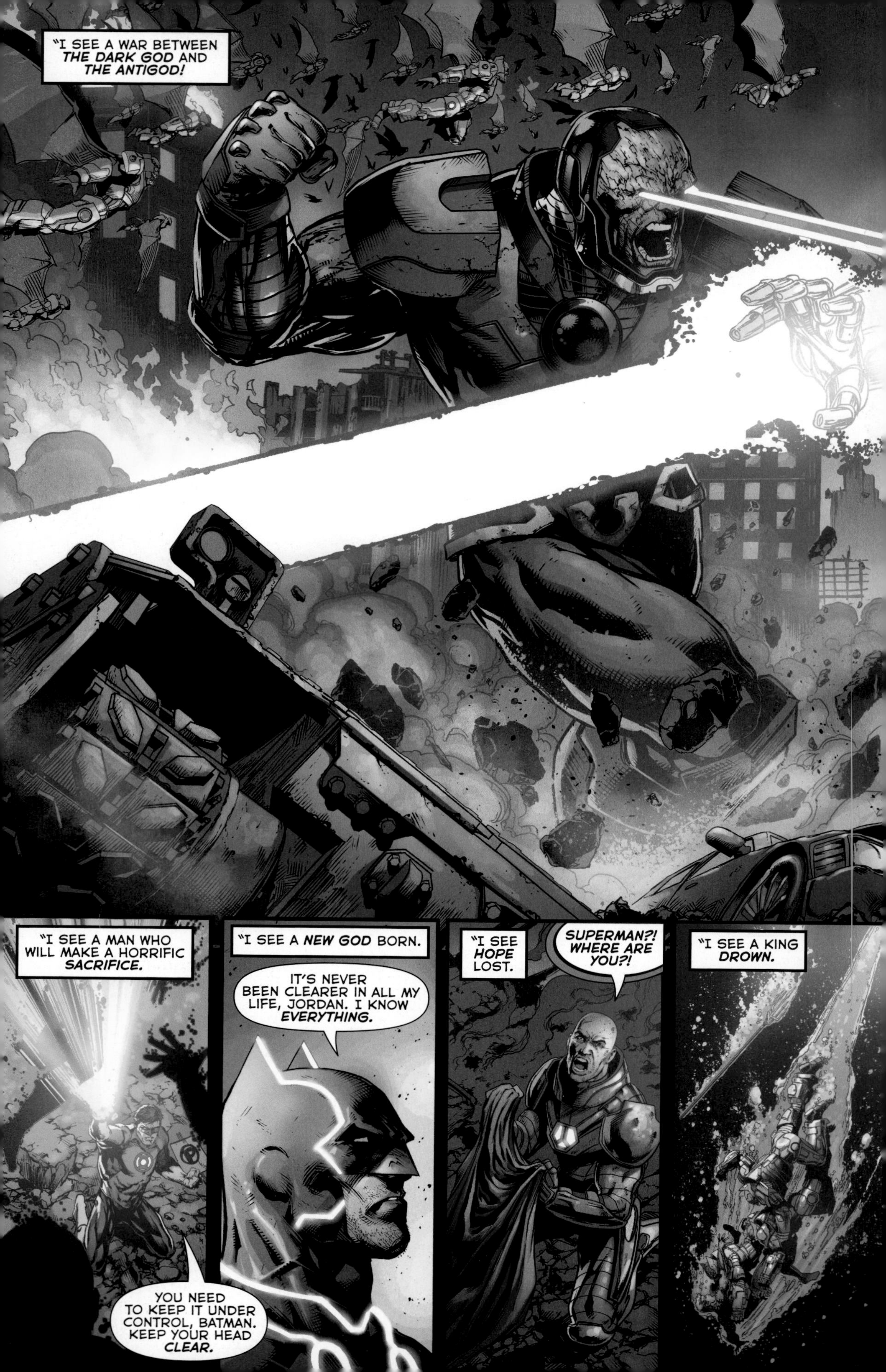
"I SEE A WAR BETWEEN *THE DARK GOD* AND *THE ANTIGOD!*
"I SEE A MAN WHO WILL MAKE A HORRIFIC *SACRIFICE.*
YOU NEED TO KEEP IT UNDER CONTROL, BATMAN. KEEP YOUR HEAD *CLEAR.*
"I SEE A *NEW GOD* BORN.
IT'S NEVER BEEN CLEARER IN ALL MY LIFE, JORDAN. I KNOW *EVERYTHING.*
"I SEE *HOPE* LOST.
SUPERMAN?! WHERE ARE YOU?!
"I SEE A KING *DROWN.*

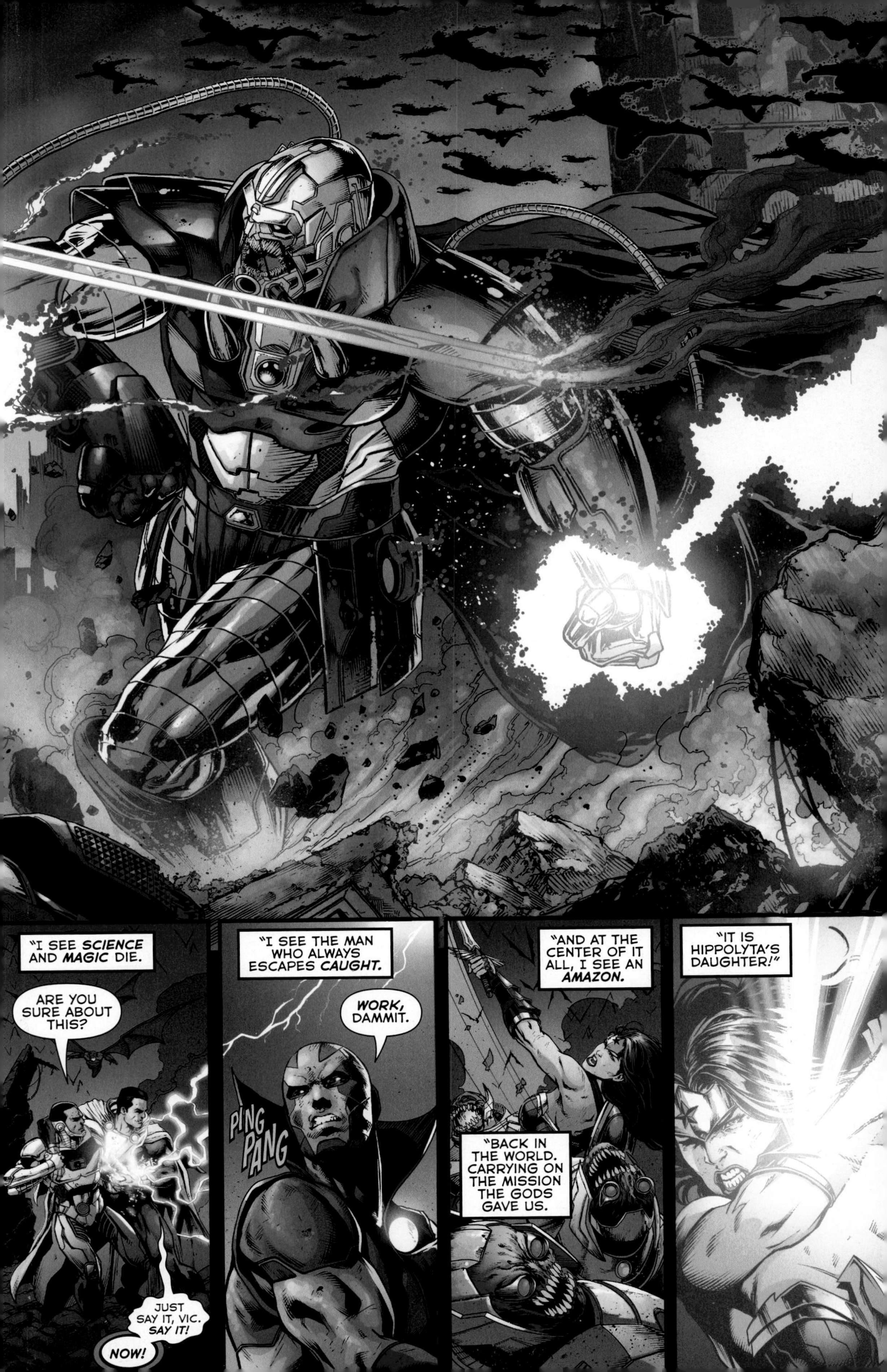
"I SEE SCIENCE AND MAGIC DIE.
ARE YOU SURE ABOUT THIS?
JUST SAY IT, VIC. SAY IT!
NOW!
"I SEE THE MAN WHO ALWAYS ESCAPES CAUGHT.
WORK, DAMMIT.
PING
PANG
"AND AT THE CENTER OF IT ALL, I SEE AN AMAZON.
"BACK IN THE WORLD. CARRYING ON THE MISSION THE GODS GAVE US.
"IT IS HIPPOLYTA'S DAUGHTER!"

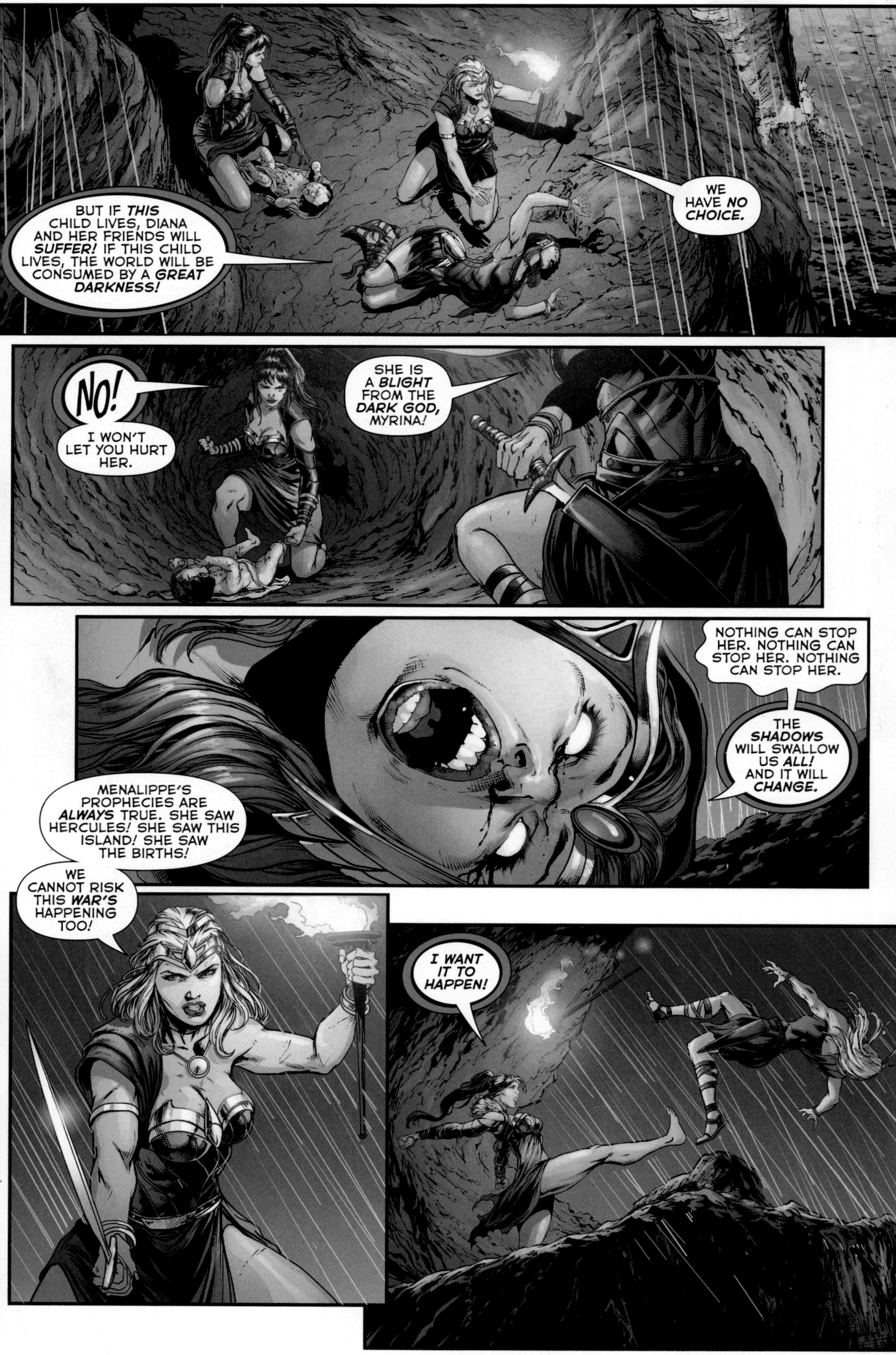
BUT IF THIS CHILD LIVES, DIANA AND HER FRIENDS WILL SUFFER! IF THIS CHILD LIVES, THE WORLD WILL BE CONSUMED BY A GREAT DARKNESS!
WE HAVE NO CHOICE.
NO!
I WON'T LET YOU HURT HER.
SHE IS A BLIGHT FROM THE DARK GOD, MYRINA!
NOTHING CAN STOP HER. NOTHING CAN STOP HER. NOTHING CAN STOP HER.
THE SHADOWS WILL SWALLOW US ALL! AND IT WILL CHANGE.
MENALIPPE'S PROPHECIES ARE ALWAYS TRUE. SHE SAW HERCULES! SHE SAW THIS ISLAND! SHE SAW THE BIRTHS!
WE CANNOT RISK THIS WAR'S HAPPENING TOO!
I WANT IT TO HAPPEN!

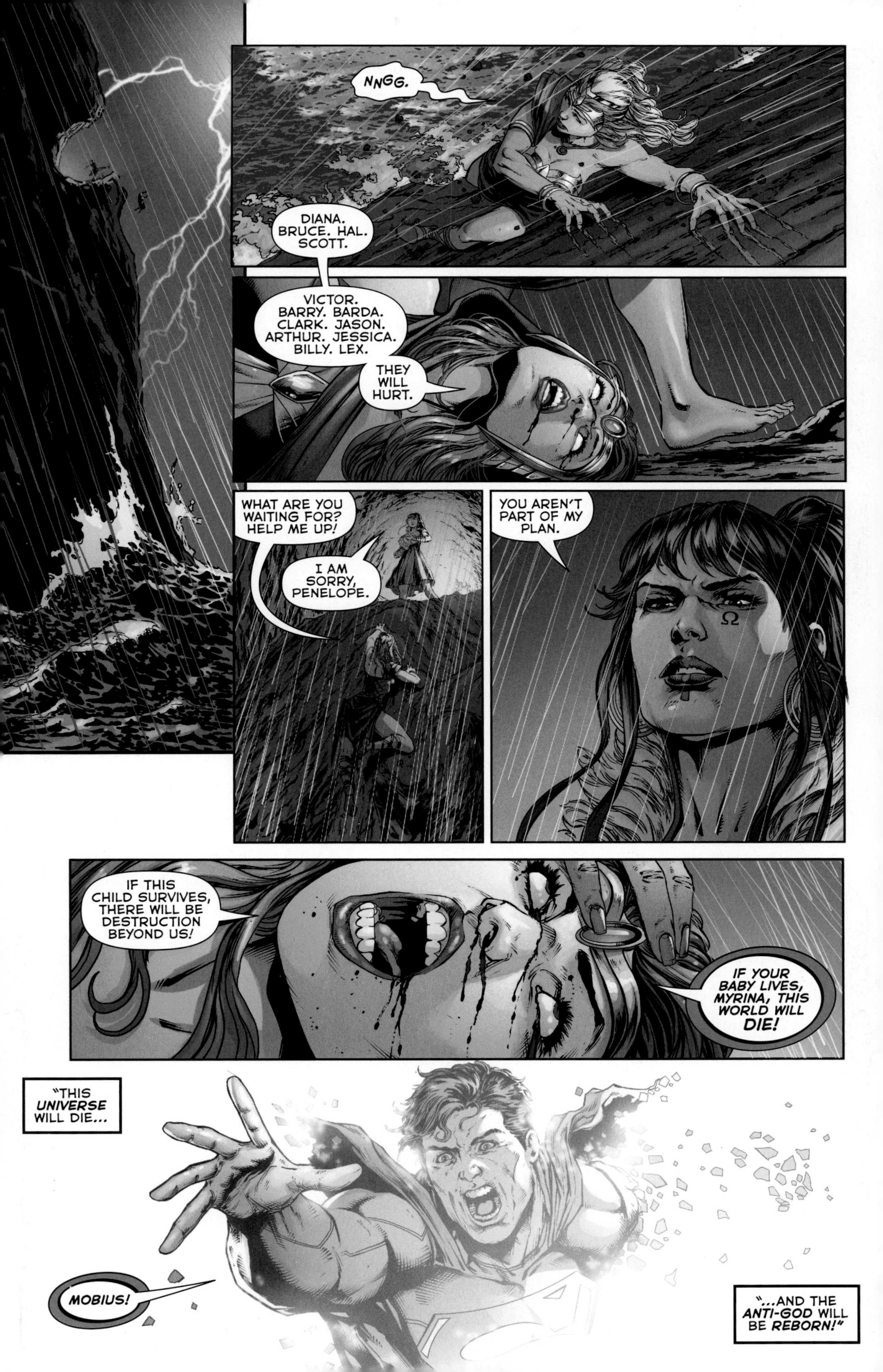

NNGG.
DIANA. BRUCE. HAL. SCOTT.
VICTOR. BARRY. BARDA. CLARK. JASON. ARTHUR. JESSICA. BILLY. LEX.
THEY WILL HURT.
WHAT ARE YOU WAITING FOR? HELP ME UP!
I AM SORRY, PENELOPE.
YOU AREN'T PART OF MY PLAN.
IF THIS CHILD SURVIVES, THERE WILL BE DESTRUCTION BEYOND US!
IF YOUR BABY LIVES, MYRINA, THIS WORLD WILL DIE!
"THIS UNIVERSE WILL DIE...
MOBIUS!
"...AND THE ANTI-GOD WILL BE REBORN!"

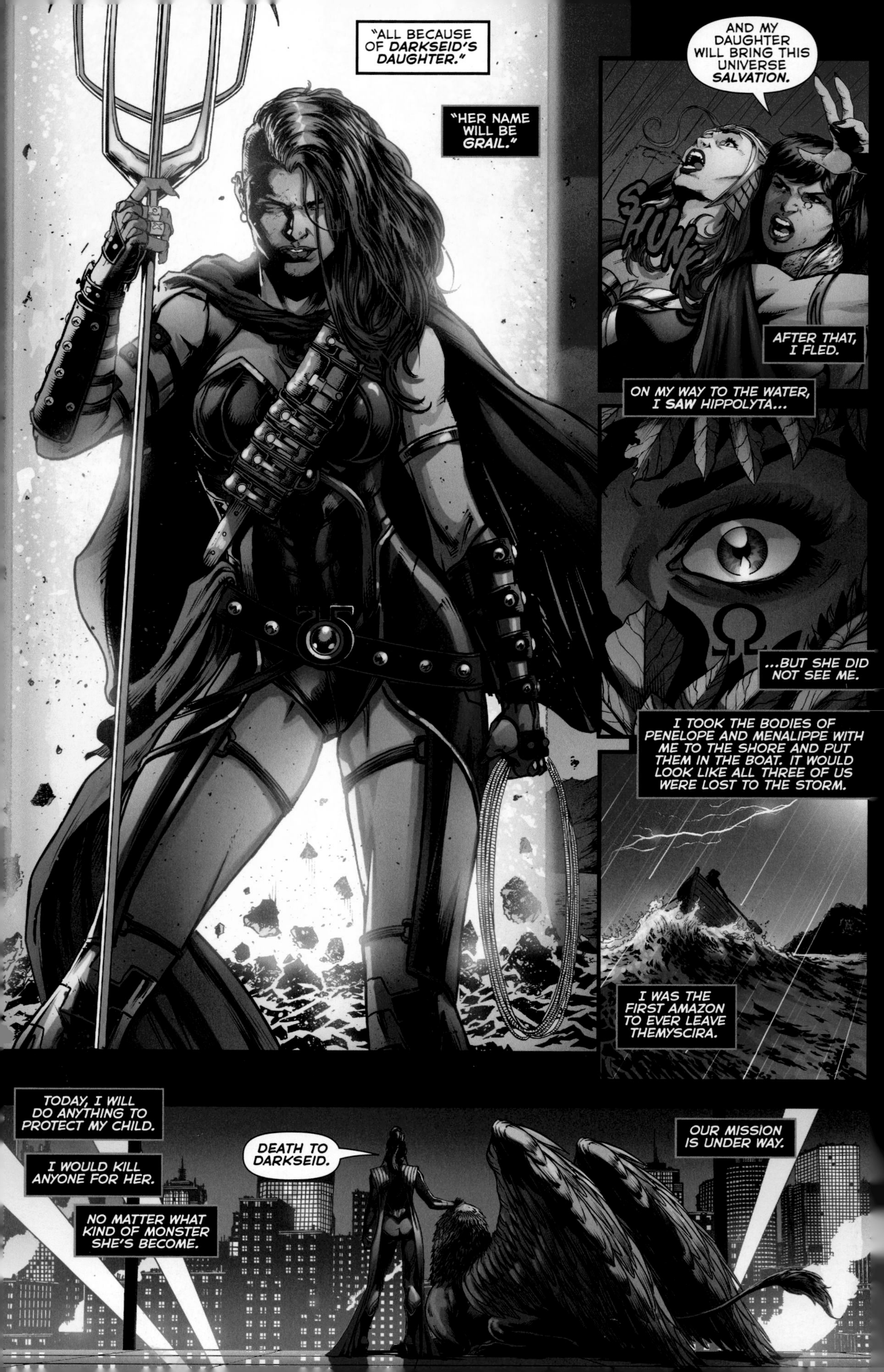
"ALL BECAUSE OF DARKSEID'S DAUGHTER."
"HER NAME WILL BE GRAIL."
AND MY DAUGHTER WILL BRING THIS UNIVERSE SALVATION.
SHUNK
AFTER THAT, I FLED.
ON MY WAY TO THE WATER, I SAW HIPPOLYTA...
...BUT SHE DID NOT SEE ME.
I TOOK THE BODIES OF PENELOPE AND MENALIPPE WITH ME TO THE SHORE AND PUT THEM IN THE BOAT. IT WOULD LOOK LIKE ALL THREE OF US WERE LOST TO THE STORM.
I WAS THE FIRST AMAZON TO EVER LEAVE THEMYSCIRA.
TODAY, I WILL DO ANYTHING TO PROTECT MY CHILD.
I WOULD KILL ANYONE FOR HER.
NO MATTER WHAT KIND OF MONSTER SHE'S BECOME.
DEATH TO DARKSEID.
OUR MISSION IS UNDER WAY.

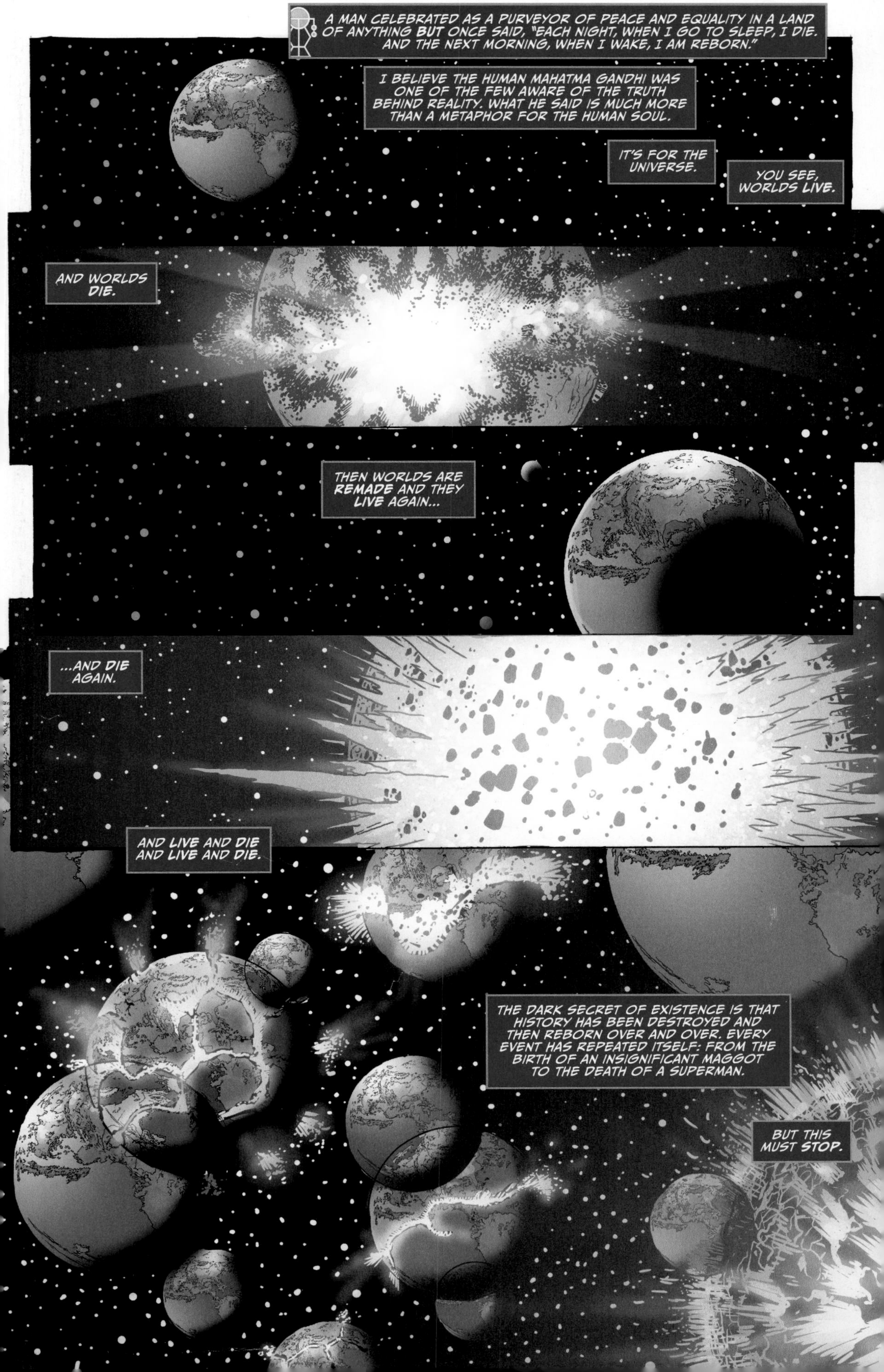
A MAN CELEBRATED AS A PURVEYOR OF PEACE AND EQUALITY IN A LAND OF ANYTHING BUT ONCE SAID, "EACH NIGHT, WHEN I GO TO SLEEP, I DIE. AND THE NEXT MORNING, WHEN I WAKE, I AM REBORN."
I BELIEVE THE HUMAN MAHATMA GANDHI WAS ONE OF THE FEW AWARE OF THE TRUTH BEHIND REALITY. WHAT HE SAID IS MUCH MORE THAN A METAPHOR FOR THE HUMAN SOUL.
IT'S FOR THE UNIVERSE.
YOU SEE, WORLDS LIVE.
AND WORLDS DIE.
THEN WORLDS ARE REMADE AND THEY LIVE AGAIN...
...AND DIE AGAIN.
AND LIVE AND DIE AND LIVE AND DIE.
THE DARK SECRET OF EXISTENCE IS THAT HISTORY HAS BEEN DESTROYED AND THEN REBORN OVER AND OVER. EVERY EVENT HAS REPEATED ITSELF: FROM THE BIRTH OF AN INSIGNIFICANT MAGGOT TO THE DEATH OF A SUPERMAN.
BUT THIS MUST STOP.

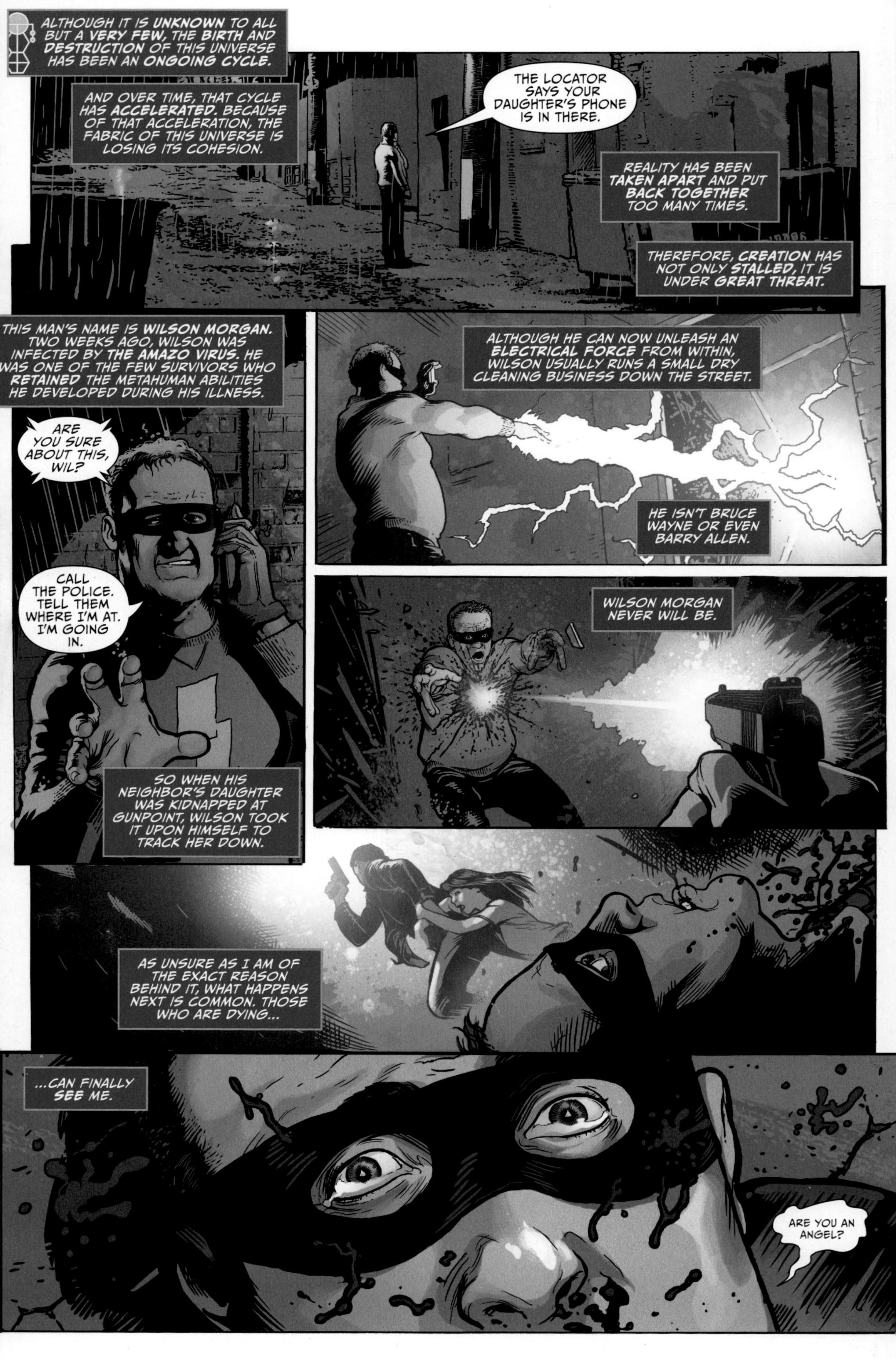
ALTHOUGH IT IS UNKNOWN TO ALL BUT A VERY FEW, THE BIRTH AND DESTRUCTION OF THIS UNIVERSE HAS BEEN AN ONGOING CYCLE.
AND OVER TIME, THAT CYCLE HAS ACCELERATED. BECAUSE OF THAT ACCELERATION, THE FABRIC OF THIS UNIVERSE IS LOSING ITS COHESION.
THE LOCATOR SAYS YOUR DAUGHTER'S PHONE IS IN THERE.
REALITY HAS BEEN TAKEN APART AND PUT BACK TOGETHER TOO MANY TIMES.
THEREFORE, CREATION HAS NOT ONLY STALLED, IT IS UNDER GREAT THREAT.
THIS MAN'S NAME IS WILSON MORGAN. TWO WEEKS AGO, WILSON WAS INFECTED BY THE AMAZO VIRUS. HE WAS ONE OF THE FEW SURVIVORS WHO RETAINED THE METAHUMAN ABILITIES HE DEVELOPED DURING HIS ILLNESS.
ARE YOU SURE ABOUT THIS, WIL?
CALL THE POLICE. TELL THEM WHERE I'M AT. I'M GOING IN.
SO WHEN HIS NEIGHBOR'S DAUGHTER WAS KIDNAPPED AT GUNPOINT, WILSON TOOK IT UPON HIMSELF TO TRACK HER DOWN.
ALTHOUGH HE CAN NOW UNLEASH AN ELECTRICAL FORCE FROM WITHIN, WILSON USUALLY RUNS A SMALL DRY CLEANING BUSINESS DOWN THE STREET.
HE ISN'T BRUCE WAYNE OR EVEN BARRY ALLEN.
WILSON MORGAN NEVER WILL BE.
AS UNSURE AS I AM OF THE EXACT REASON BEHIND IT, WHAT HAPPENS NEXT IS COMMON. THOSE WHO ARE DYING...
...CAN FINALLY SEE ME.
ARE YOU AN ANGEL?

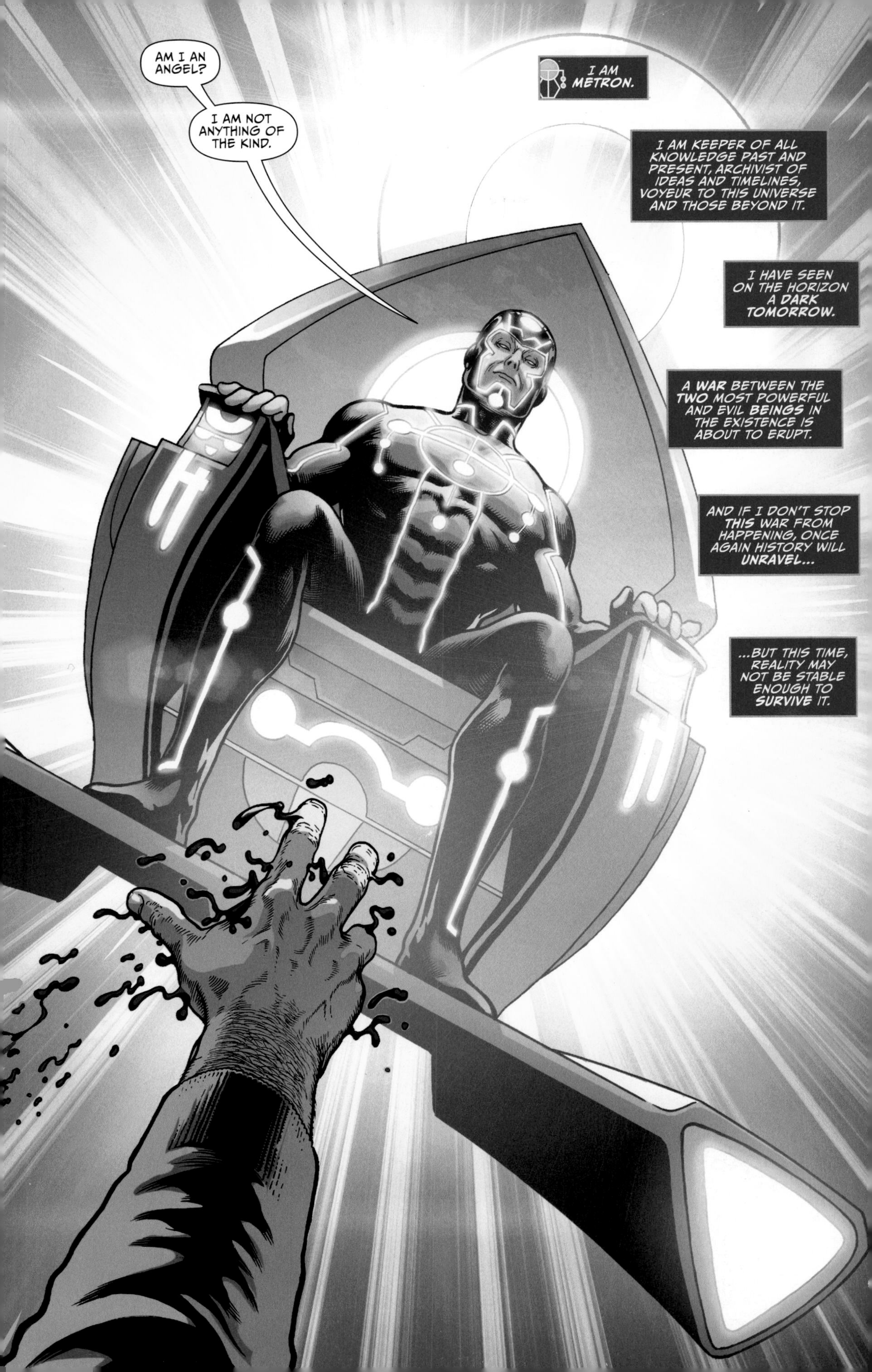
AM I AN ANGEL?
I AM NOT ANYTHING OF THE KIND.
I AM METRON.
I AM KEEPER OF ALL KNOWLEDGE PAST AND PRESENT, ARCHIVIST OF IDEAS AND TIMELINES, VOYEUR TO THIS UNIVERSE AND THOSE BEYOND IT.
I HAVE SEEN ON THE HORIZON A DARK TOMORROW.
A WAR BETWEEN THE TWO MOST POWERFUL AND EVIL BEINGS IN THE EXISTENCE IS ABOUT TO ERUPT.
AND IF I DON'T STOP THIS WAR FROM HAPPENING, ONCE AGAIN HISTORY WILL UNRAVEL...
...BUT THIS TIME, REALITY MAY NOT BE STABLE ENOUGH TO SURVIVE IT.

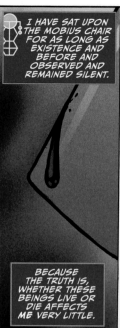

I HAVE SAT UPON THE MOBIUS CHAIR FOR AS LONG AS EXISTENCE AND BEFORE AND OBSERVED AND REMAINED SILENT.

BECAUSE THE TRUTH IS, WHETHER THESE BEINGS LIVE OR DIE AFFECTS ME VERY LITTLE.

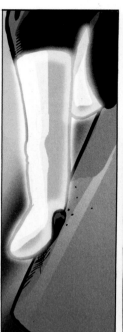

STILL. WITHOUT THEM TO OBSERVE, I LOSE PURPOSE.

I OBSERVE EMPTINESS.

SO ALTHOUGH I HAVE BEEN FORBIDDEN TO USE MY KNOWLEDGE TO INTERFERE, I HAVE DISOBEYED ON OCCASION WHEN I BELIEVE THE THREAT IS GREAT ENOUGH.

THE FIRST TIME I BROKE MY WORD WAS FAR AWAY FROM HERE, IN ANOTHER SOLAR SYSTEM.

THERE, YOU COULD NOT FIND TWO WORLDS TO BE MORE OPPOSITE IN TERRAIN AND SOUL.

APOKOLIPS.

A PIT OF SLAVERY AND OPPRESSION, RULED BY FEAR AND FUELED BY DESPAIR.

AND NEW GENESIS.

A HAVEN OF CULTURE AND SCIENCE, THOUGH NOT A WORLD WITHOUT HIDDEN AND INSIDIOUS PROBLEMS OF ITS OWN.

EVEN NOW, MANY WOULD MISTAKE MY ALLEGIANCES TO BE WITH NEW GENESIS.

BUT MY ALLEGIANCES ARE TO NO ONE.

IT WOULD BE GOOD TO REMEMBER THAT.

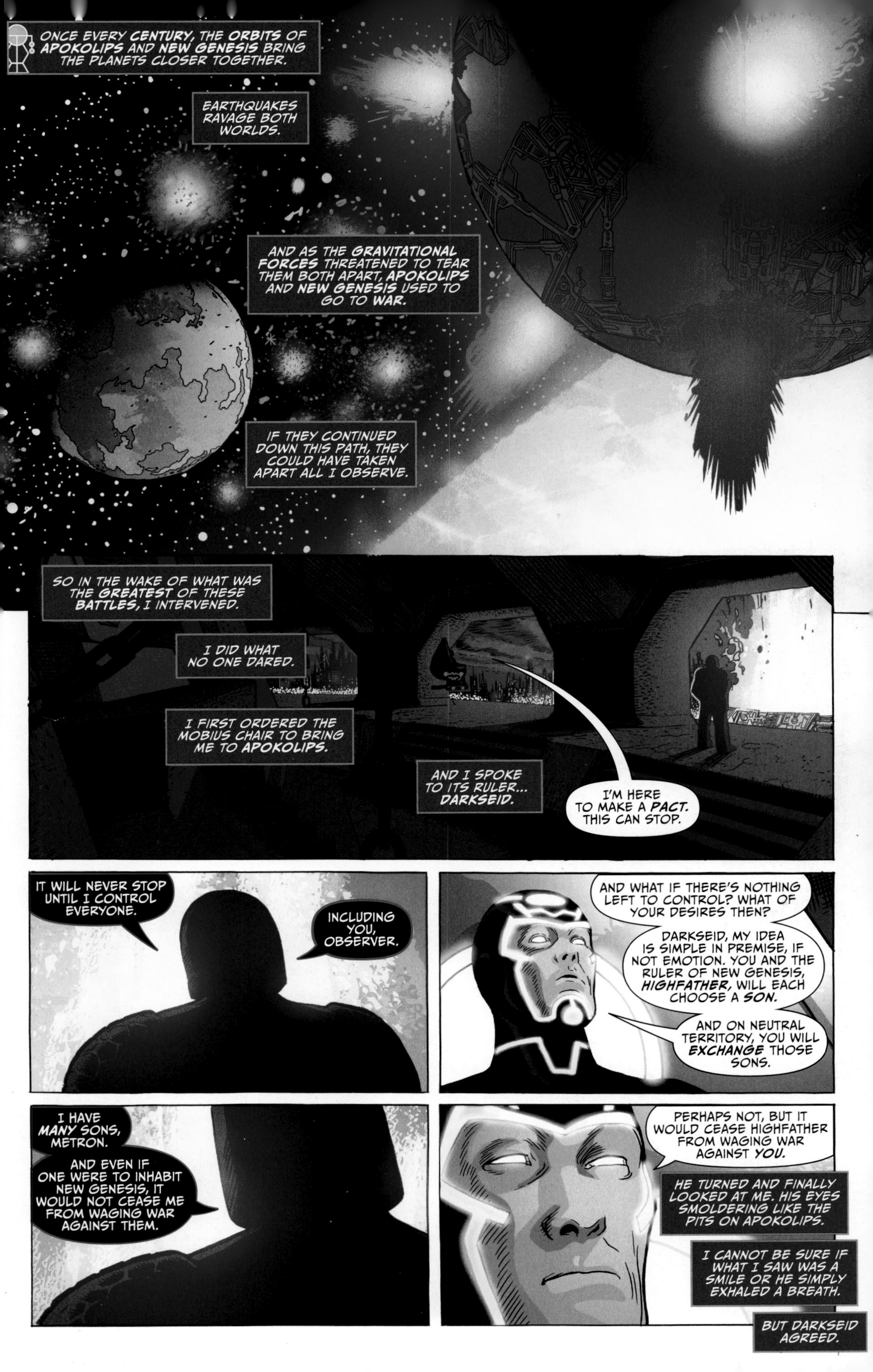
ONCE EVERY CENTURY, THE ORBITS OF APOKOLIPS AND NEW GENESIS BRING THE PLANETS CLOSER TOGETHER.
EARTHQUAKES RAVAGE BOTH WORLDS.
AND AS THE GRAVITATIONAL FORCES THREATENED TO TEAR THEM BOTH APART, APOKOLIPS AND NEW GENESIS USED TO GO TO WAR.
IF THEY CONTINUED DOWN THIS PATH, THEY COULD HAVE TAKEN APART ALL I OBSERVE.
SO IN THE WAKE OF WHAT WAS THE GREATEST OF THESE BATTLES, I INTERVENED.
I DID WHAT NO ONE DARED.
I FIRST ORDERED THE MOBIUS CHAIR TO BRING ME TO APOKOLIPS.
AND I SPOKE TO ITS RULER... DARKSEID.
I'M HERE TO MAKE A PACT. THIS CAN STOP.
IT WILL NEVER STOP UNTIL I CONTROL EVERYONE.
INCLUDING YOU, OBSERVER.
AND WHAT IF THERE'S NOTHING LEFT TO CONTROL? WHAT OF YOUR DESIRES THEN?
DARKSEID, MY IDEA IS SIMPLE IN PREMISE, IF NOT EMOTION. YOU AND THE RULER OF NEW GENESIS, HIGHFATHER, WILL EACH CHOOSE A SON.
AND ON NEUTRAL TERRITORY, YOU WILL EXCHANGE THOSE SONS.
I HAVE MANY SONS, METRON.
AND EVEN IF ONE WERE TO INHABIT NEW GENESIS, IT WOULD NOT CEASE ME FROM WAGING WAR AGAINST THEM.
PERHAPS NOT, BUT IT WOULD CEASE HIGHFATHER FROM WAGING WAR AGAINST YOU.
HE TURNED AND FINALLY LOOKED AT ME. HIS EYES SMOLDERING LIKE THE PITS ON APOKOLIPS.
I CANNOT BE SURE IF WHAT I SAW WAS A SMILE OR HE SIMPLY EXHALED A BREATH.
BUT DARKSEID AGREED.

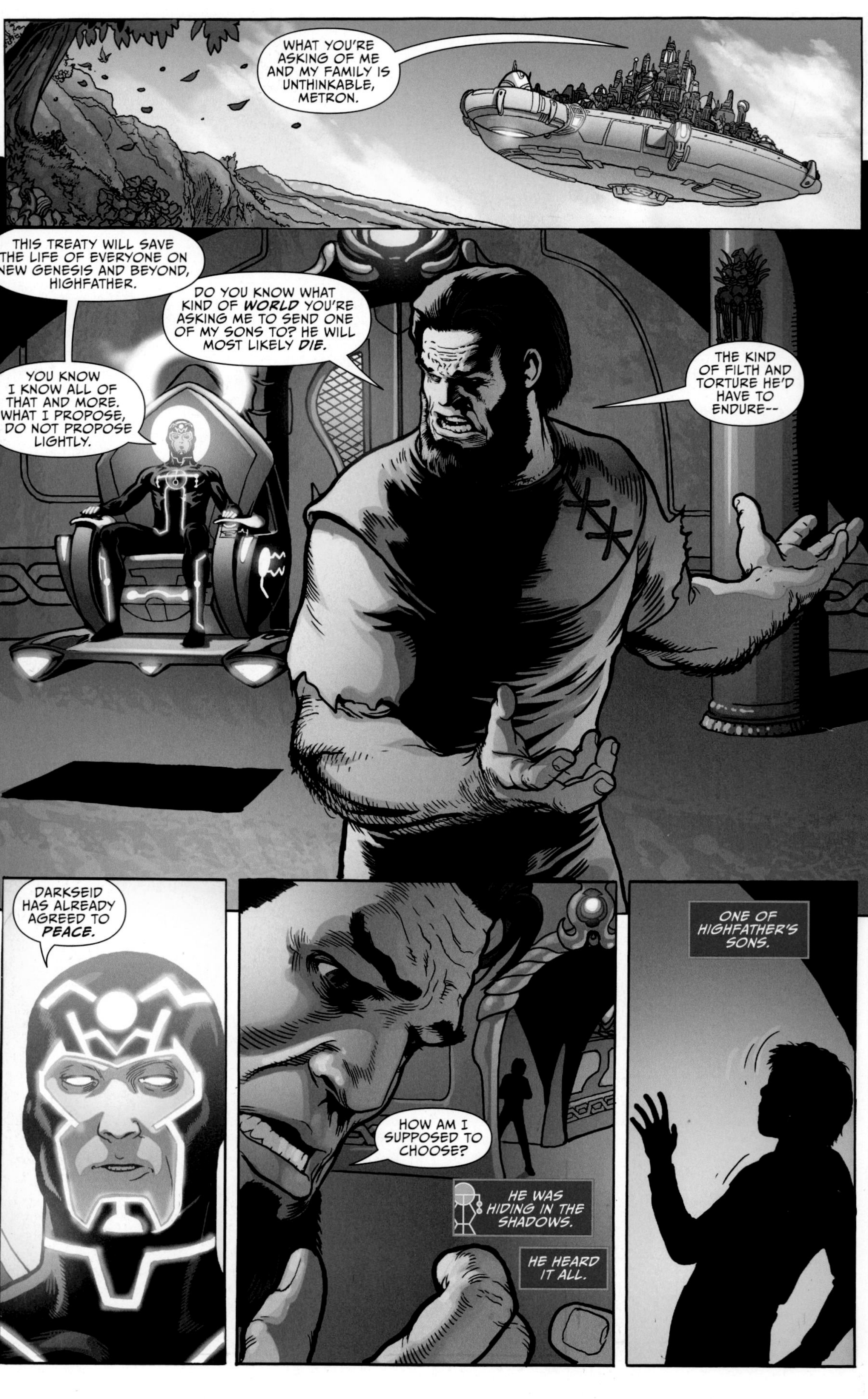
WHAT YOU'RE ASKING OF ME AND MY FAMILY IS UNTHINKABLE, METRON.
THIS TREATY WILL SAVE THE LIFE OF EVERYONE ON NEW GENESIS AND BEYOND, HIGHFATHER.
DO YOU KNOW WHAT KIND OF WORLD YOU'RE ASKING ME TO SEND ONE OF MY SONS TO? HE WILL MOST LIKELY DIE.
YOU KNOW I KNOW ALL OF THAT AND MORE. WHAT I PROPOSE, I DO NOT PROPOSE LIGHTLY.
THE KIND OF FILTH AND TORTURE HE'D HAVE TO ENDURE--
DARKSEID HAS ALREADY AGREED TO PEACE.
HOW AM I SUPPOSED TO CHOOSE?
HE WAS HIDING IN THE SHADOWS.
HE HEARD IT ALL.
ONE OF HIGHFATHER'S SONS.

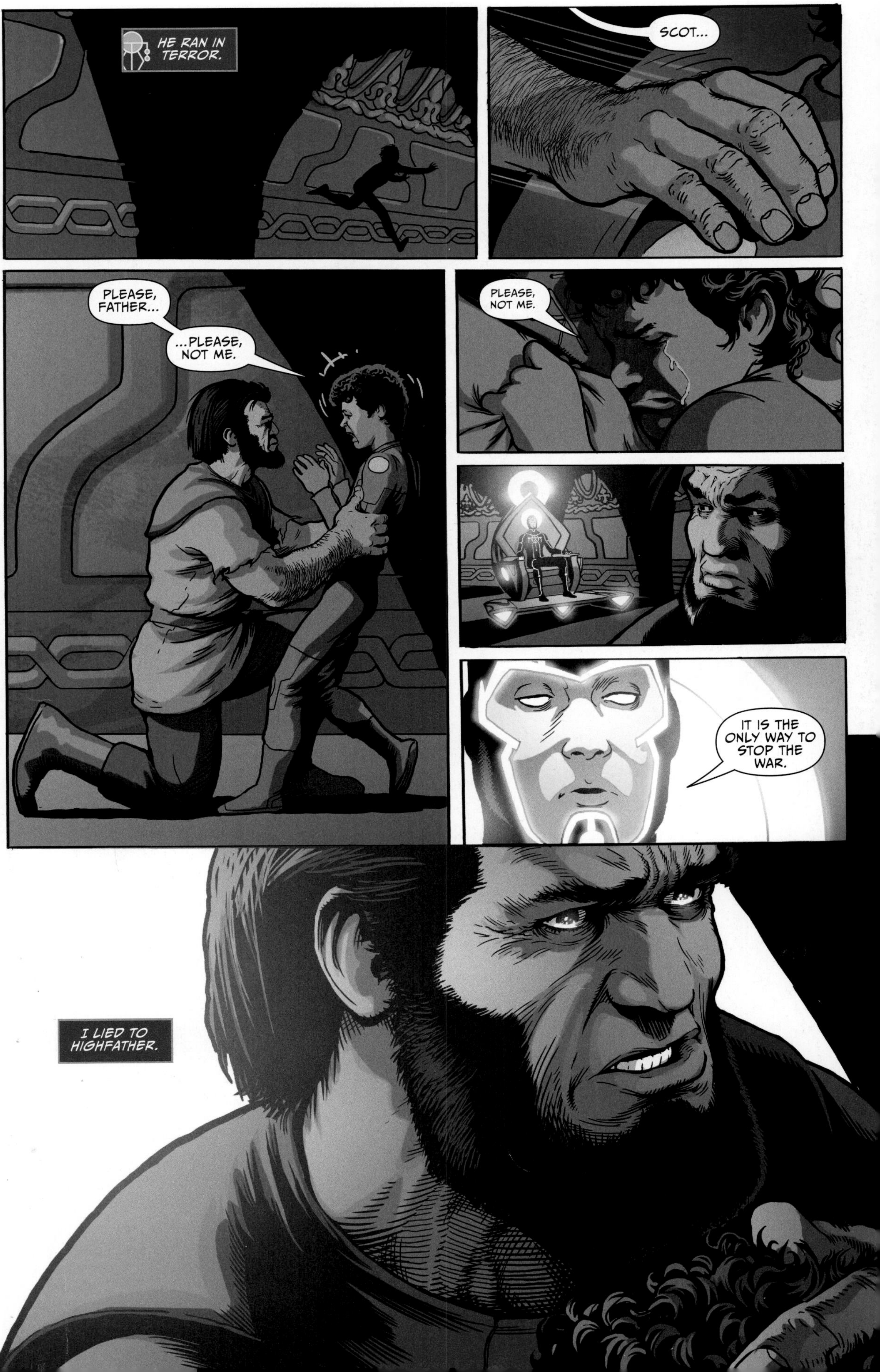
HE RAN IN TERROR.
SCOT...
PLEASE, FATHER...
...PLEASE, NOT ME.
PLEASE, NOT ME.
IT IS THE ONLY WAY TO STOP THE WAR.
I LIED TO HIGHFATHER.

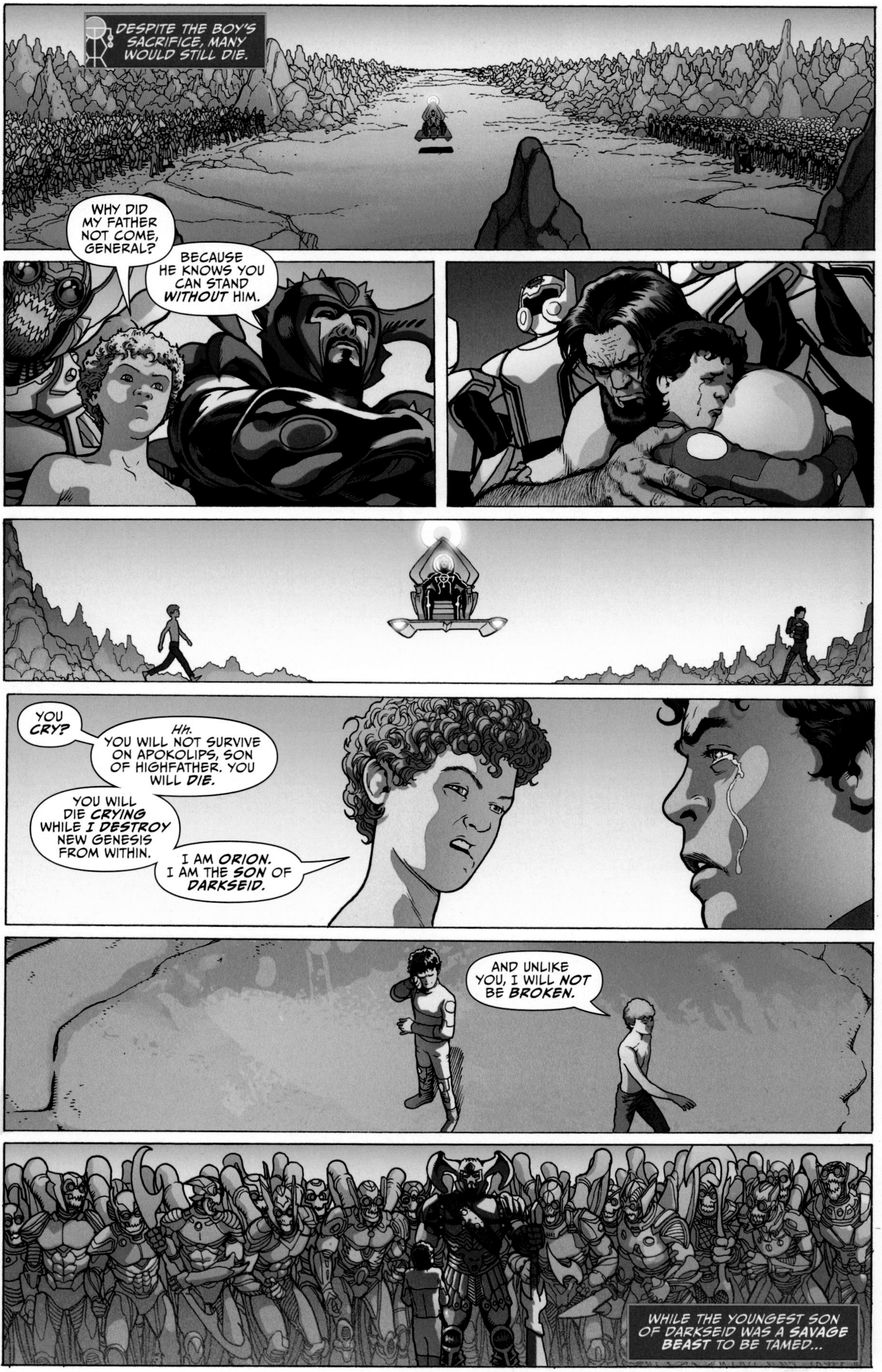
DESPITE THE BOY'S SACRIFICE, MANY WOULD STILL DIE.
WHY DID MY FATHER NOT COME, GENERAL?
BECAUSE HE KNOWS YOU CAN STAND *WITHOUT* HIM.
YOU *CRY?*
Hh. YOU WILL NOT SURVIVE ON APOKOLIPS, SON OF HIGHFATHER. YOU WILL *DIE.*
YOU WILL DIE *CRYING* WHILE *I DESTROY* NEW GENESIS FROM WITHIN.
I AM *ORION.* I AM THE *SON* OF *DARKSEID.*
AND UNLIKE YOU, I WILL *NOT* BE *BROKEN.*
WHILE THE YOUNGEST SON OF DARKSEID WAS A *SAVAGE BEAST* TO BE TAMED...

...THE SON OF HIGHFATHER WAS THROWN INTO THE SLAVE CAMPS. HE SUFFERED GREATLY.

BUT EXISTENCE WOULD CARRY ON, AND I COULD CONTINUE TO OBSERVE THE KNOWN AND UNKNOWN UNIVERSES.

A PACT WAS MADE.

AND WHETHER SCOT WOULD SURVIVE WAS IRRELEVANT TO ME.

AS LONG AS THE WAR WAS AVERTED, I COULD CONTINUE.

THEN, YEARS LATER, IT HAPPENED FOR THE FIRST TIME.

I WAS UNPREPARED...

AAAARGHHHH!!

...TO SEE THE END.

THE MYSTERIOUS BEING OTHERS CALLED THE ANTI-MONITOR HAD RISEN.

FOR REASONS UNKNOWN TO THEM... HE HAD THE POWER TO CONSUME ENTIRE UNIVERSES.

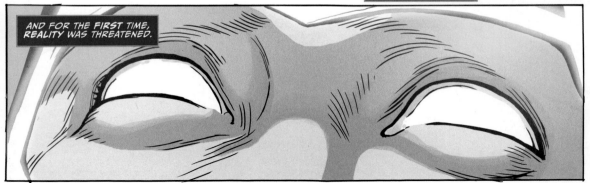

AND FOR THE FIRST TIME, REALITY WAS THREATENED.

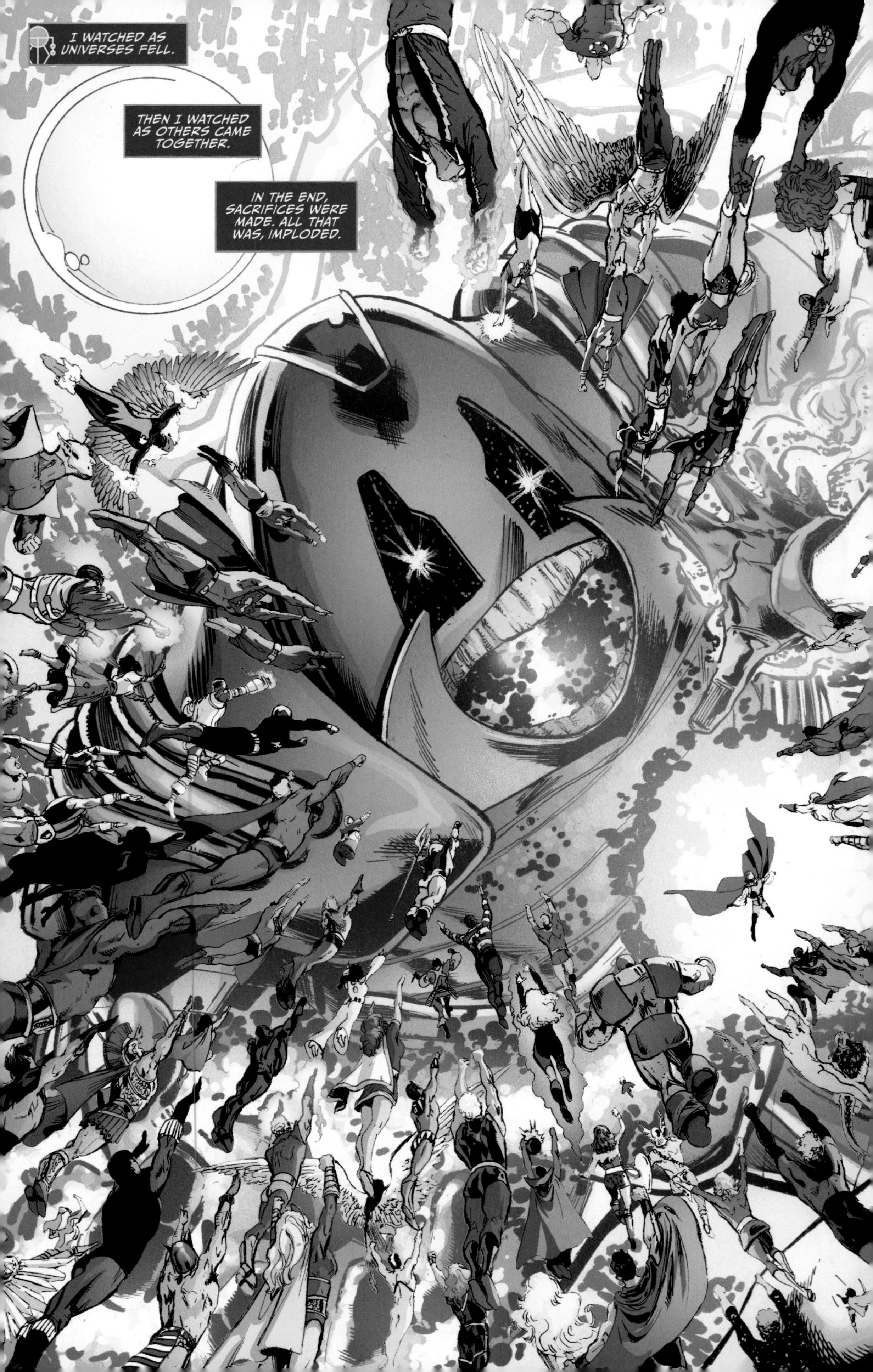
I WATCHED AS UNIVERSES FELL.
THEN I WATCHED AS OTHERS CAME TOGETHER.
IN THE END, SACRIFICES WERE MADE. ALL THAT WAS, IMPLODED.

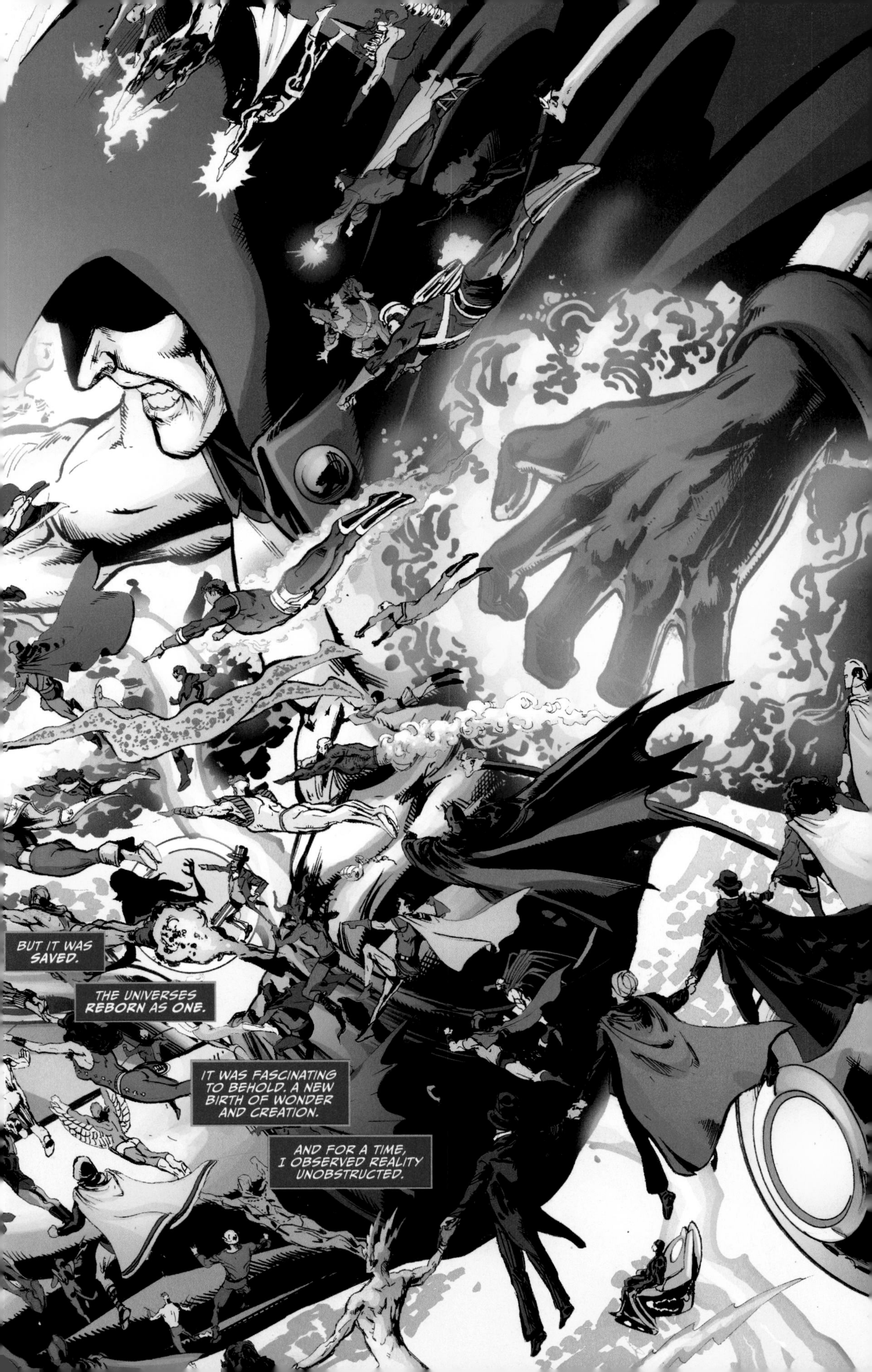
BUT IT WAS SAVED.
THE UNIVERSES REBORN AS ONE.
IT WAS FASCINATING TO BEHOLD. A NEW BIRTH OF WONDER AND CREATION.
AND FOR A TIME, I OBSERVED REALITY UNOBSTRUCTED.

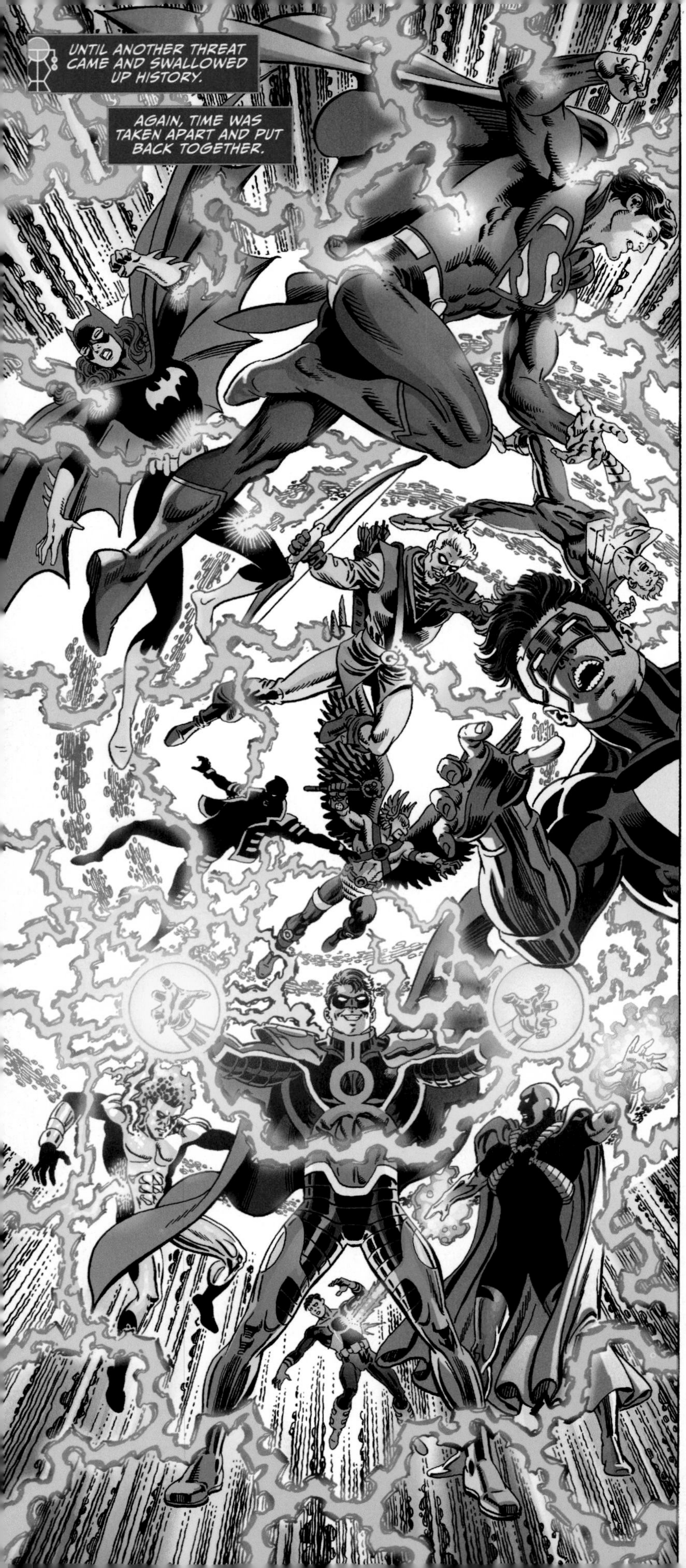
UNTIL ANOTHER THREAT CAME AND SWALLOWED UP HISTORY.
AGAIN, TIME WAS TAKEN APART AND PUT BACK TOGETHER.
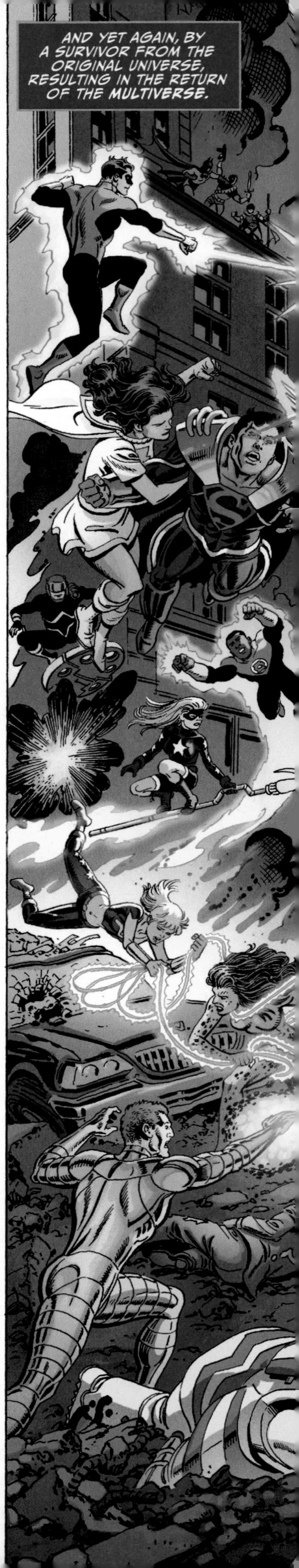
AND YET AGAIN, BY A SURVIVOR FROM THE ORIGINAL UNIVERSE, RESULTING IN THE RETURN OF THE MULTIVERSE.

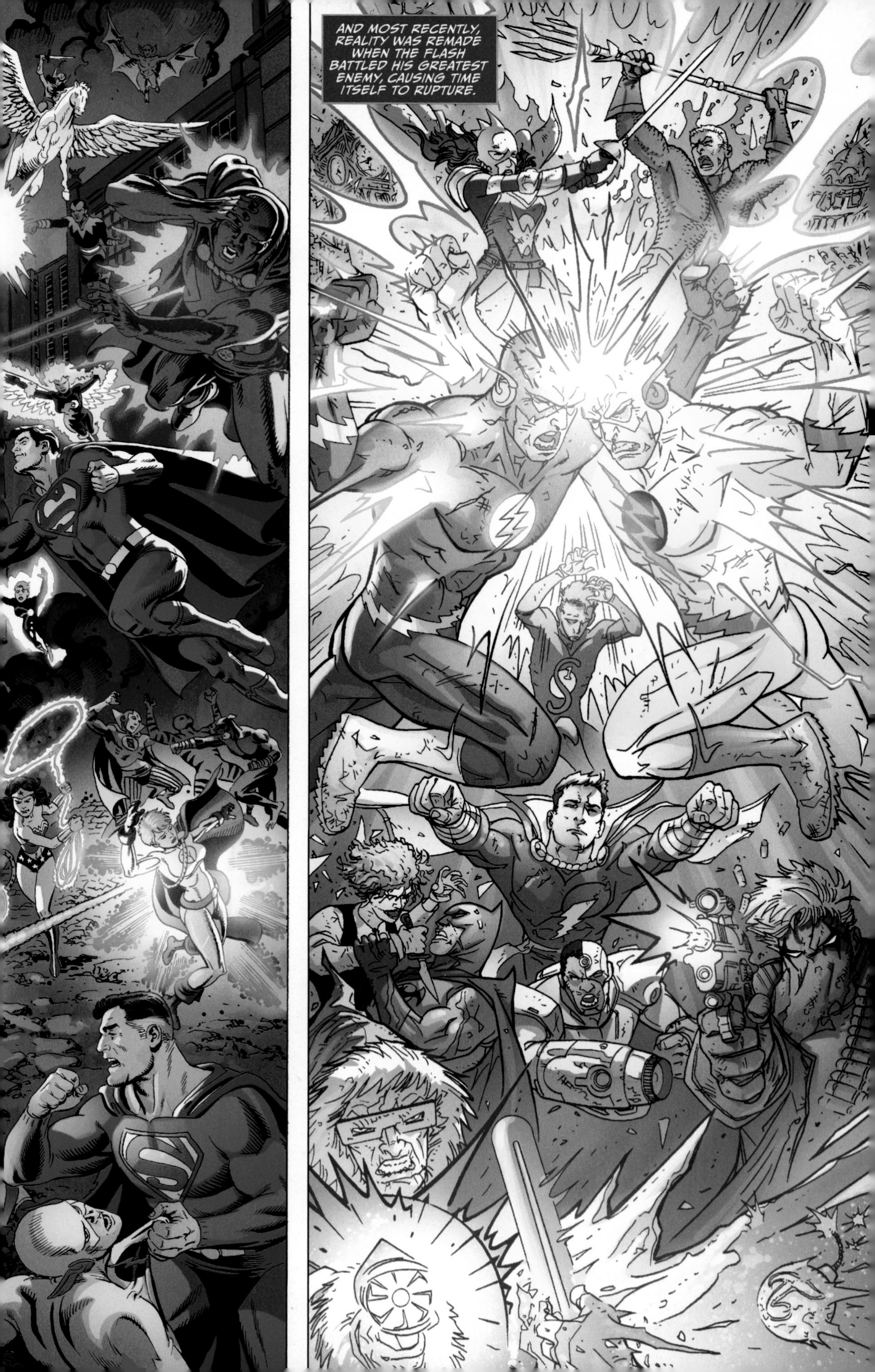
AND MOST RECENTLY, REALITY WAS REMADE WHEN THE FLASH BATTLED HIS GREATEST ENEMY, CAUSING TIME ITSELF TO RUPTURE.

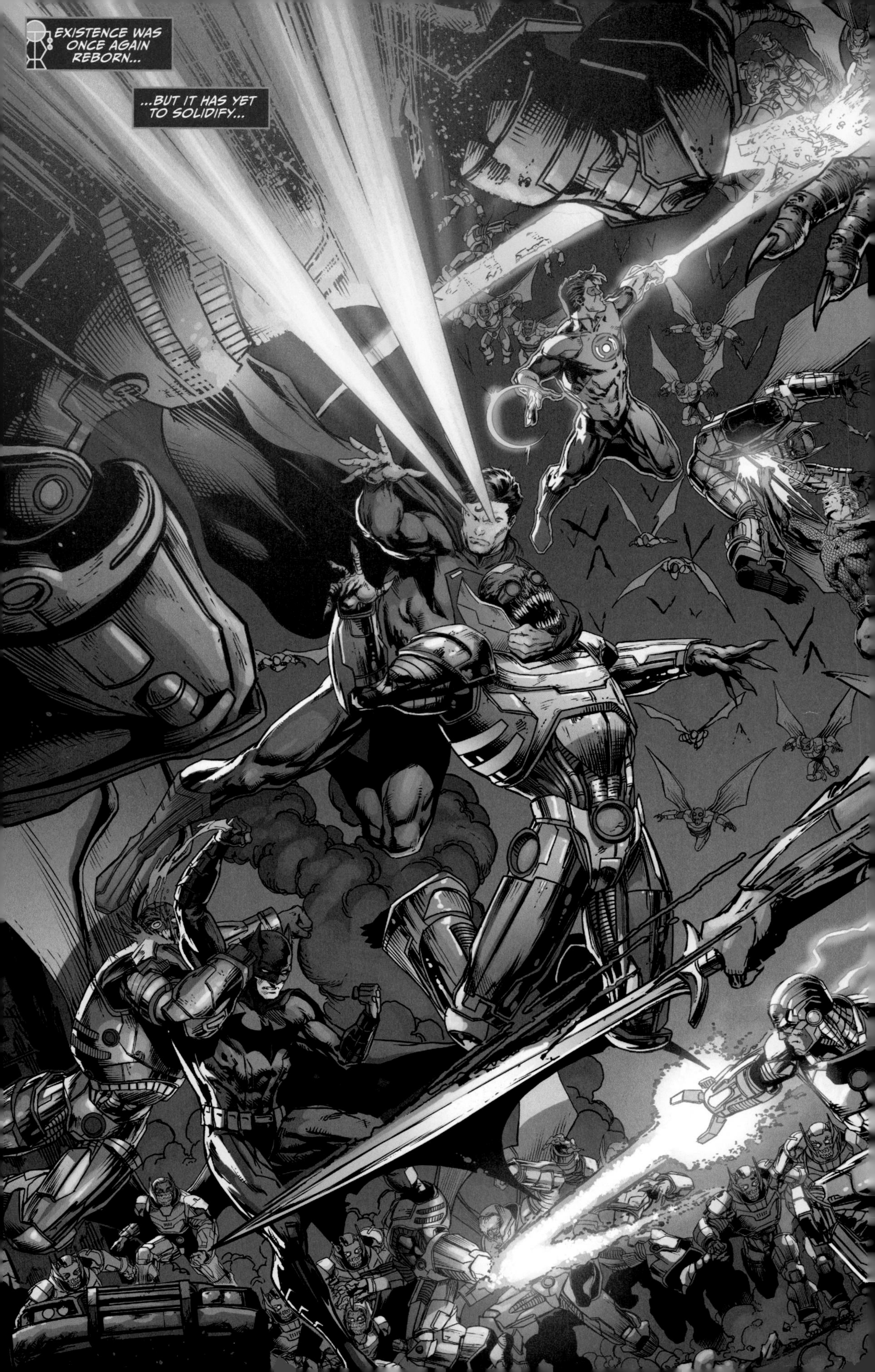
EXISTENCE WAS ONCE AGAIN REBORN...
...BUT IT HAS YET TO SOLIDIFY...

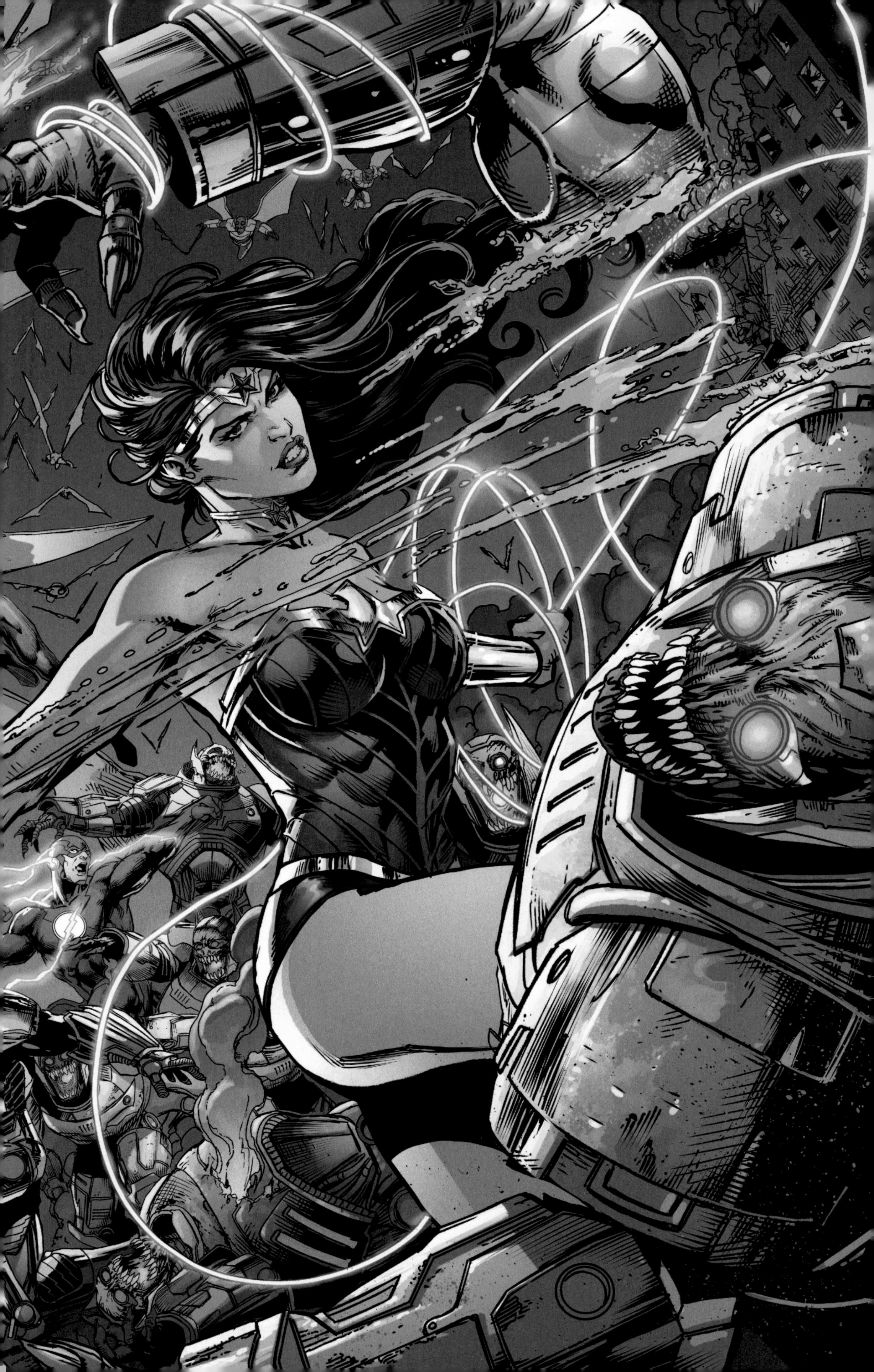

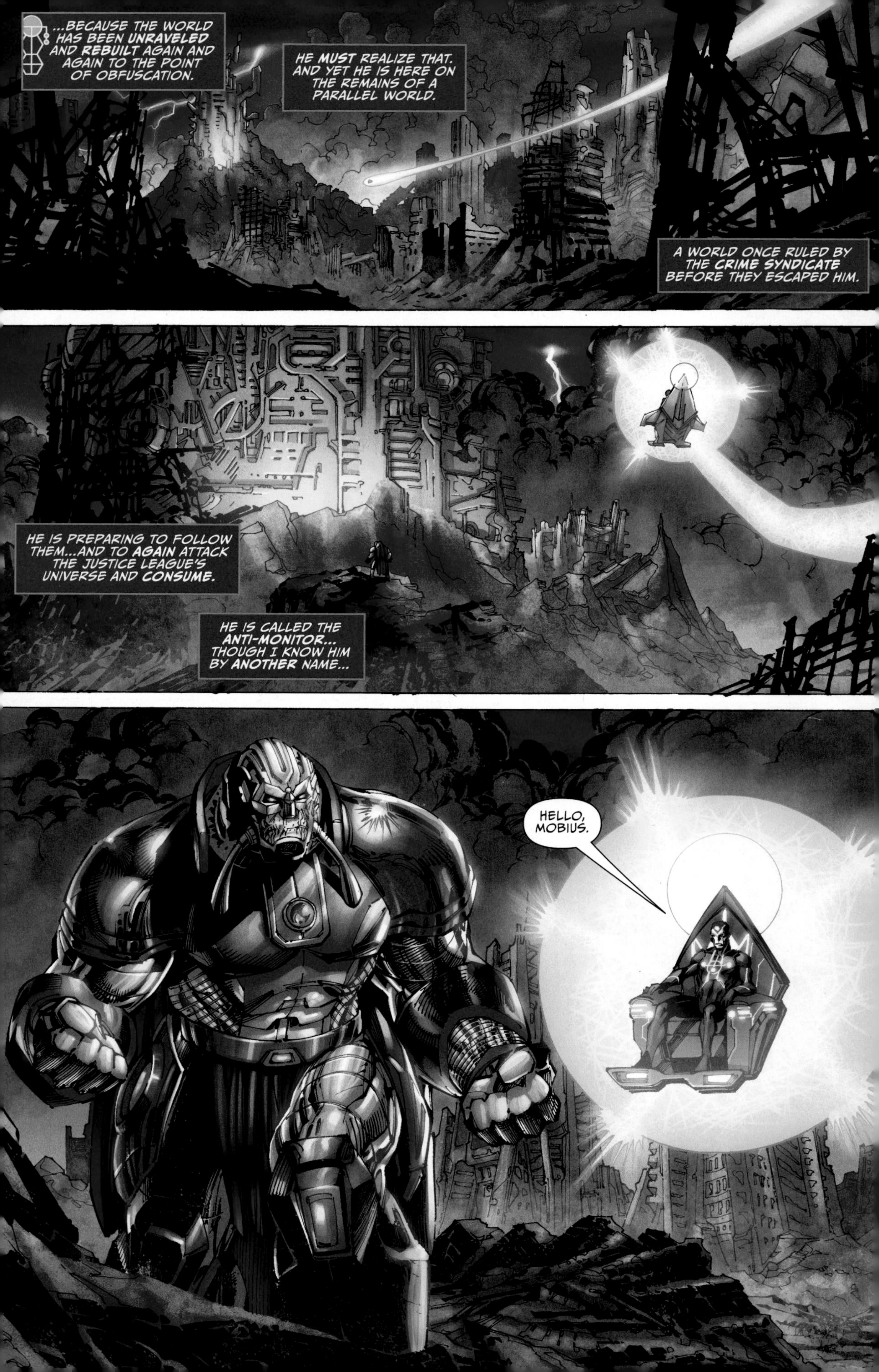
...BECAUSE THE WORLD HAS BEEN UNRAVELED AND REBUILT AGAIN AND AGAIN TO THE POINT OF OBFUSCATION.
HE MUST REALIZE THAT. AND YET HE IS HERE ON THE REMAINS OF A PARALLEL WORLD.
A WORLD ONCE RULED BY THE CRIME SYNDICATE BEFORE THEY ESCAPED HIM.
HE IS PREPARING TO FOLLOW THEM...AND TO AGAIN ATTACK THE JUSTICE LEAGUE'S UNIVERSE AND CONSUME.
HE IS CALLED THE ANTI-MONITOR... THOUGH I KNOW HIM BY ANOTHER NAME...
HELLO, MOBIUS.

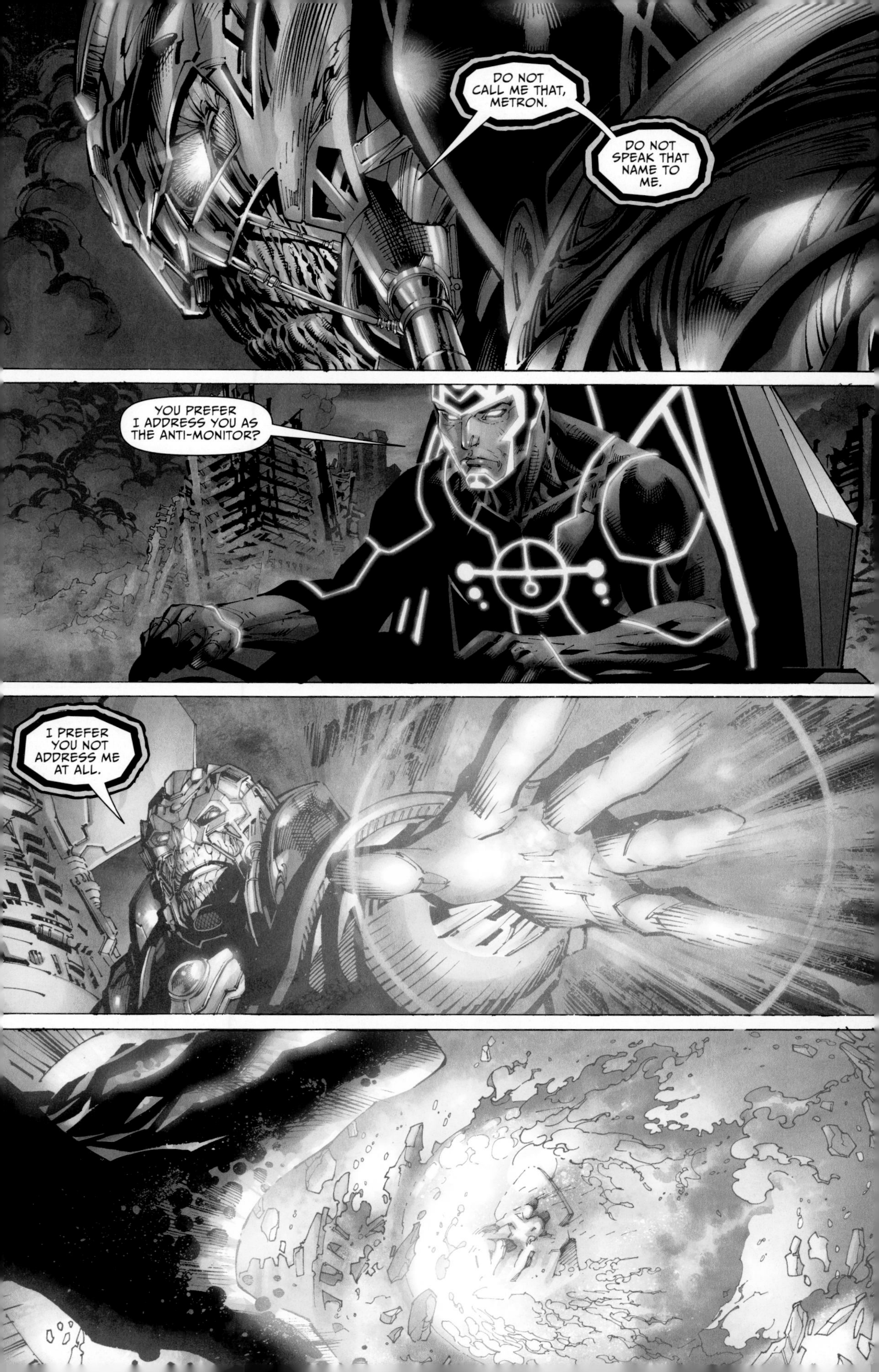
DO NOT CALL ME THAT, METRON.
DO NOT SPEAK THAT NAME TO ME.
YOU PREFER I ADDRESS YOU AS THE ANTI-MONITOR?
I PREFER YOU NOT ADDRESS ME AT ALL.

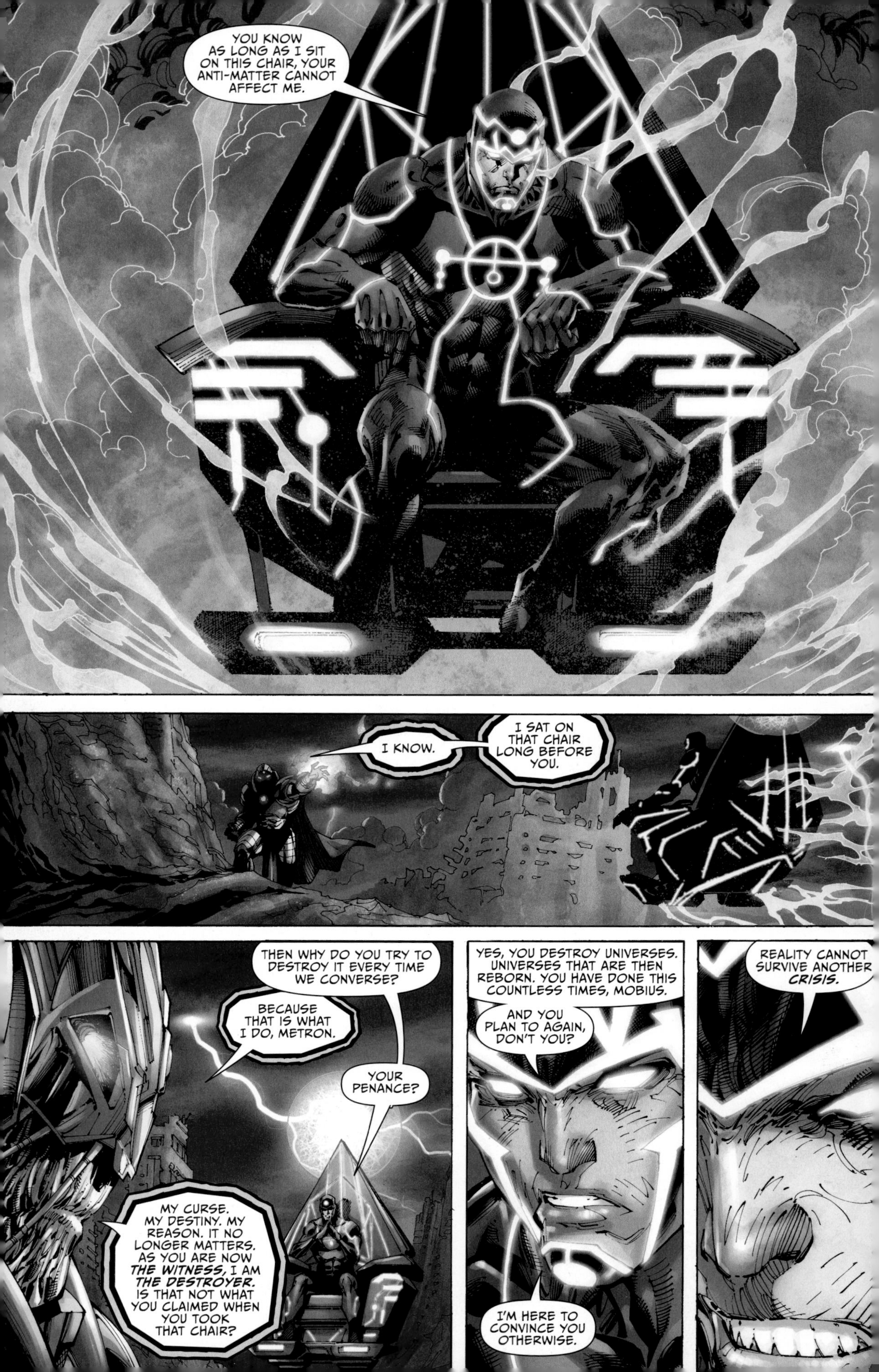
YOU KNOW AS LONG AS I SIT ON THIS CHAIR, YOUR ANTI-MATTER CANNOT AFFECT ME.
I KNOW.
I SAT ON THAT CHAIR LONG BEFORE YOU.
THEN WHY DO YOU TRY TO DESTROY IT EVERY TIME WE CONVERSE?
BECAUSE THAT IS WHAT I DO, METRON.
YOUR PENANCE?
MY CURSE. MY DESTINY. MY REASON. IT NO LONGER MATTERS. AS YOU ARE NOW THE WITNESS, I AM THE DESTROYER. IS THAT NOT WHAT YOU CLAIMED WHEN YOU TOOK THAT CHAIR?
YES, YOU DESTROY UNIVERSES. UNIVERSES THAT ARE THEN REBORN. YOU HAVE DONE THIS COUNTLESS TIMES, MOBIUS.
AND YOU PLAN TO AGAIN, DON'T YOU?
I'M HERE TO CONVINCE YOU OTHERWISE.
REALITY CANNOT SURVIVE ANOTHER CRISIS.

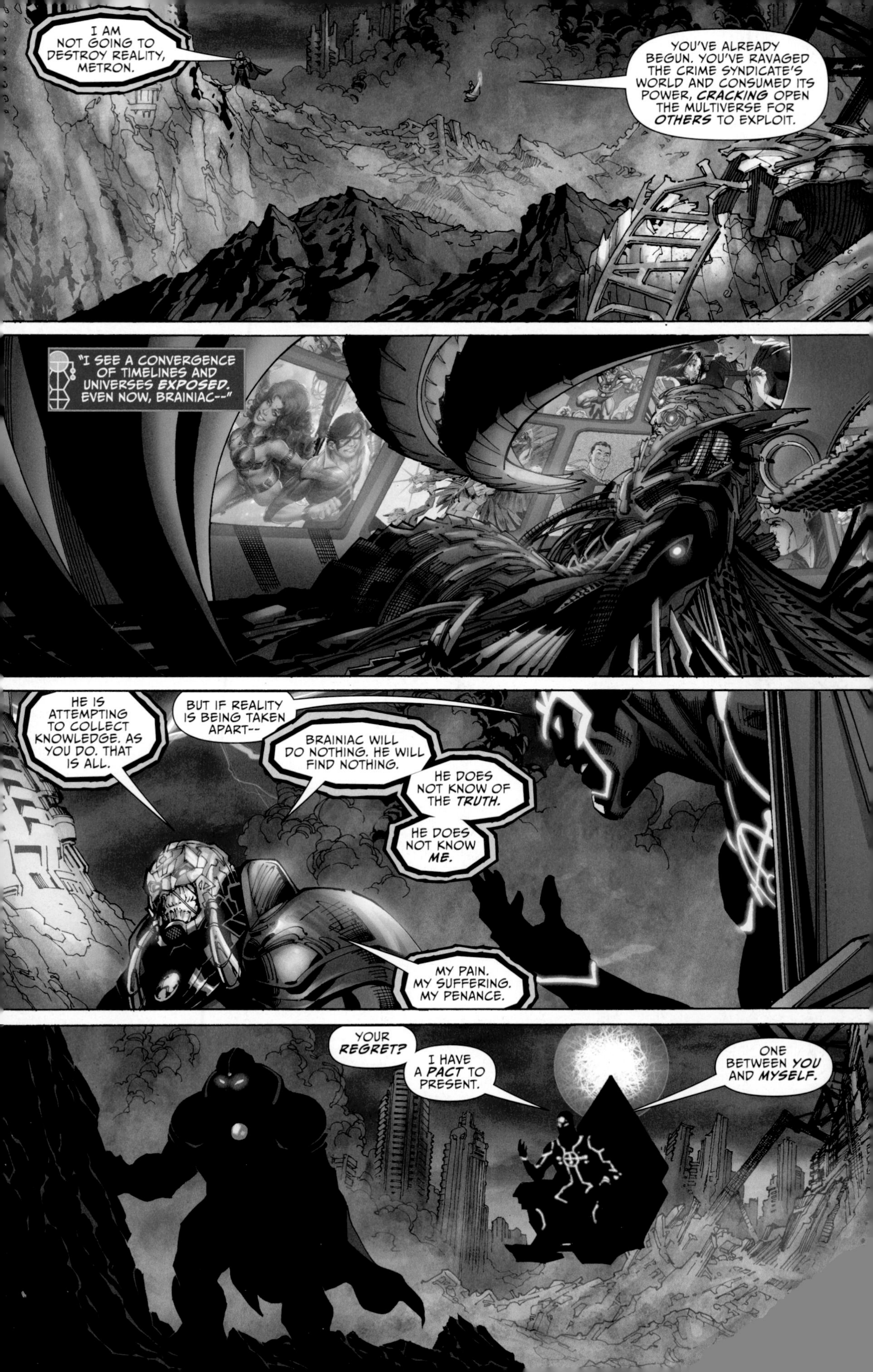
I AM NOT GOING TO DESTROY REALITY, METRON.
YOU'VE ALREADY BEGUN. YOU'VE RAVAGED THE CRIME SYNDICATE'S WORLD AND CONSUMED ITS POWER, *CRACKING* OPEN THE MULTIVERSE FOR *OTHERS* TO EXPLOIT.
"I SEE A CONVERGENCE OF TIMELINES AND UNIVERSES *EXPOSED.* EVEN NOW, BRAINIAC--"
HE IS ATTEMPTING TO COLLECT KNOWLEDGE. AS YOU DO. THAT IS ALL.
BUT IF REALITY IS BEING TAKEN APART--
BRAINIAC WILL DO NOTHING. HE WILL FIND NOTHING.
HE DOES NOT KNOW OF THE *TRUTH.*
HE DOES NOT KNOW *ME.*
MY PAIN. MY SUFFERING. MY PENANCE.
YOUR *REGRET?*
I HAVE A *PACT* TO PRESENT.
ONE BETWEEN *YOU* AND *MYSELF.*

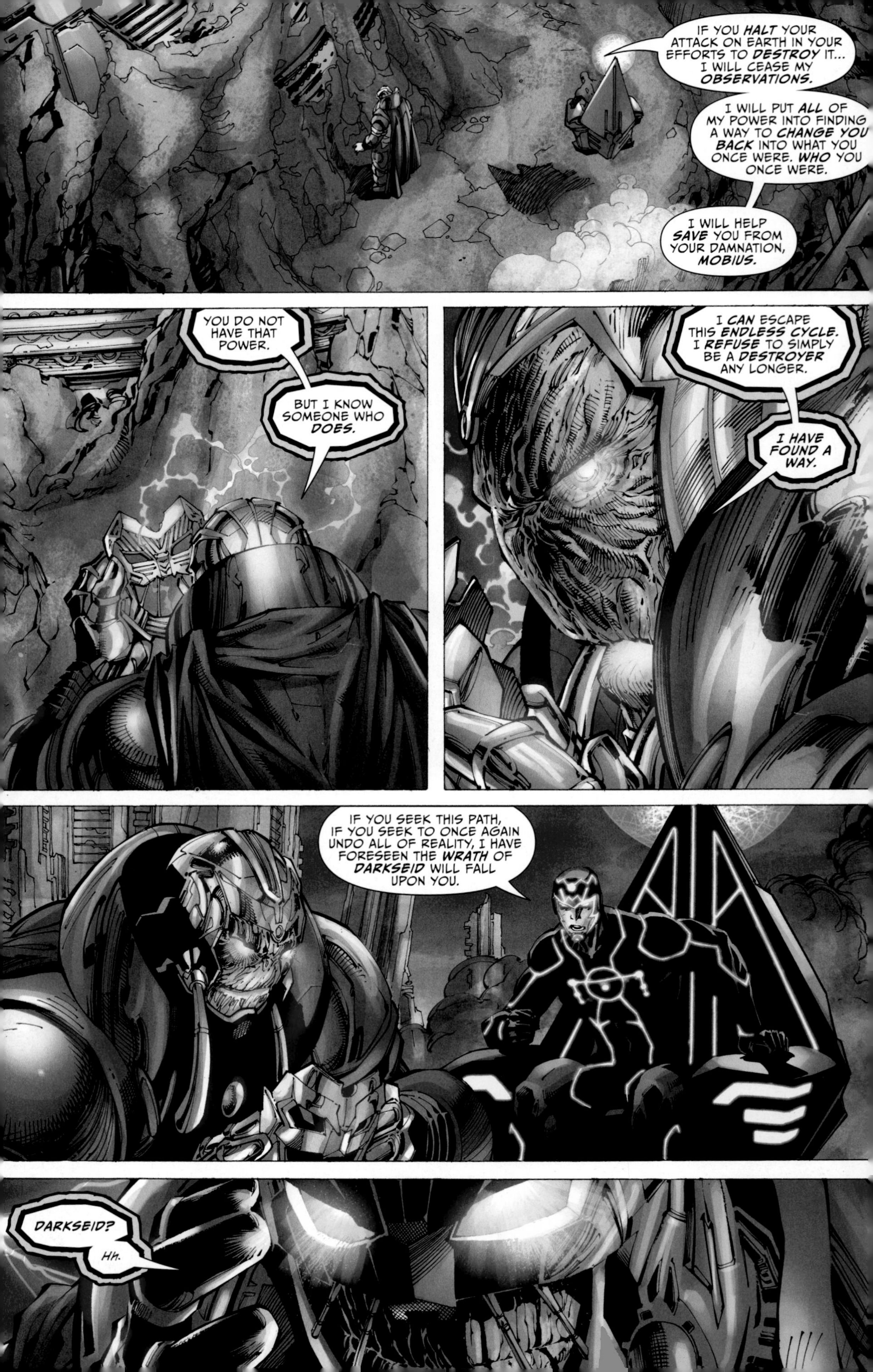
IF YOU HALT YOUR ATTACK ON EARTH IN YOUR EFFORTS TO DESTROY IT... I WILL CEASE MY OBSERVATIONS.
I WILL PUT ALL OF MY POWER INTO FINDING A WAY TO CHANGE YOU BACK INTO WHAT YOU ONCE WERE. WHO YOU ONCE WERE.
I WILL HELP SAVE YOU FROM YOUR DAMNATION, MOBIUS.
YOU DO NOT HAVE THAT POWER.
BUT I KNOW SOMEONE WHO DOES.
I CAN ESCAPE THIS ENDLESS CYCLE. I REFUSE TO SIMPLY BE A DESTROYER ANY LONGER.
I HAVE FOUND A WAY.
IF YOU SEEK THIS PATH, IF YOU SEEK TO ONCE AGAIN UNDO ALL OF REALITY, I HAVE FORESEEN THE WRATH OF DARKSEID WILL FALL UPON YOU.
DARKSEID?
Hn.

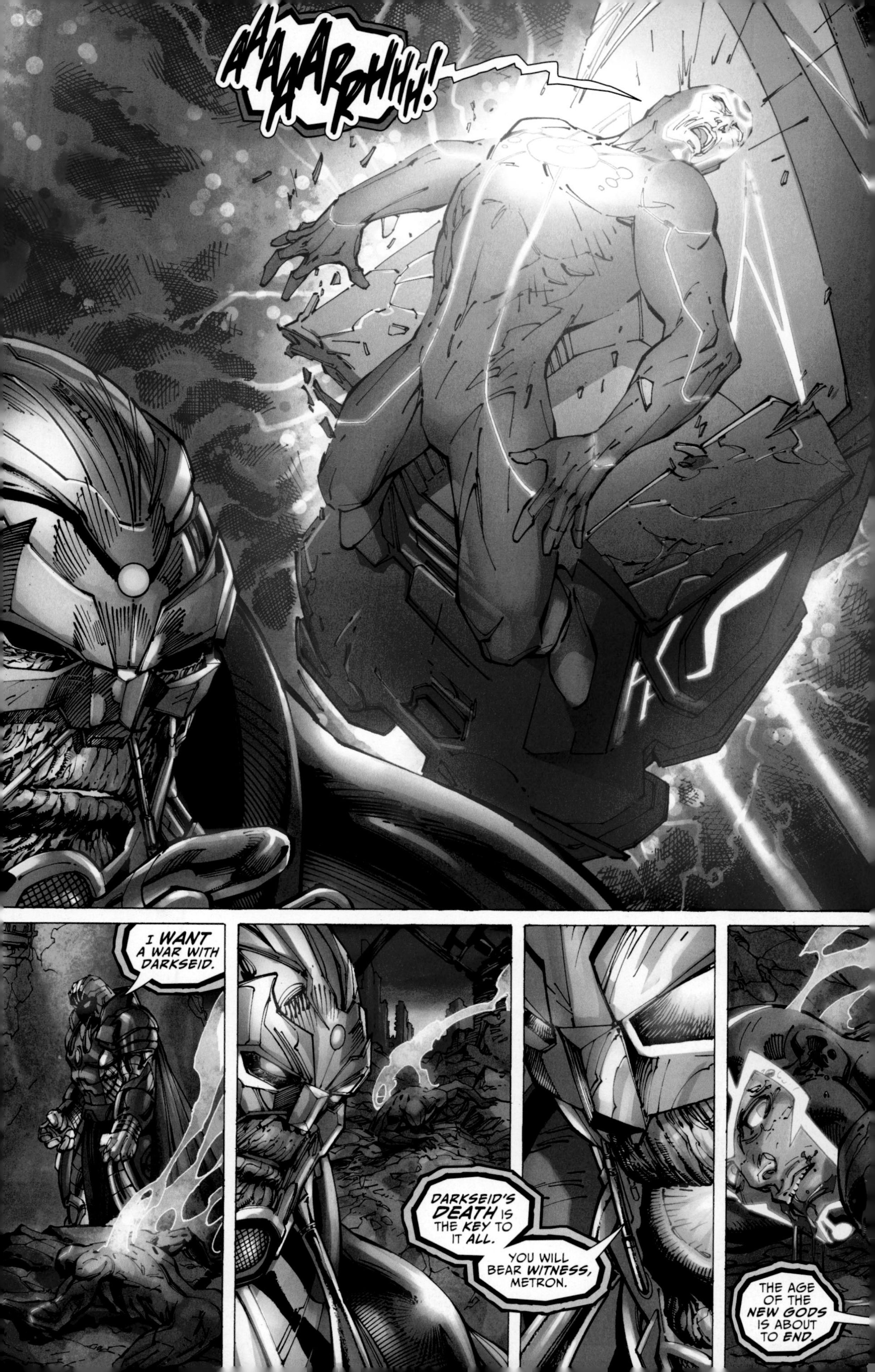
AAAAARRHHH!
I WANT A WAR WITH DARKSEID.
DARKSEID'S DEATH IS THE KEY TO IT ALL.
YOU WILL BEAR WITNESS, METRON.
THE AGE OF THE NEW GODS IS ABOUT TO END.

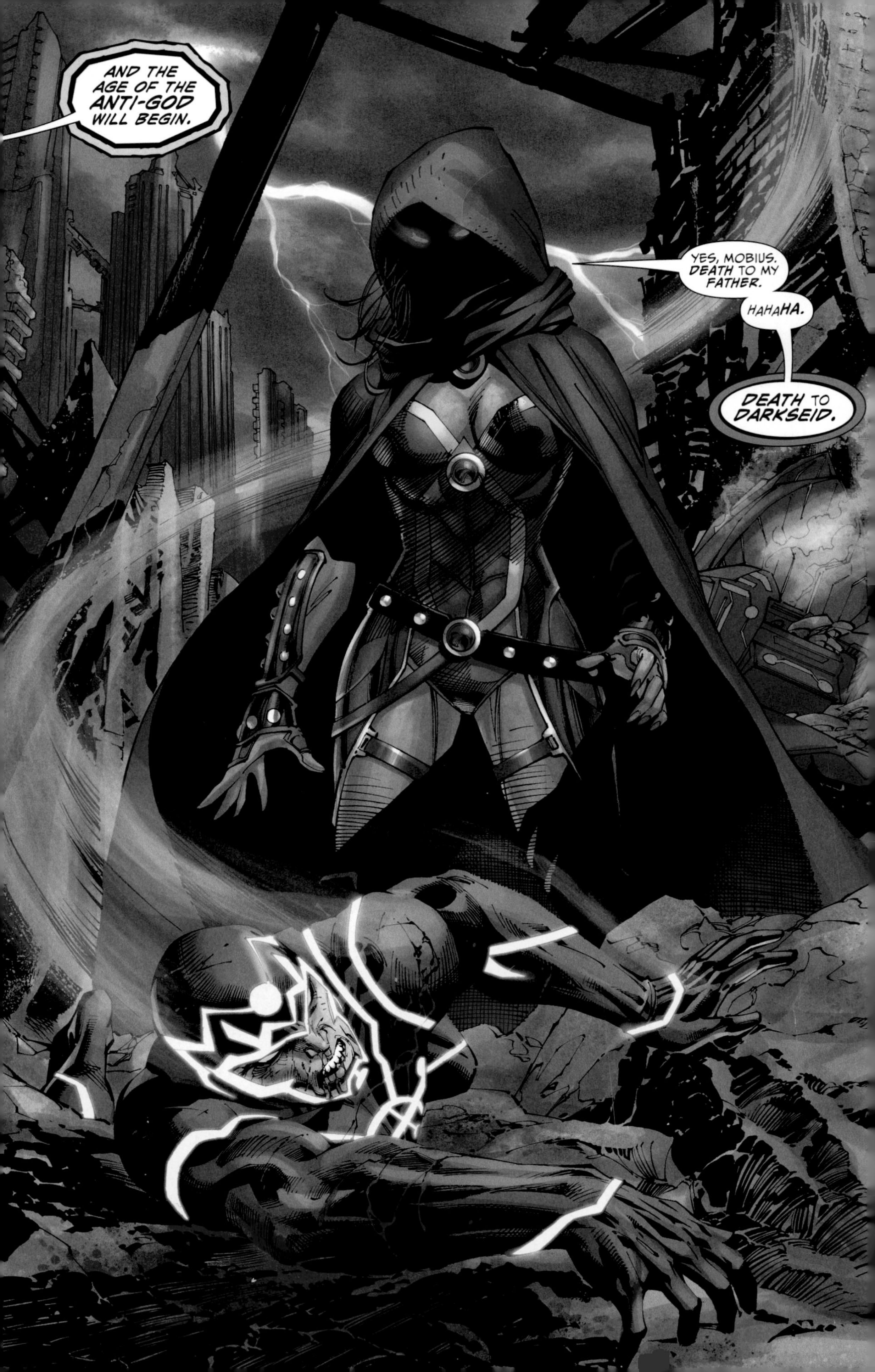
AND THE AGE OF THE ANTI-GOD WILL BEGIN.
YES, MOBIUS. DEATH TO MY FATHER.
HAHAHA.
DEATH TO DARKSEID.

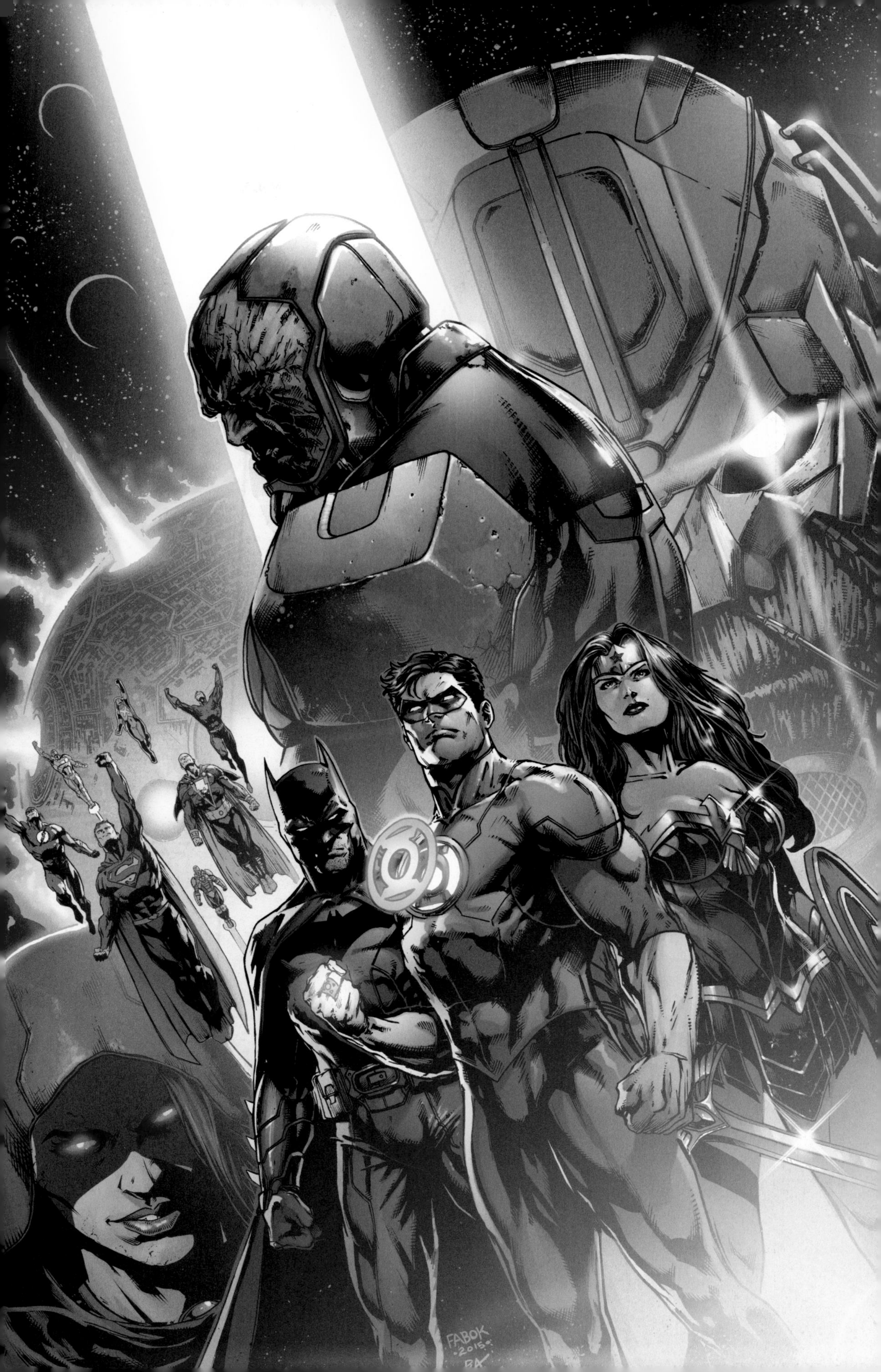
FABOK
2015
BA

DARKSEID WAR CHAPTER ONE: GOD VS. MAN

GEOFF JOHNS writer JASON FABOK artist BRAD ANDERSON colorist ROB LEIGH letterer cover by JASON FABOK and BRAD ANDERSON

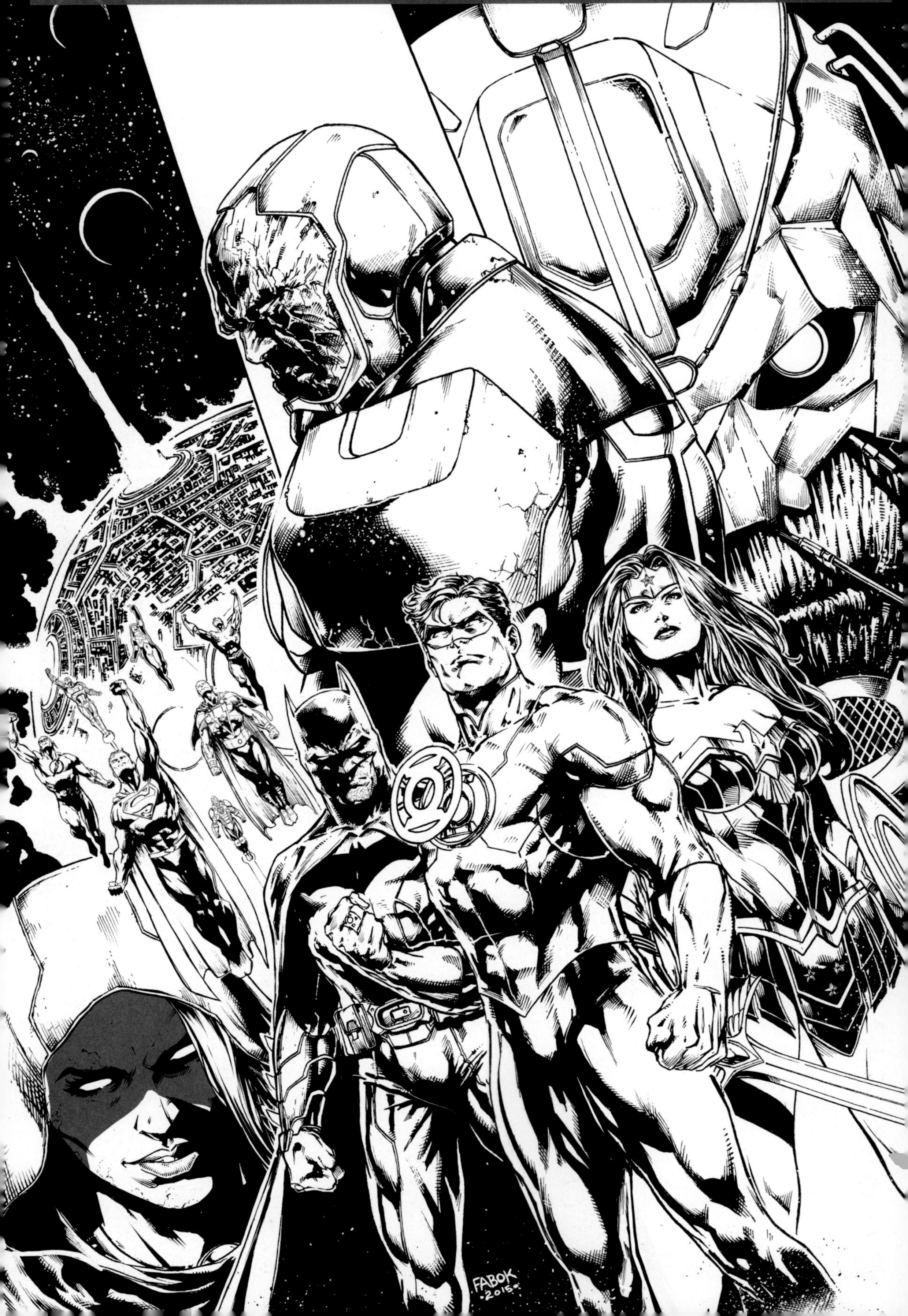
FABOK
2015

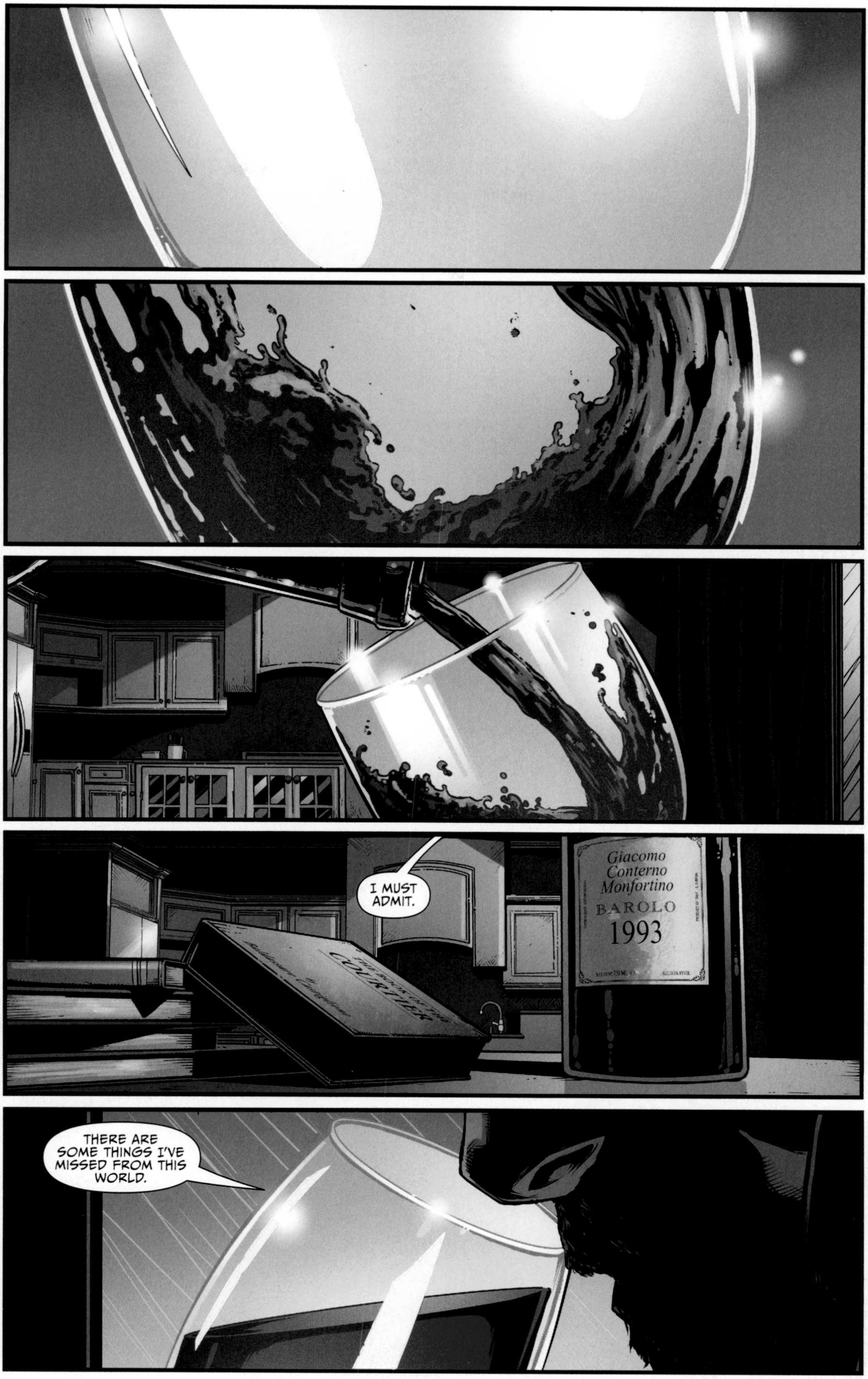
THE BOOK OF THE COURTIER
I MUST ADMIT.
Giacomo Conterno Monfortino
BAROLO
1993
THERE ARE SOME THINGS I'VE MISSED FROM THIS WORLD.

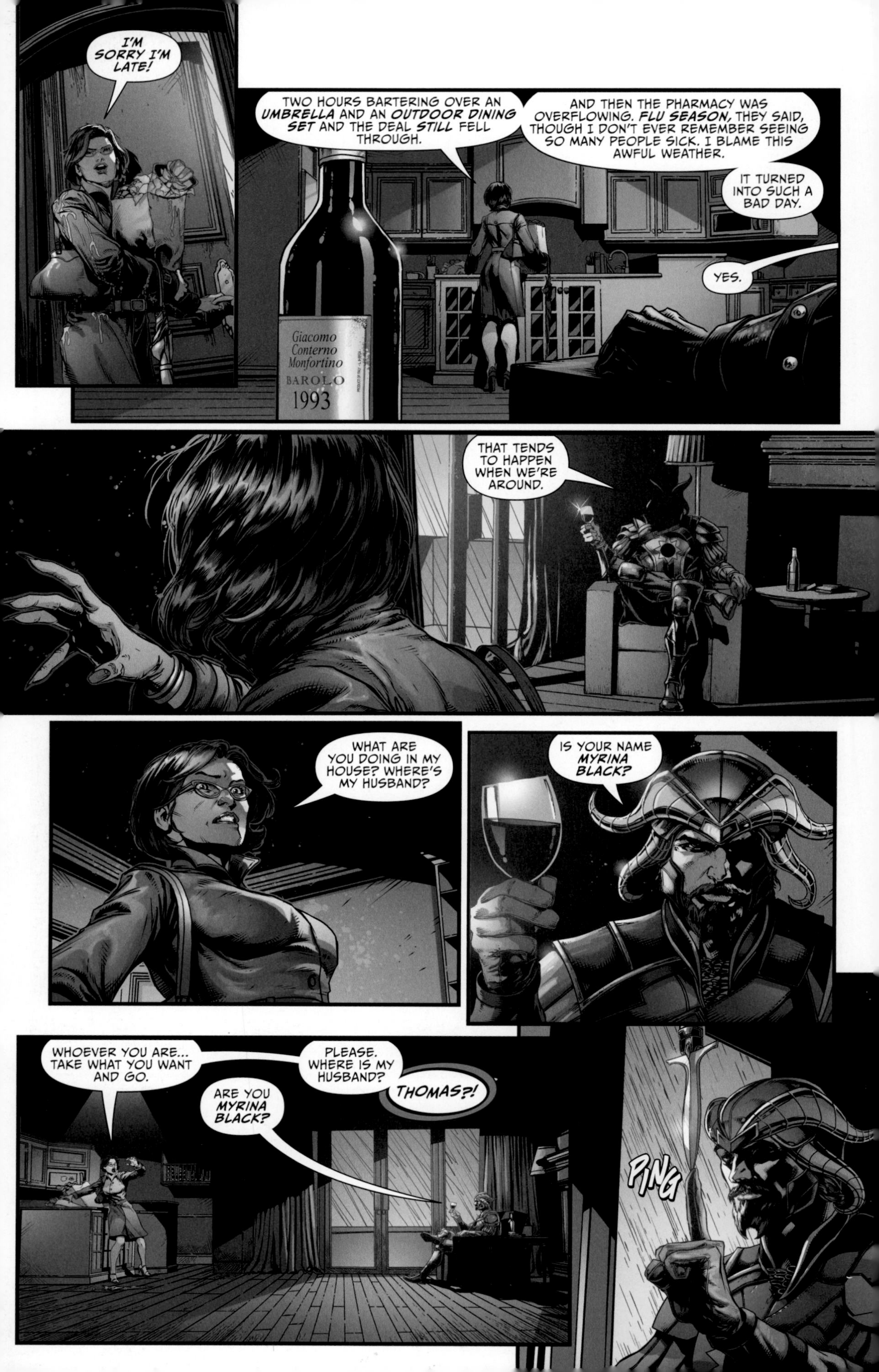
I'M SORRY I'M LATE!
TWO HOURS BARTERING OVER AN UMBRELLA AND AN OUTDOOR DINING SET AND THE DEAL STILL FELL THROUGH.
AND THEN THE PHARMACY WAS OVERFLOWING. FLU SEASON, THEY SAID, THOUGH I DON'T EVER REMEMBER SEEING SO MANY PEOPLE SICK. I BLAME THIS AWFUL WEATHER.
IT TURNED INTO SUCH A BAD DAY.
YES.
Giacomo Conterno Monfortino BAROLO 1993
THAT TENDS TO HAPPEN WHEN WE'RE AROUND.
WHAT ARE YOU DOING IN MY HOUSE? WHERE'S MY HUSBAND?
IS YOUR NAME MYRINA BLACK?
WHOEVER YOU ARE... TAKE WHAT YOU WANT AND GO.
PLEASE. WHERE IS MY HUSBAND?
THOMAS?!
ARE YOU MYRINA BLACK?
PING

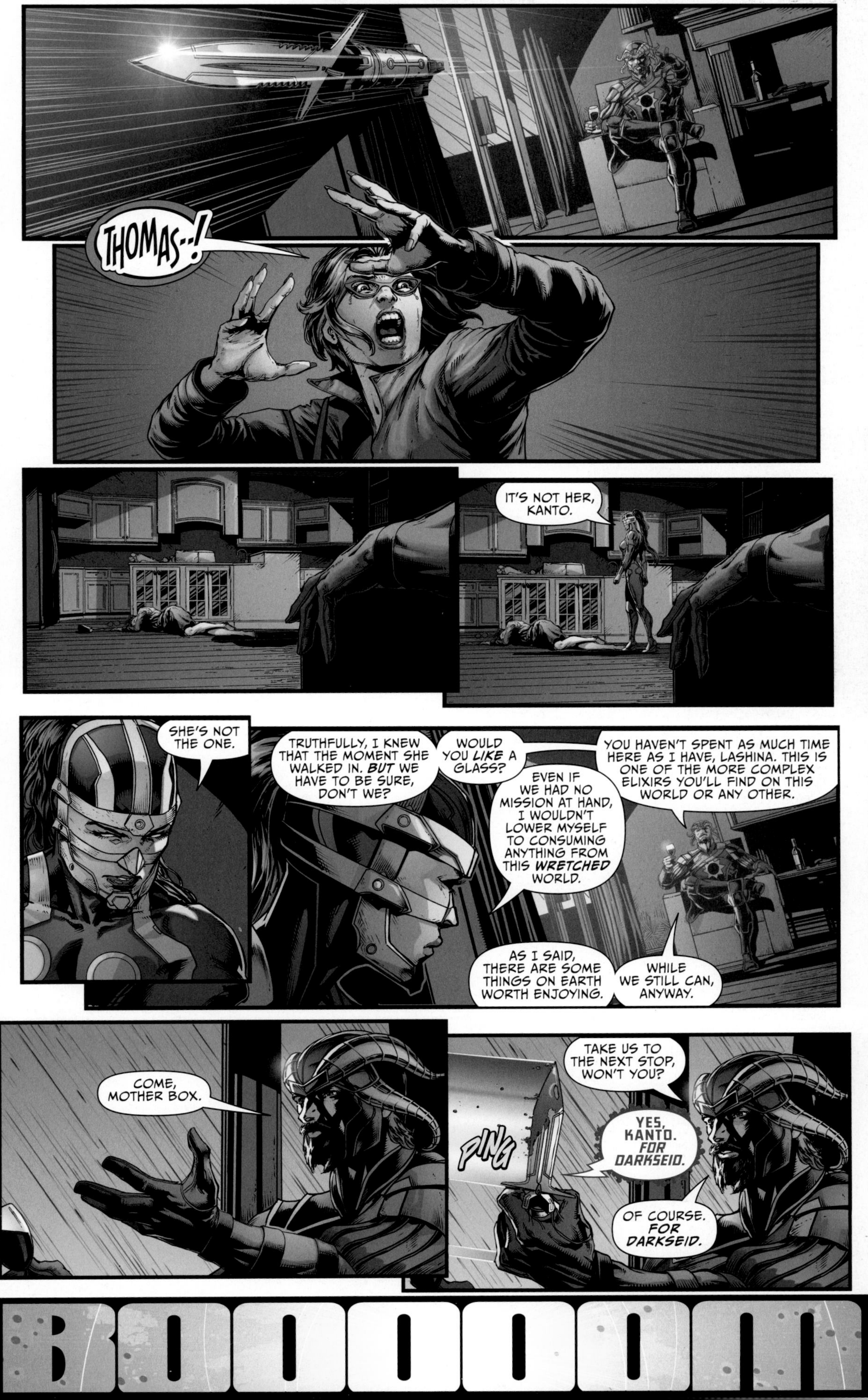

THOMAS--!
IT'S NOT HER, KANTO.
SHE'S NOT THE ONE.
TRUTHFULLY, I KNEW THAT THE MOMENT SHE WALKED IN. *BUT* WE HAVE TO BE SURE, DON'T WE?
WOULD YOU *LIKE* A GLASS?
EVEN IF WE HAD NO MISSION AT HAND, I WOULDN'T LOWER MYSELF TO CONSUMING ANYTHING FROM THIS *WRETCHED* WORLD.
YOU HAVEN'T SPENT AS MUCH TIME HERE AS I HAVE, LASHINA. THIS IS ONE OF THE MORE COMPLEX ELIXIRS YOU'LL FIND ON THIS WORLD OR ANY OTHER.
AS I SAID, THERE ARE SOME THINGS ON EARTH WORTH ENJOYING.
WHILE WE STILL CAN, ANYWAY.
COME, MOTHER BOX.
TAKE US TO THE NEXT STOP, WON'T YOU?
PING
YES, KANTO. *FOR DARKSEID.*
OF COURSE. *FOR DARKSEID.*
BOOOOOM

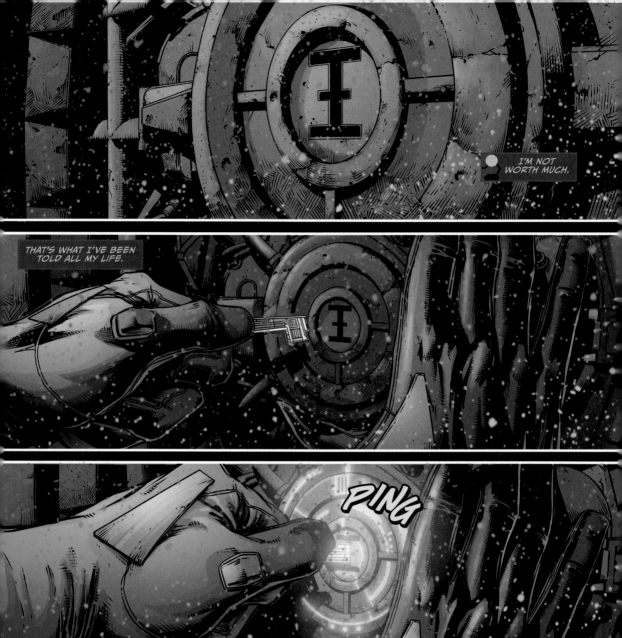

I'M NOT WORTH MUCH.

THAT'S WHAT I'VE BEEN TOLD ALL MY LIFE.

PING

WHEN I WAS SEVEN, MY FATHER WAS TOLD THE ONLY WAY TO END THE WAR BETWEEN NEW GENESIS AND APOKOLIPS WAS IF HE EXCHANGED SONS WITH DARKSEID.

I BEGGED NOT TO BE CHOSEN.

BUT I WAS.

AND WHILE MY FATHER WELCOMED DARKSEID'S SAVAGE SON TO THE FAMILY DINNER TABLE AND TAUGHT HIM HOW TO USE A FORK, I WAS TAKEN TO APOKOLIPS, THROWN INTO THE SLAVE PITS AND FORGOTTEN.

BUT EVENTUALLY, BEING FORGOTTEN BECAME AN ADVANTAGE.

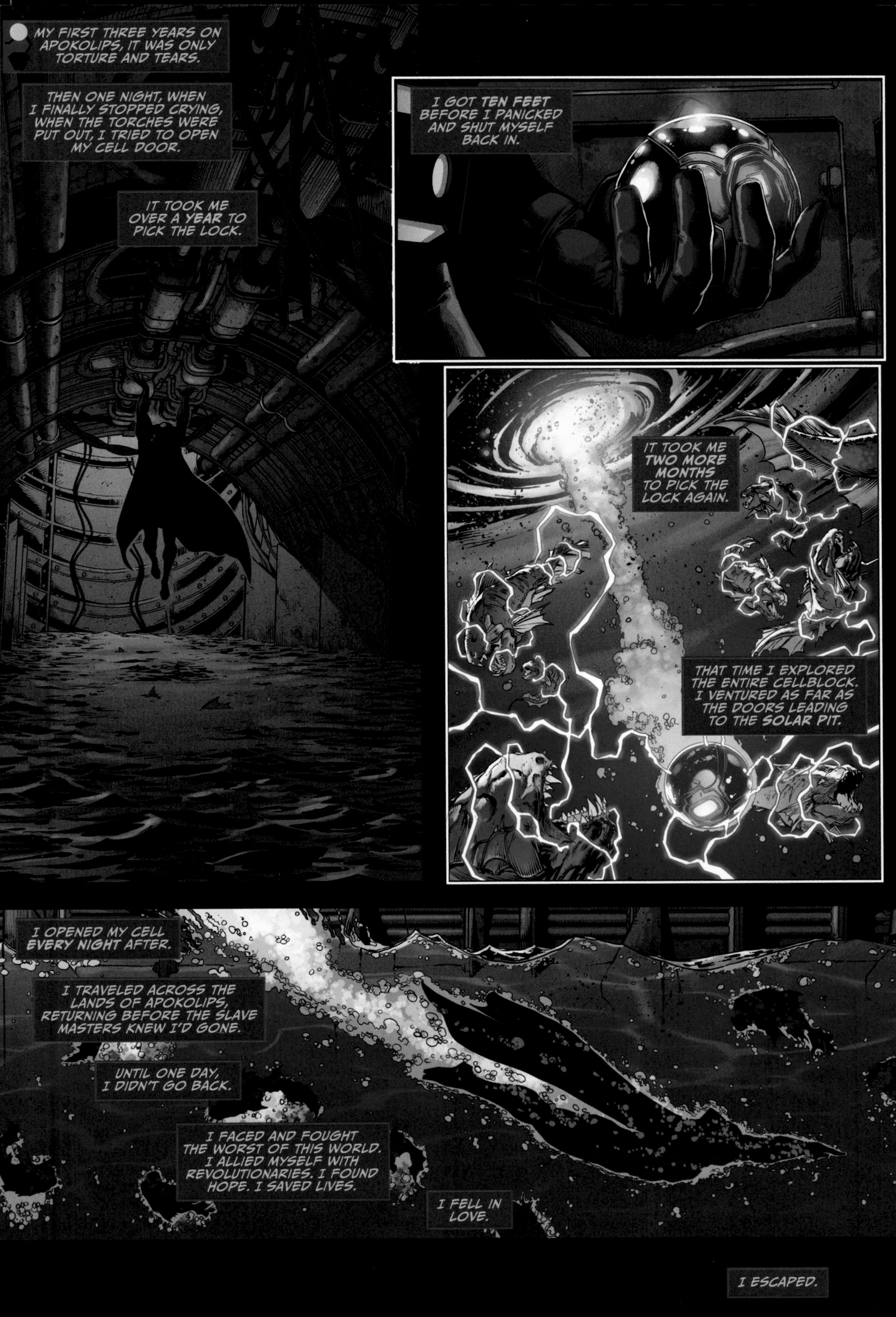
MY FIRST THREE YEARS ON APOKOLIPS, IT WAS ONLY TORTURE AND TEARS.
THEN ONE NIGHT, WHEN I FINALLY STOPPED CRYING, WHEN THE TORCHES WERE PUT OUT, I TRIED TO OPEN MY CELL DOOR.
IT TOOK ME OVER A YEAR TO PICK THE LOCK.
I GOT TEN FEET BEFORE I PANICKED AND SHUT MYSELF BACK IN.
IT TOOK ME TWO MORE MONTHS TO PICK THE LOCK AGAIN.
THAT TIME I EXPLORED THE ENTIRE CELLBLOCK. I VENTURED AS FAR AS THE DOORS LEADING TO THE SOLAR PIT.
I OPENED MY CELL EVERY NIGHT AFTER.
I TRAVELED ACROSS THE LANDS OF APOKOLIPS, RETURNING BEFORE THE SLAVE MASTERS KNEW I'D GONE.
UNTIL ONE DAY, I DIDN'T GO BACK.
I FACED AND FOUGHT THE WORST OF THIS WORLD. I ALLIED MYSELF WITH REVOLUTIONARIES. I FOUND HOPE. I SAVED LIVES.
I FELL IN LOVE.
I ESCAPED.

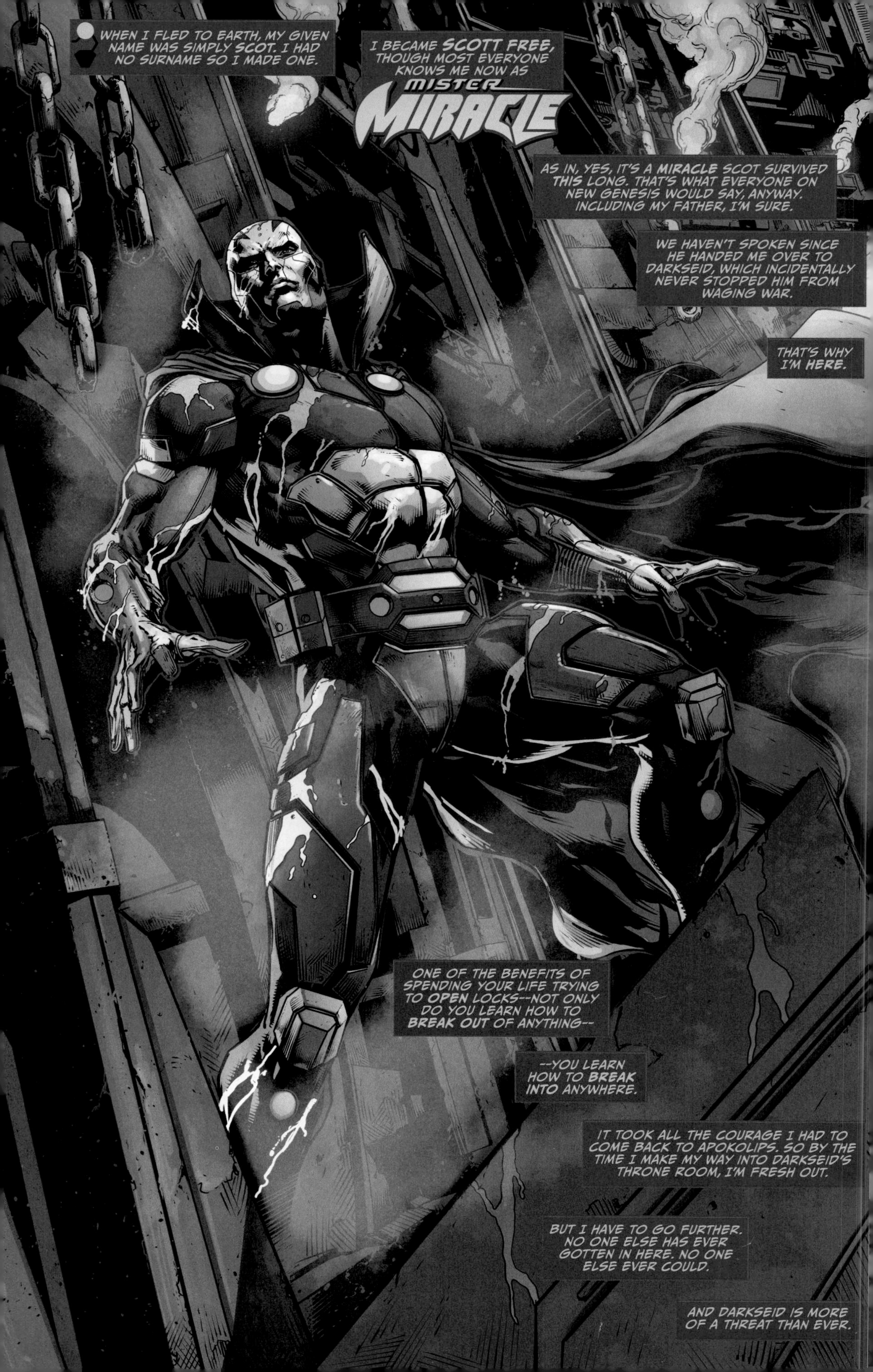
WHEN I FLED TO EARTH, MY GIVEN NAME WAS SIMPLY SCOT. I HAD NO SURNAME SO I MADE ONE.
I BECAME SCOTT FREE, THOUGH MOST EVERYONE KNOWS ME NOW AS
MISTER MIRACLE
AS IN, YES, IT'S A MIRACLE SCOT SURVIVED THIS LONG. THAT'S WHAT EVERYONE ON NEW GENESIS WOULD SAY, ANYWAY. INCLUDING MY FATHER, I'M SURE.
WE HAVEN'T SPOKEN SINCE HE HANDED ME OVER TO DARKSEID, WHICH INCIDENTALLY NEVER STOPPED HIM FROM WAGING WAR.
THAT'S WHY I'M HERE.
ONE OF THE BENEFITS OF SPENDING YOUR LIFE TRYING TO OPEN LOCKS--NOT ONLY DO YOU LEARN HOW TO BREAK OUT OF ANYTHING--
--YOU LEARN HOW TO BREAK INTO ANYWHERE.
IT TOOK ALL THE COURAGE I HAD TO COME BACK TO APOKOLIPS. SO BY THE TIME I MAKE MY WAY INTO DARKSEID'S THRONE ROOM, I'M FRESH OUT.
BUT I HAVE TO GO FURTHER. NO ONE ELSE HAS EVER GOTTEN IN HERE. NO ONE ELSE EVER COULD.
AND DARKSEID IS MORE OF A THREAT THAN EVER.

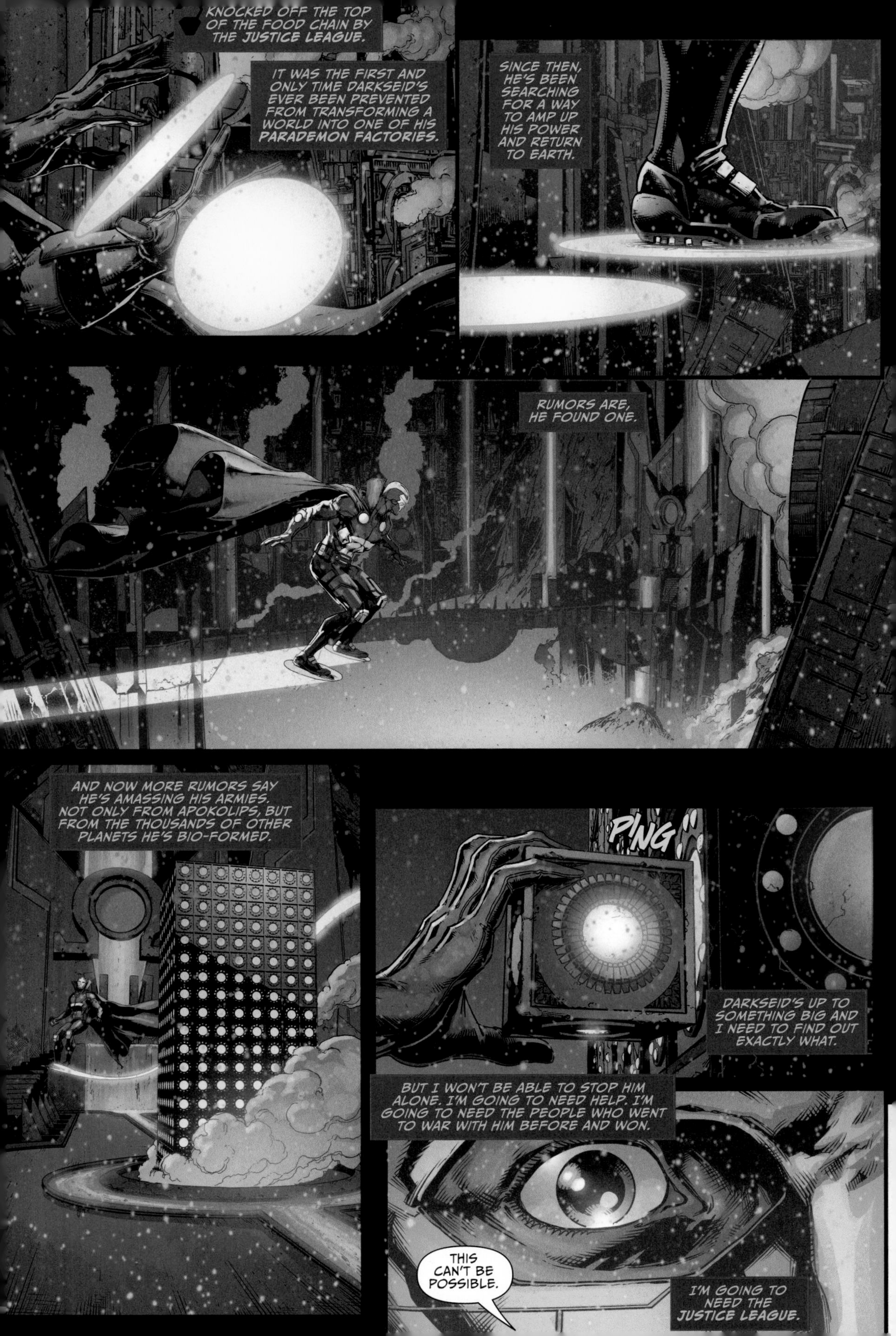
KNOCKED OFF THE TOP OF THE FOOD CHAIN BY THE JUSTICE LEAGUE.
IT WAS THE FIRST AND ONLY TIME DARKSEID'S EVER BEEN PREVENTED FROM TRANSFORMING A WORLD INTO ONE OF HIS PARADEMON FACTORIES.
SINCE THEN, HE'S BEEN SEARCHING FOR A WAY TO AMP UP HIS POWER AND RETURN TO EARTH.
RUMORS ARE, HE FOUND ONE.
AND NOW MORE RUMORS SAY HE'S AMASSING HIS ARMIES. NOT ONLY FROM APOKOLIPS, BUT FROM THE THOUSANDS OF OTHER PLANETS HE'S BIO-FORMED.
PING
DARKSEID'S UP TO SOMETHING BIG AND I NEED TO FIND OUT EXACTLY WHAT.
BUT I WON'T BE ABLE TO STOP HIM ALONE. I'M GOING TO NEED HELP. I'M GOING TO NEED THE PEOPLE WHO WENT TO WAR WITH HIM BEFORE AND WON.
THIS CAN'T BE POSSIBLE.
I'M GOING TO NEED THE JUSTICE LEAGUE.

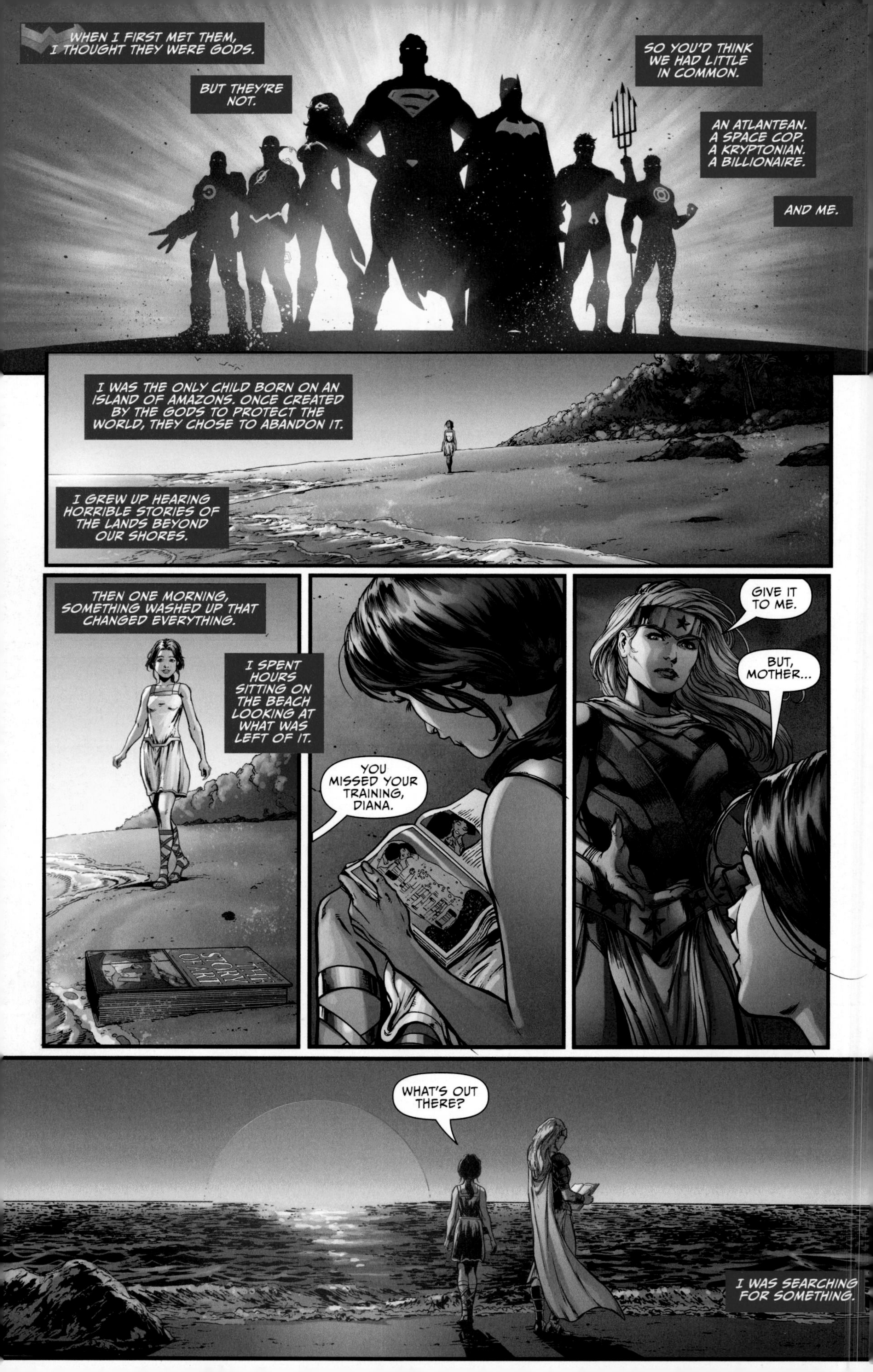
WHEN I FIRST MET THEM, I THOUGHT THEY WERE GODS.
BUT THEY'RE NOT.
SO YOU'D THINK WE HAD LITTLE IN COMMON.
AN ATLANTEAN. A SPACE COP. A KRYPTONIAN. A BILLIONAIRE.
AND ME.
I WAS THE ONLY CHILD BORN ON AN ISLAND OF AMAZONS. ONCE CREATED BY THE GODS TO PROTECT THE WORLD, THEY CHOSE TO ABANDON IT.
I GREW UP HEARING HORRIBLE STORIES OF THE LANDS BEYOND OUR SHORES.
THEN ONE MORNING, SOMETHING WASHED UP THAT CHANGED EVERYTHING.
I SPENT HOURS SITTING ON THE BEACH LOOKING AT WHAT WAS LEFT OF IT.
THE STORY OF ART
YOU MISSED YOUR TRAINING, DIANA.
GIVE IT TO ME.
BUT, MOTHER...
WHAT'S OUT THERE?
I WAS SEARCHING FOR SOMETHING.

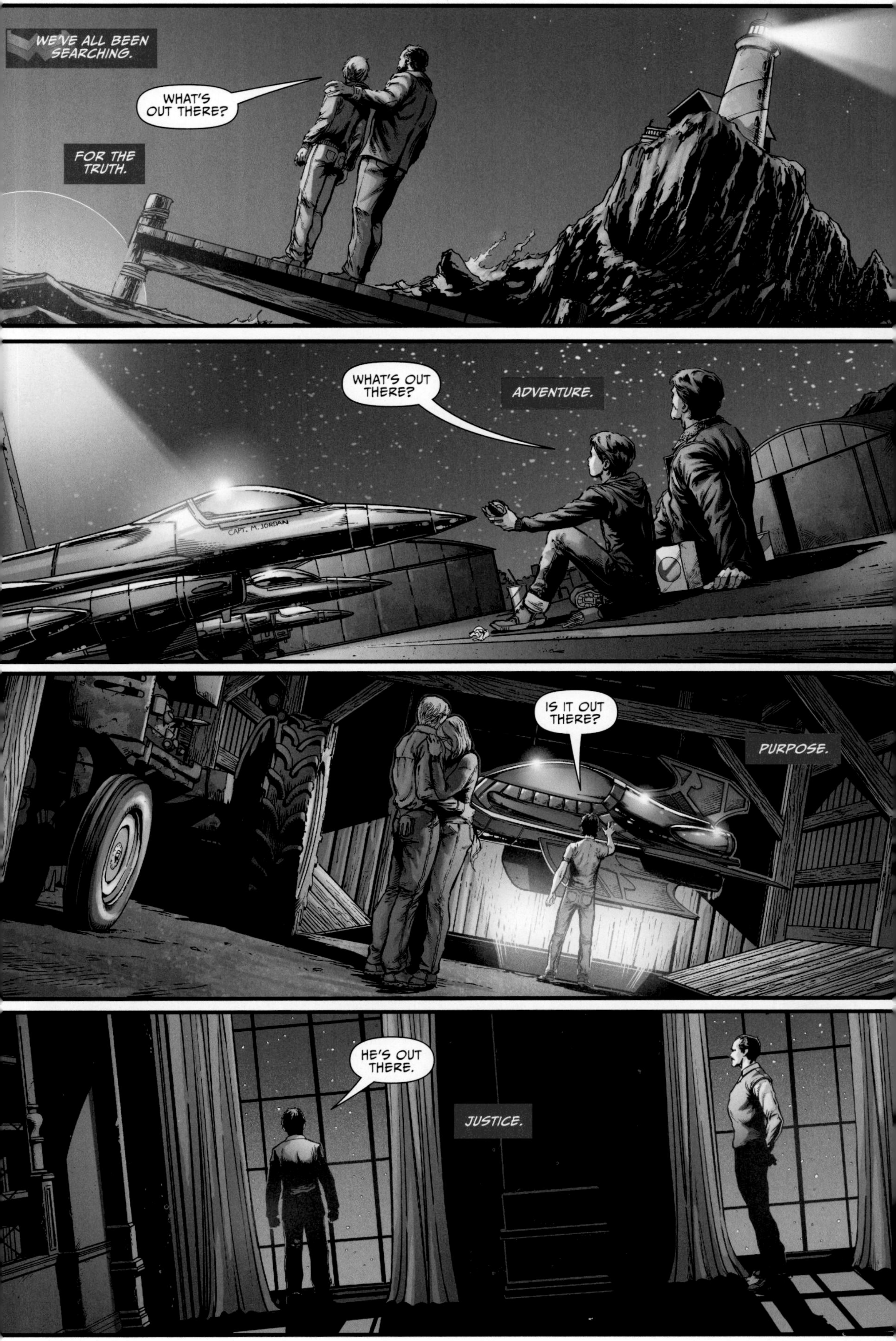

WE'VE ALL BEEN SEARCHING.
WHAT'S OUT THERE?
FOR THE TRUTH.
WHAT'S OUT THERE?
ADVENTURE.
CAPT. M. JORDAN
IS IT OUT THERE?
PURPOSE.
HE'S OUT THERE.
JUSTICE.

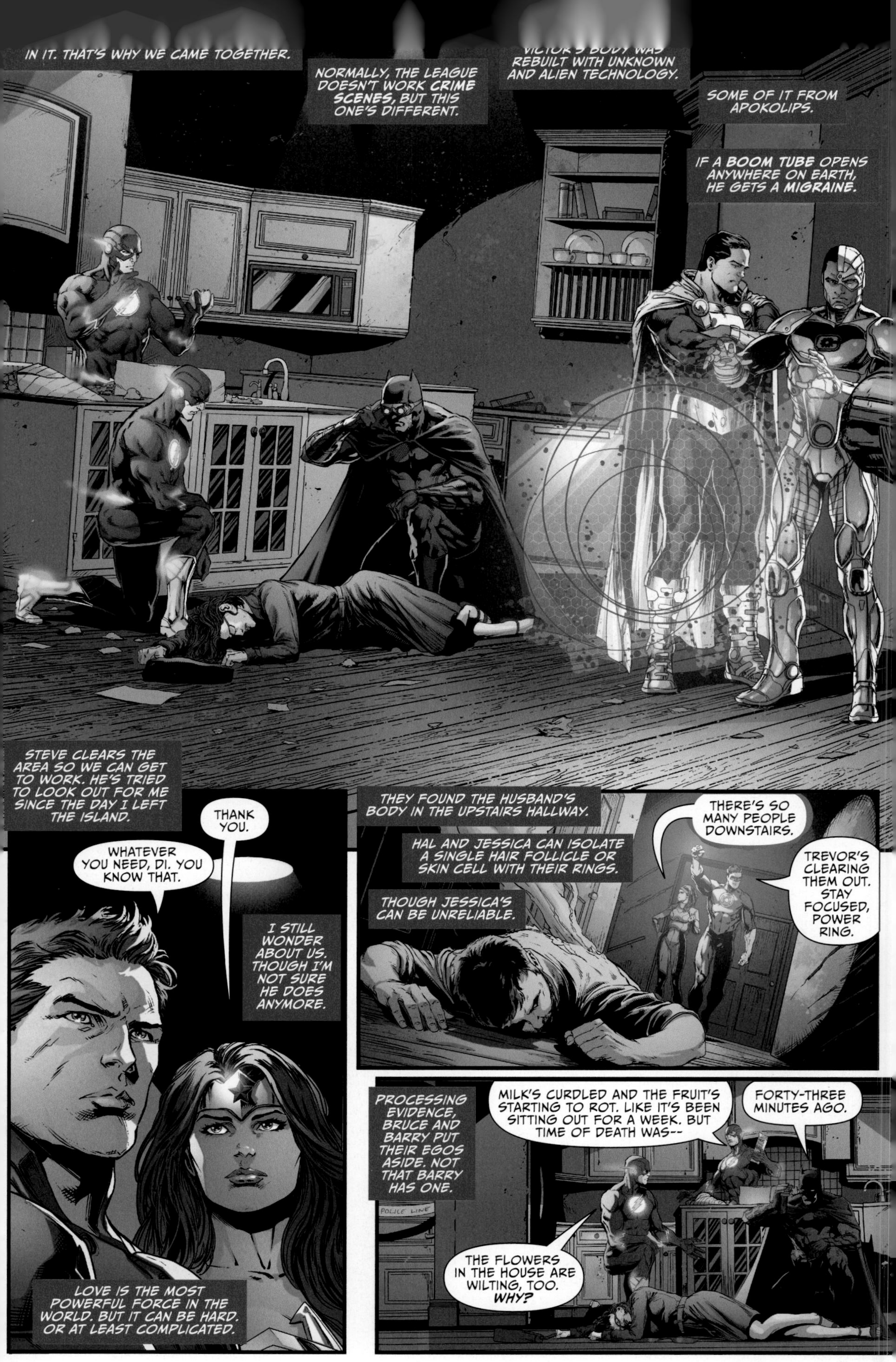
IN IT. THAT'S WHY WE CAME TOGETHER.
NORMALLY, THE LEAGUE DOESN'T WORK CRIME SCENES, BUT THIS ONE'S DIFFERENT.
VICTOR'S BODY WAS REBUILT WITH UNKNOWN AND ALIEN TECHNOLOGY.
SOME OF IT FROM APOKOLIPS.
IF A BOOM TUBE OPENS ANYWHERE ON EARTH, HE GETS A MIGRAINE.
STEVE CLEARS THE AREA SO WE CAN GET TO WORK. HE'S TRIED TO LOOK OUT FOR ME SINCE THE DAY I LEFT THE ISLAND.
WHATEVER YOU NEED, DI. YOU KNOW THAT.
THANK YOU.
I STILL WONDER ABOUT US. THOUGH I'M NOT SURE HE DOES ANYMORE.
LOVE IS THE MOST POWERFUL FORCE IN THE WORLD. BUT IT CAN BE HARD. OR AT LEAST COMPLICATED.
THEY FOUND THE HUSBAND'S BODY IN THE UPSTAIRS HALLWAY.
HAL AND JESSICA CAN ISOLATE A SINGLE HAIR FOLLICLE OR SKIN CELL WITH THEIR RINGS.
THOUGH JESSICA'S CAN BE UNRELIABLE.
THERE'S SO MANY PEOPLE DOWNSTAIRS.
TREVOR'S CLEARING THEM OUT. STAY FOCUSED, POWER RING.
PROCESSING EVIDENCE, BRUCE AND BARRY PUT THEIR EGOS ASIDE. NOT THAT BARRY HAS ONE.
MILK'S CURDLED AND THE FRUIT'S STARTING TO ROT. LIKE IT'S BEEN SITTING OUT FOR A WEEK. BUT TIME OF DEATH WAS--
FORTY-THREE MINUTES AGO.
THE FLOWERS IN THE HOUSE ARE WILTING, TOO. WHY?
POLICE LINE

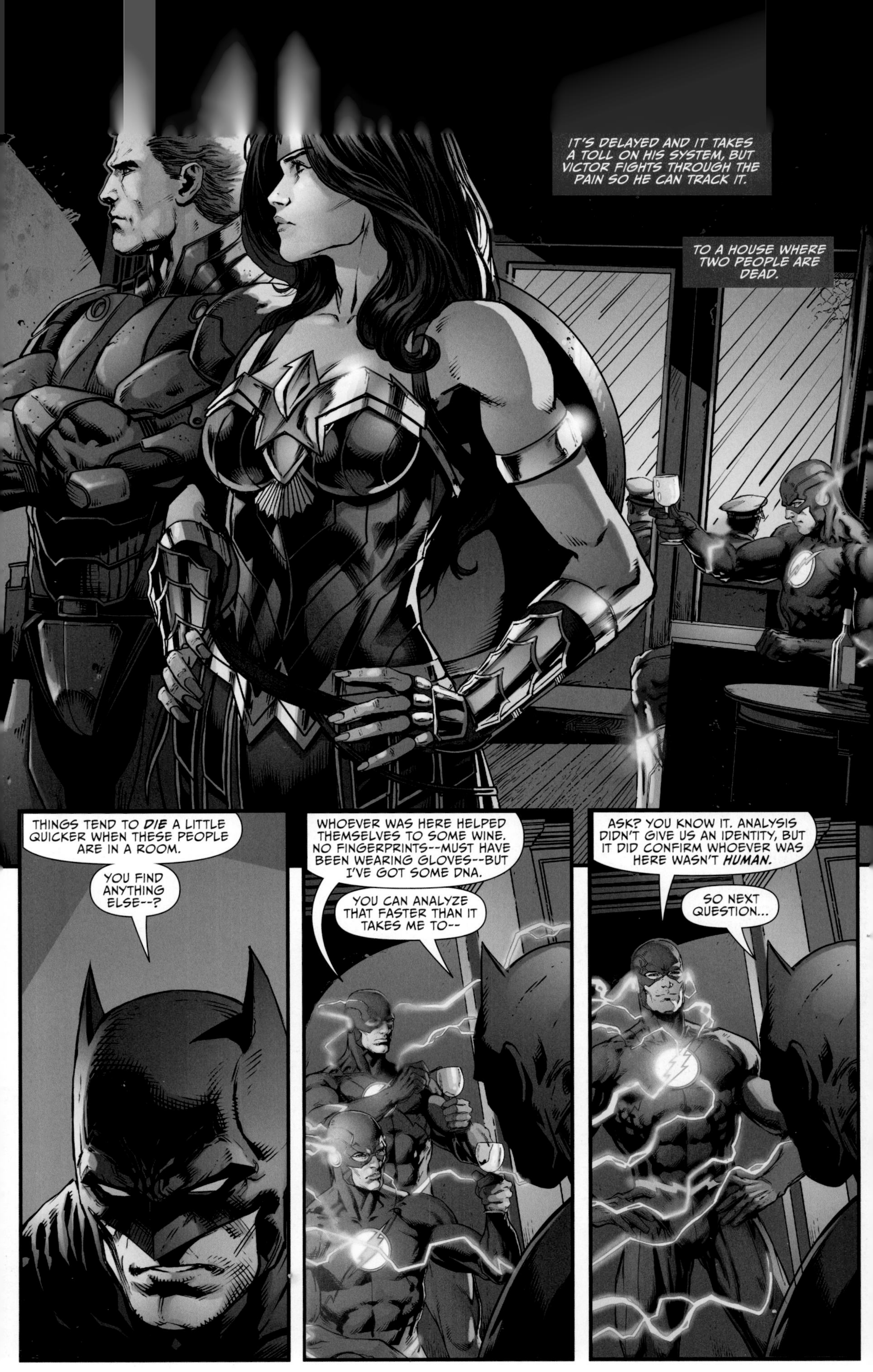
IT'S DELAYED AND IT TAKES A TOLL ON HIS SYSTEM, BUT VICTOR FIGHTS THROUGH THE PAIN SO HE CAN TRACK IT.
TO A HOUSE WHERE TWO PEOPLE ARE DEAD.
THINGS TEND TO *DIE* A LITTLE QUICKER WHEN THESE PEOPLE ARE IN A ROOM.
YOU FIND ANYTHING ELSE--?
WHOEVER WAS HERE HELPED THEMSELVES TO SOME WINE. NO FINGERPRINTS--MUST HAVE BEEN WEARING GLOVES--BUT I'VE GOT SOME DNA.
YOU CAN ANALYZE THAT FASTER THAN IT TAKES ME TO--
ASK? YOU KNOW IT. ANALYSIS DIDN'T GIVE US AN IDENTITY, BUT IT DID CONFIRM WHOEVER WAS HERE WASN'T *HUMAN.*
SO NEXT QUESTION...

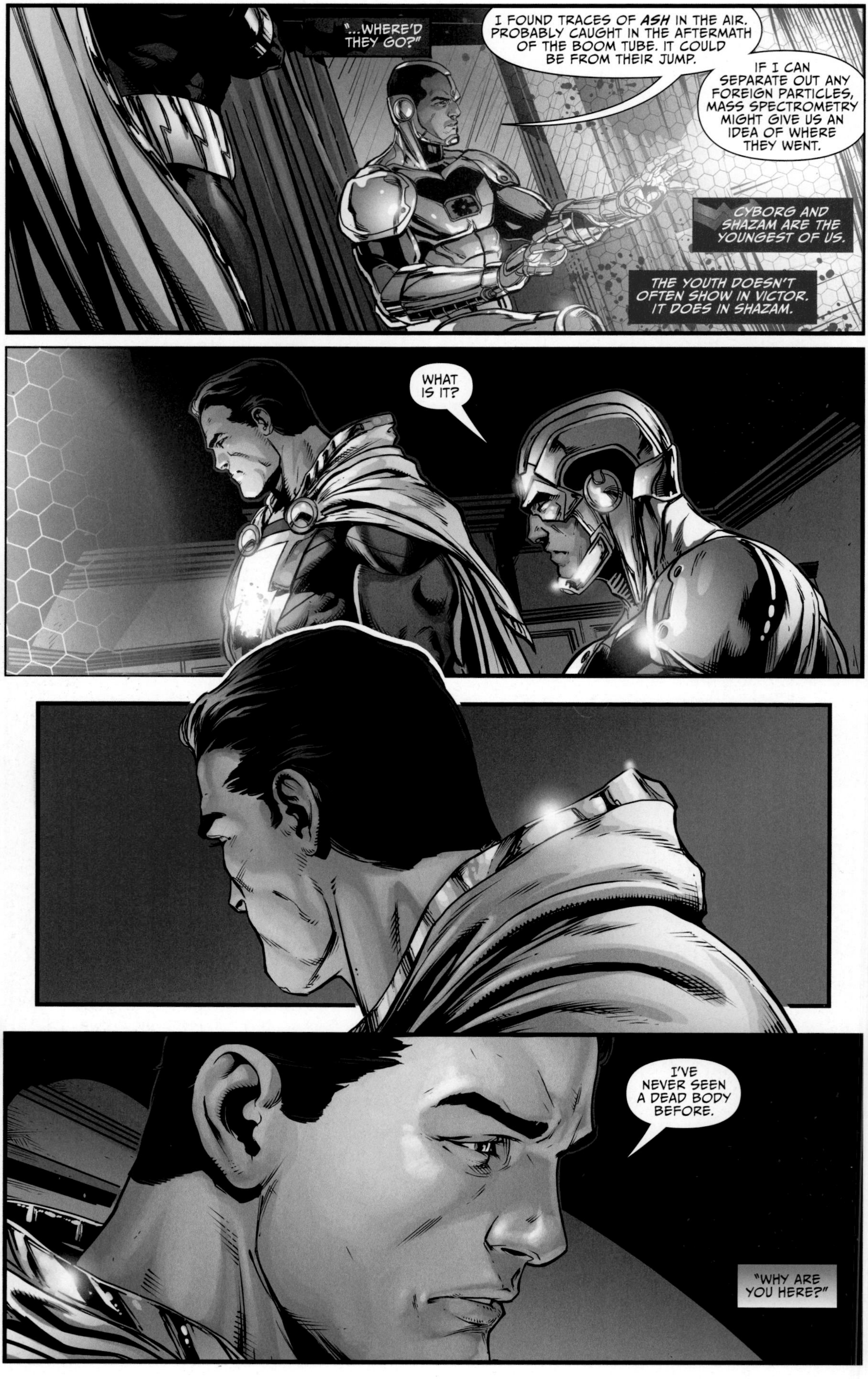
"...WHERE'D THEY GO?"
I FOUND TRACES OF ASH IN THE AIR. PROBABLY CAUGHT IN THE AFTERMATH OF THE BOOM TUBE. IT COULD BE FROM THEIR JUMP.
IF I CAN SEPARATE OUT ANY FOREIGN PARTICLES, MASS SPECTROMETRY MIGHT GIVE US AN IDEA OF WHERE THEY WENT.
CYBORG AND SHAZAM ARE THE YOUNGEST OF US.
THE YOUTH DOESN'T OFTEN SHOW IN VICTOR. IT DOES IN SHAZAM.
WHAT IS IT?
I'VE NEVER SEEN A DEAD BODY BEFORE.
"WHY ARE YOU HERE?"

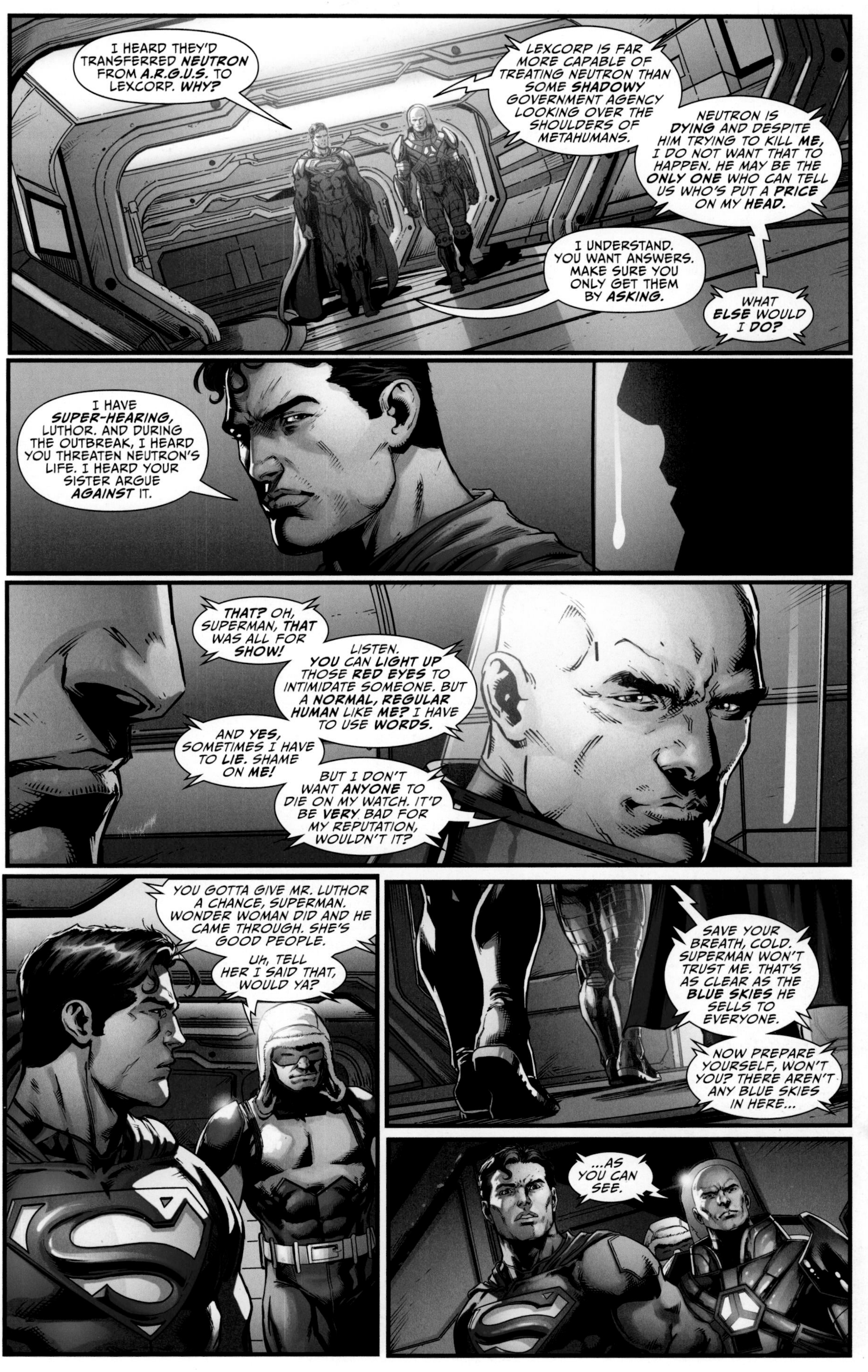
I HEARD THEY'D TRANSFERRED NEUTRON FROM A.R.G.U.S. TO LEXCORP. WHY?
LEXCORP IS FAR MORE CAPABLE OF TREATING NEUTRON THAN SOME SHADOWY GOVERNMENT AGENCY LOOKING OVER THE SHOULDERS OF METAHUMANS.
NEUTRON IS DYING AND DESPITE HIM TRYING TO KILL ME, I DO NOT WANT THAT TO HAPPEN. HE MAY BE THE ONLY ONE WHO CAN TELL US WHO'S PUT A PRICE ON MY HEAD.
I UNDERSTAND. YOU WANT ANSWERS. MAKE SURE YOU ONLY GET THEM BY ASKING.
WHAT ELSE WOULD I DO?
I HAVE SUPER-HEARING, LUTHOR. AND DURING THE OUTBREAK, I HEARD YOU THREATEN NEUTRON'S LIFE. I HEARD YOUR SISTER ARGUE AGAINST IT.
THAT? OH, SUPERMAN, THAT WAS ALL FOR SHOW!
LISTEN. YOU CAN LIGHT UP THOSE RED EYES TO INTIMIDATE SOMEONE. BUT A NORMAL, REGULAR HUMAN LIKE ME? I HAVE TO USE WORDS.
AND YES, SOMETIMES I HAVE TO LIE. SHAME ON ME!
BUT I DON'T WANT ANYONE TO DIE ON MY WATCH. IT'D BE VERY BAD FOR MY REPUTATION, WOULDN'T IT?
YOU GOTTA GIVE MR. LUTHOR A CHANCE, SUPERMAN. WONDER WOMAN DID AND HE CAME THROUGH. SHE'S GOOD PEOPLE.
UH, TELL HER I SAID THAT, WOULD YA?
SAVE YOUR BREATH, COLD. SUPERMAN WON'T TRUST ME. THAT'S AS CLEAR AS THE BLUE SKIES HE SELLS TO EVERYONE.
NOW PREPARE YOURSELF, WON'T YOU? THERE AREN'T ANY BLUE SKIES IN HERE...
...AS YOU CAN SEE.

HE'S NOT RESPONDING WELL, MR. LUTHOR.

EVER SINCE NEUTRON'S RADIOACTIVE POWERS WERE SHUT DOWN BY THE AMAZO VIRUS HIS BODY'S BECOME RAVAGED BY CANCER.

WE'VE TRIED X-RAYS, GAMMA RAYS, SYSTEMIC AND BRACHYTHERAPY. NONE OF IT'S HAVING ANY POSITIVE EFFECT.

HOW TRAGIC.

HIS EX-WIFE REQUESTED TO SEE HIM, BUT HE'S BEEN UNRESPONSIVE. AND IF WE CAN'T FIGURE SOMETHING OUT SOON, HE COULD BE DEAD BY TOMORROW.

THEN WE NEED TO WAKE HIM UP NOW.

WE DO THAT AND HE COULD DIE, MR. LUTHOR.

THEN YOU CAN'T WAKE HIM UP.

HE'S AS GOOD AS DEAD.

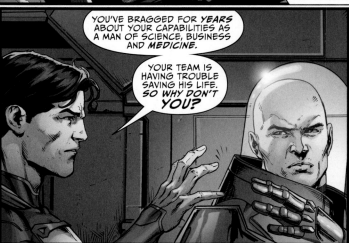

YOU'VE BRAGGED FOR YEARS ABOUT YOUR CAPABILITIES AS A MAN OF SCIENCE, BUSINESS AND MEDICINE.

YOUR TEAM IS HAVING TROUBLE SAVING HIS LIFE. SO WHY DON'T YOU?

UNLESS YOU CAN'T.

CAN'T--?! MOVE ASIDE.

HONESTLY. WHAT AM I EVEN PAYING YOU ALL FOR?

SUPERMAN JUST CHALLENGED LEX LUTHOR TO CURE CANCER AND I GET TO WATCH?

I GOT THE BEST SEAT IN THE WORLD.

IT'S HARD TO TRUST PEOPLE.

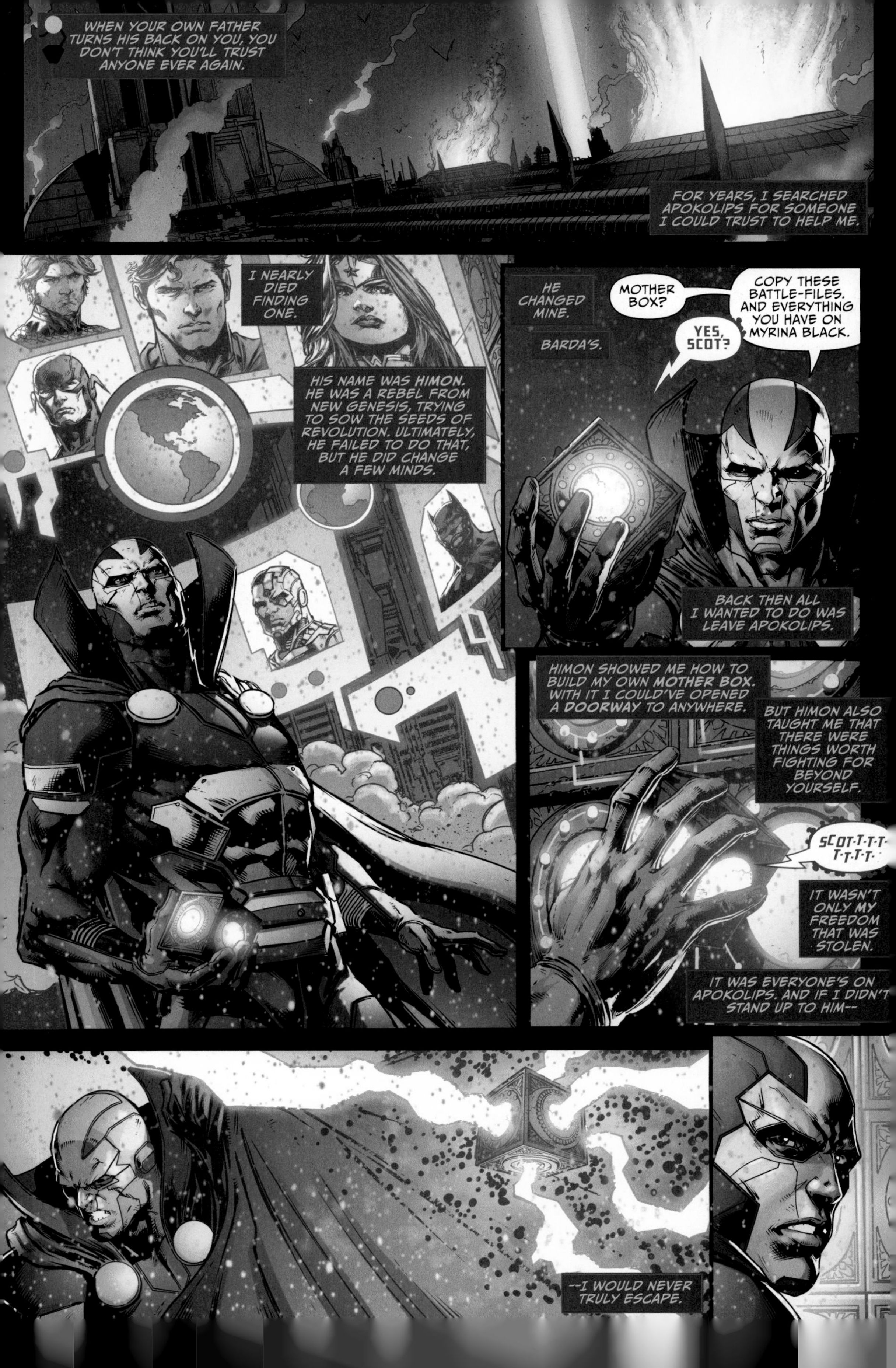
WHEN YOUR OWN FATHER TURNS HIS BACK ON YOU, YOU DON'T THINK YOU'LL TRUST ANYONE EVER AGAIN.
FOR YEARS, I SEARCHED APOKOLIPS FOR SOMEONE I COULD TRUST TO HELP ME.
I NEARLY DIED FINDING ONE.
HIS NAME WAS HIMON. HE WAS A REBEL FROM NEW GENESIS, TRYING TO SOW THE SEEDS OF REVOLUTION. ULTIMATELY, HE FAILED TO DO THAT, BUT HE DID CHANGE A FEW MINDS.
HE CHANGED MINE.
BARDA'S.
MOTHER BOX?
YES, SCOT?
COPY THESE BATTLE-FILES. AND EVERYTHING YOU HAVE ON MYRINA BLACK.
BACK THEN ALL I WANTED TO DO WAS LEAVE APOKOLIPS.
HIMON SHOWED ME HOW TO BUILD MY OWN MOTHER BOX. WITH IT I COULD'VE OPENED A DOORWAY TO ANYWHERE.
BUT HIMON ALSO TAUGHT ME THAT THERE WERE THINGS WORTH FIGHTING FOR BEYOND YOURSELF.
SCOT-T-T-T-T-T-T-T-
IT WASN'T ONLY MY FREEDOM THAT WAS STOLEN.
IT WAS EVERYONE'S ON APOKOLIPS. AND IF I DIDN'T STAND UP TO HIM--
--I WOULD NEVER TRULY ESCAPE.

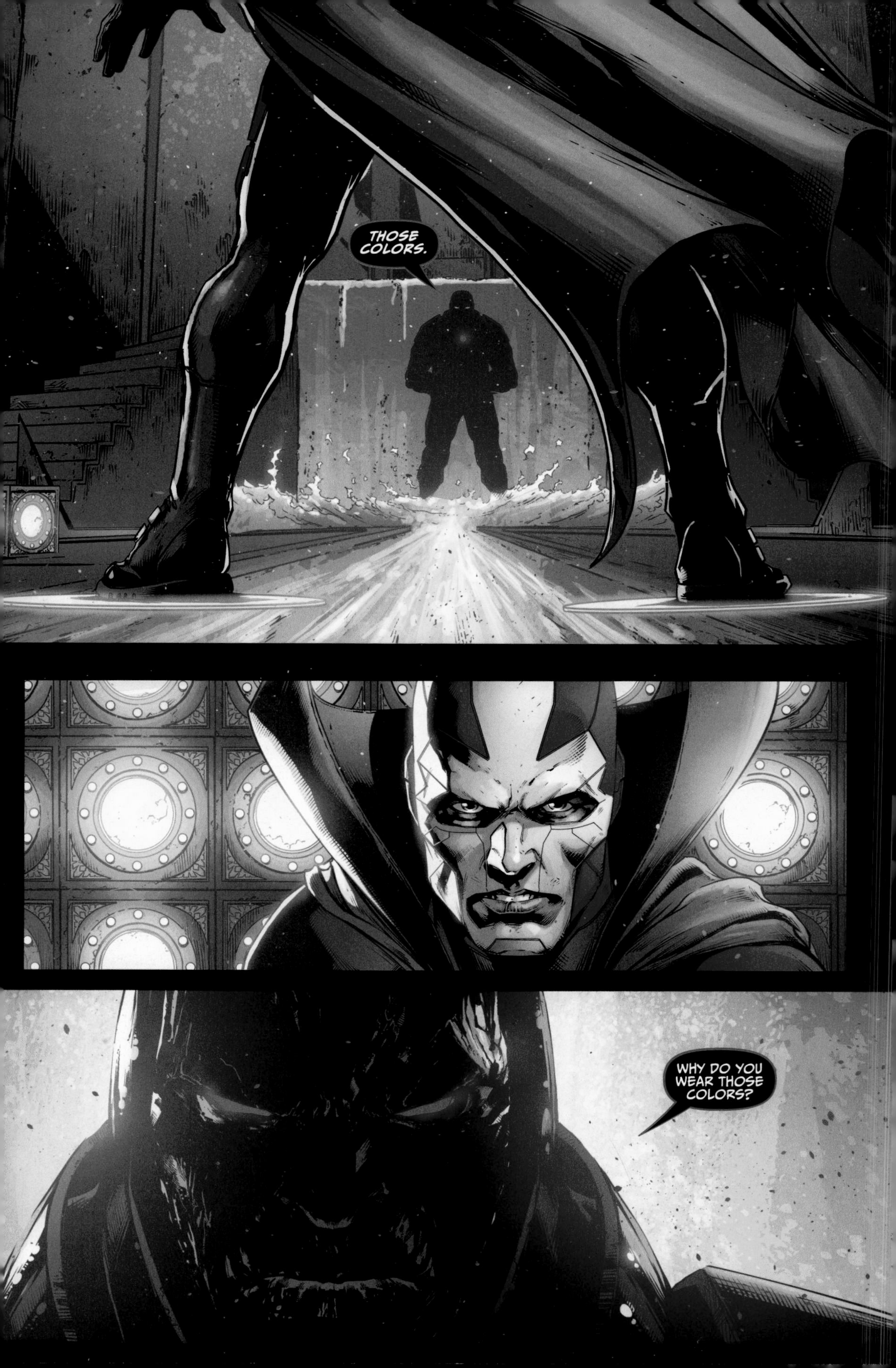
THOSE COLORS.
WHY DO YOU WEAR THOSE COLORS?

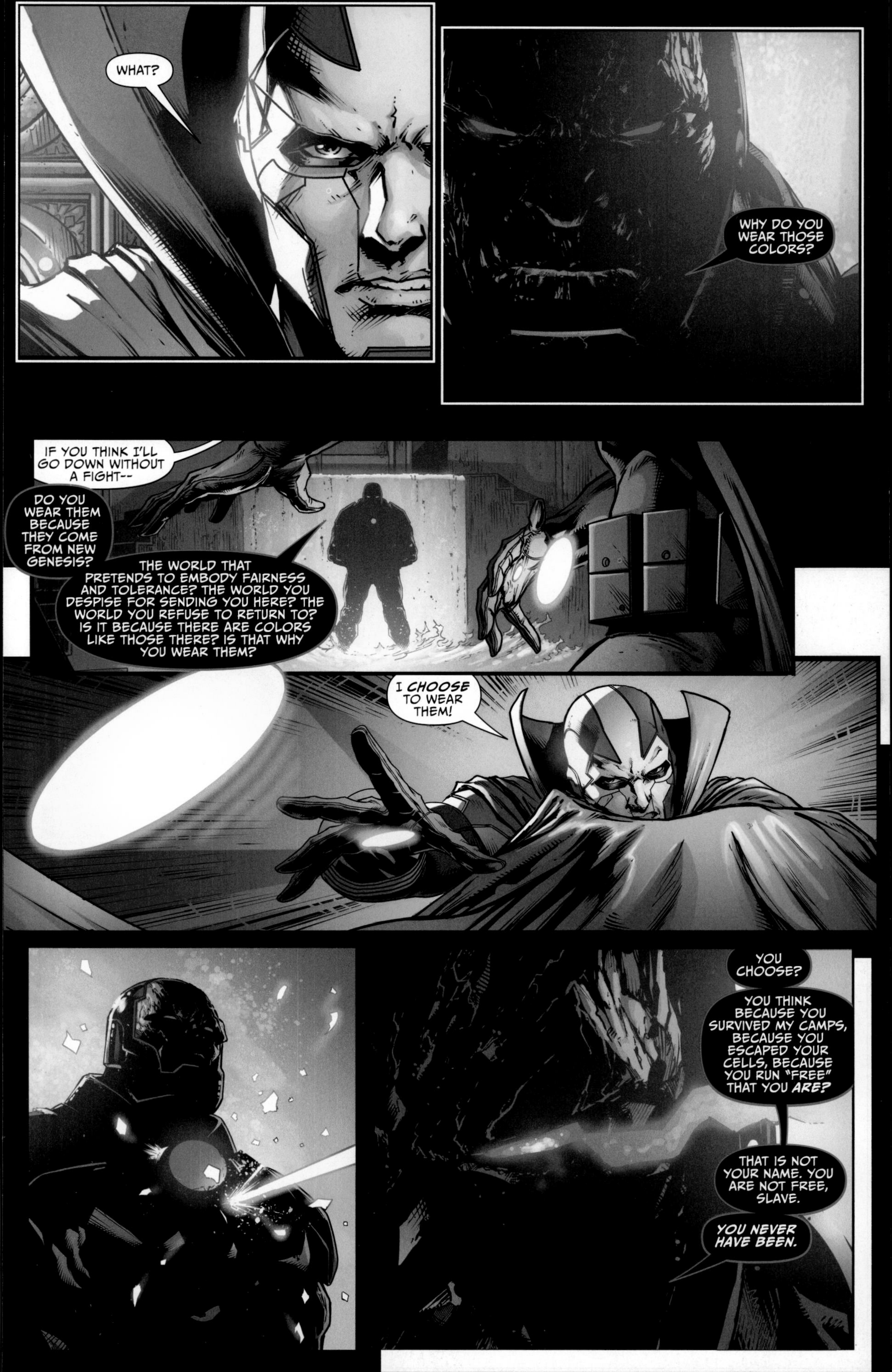
WHAT?
WHY DO YOU WEAR THOSE COLORS?
IF YOU THINK I'LL GO DOWN WITHOUT A FIGHT--
DO YOU WEAR THEM BECAUSE THEY COME FROM NEW GENESIS?
THE WORLD THAT PRETENDS TO EMBODY FAIRNESS AND TOLERANCE? THE WORLD YOU DESPISE FOR SENDING YOU HERE? THE WORLD YOU REFUSE TO RETURN TO? IS IT BECAUSE THERE ARE COLORS LIKE THOSE THERE? IS THAT WHY YOU WEAR THEM?
I *CHOOSE* TO WEAR THEM!
YOU CHOOSE?
YOU THINK BECAUSE YOU SURVIVED MY CAMPS, BECAUSE YOU ESCAPED YOUR CELLS, BECAUSE YOU RUN "FREE" THAT YOU *ARE?*
THAT IS NOT YOUR NAME. YOU ARE NOT FREE, SLAVE.
YOU NEVER HAVE BEEN.

AAAHHH!!

THERE WAS ANOTHER MAN LONG AGO ON APOKOLIPS WHO RESISTED MY WILL FOR A TIME.

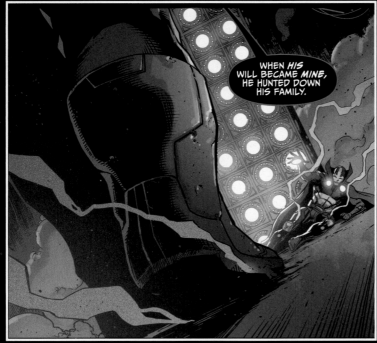

WHEN *HIS* WILL BECAME *MINE*, HE HUNTED DOWN HIS FAMILY.

HE CRUSHED THEIR SKULLS WITH A ROCK.

YOU HAVE MANY YOU CARE ABOUT. FRIENDS...AND A LOVER.

I KNOW ABOUT BARDA, SLAVE. YOU STOLE HER FROM MY FURIES.

AND I... KN-KNOW WHAT YOU'RE AFTER, DARKSEID.

DO YOU THINK THAT MATTERS?

MOTHER BOX... G-GET ME OUT.

YES, SCOT.

PING

BOOM

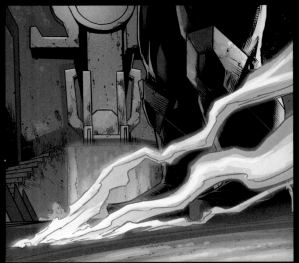

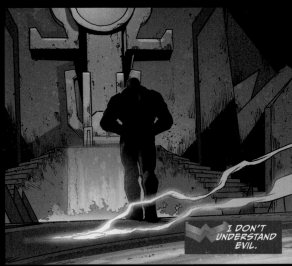

I DON'T UNDERSTAND EVIL.

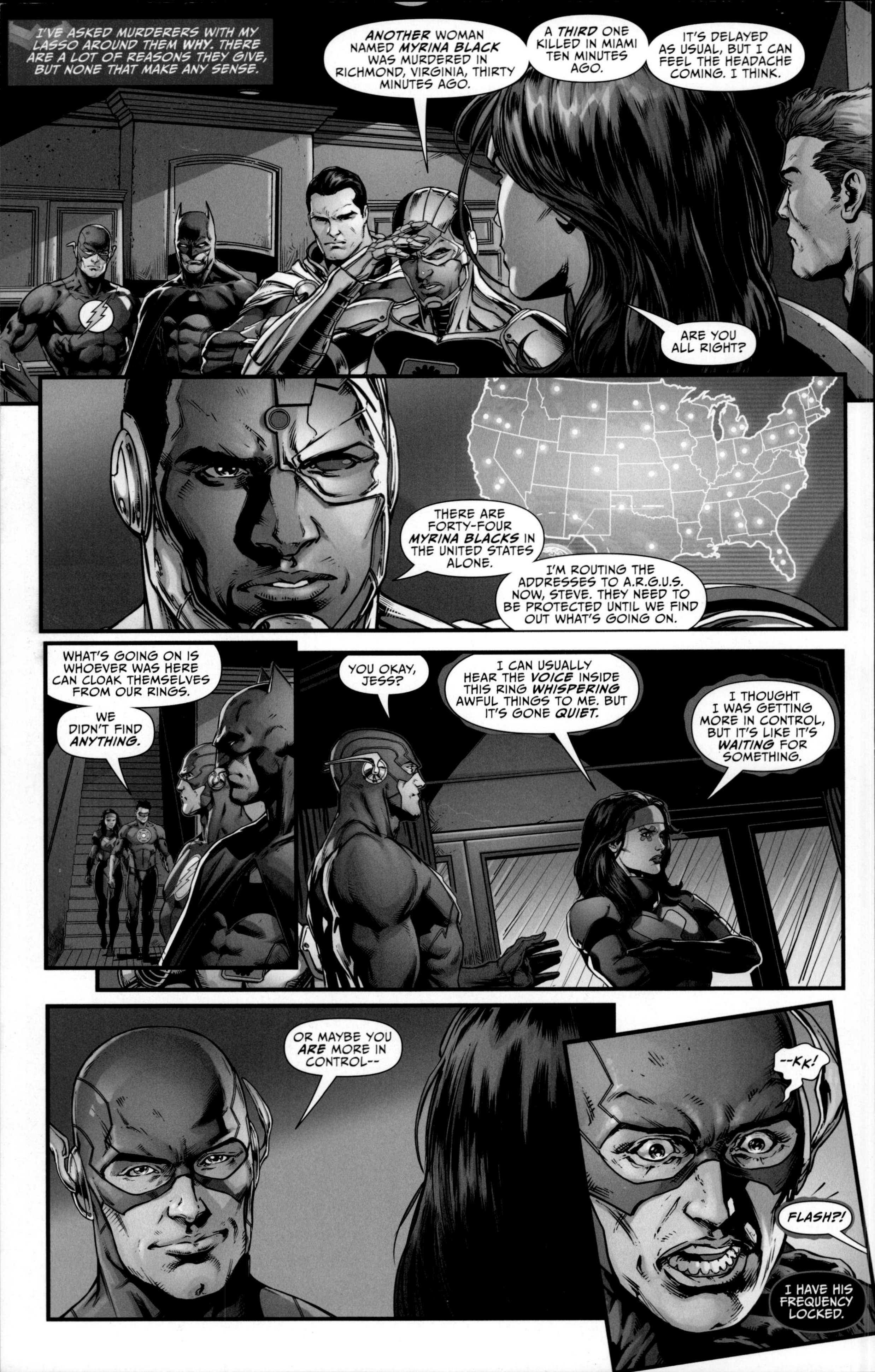
I'VE ASKED MURDERERS WITH MY LASSO AROUND THEM WHY. THERE ARE A LOT OF REASONS THEY GIVE, BUT NONE THAT MAKE ANY SENSE.
ANOTHER WOMAN NAMED MYRINA BLACK WAS MURDERED IN RICHMOND, VIRGINIA, THIRTY MINUTES AGO.
A THIRD ONE KILLED IN MIAMI TEN MINUTES AGO.
IT'S DELAYED AS USUAL, BUT I CAN FEEL THE HEADACHE COMING. I THINK.
ARE YOU ALL RIGHT?
THERE ARE FORTY-FOUR MYRINA BLACKS IN THE UNITED STATES ALONE.
I'M ROUTING THE ADDRESSES TO A.R.G.U.S. NOW, STEVE. THEY NEED TO BE PROTECTED UNTIL WE FIND OUT WHAT'S GOING ON.
WHAT'S GOING ON IS WHOEVER WAS HERE CAN CLOAK THEMSELVES FROM OUR RINGS.
WE DIDN'T FIND ANYTHING.
YOU OKAY, JESS?
I CAN USUALLY HEAR THE VOICE INSIDE THIS RING WHISPERING AWFUL THINGS TO ME. BUT IT'S GONE QUIET.
I THOUGHT I WAS GETTING MORE IN CONTROL, BUT IT'S LIKE IT'S WAITING FOR SOMETHING.
OR MAYBE YOU ARE MORE IN CONTROL--
--KK!
FLASH?!
I HAVE HIS FREQUENCY LOCKED.

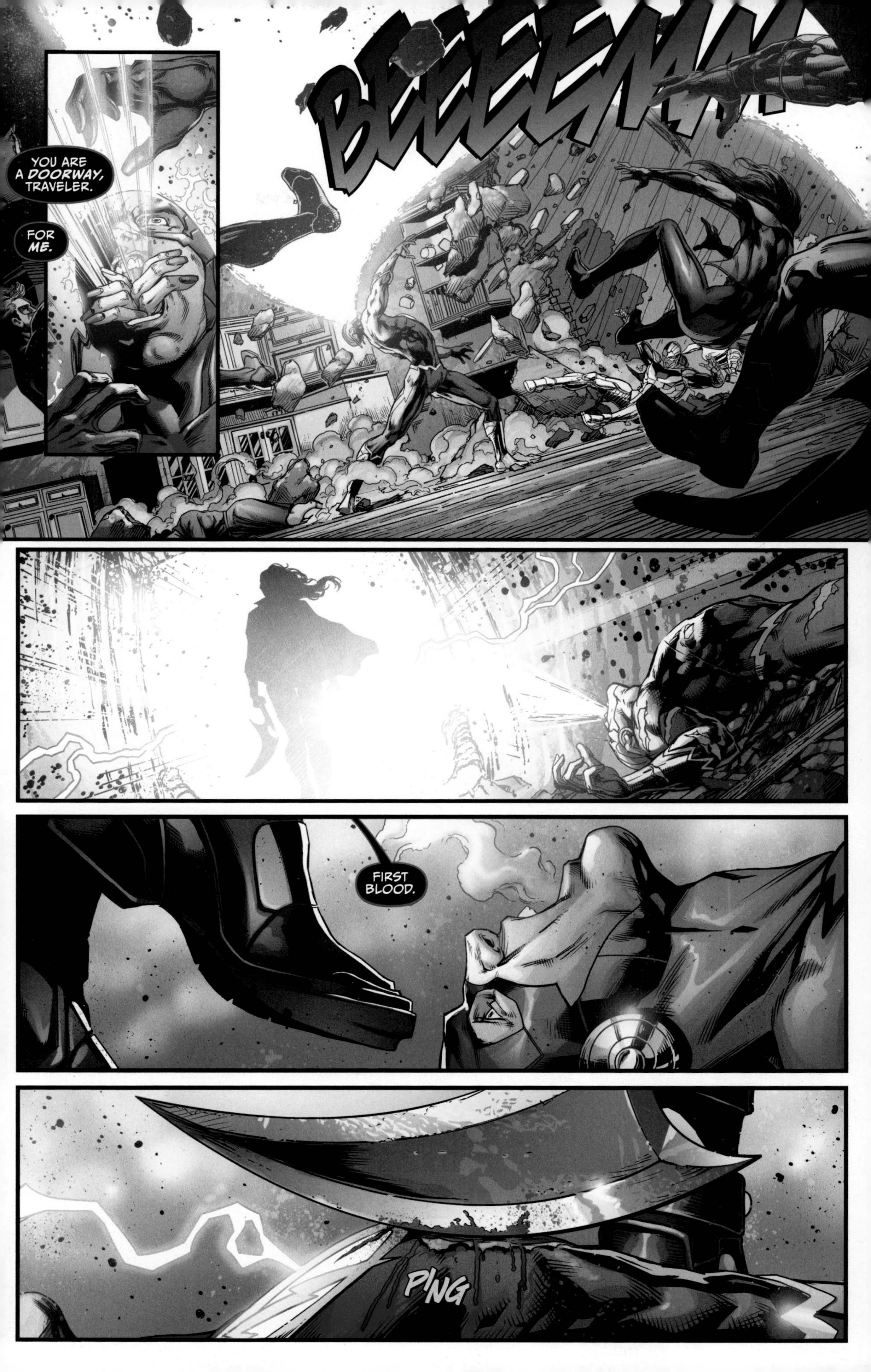
BEEEMM!
YOU ARE A *DOORWAY*, TRAVELER.
FOR *ME*.
FIRST BLOOD.
PING

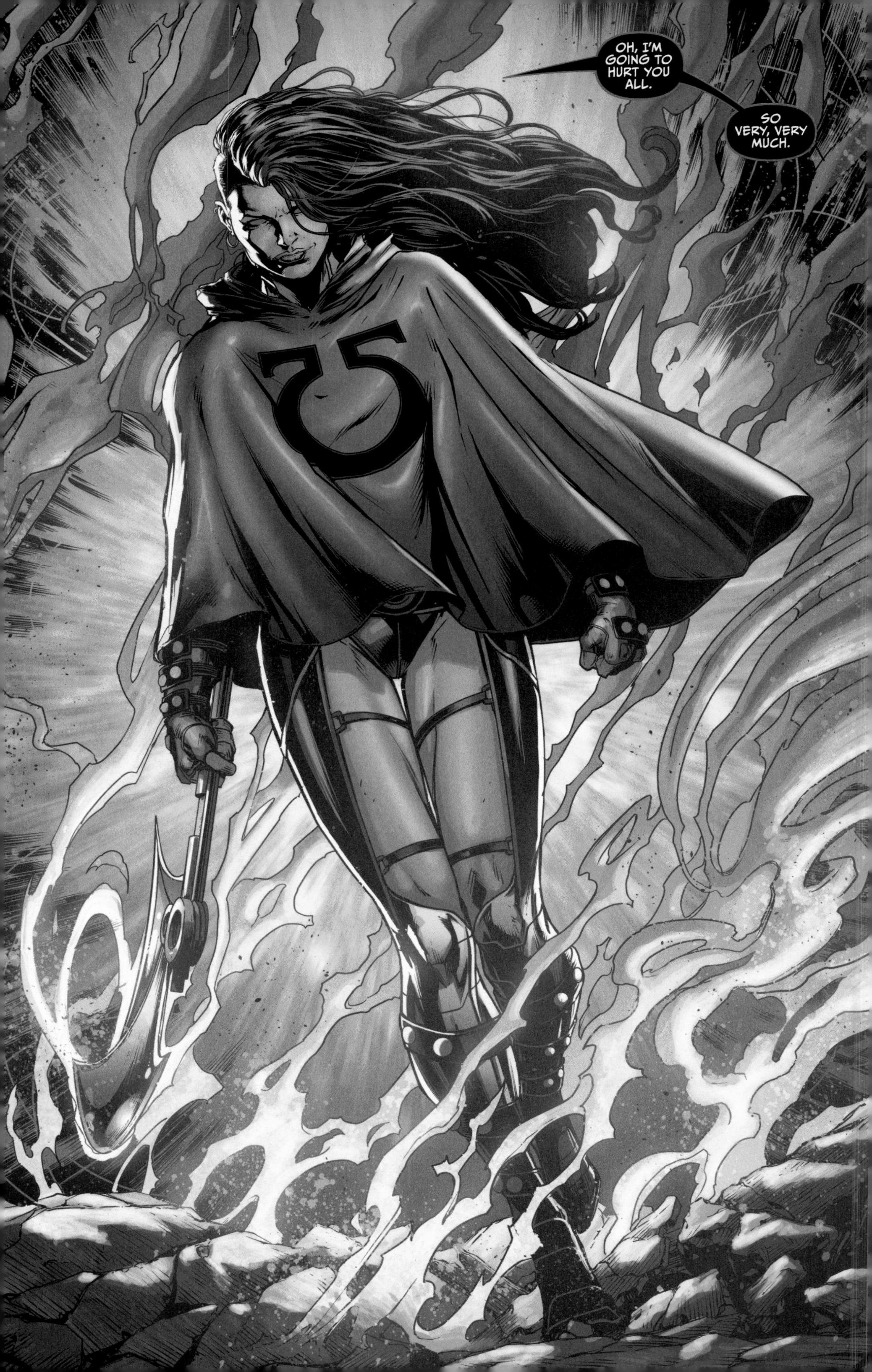
OH, I'M GOING TO HURT YOU ALL.
SO VERY, VERY MUCH.

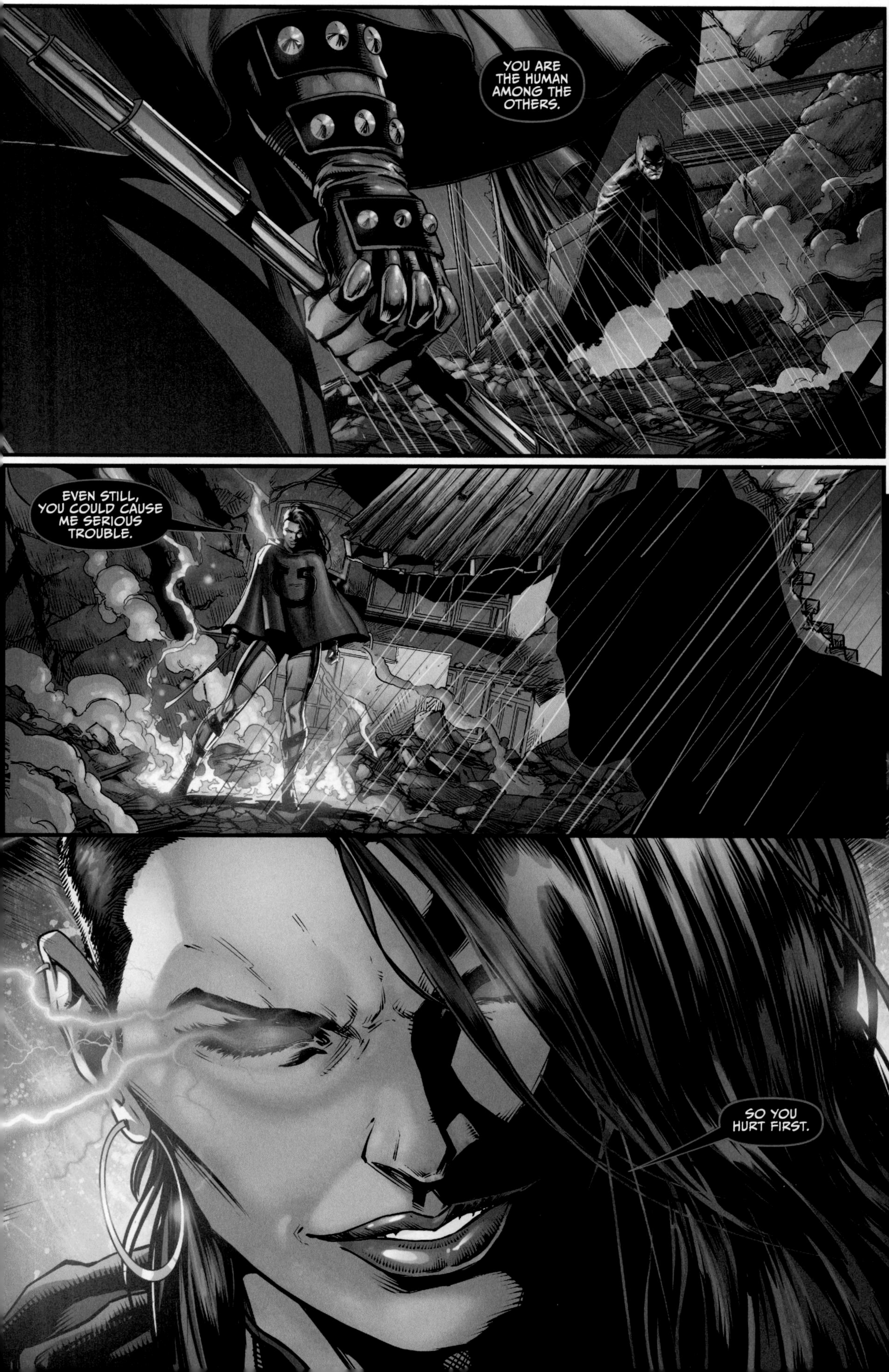
YOU ARE THE HUMAN AMONG THE OTHERS.
EVEN STILL, YOU COULD CAUSE ME SERIOUS TROUBLE.
SO YOU HURT FIRST.

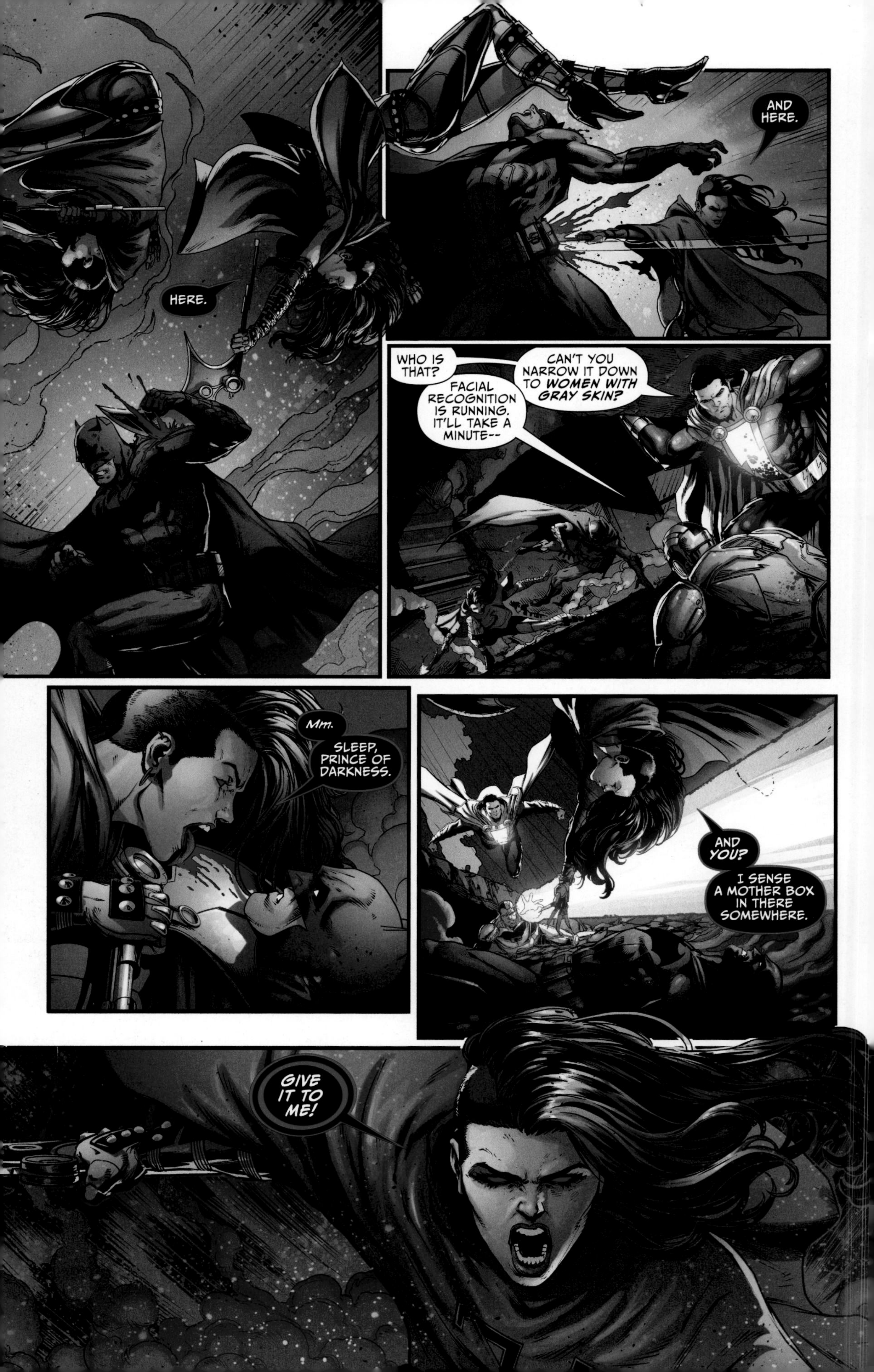
HERE.
AND HERE.
WHO IS THAT?
CAN'T YOU NARROW IT DOWN TO *WOMEN WITH GRAY SKIN?*
FACIAL RECOGNITION IS RUNNING. IT'LL TAKE A MINUTE--
Mm.
SLEEP, PRINCE OF DARKNESS.
AND *YOU?*
I SENSE A MOTHER BOX IN THERE SOMEWHERE.
GIVE IT TO ME!

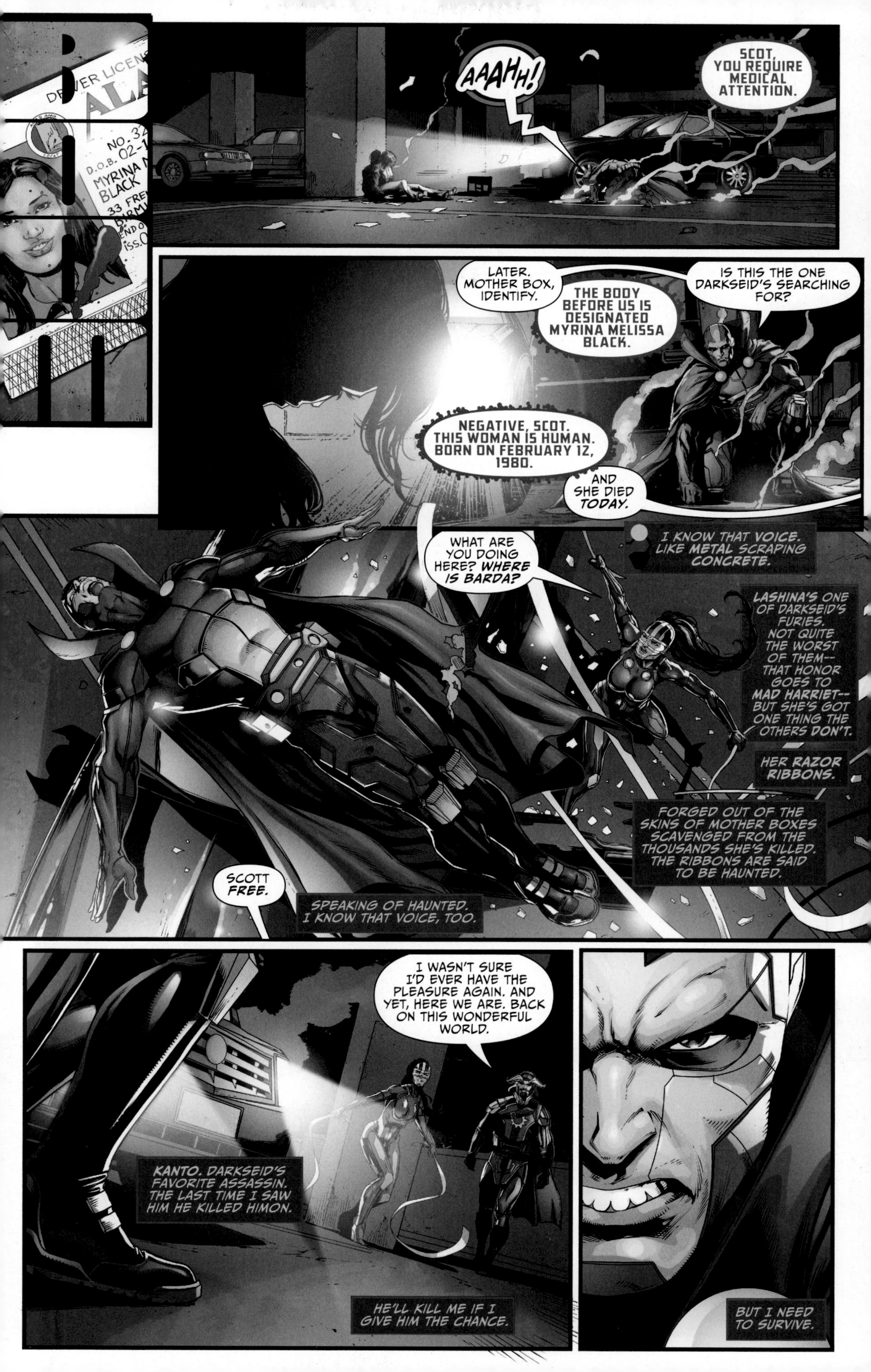
DRIVER LICENSE
ALA
NO.32
D.O.B. 02-1
MYRINA
BLACK
AAAHH!
SCOT, YOU REQUIRE MEDICAL ATTENTION.
LATER. MOTHER BOX, IDENTIFY.
IS THIS THE ONE DARKSEID'S SEARCHING FOR?
THE BODY BEFORE US IS DESIGNATED MYRINA MELISSA BLACK.
NEGATIVE, SCOT. THIS WOMAN IS HUMAN. BORN ON FEBRUARY 12, 1980.
AND SHE DIED *TODAY.*
WHAT ARE YOU DOING HERE? ***WHERE IS BARDA?***
I KNOW THAT VOICE. LIKE METAL SCRAPING CONCRETE.
LASHINA'S ONE OF DARKSEID'S FURIES. NOT QUITE THE WORST OF THEM-- THAT HONOR GOES TO MAD HARRIET-- BUT SHE'S GOT ONE THING THE OTHERS DON'T.
HER RAZOR RIBBONS.
FORGED OUT OF THE SKINS OF MOTHER BOXES SCAVENGED FROM THE THOUSANDS SHE'S KILLED. THE RIBBONS ARE SAID TO BE HAUNTED.
SCOTT ***FREE.***
SPEAKING OF HAUNTED. I KNOW THAT VOICE, TOO.
I WASN'T SURE I'D EVER HAVE THE PLEASURE AGAIN. AND YET, HERE WE ARE. BACK ON THIS WONDERFUL WORLD.
KANTO. DARKSEID'S FAVORITE ASSASSIN. THE LAST TIME I SAW HIM HE KILLED HIMON.
HE'LL KILL ME IF I GIVE HIM THE CHANCE.
BUT I NEED TO SURVIVE.

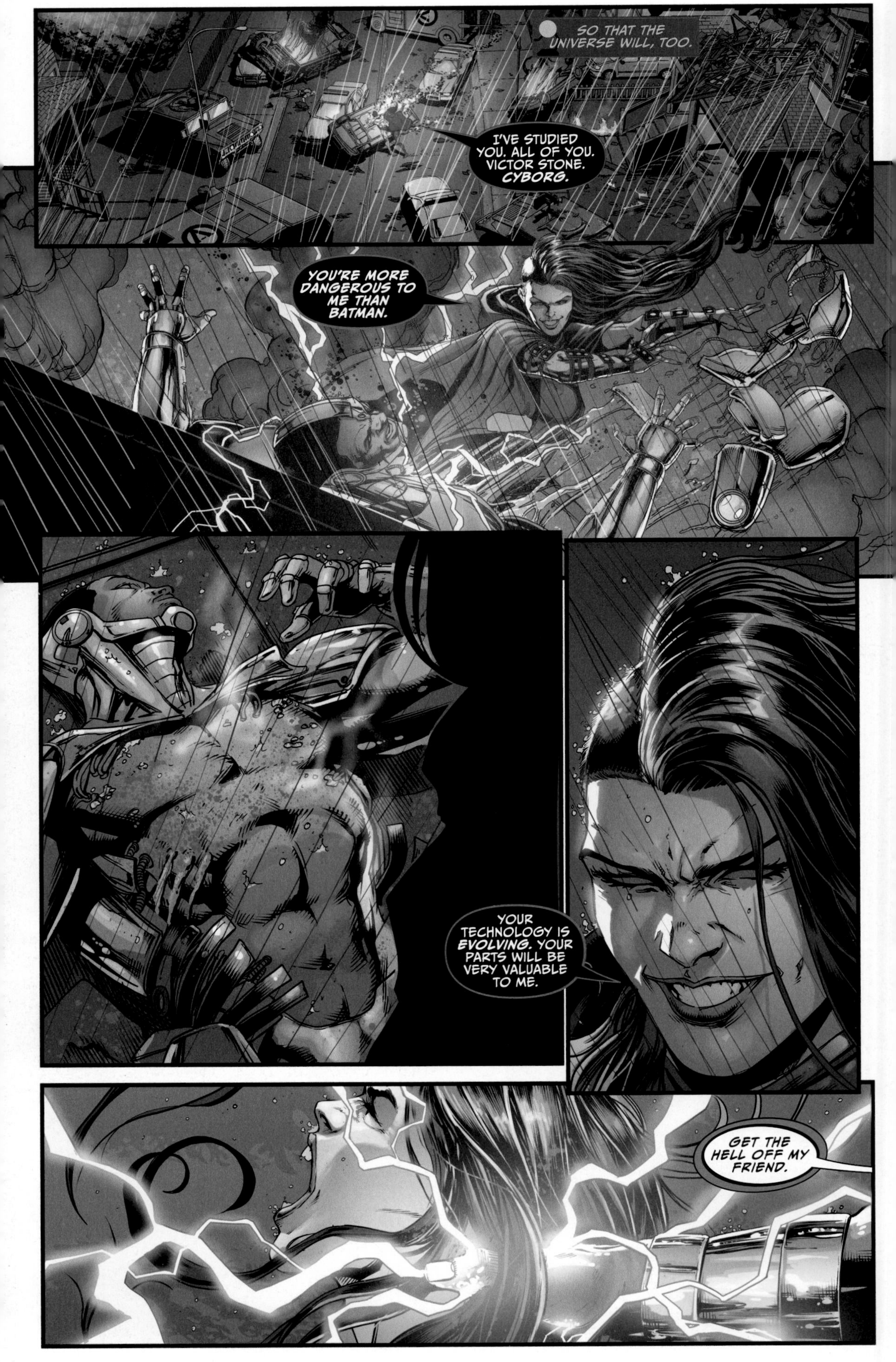

SO THAT THE UNIVERSE WILL, TOO.
I'VE STUDIED YOU. ALL OF YOU. VICTOR STONE. CYBORG.
YOU'RE MORE DANGEROUS TO ME THAN BATMAN.
YOUR TECHNOLOGY IS EVOLVING. YOUR PARTS WILL BE VERY VALUABLE TO ME.
GET THE HELL OFF MY FRIEND.

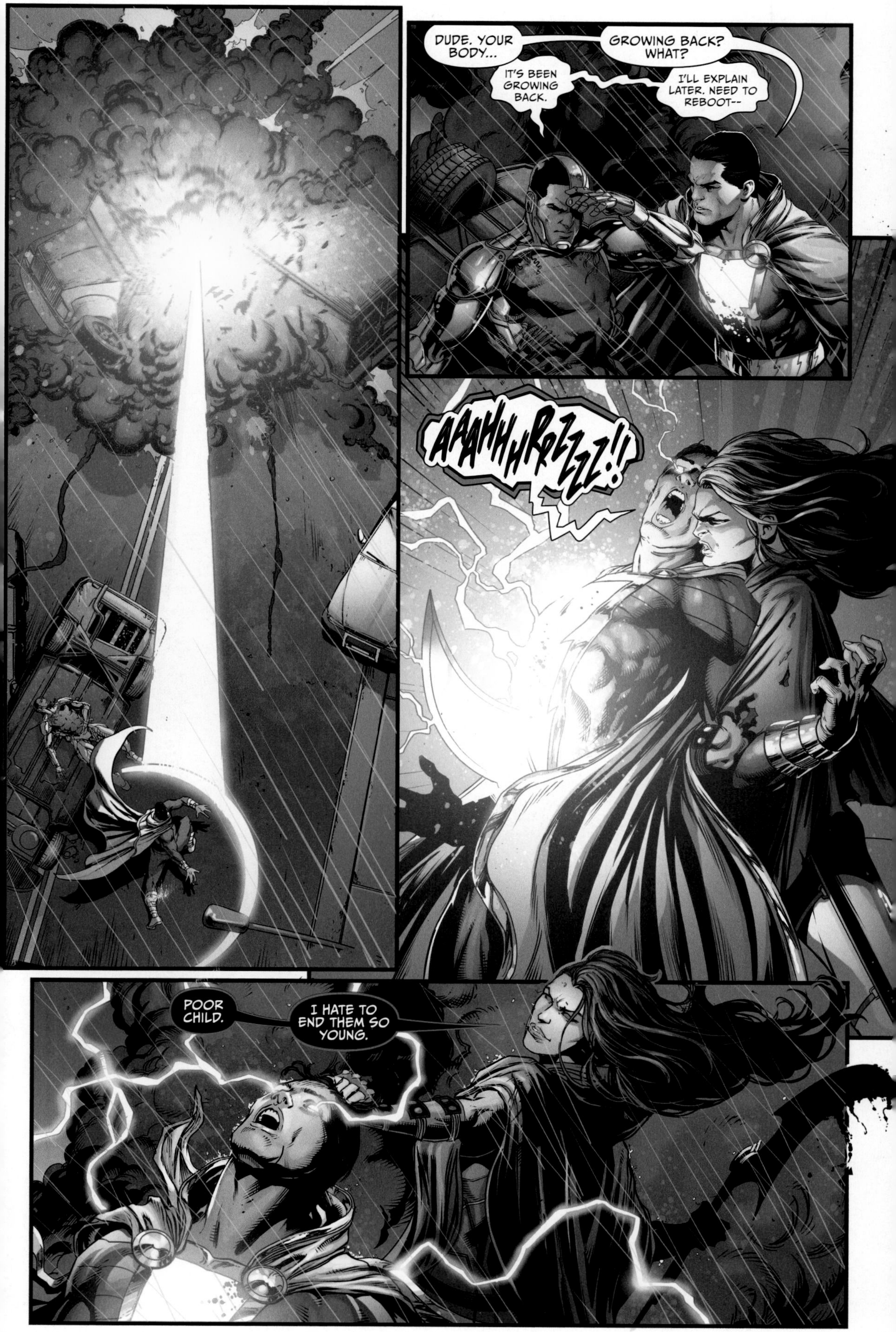
DUDE. YOUR BODY...
IT'S BEEN GROWING BACK.
GROWING BACK? WHAT?
I'LL EXPLAIN LATER. NEED TO REBOOT--
AAAHHHRRZZZZZ!!
POOR CHILD.
I HATE TO END THEM SO YOUNG.

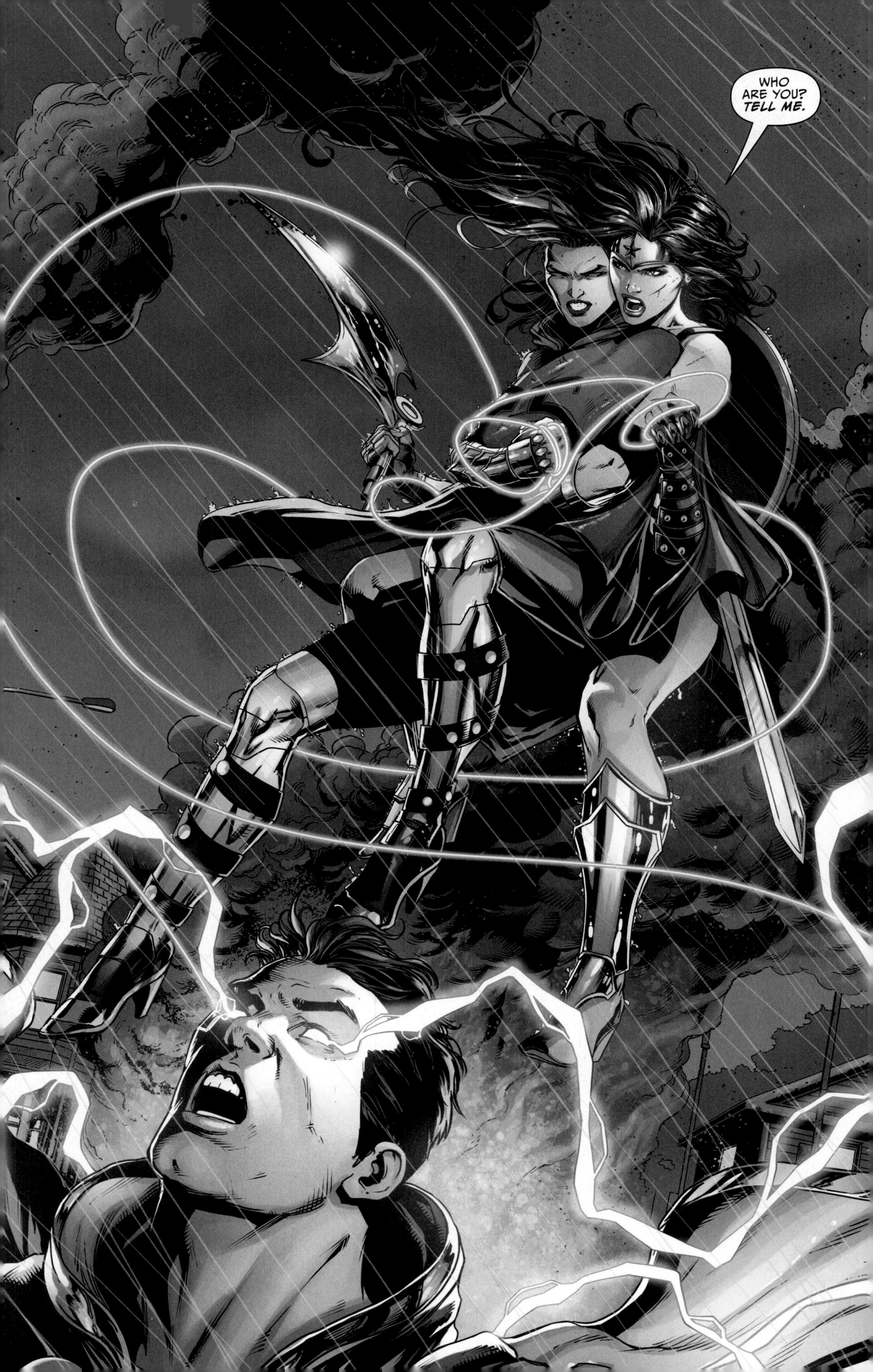
WHO ARE YOU? TELL ME.

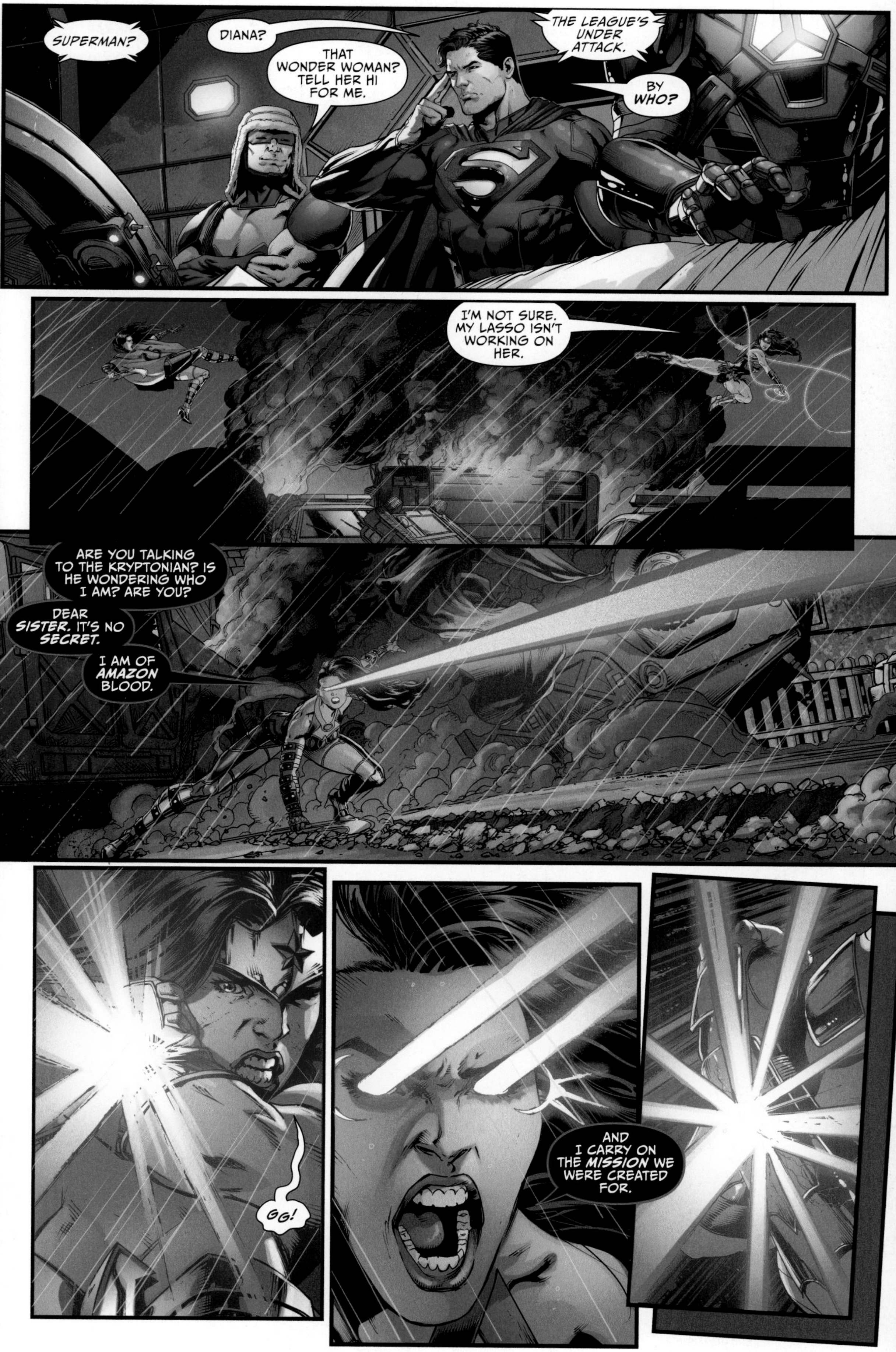
SUPERMAN?
DIANA?
THAT WONDER WOMAN? TELL HER HI FOR ME.
THE LEAGUE'S UNDER ATTACK.
BY WHO?
I'M NOT SURE. MY LASSO ISN'T WORKING ON HER.
ARE YOU TALKING TO THE KRYPTONIAN? IS HE WONDERING WHO I AM? ARE YOU?
DEAR SISTER. IT'S NO SECRET.
I AM OF AMAZON BLOOD.
GG!
AND I CARRY ON THE MISSION WE WERE CREATED FOR.

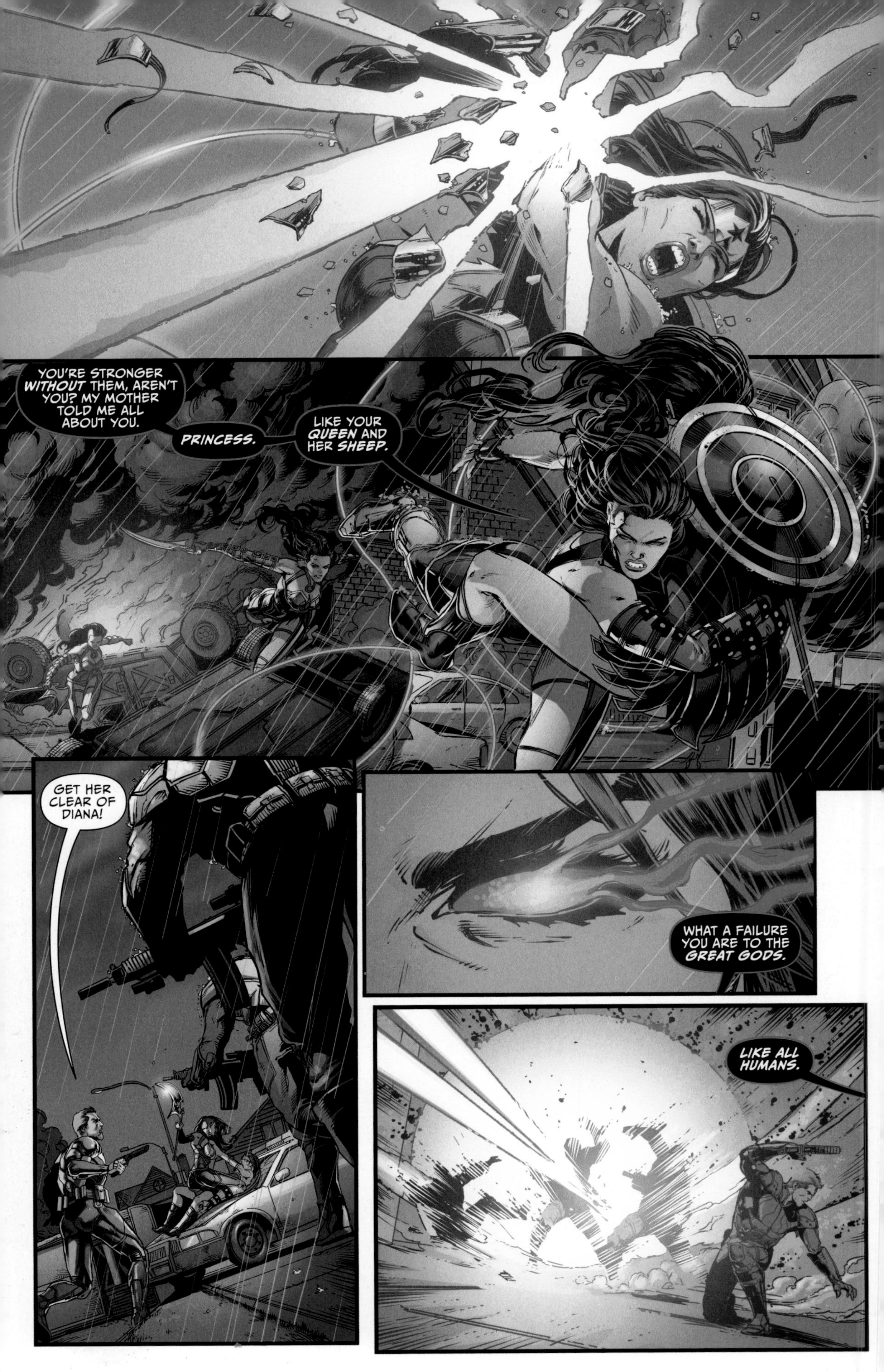
YOU'RE STRONGER WITHOUT THEM, AREN'T YOU? MY MOTHER TOLD ME ALL ABOUT YOU.
PRINCESS.
LIKE YOUR QUEEN AND HER SHEEP.
GET HER CLEAR OF DIANA!
WHAT A FAILURE YOU ARE TO THE GREAT GODS.
LIKE ALL HUMANS.

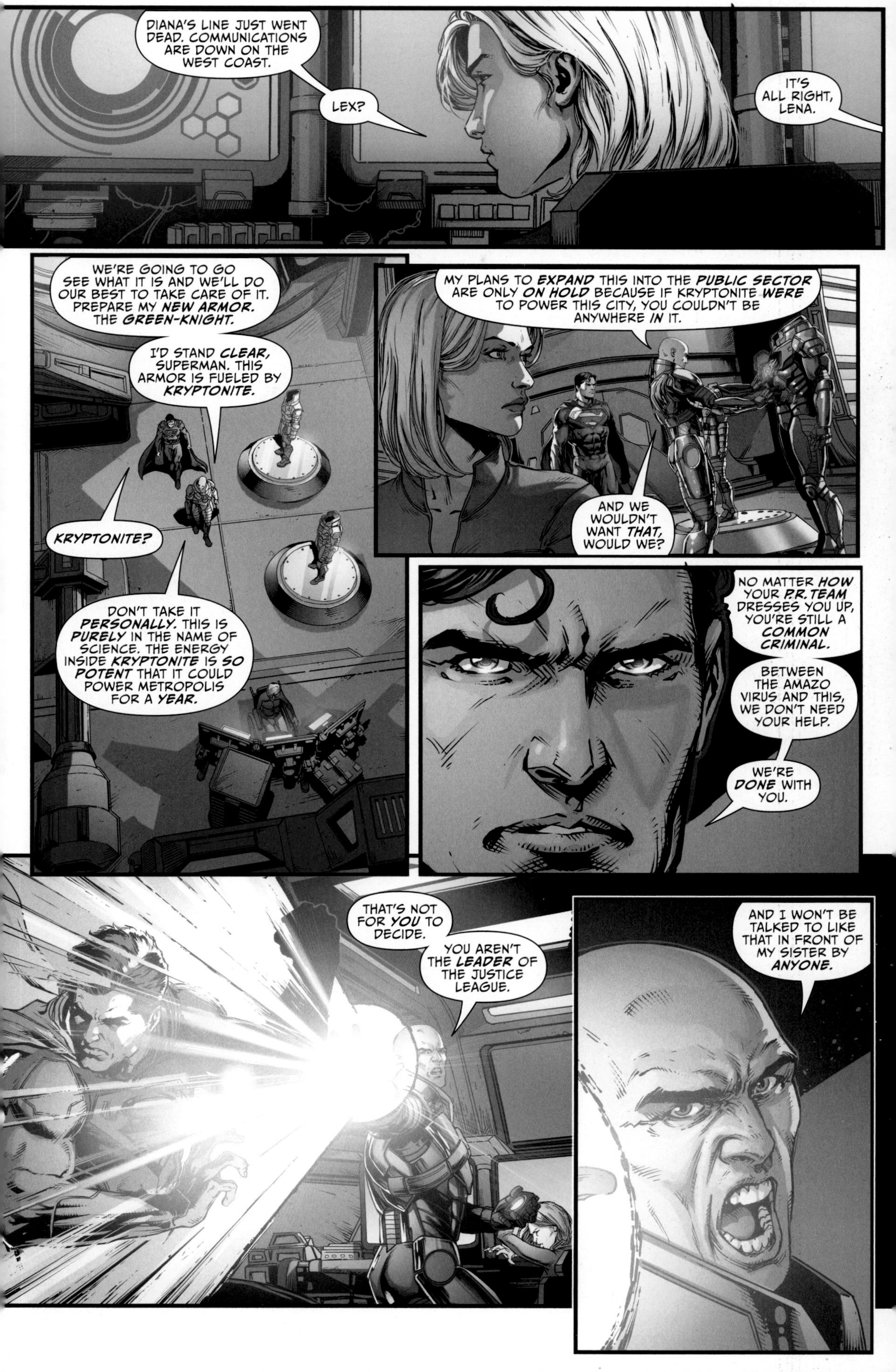

DIANA'S LINE JUST WENT DEAD. COMMUNICATIONS ARE DOWN ON THE WEST COAST.
LEX?
IT'S ALL RIGHT, LENA.
WE'RE GOING TO GO SEE WHAT IT IS AND WE'LL DO OUR BEST TO TAKE CARE OF IT. PREPARE MY NEW ARMOR. THE GREEN-KNIGHT.
I'D STAND CLEAR, SUPERMAN. THIS ARMOR IS FUELED BY KRYPTONITE.
KRYPTONITE?
DON'T TAKE IT PERSONALLY. THIS IS PURELY IN THE NAME OF SCIENCE. THE ENERGY INSIDE KRYPTONITE IS SO POTENT THAT IT COULD POWER METROPOLIS FOR A YEAR.
MY PLANS TO EXPAND THIS INTO THE PUBLIC SECTOR ARE ONLY ON HOLD BECAUSE IF KRYPTONITE WERE TO POWER THIS CITY, YOU COULDN'T BE ANYWHERE IN IT.
AND WE WOULDN'T WANT THAT, WOULD WE?
NO MATTER HOW YOUR P.R. TEAM DRESSES YOU UP, YOU'RE STILL A COMMON CRIMINAL.
BETWEEN THE AMAZO VIRUS AND THIS, WE DON'T NEED YOUR HELP.
WE'RE DONE WITH YOU.
THAT'S NOT FOR YOU TO DECIDE.
YOU AREN'T THE LEADER OF THE JUSTICE LEAGUE.
AND I WON'T BE TALKED TO LIKE THAT IN FRONT OF MY SISTER BY ANYONE.

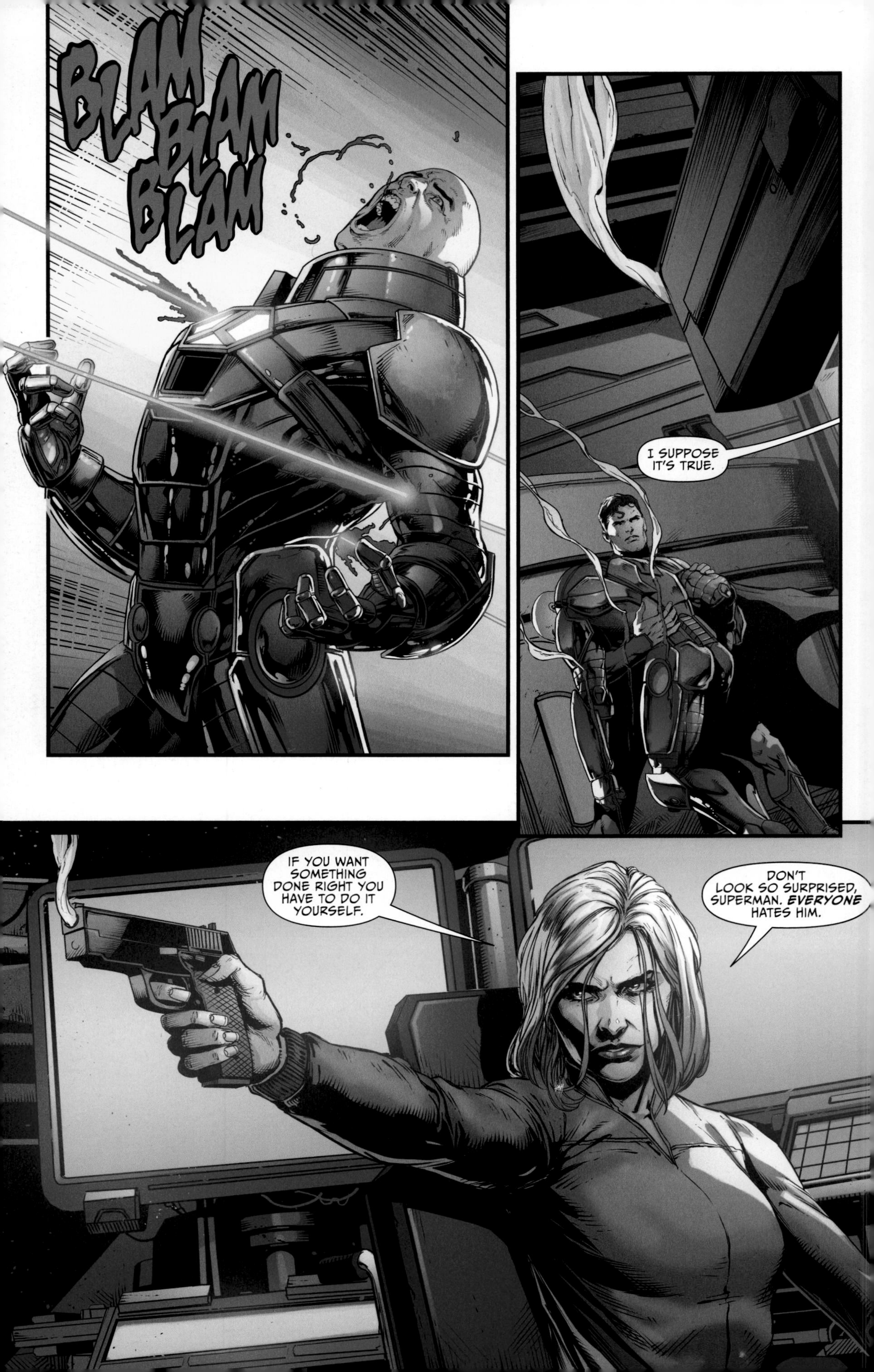
BLAM BLAM BLAM
I SUPPOSE IT'S TRUE.
IF YOU WANT SOMETHING DONE RIGHT YOU HAVE TO DO IT YOURSELF.
DON'T LOOK SO SURPRISED, SUPERMAN. *EVERYONE* HATES HIM.

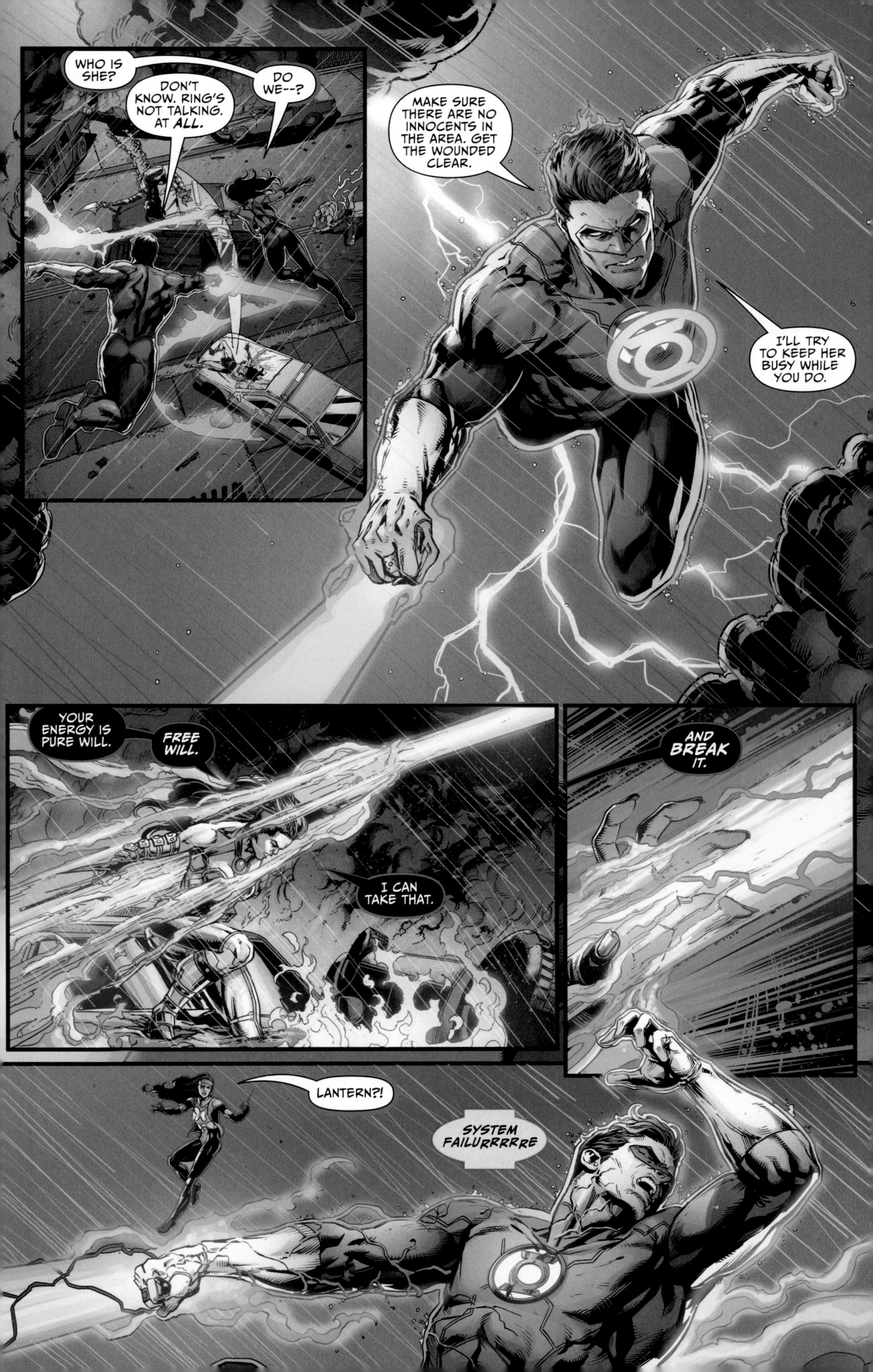
WHO IS SHE?
DON'T KNOW. RING'S NOT TALKING. AT ALL.
DO WE--?
MAKE SURE THERE ARE NO INNOCENTS IN THE AREA. GET THE WOUNDED CLEAR.
I'LL TRY TO KEEP HER BUSY WHILE YOU DO.
YOUR ENERGY IS PURE WILL.
FREE WILL.
I CAN TAKE THAT.
AND BREAK IT.
LANTERN?!
SYSTEM FAILURRRRRE

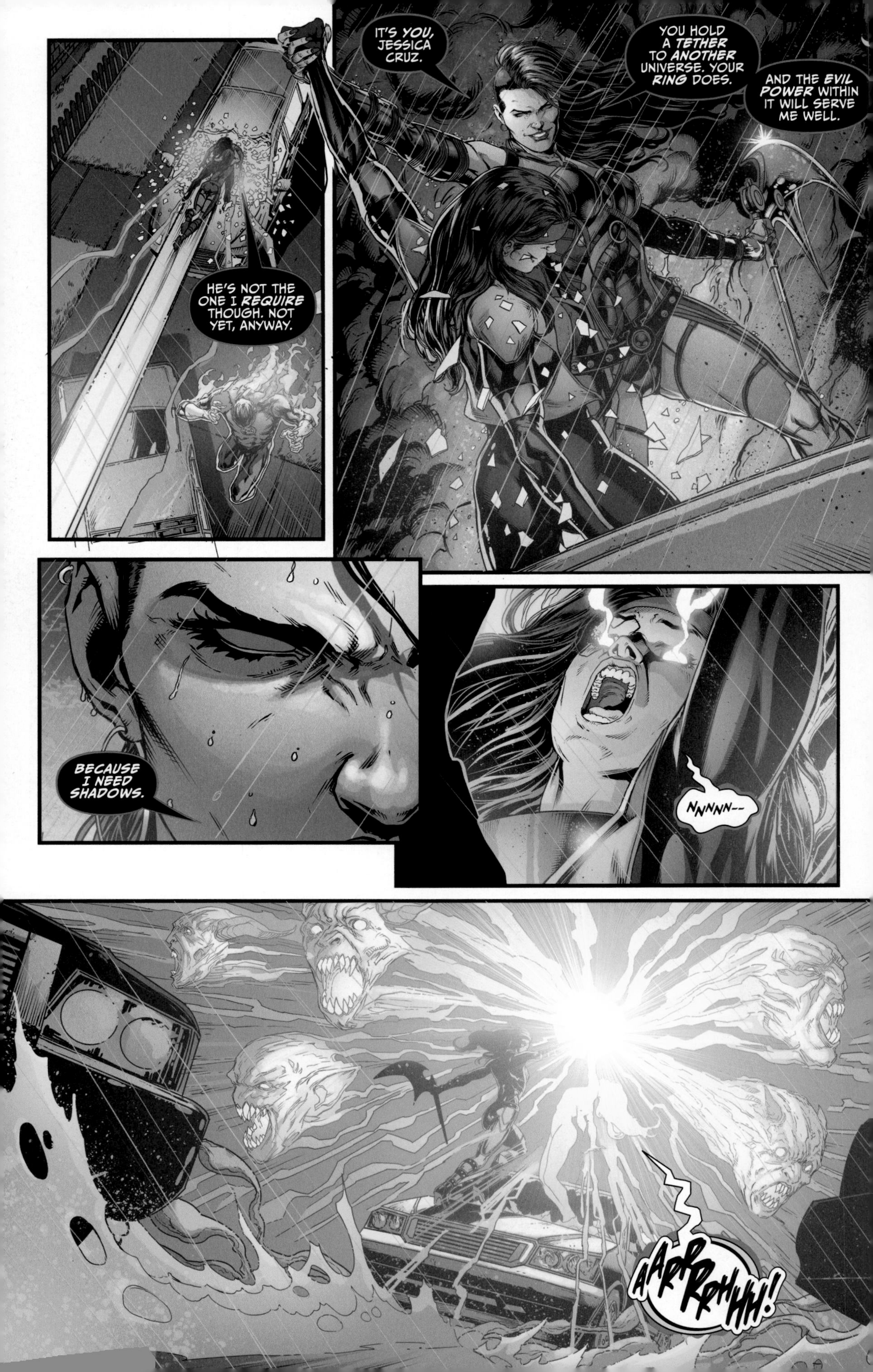
IT'S YOU, JESSICA CRUZ.
YOU HOLD A TETHER TO ANOTHER UNIVERSE. YOUR RING DOES.
AND THE EVIL POWER WITHIN IT WILL SERVE ME WELL.
HE'S NOT THE ONE I REQUIRE THOUGH. NOT YET, ANYWAY.
BECAUSE I NEED SHADOWS.
NNNNN--
AARRRHHHH!

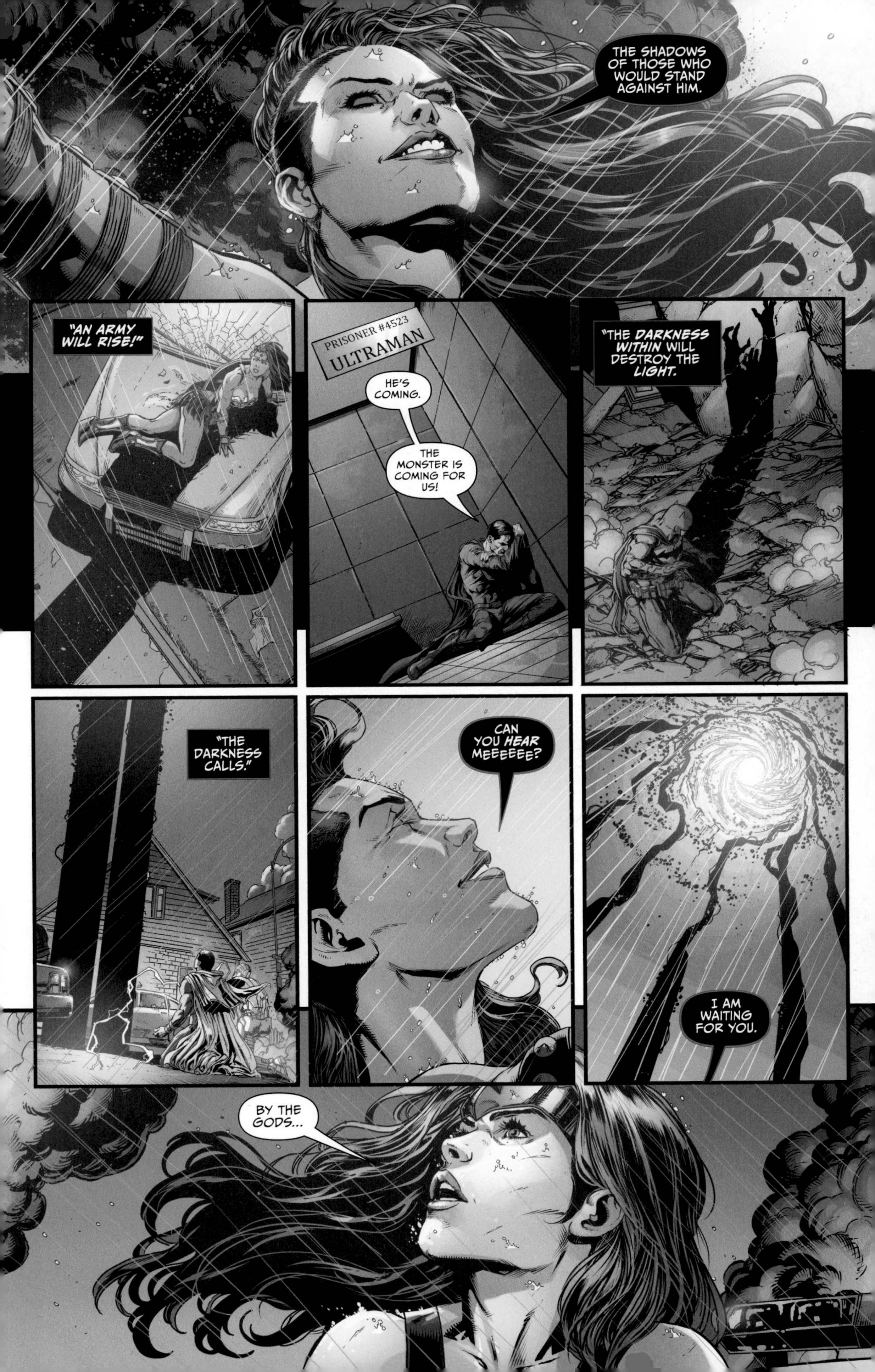
THE SHADOWS OF THOSE WHO WOULD STAND AGAINST HIM.
"AN ARMY WILL RISE!"
PRISONER #4523
ULTRAMAN
HE'S COMING.
THE MONSTER IS COMING FOR US!
"THE DARKNESS WITHIN WILL DESTROY THE LIGHT.
"THE DARKNESS CALLS."
CAN YOU HEAR MEEEEEE?
I AM WAITING FOR YOU.
BY THE GODS...

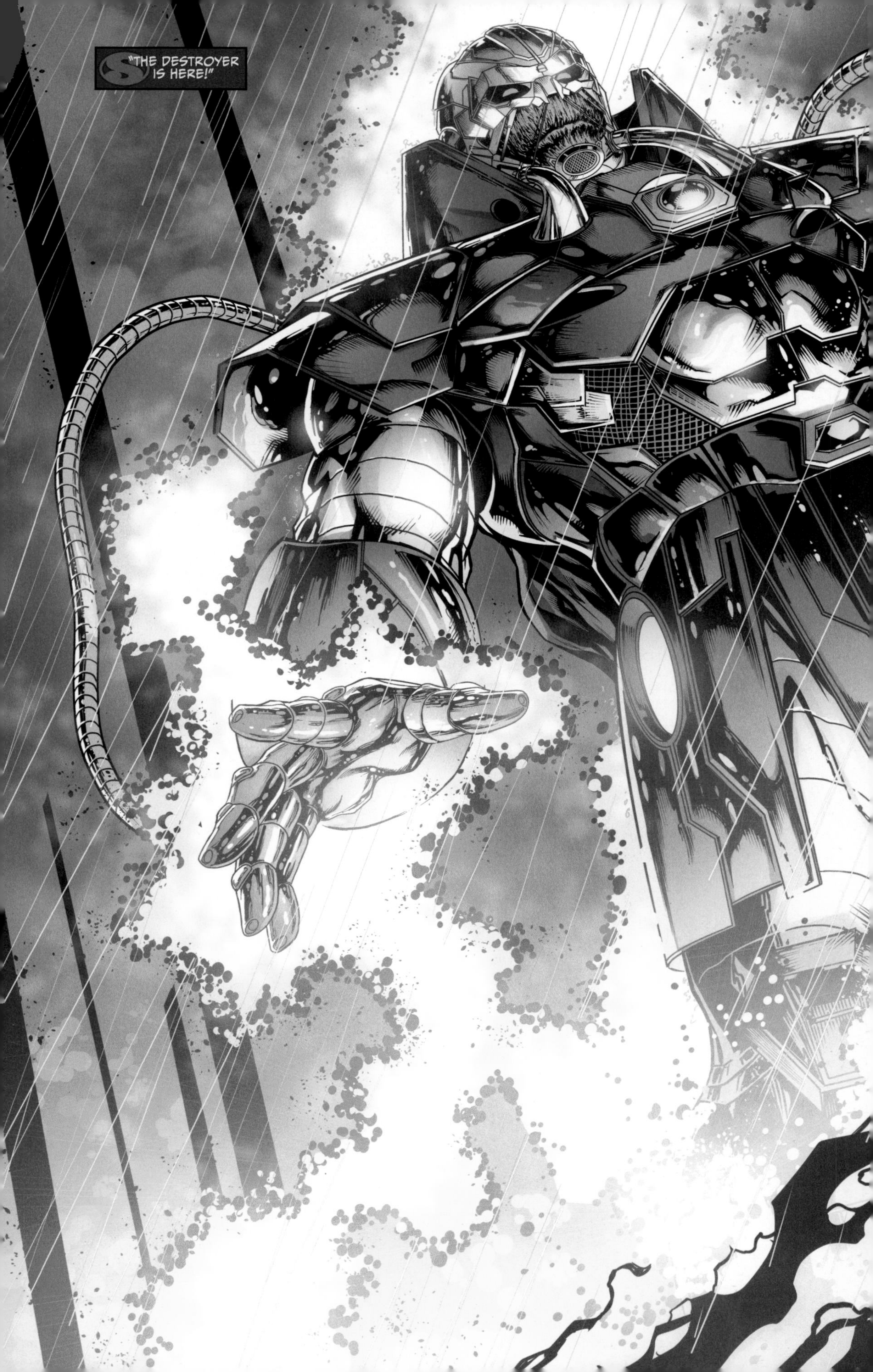
"THE DESTROYER IS HERE!"

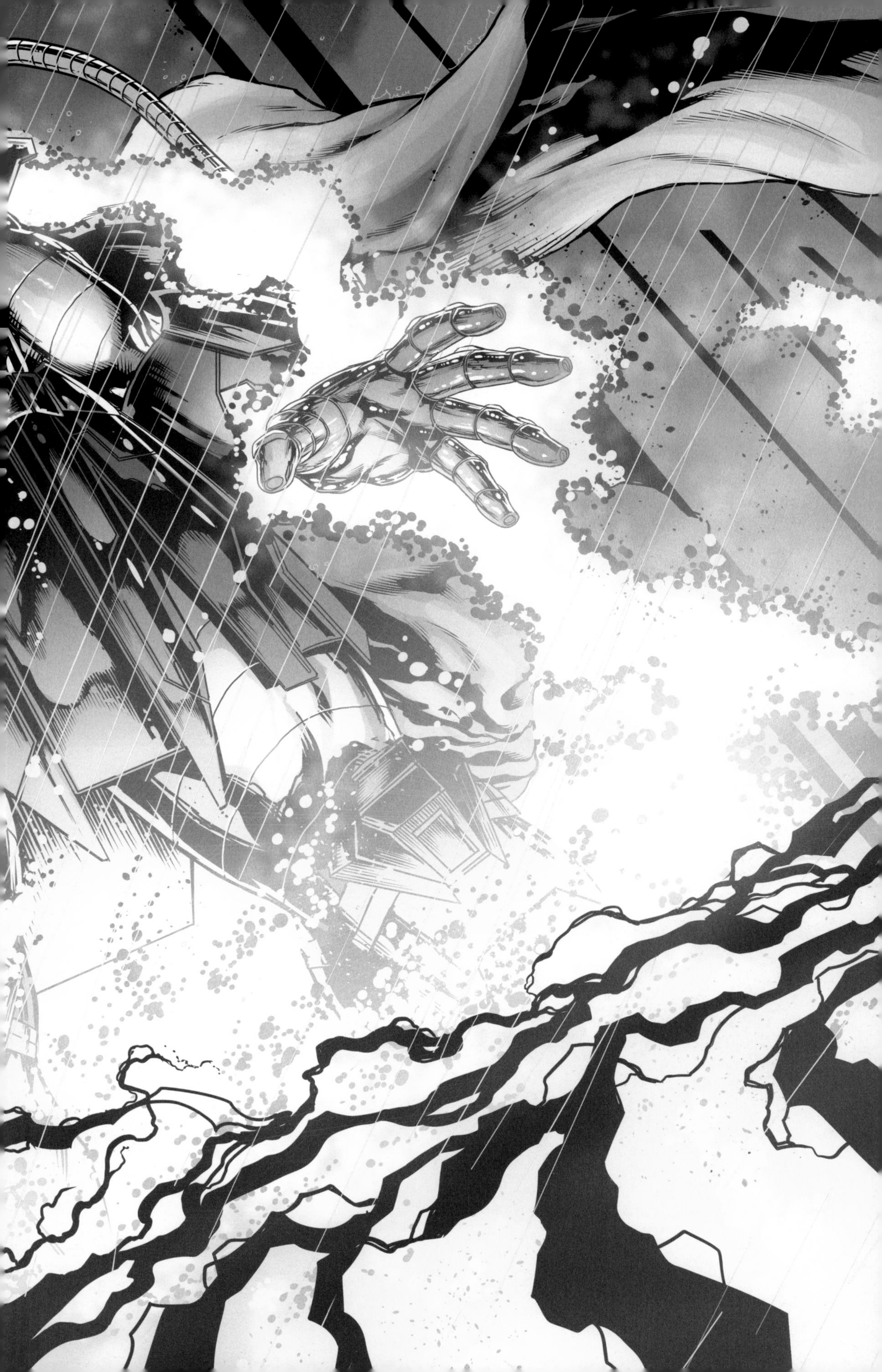

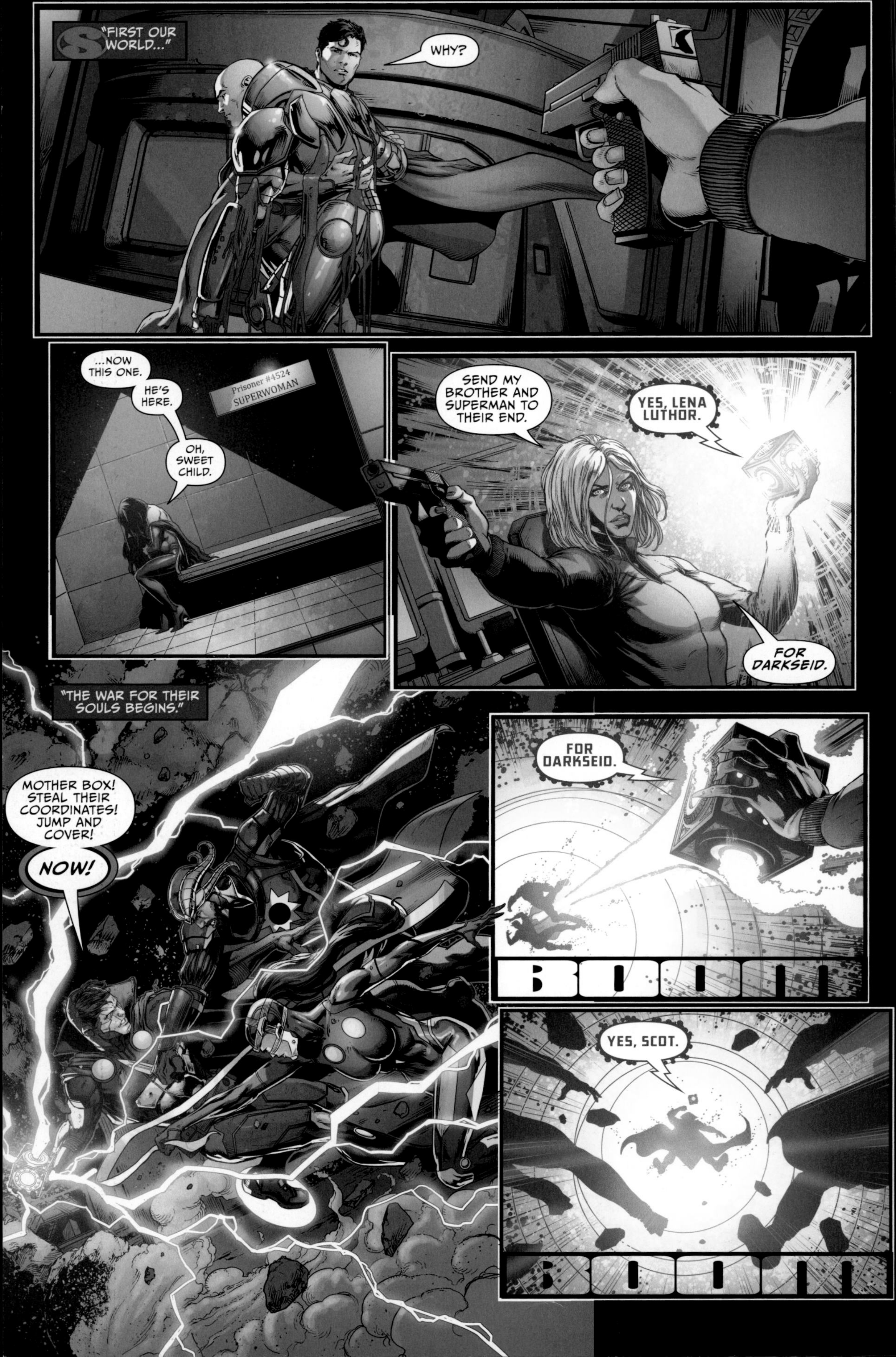
"FIRST OUR WORLD..."
WHY?
...NOW THIS ONE.
HE'S HERE.
Prisoner #4524 SUPERWOMAN
OH, SWEET CHILD.
SEND MY BROTHER AND SUPERMAN TO THEIR END.
YES, LENA LUTHOR.
FOR DARKSEID.
"THE WAR FOR THEIR SOULS BEGINS."
MOTHER BOX! STEAL THEIR COORDINATES! JUMP AND COVER!
NOW!
FOR DARKSEID.
BOOM
YES, SCOT.
BOOM

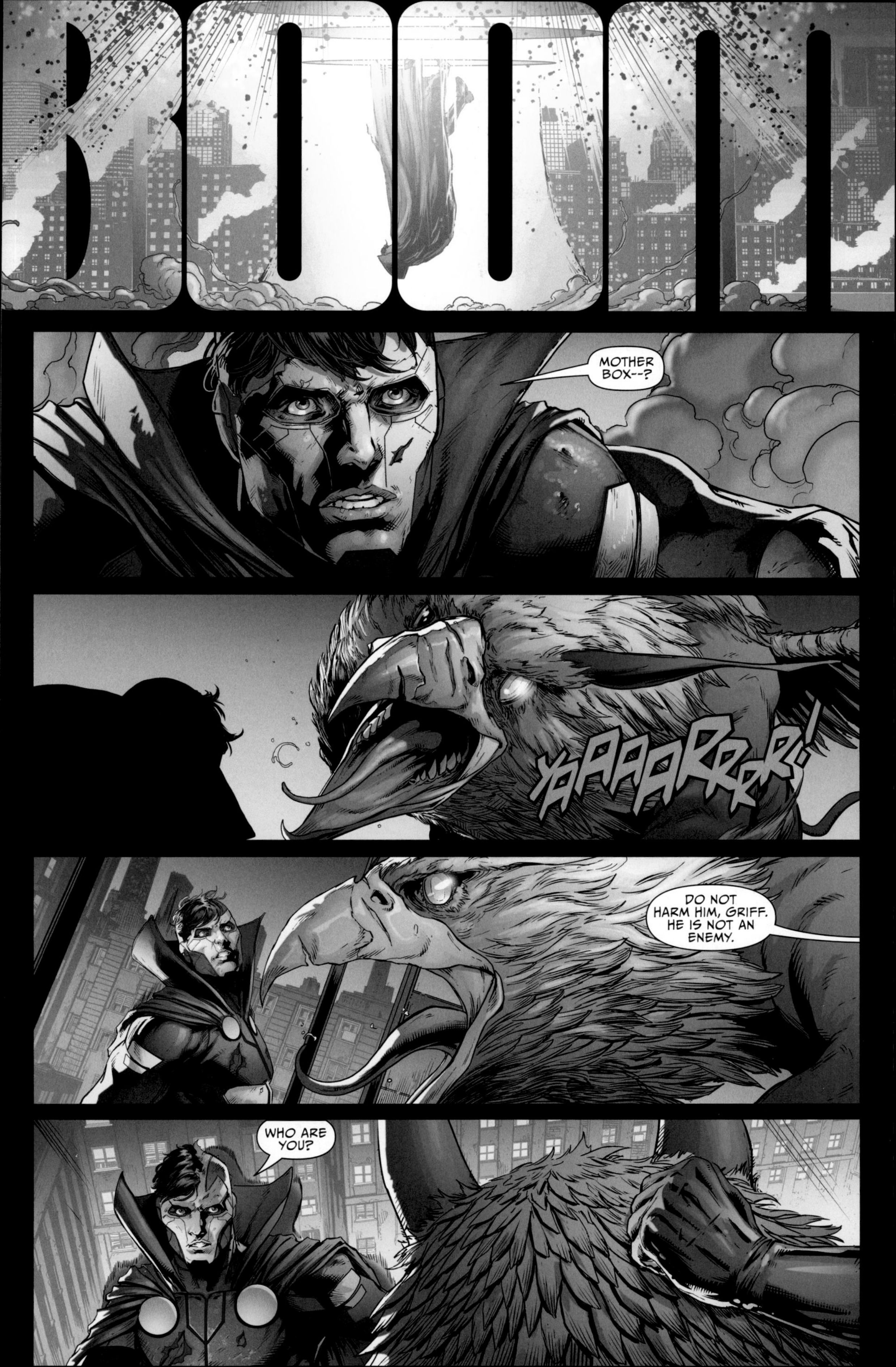
BOOOM
MOTHER BOX--?
YAAAARRRR!
DO NOT HARM HIM, GRIFF. HE IS NOT AN ENEMY.
WHO ARE YOU?

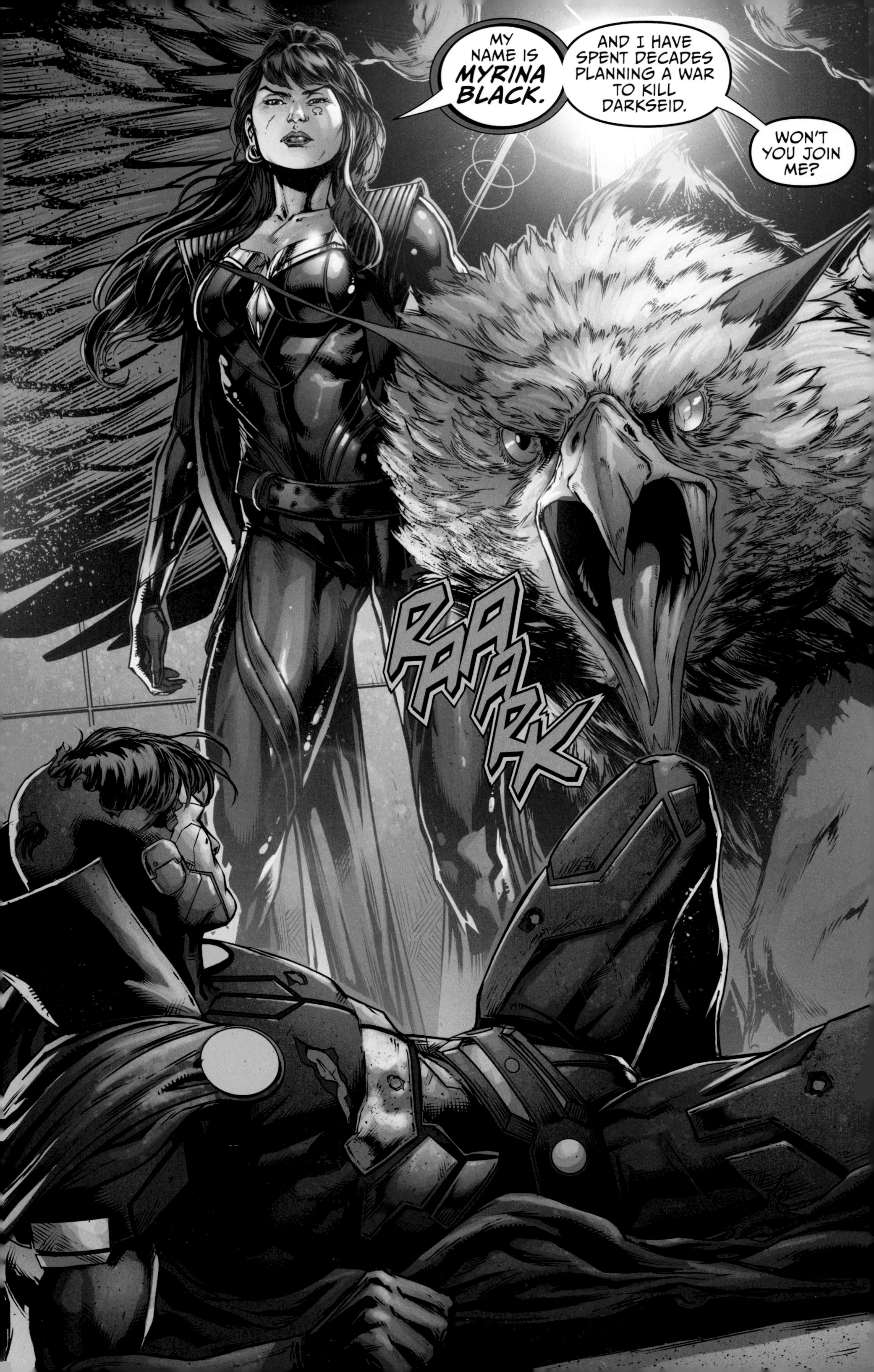
MY NAME IS MYRINA BLACK.
AND I HAVE SPENT DECADES PLANNING A WAR TO KILL DARKSEID.
WON'T YOU JOIN ME?
RAAARK

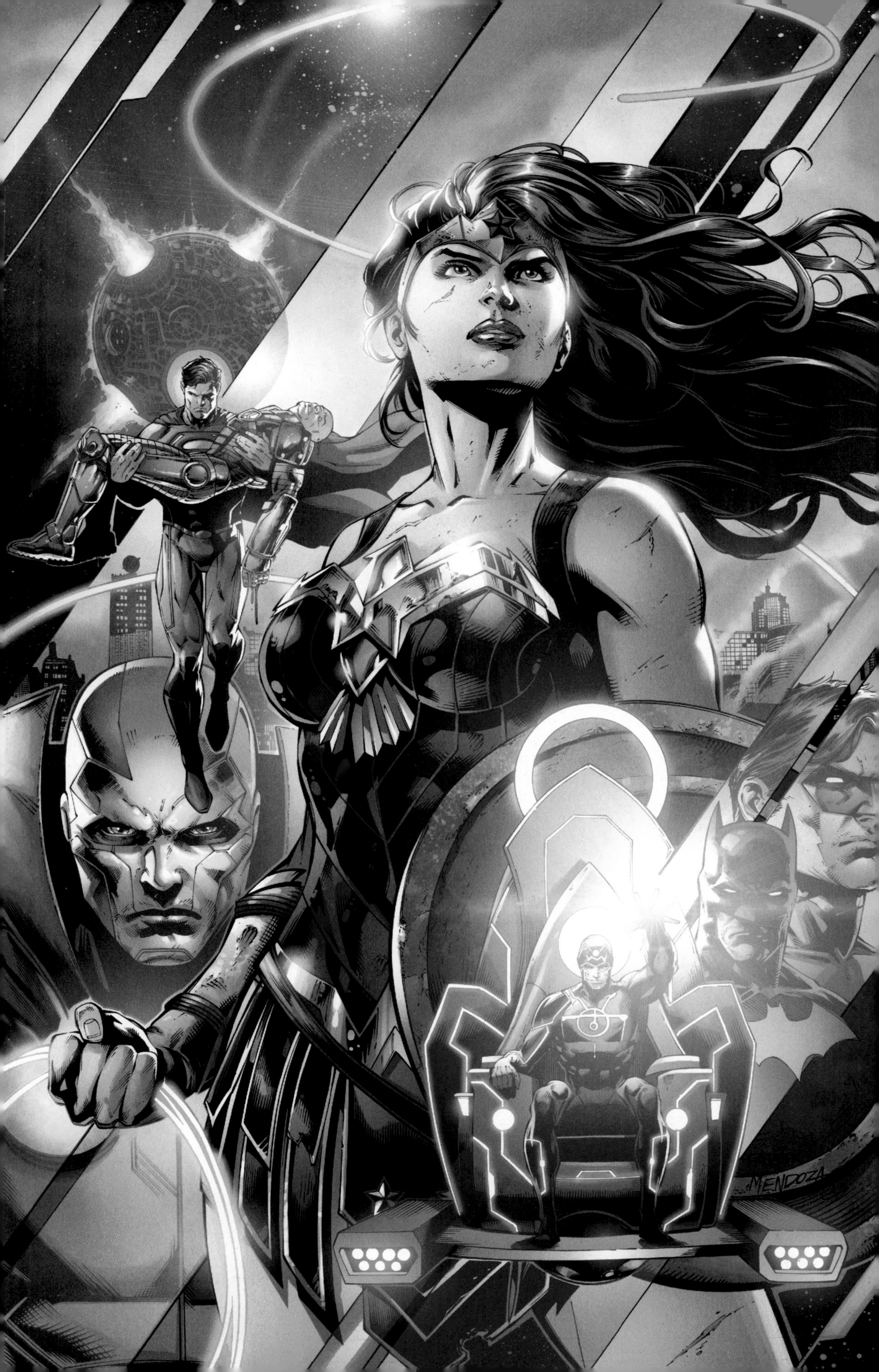
MENDOZA

DARKSEID WAR CHAPTER TWO: THE NEW GOD

GEOFF JOHNS writer JASON FABOK artist BRAD ANDERSON colorist ROB LEIGH letterer cover by JASON FABOK, JAIME MENDOZA and BRAD ANDERSON

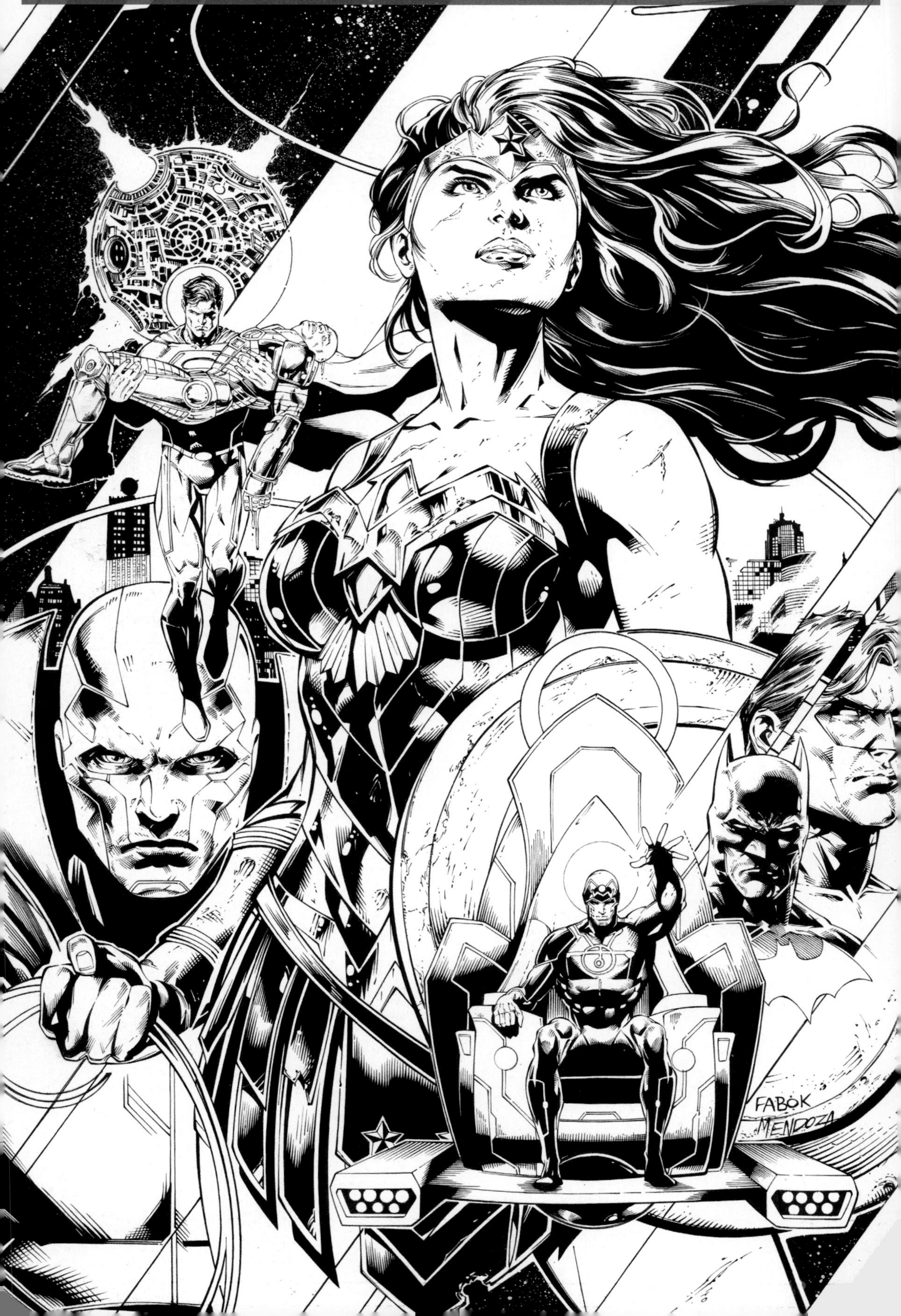
FABOK
MENDOZA

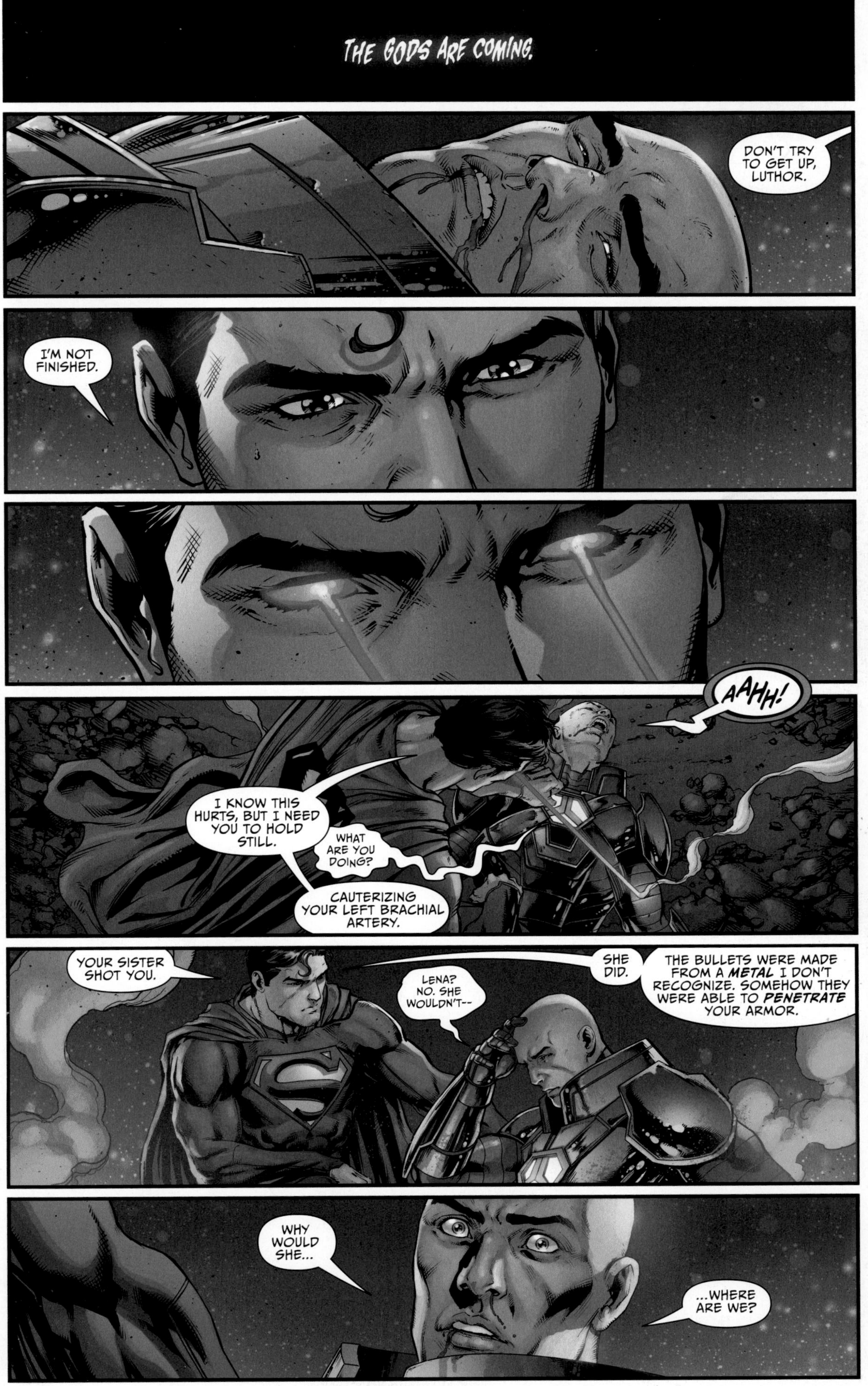
THE GODS ARE COMING.
DON'T TRY TO GET UP, LUTHOR.
I'M NOT FINISHED.
AAHH!
I KNOW THIS HURTS, BUT I NEED YOU TO HOLD STILL.
WHAT ARE YOU DOING?
CAUTERIZING YOUR LEFT BRACHIAL ARTERY.
YOUR SISTER SHOT YOU.
LENA? NO. SHE WOULDN'T--
SHE DID.
THE BULLETS WERE MADE FROM A METAL I DON'T RECOGNIZE. SOMEHOW THEY WERE ABLE TO PENETRATE YOUR ARMOR.
WHY WOULD SHE...
...WHERE ARE WE?

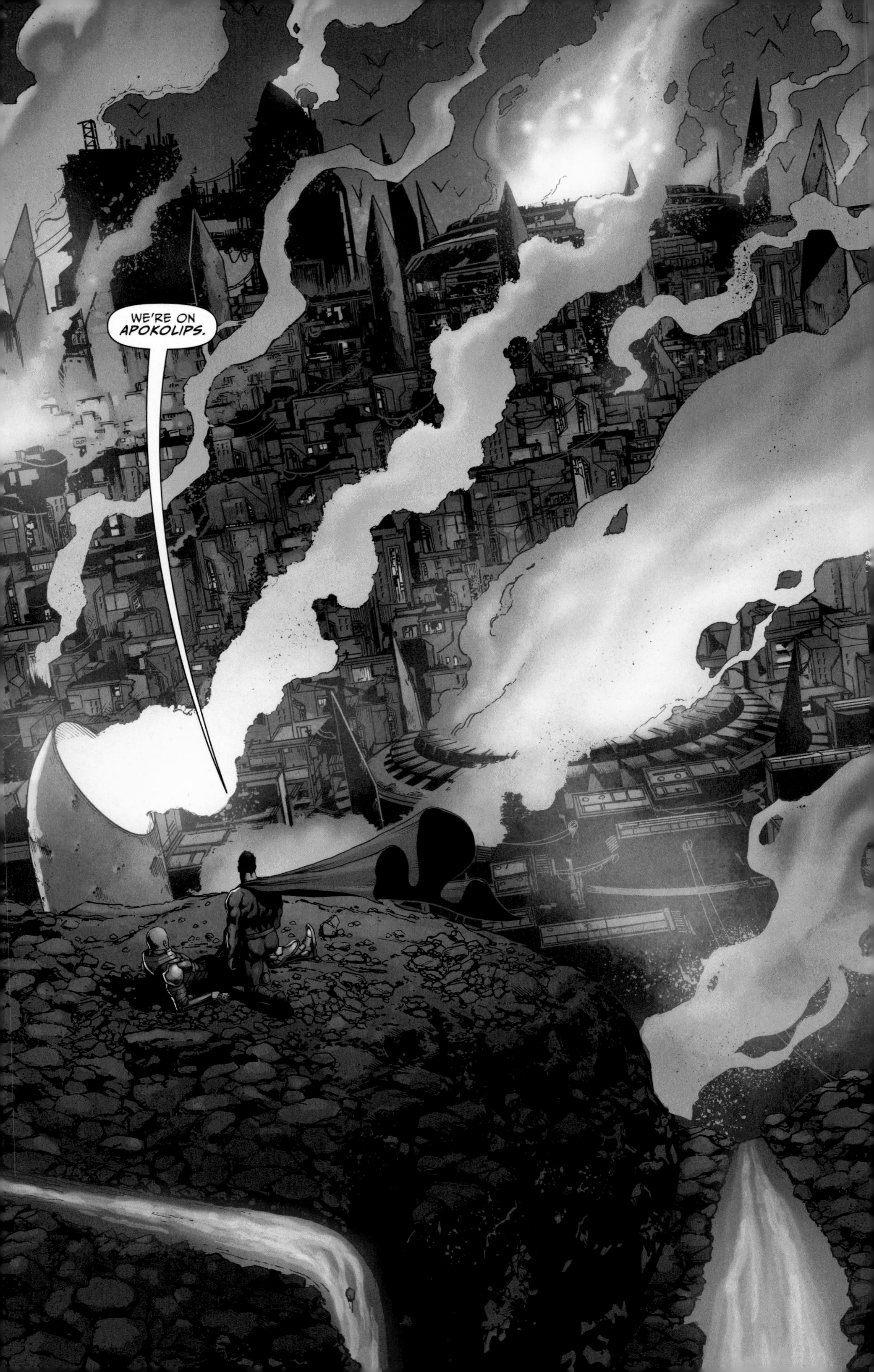
WE'RE ON APOKOLIPS.

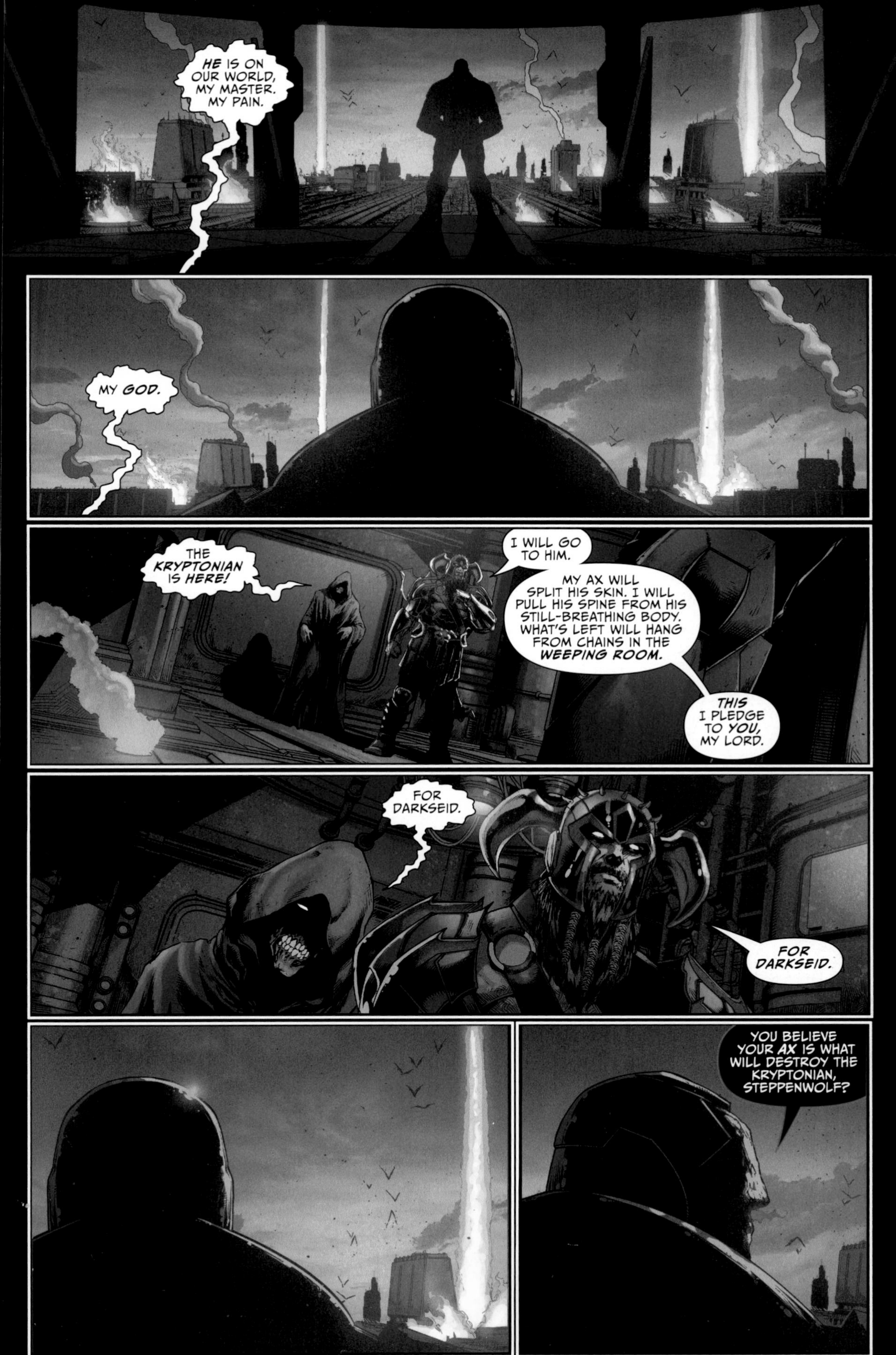
HE IS ON OUR WORLD, MY MASTER. MY PAIN.
MY GOD.
THE KRYPTONIAN IS HERE!
I WILL GO TO HIM.
MY AX WILL SPLIT HIS SKIN. I WILL PULL HIS SPINE FROM HIS STILL-BREATHING BODY. WHAT'S LEFT WILL HANG FROM CHAINS IN THE WEEPING ROOM.
THIS I PLEDGE TO YOU, MY LORD.
FOR DARKSEID.
FOR DARKSEID.
YOU BELIEVE YOUR AX IS WHAT WILL DESTROY THE KRYPTONIAN, STEPPENWOLF?

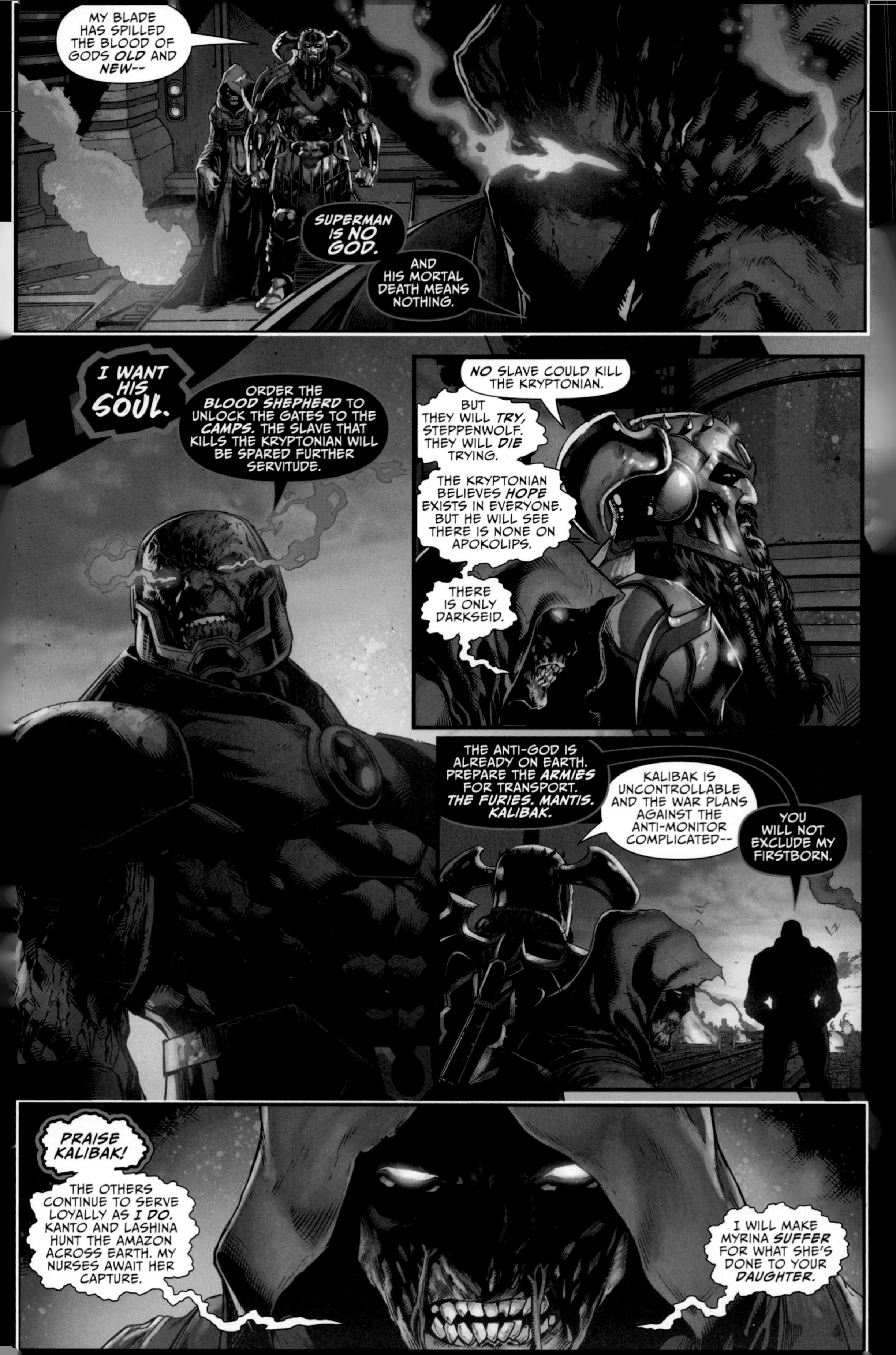

MY BLADE HAS SPILLED THE BLOOD OF GODS OLD AND NEW--
SUPERMAN IS NO GOD.
AND HIS MORTAL DEATH MEANS NOTHING.
I WANT HIS SOUL.
ORDER THE BLOOD SHEPHERD TO UNLOCK THE GATES TO THE CAMPS. THE SLAVE THAT KILLS THE KRYPTONIAN WILL BE SPARED FURTHER SERVITUDE.
NO SLAVE COULD KILL THE KRYPTONIAN.
BUT THEY WILL TRY, STEPPENWOLF. THEY WILL DIE TRYING.
THE KRYPTONIAN BELIEVES HOPE EXISTS IN EVERYONE. BUT HE WILL SEE THERE IS NONE ON APOKOLIPS.
THERE IS ONLY DARKSEID.
THE ANTI-GOD IS ALREADY ON EARTH. PREPARE THE ARMIES FOR TRANSPORT. THE FURIES. MANTIS. KALIBAK.
KALIBAK IS UNCONTROLLABLE AND THE WAR PLANS AGAINST THE ANTI-MONITOR COMPLICATED--
YOU WILL NOT EXCLUDE MY FIRSTBORN.
PRAISE KALIBAK!
THE OTHERS CONTINUE TO SERVE LOYALLY AS I DO. KANTO AND LASHINA HUNT THE AMAZON ACROSS EARTH. MY NURSES AWAIT HER CAPTURE.
I WILL MAKE MYRINA SUFFER FOR WHAT SHE'S DONE TO YOUR DAUGHTER.

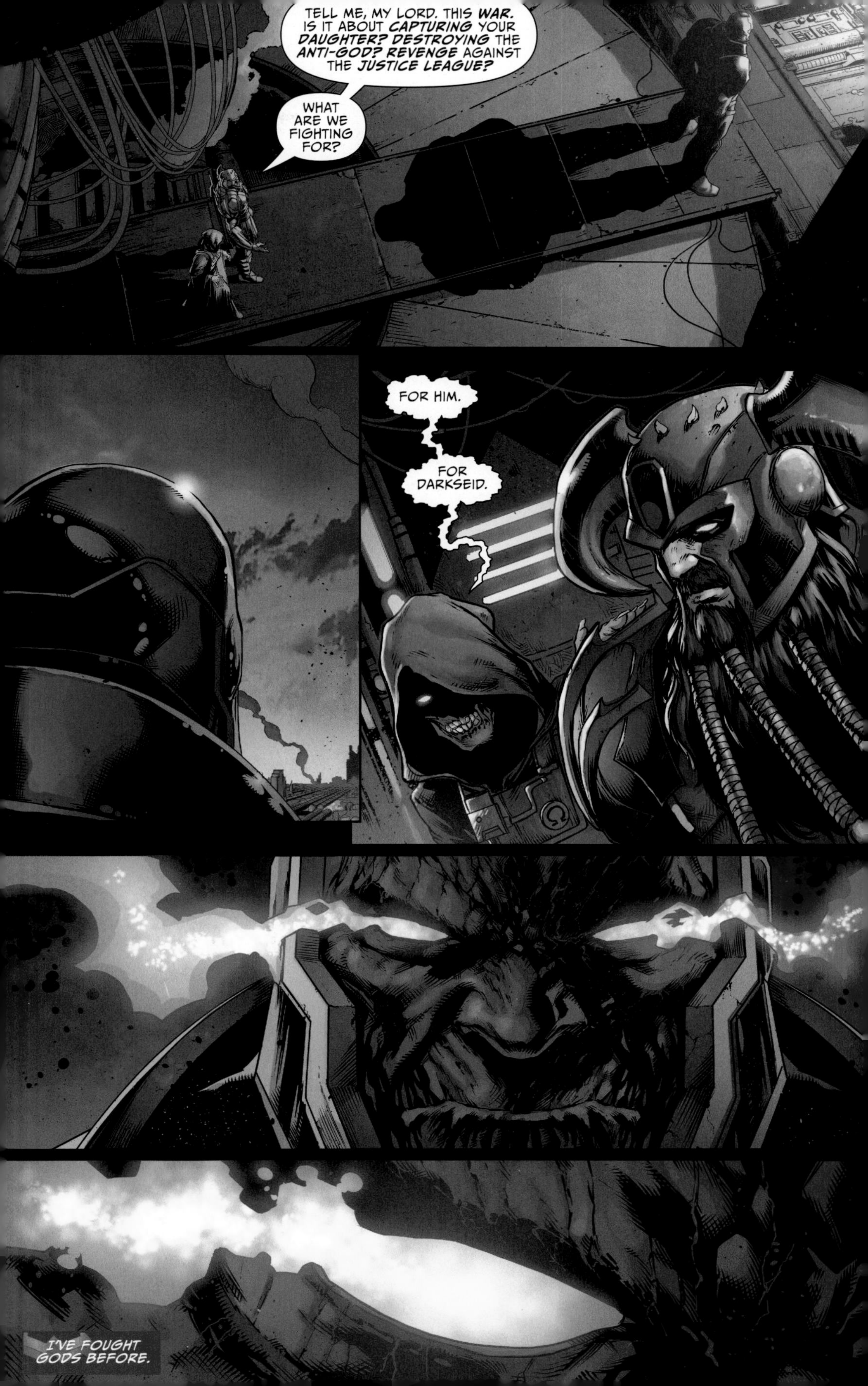
TELL ME, MY LORD. THIS WAR. IS IT ABOUT CAPTURING YOUR DAUGHTER? DESTROYING THE ANTI-GOD? REVENGE AGAINST THE JUSTICE LEAGUE?
WHAT ARE WE FIGHTING FOR?
FOR HIM.
FOR DARKSEID.
I'VE FOUGHT GODS BEFORE.

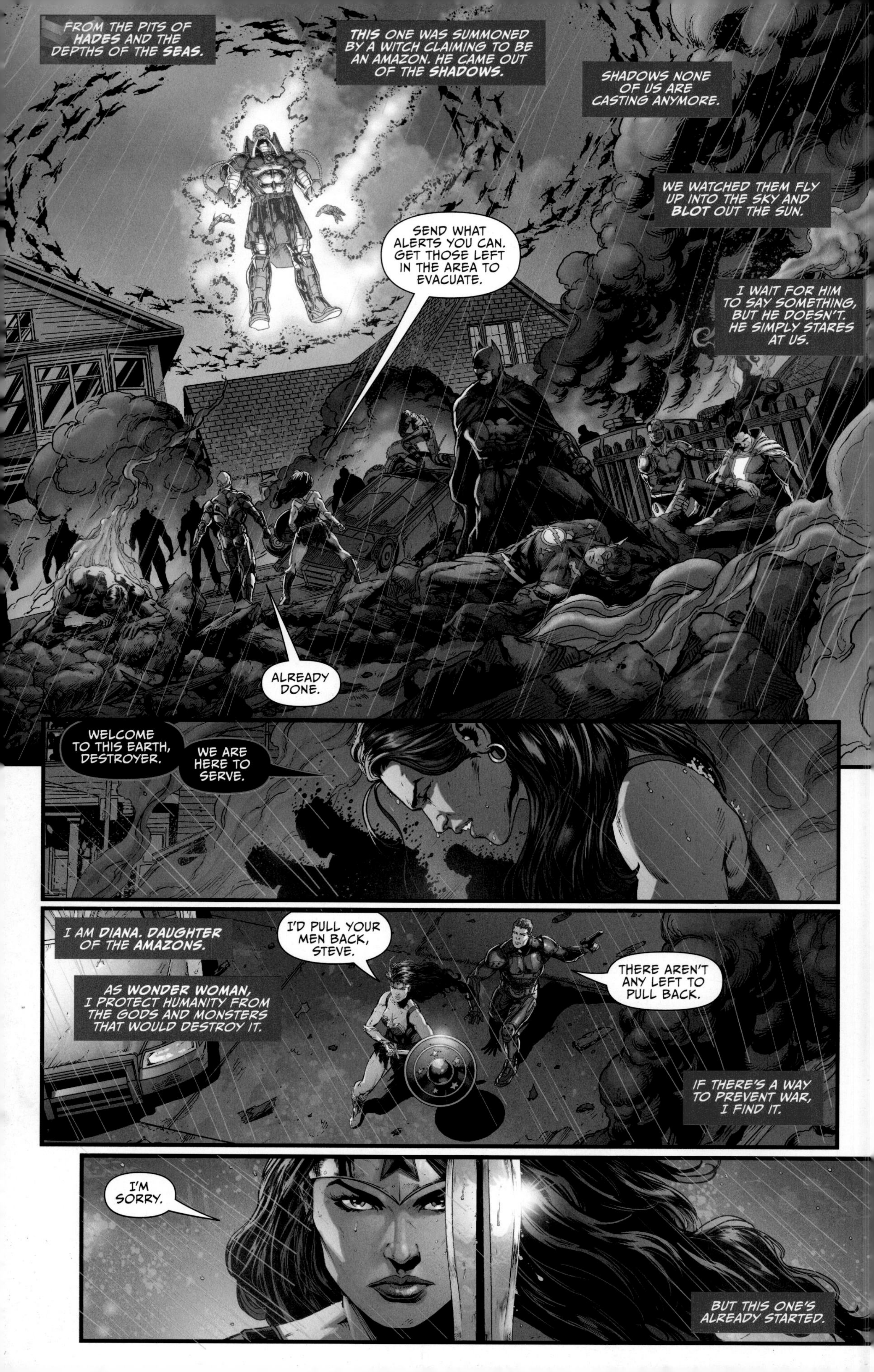
FROM THE PITS OF HADES AND THE DEPTHS OF THE SEAS.
THIS ONE WAS SUMMONED BY A WITCH CLAIMING TO BE AN AMAZON. HE CAME OUT OF THE SHADOWS.
SHADOWS NONE OF US ARE CASTING ANYMORE.
WE WATCHED THEM FLY UP INTO THE SKY AND BLOT OUT THE SUN.
SEND WHAT ALERTS YOU CAN. GET THOSE LEFT IN THE AREA TO EVACUATE.
I WAIT FOR HIM TO SAY SOMETHING, BUT HE DOESN'T. HE SIMPLY STARES AT US.
ALREADY DONE.
WELCOME TO THIS EARTH, DESTROYER.
WE ARE HERE TO SERVE.
I AM DIANA. DAUGHTER OF THE AMAZONS.
I'D PULL YOUR MEN BACK, STEVE.
AS WONDER WOMAN, I PROTECT HUMANITY FROM THE GODS AND MONSTERS THAT WOULD DESTROY IT.
THERE AREN'T ANY LEFT TO PULL BACK.
IF THERE'S A WAY TO PREVENT WAR, I FIND IT.
I'M SORRY.
BUT THIS ONE'S ALREADY STARTED.

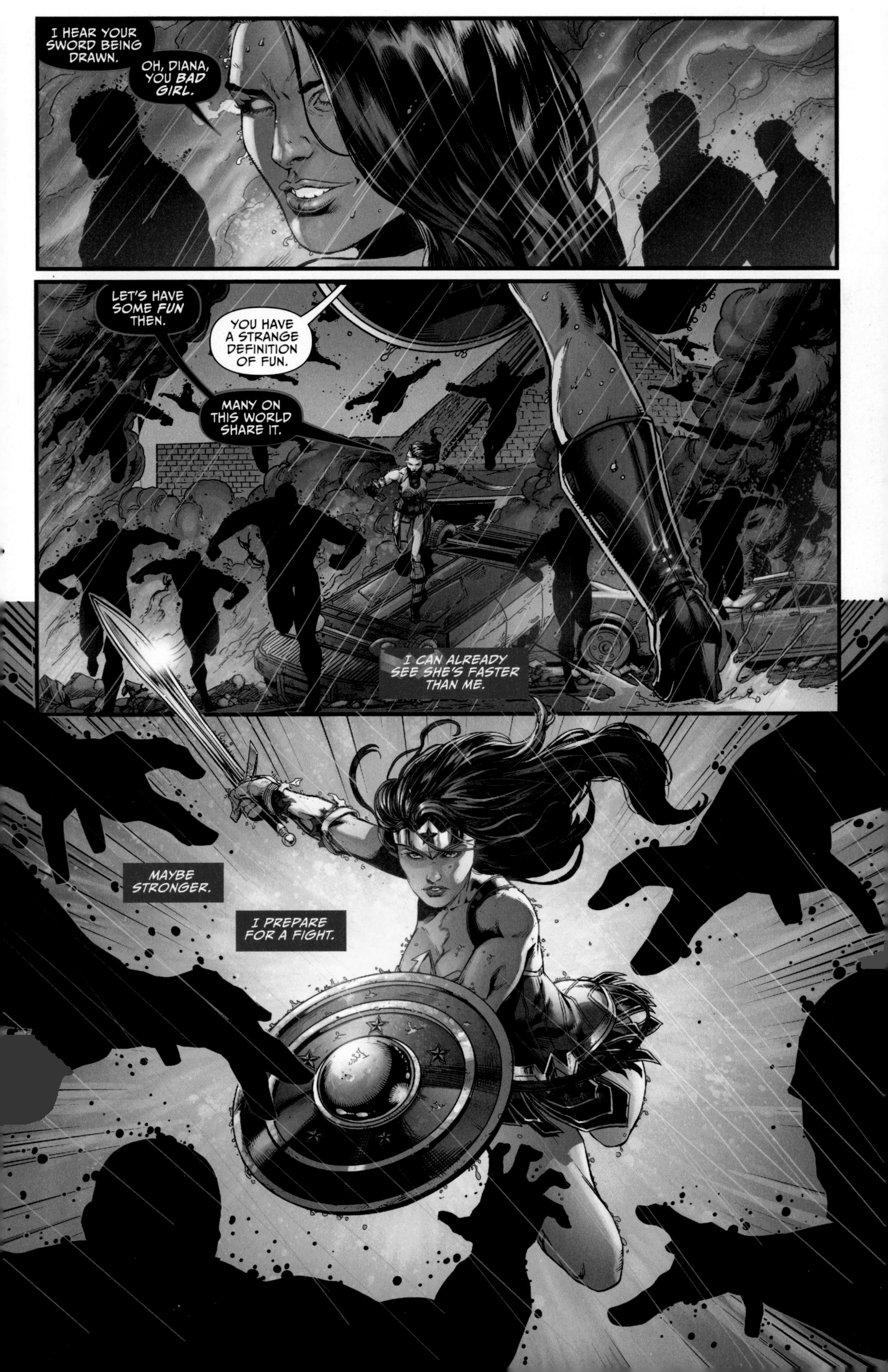
I HEAR YOUR SWORD BEING DRAWN.
OH, DIANA, YOU *BAD GIRL*.
LET'S HAVE SOME *FUN* THEN.
YOU HAVE A STRANGE DEFINITION OF FUN.
MANY ON THIS WORLD SHARE IT.
I CAN ALREADY SEE SHE'S FASTER THAN ME.
MAYBE STRONGER.
I PREPARE FOR A FIGHT.

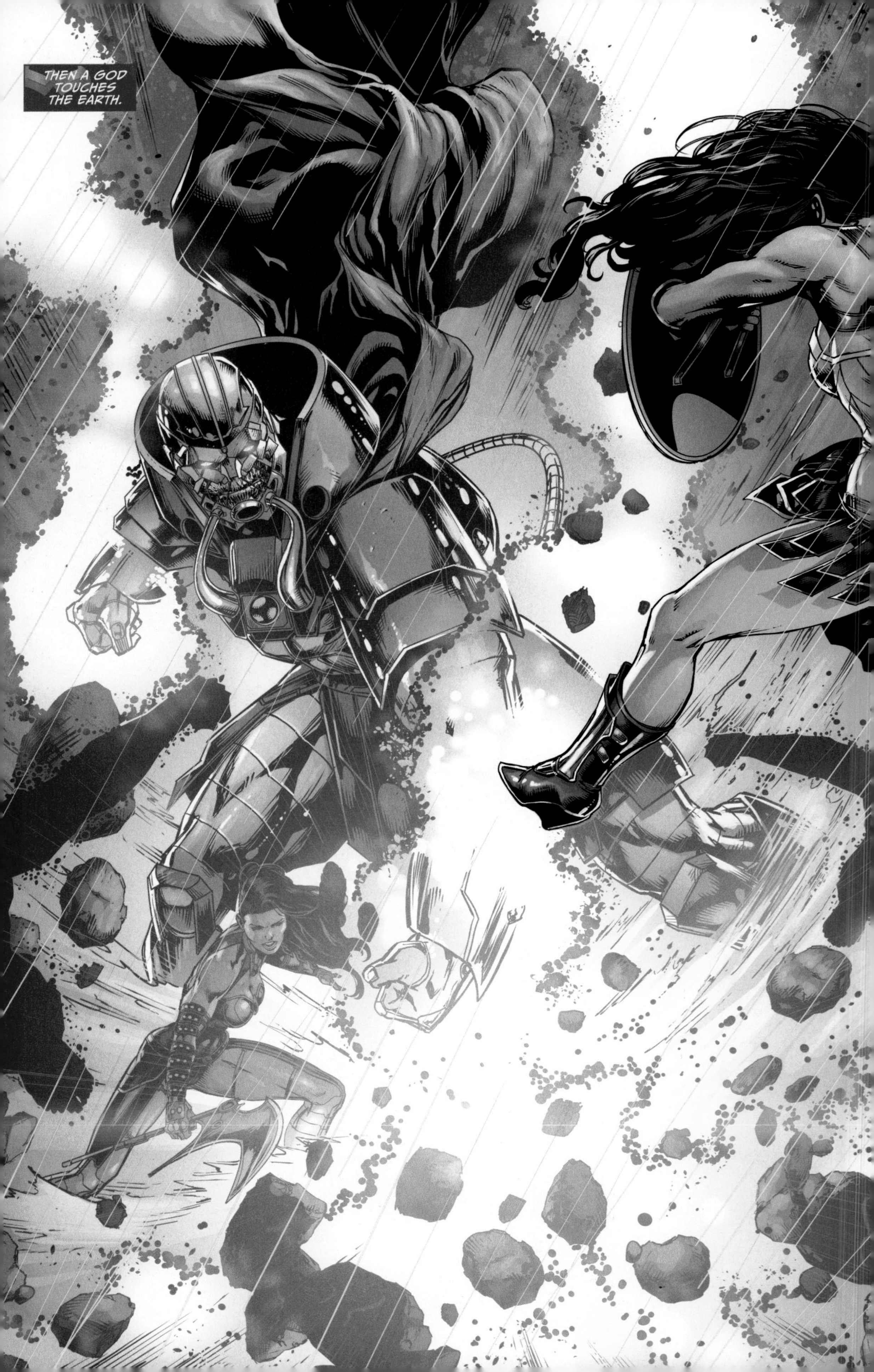
THEN A GOD TOUCHES THE EARTH.

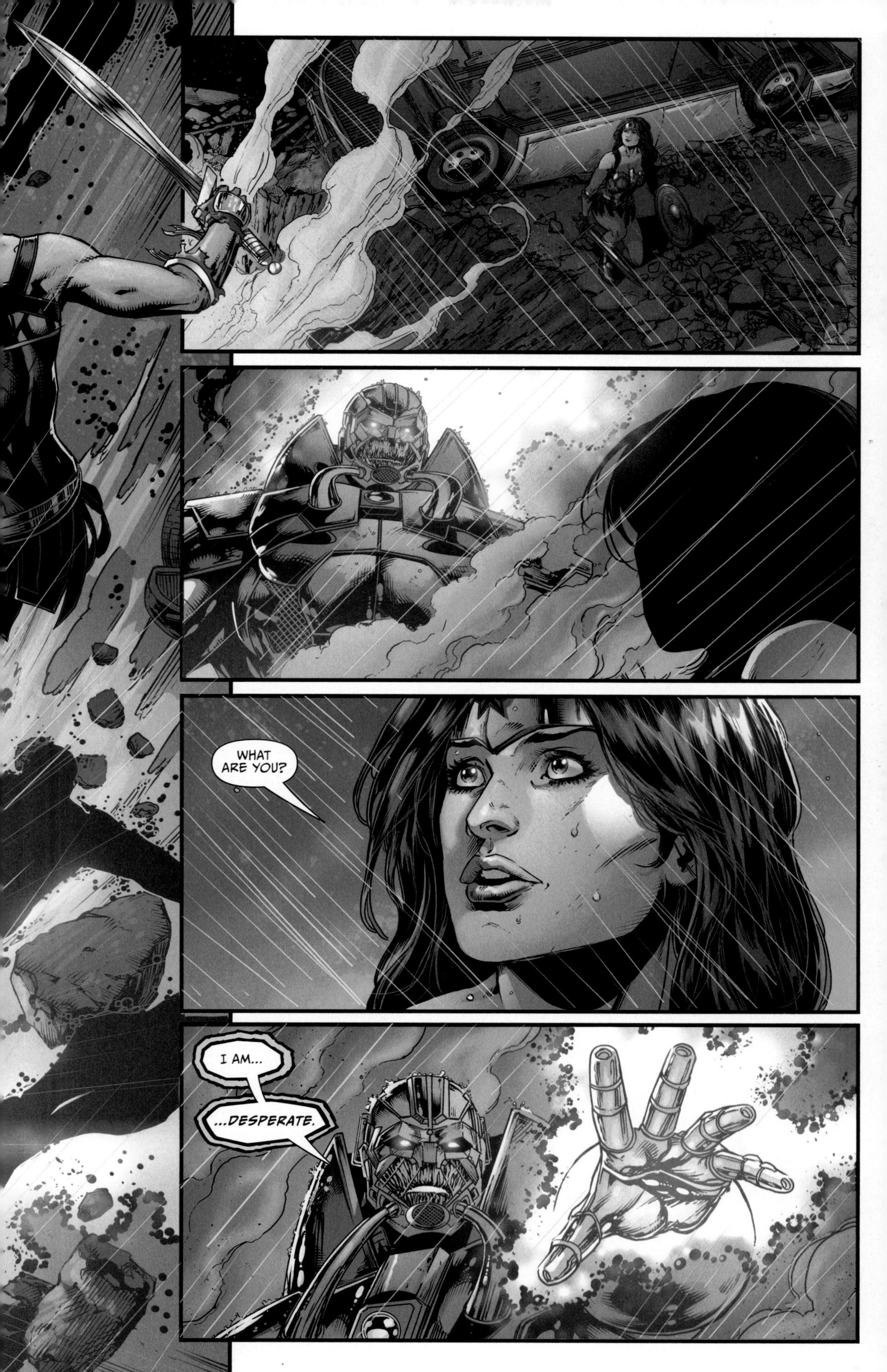
WHAT ARE YOU?
I AM...
...DESPERATE.

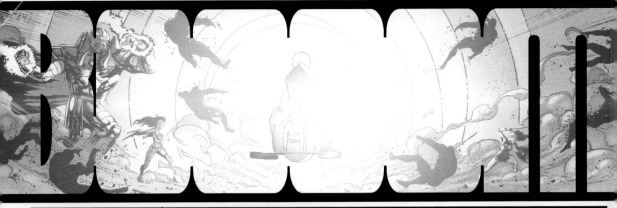

METRON! HOW DELIGHTFUL.

I AM STILL WATCHING YOU, GRAIL.

WHY? DO YOU FIND ME PRETTY?

I FIND YOU DANGEROUS, BUT ULTIMATELY PRECARIOUS.

YOU PLAY THIS GAME WELL, BUT SO DO I.

METRON BELIEVES HE CAN *HIDE* THE LEAGUE FROM ME, BUT I WILL *FIND* THEM.

I WILL *HAVE* MY TROPHIES.

FIRST, YOU WILL BRING YOUR *FATHER* TO ME.

OH, *DARKSEID* IS COMING. YOU *WILL* GET YOUR WISH, MOBIUS. YOU WILL GET YOUR *BRAND-NEW DAY.* YOUR *NEW LIFE.*

YOU WILL GET YOUR *WAR.*

MOTHER *PROMISED* ME...

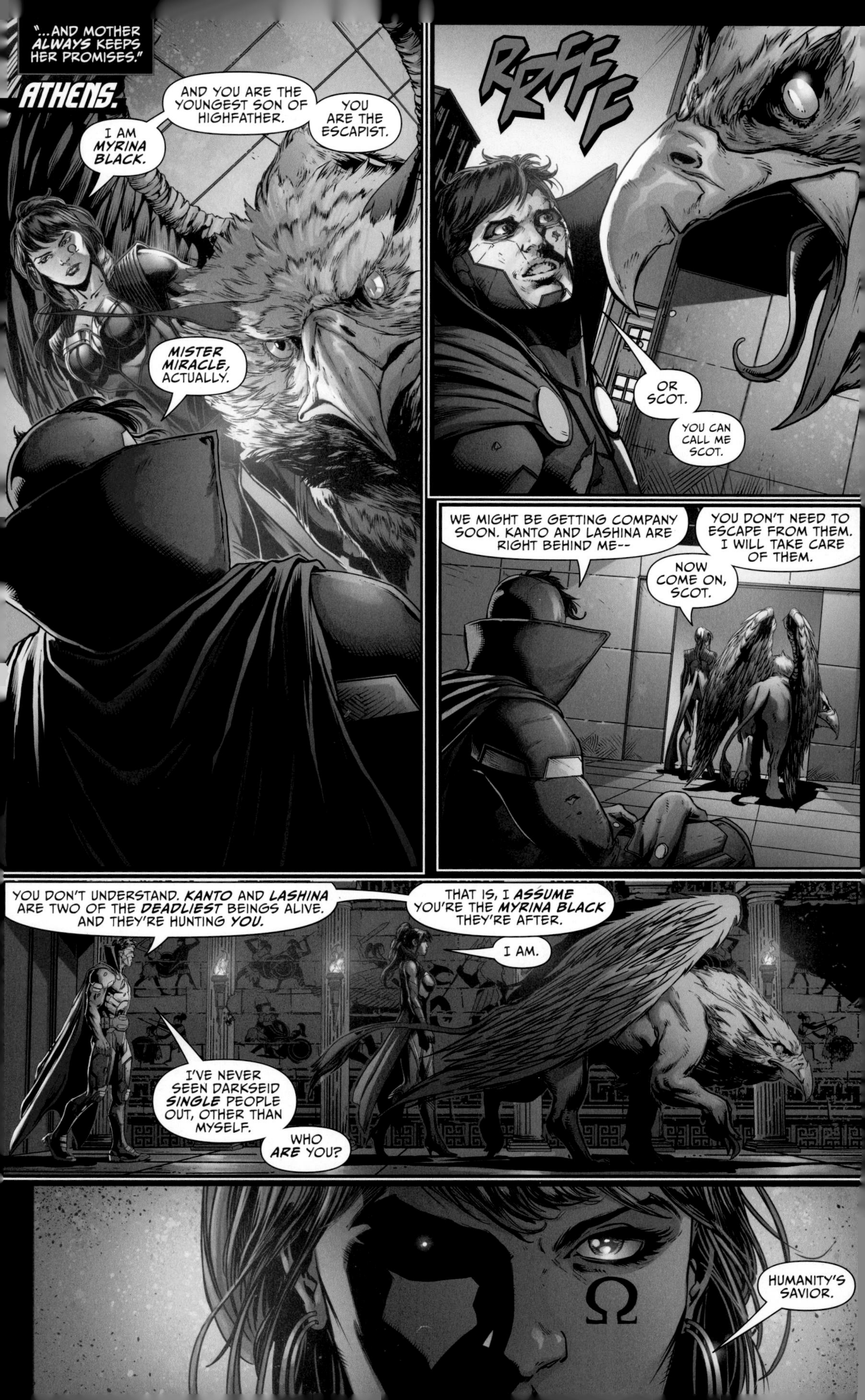
"...AND MOTHER ALWAYS KEEPS HER PROMISES."
ATHENS.
I AM MYRINA BLACK.
AND YOU ARE THE YOUNGEST SON OF HIGHFATHER.
YOU ARE THE ESCAPIST.
MISTER MIRACLE, ACTUALLY.
RRFF
OR SCOT.
YOU CAN CALL ME SCOT.
WE MIGHT BE GETTING COMPANY SOON. KANTO AND LASHINA ARE RIGHT BEHIND ME--
YOU DON'T NEED TO ESCAPE FROM THEM. I WILL TAKE CARE OF THEM.
NOW COME ON, SCOT.
YOU DON'T UNDERSTAND. KANTO AND LASHINA ARE TWO OF THE DEADLIEST BEINGS ALIVE. AND THEY'RE HUNTING YOU.
THAT IS, I ASSUME YOU'RE THE MYRINA BLACK THEY'RE AFTER.
I AM.
I'VE NEVER SEEN DARKSEID SINGLE PEOPLE OUT, OTHER THAN MYSELF.
WHO ARE YOU?
HUMANITY'S SAVIOR.

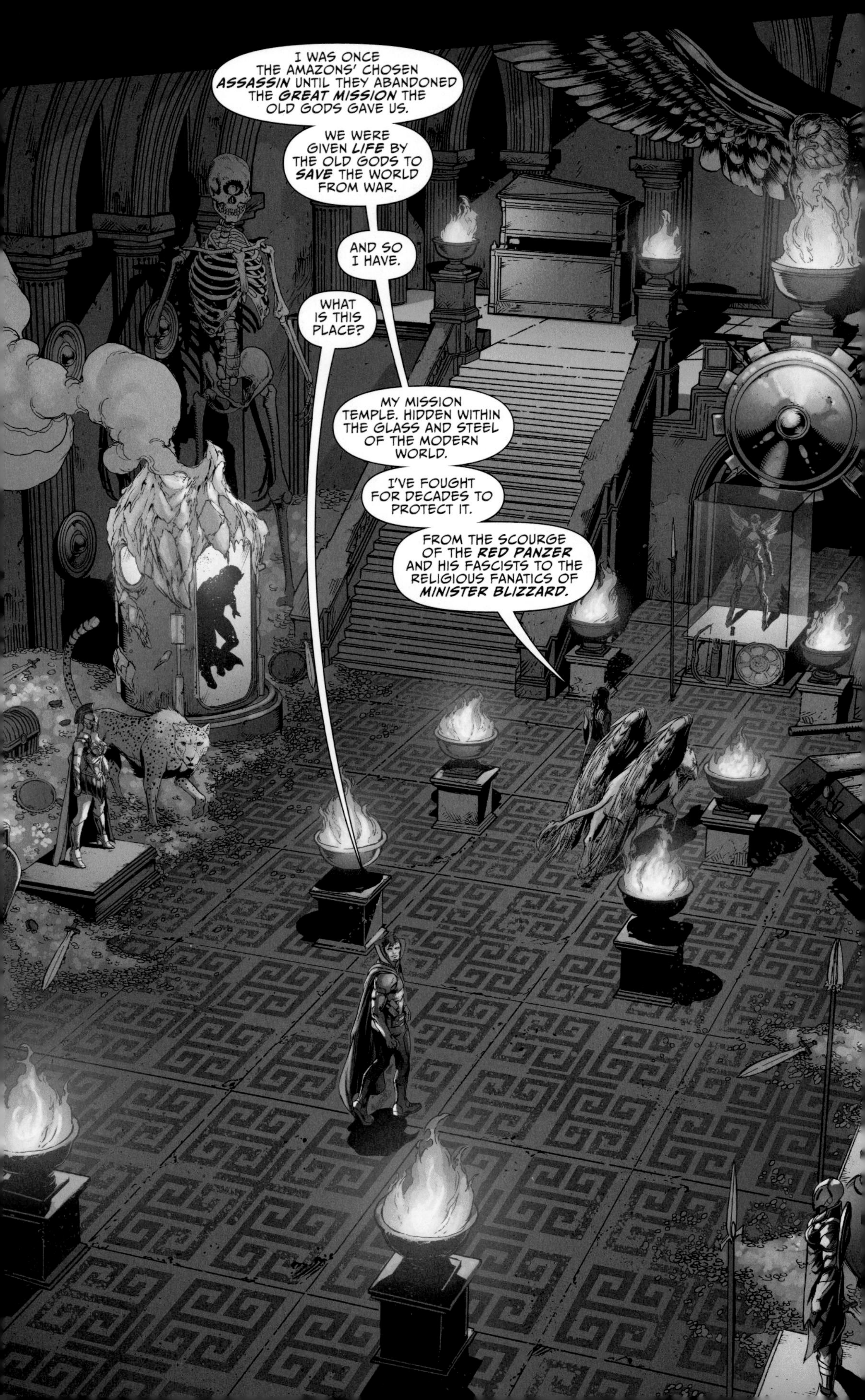
I WAS ONCE THE AMAZONS' CHOSEN ***ASSASSIN*** UNTIL THEY ABANDONED THE ***GREAT MISSION*** THE OLD GODS GAVE US.
WE WERE GIVEN ***LIFE*** BY THE OLD GODS TO ***SAVE*** THE WORLD FROM WAR.
AND SO I HAVE.
WHAT IS THIS PLACE?
MY MISSION TEMPLE. HIDDEN WITHIN THE GLASS AND STEEL OF THE MODERN WORLD.
I'VE FOUGHT FOR DECADES TO PROTECT IT.
FROM THE SCOURGE OF THE ***RED PANZER*** AND HIS FASCISTS TO THE RELIGIOUS FANATICS OF ***MINISTER BLIZZARD.***

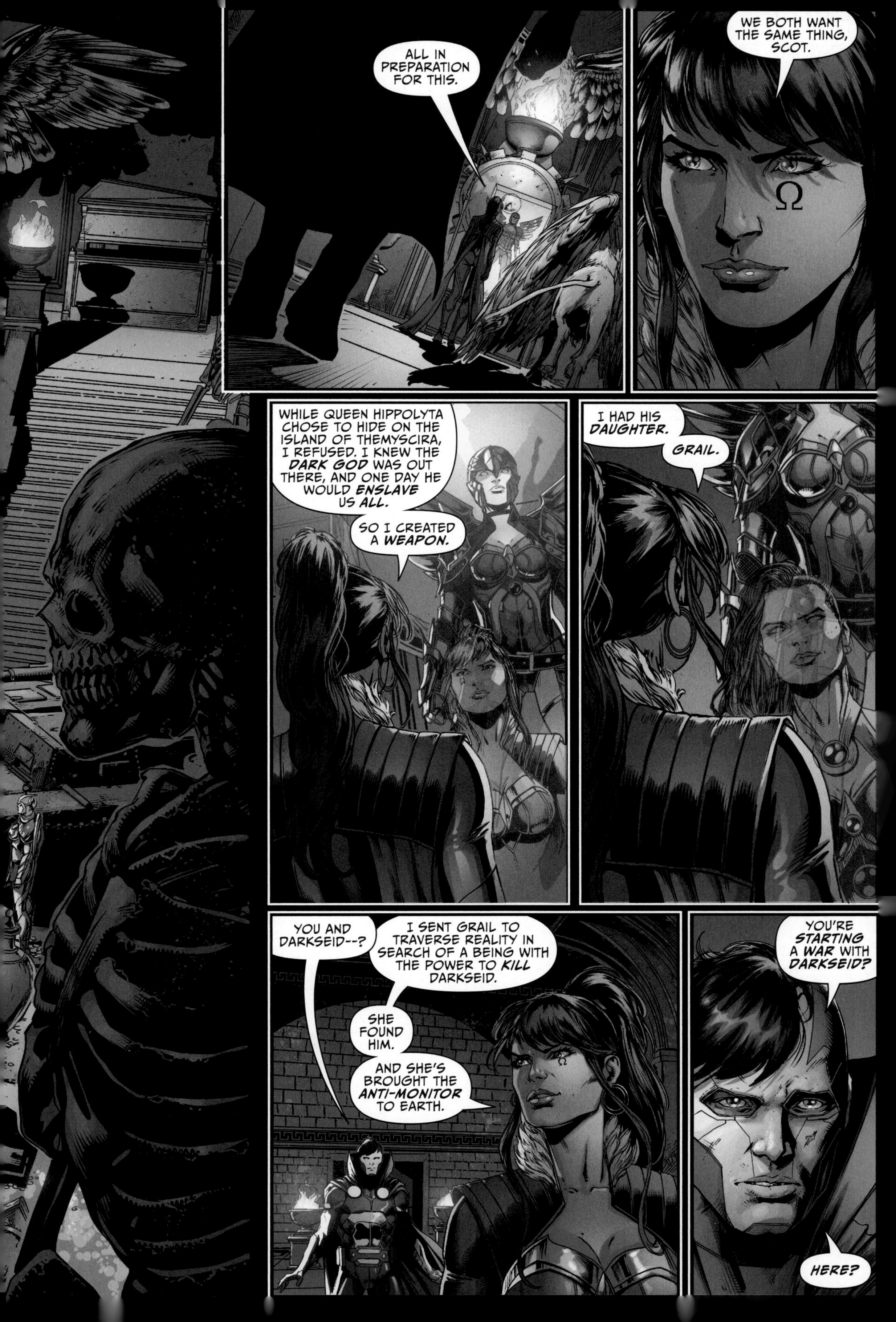

ALL IN PREPARATION FOR THIS.
WE BOTH WANT THE SAME THING, SCOT.
WHILE QUEEN HIPPOLYTA CHOSE TO HIDE ON THE ISLAND OF THEMYSCIRA, I REFUSED. I KNEW THE DARK GOD WAS OUT THERE, AND ONE DAY HE WOULD ENSLAVE US ALL.
SO I CREATED A WEAPON.
I HAD HIS DAUGHTER.
GRAIL.
YOU AND DARKSEID--?
I SENT GRAIL TO TRAVERSE REALITY IN SEARCH OF A BEING WITH THE POWER TO KILL DARKSEID.
SHE FOUND HIM.
AND SHE'S BROUGHT THE ANTI-MONITOR TO EARTH.
YOU'RE STARTING A WAR WITH DARKSEID?
HERE?

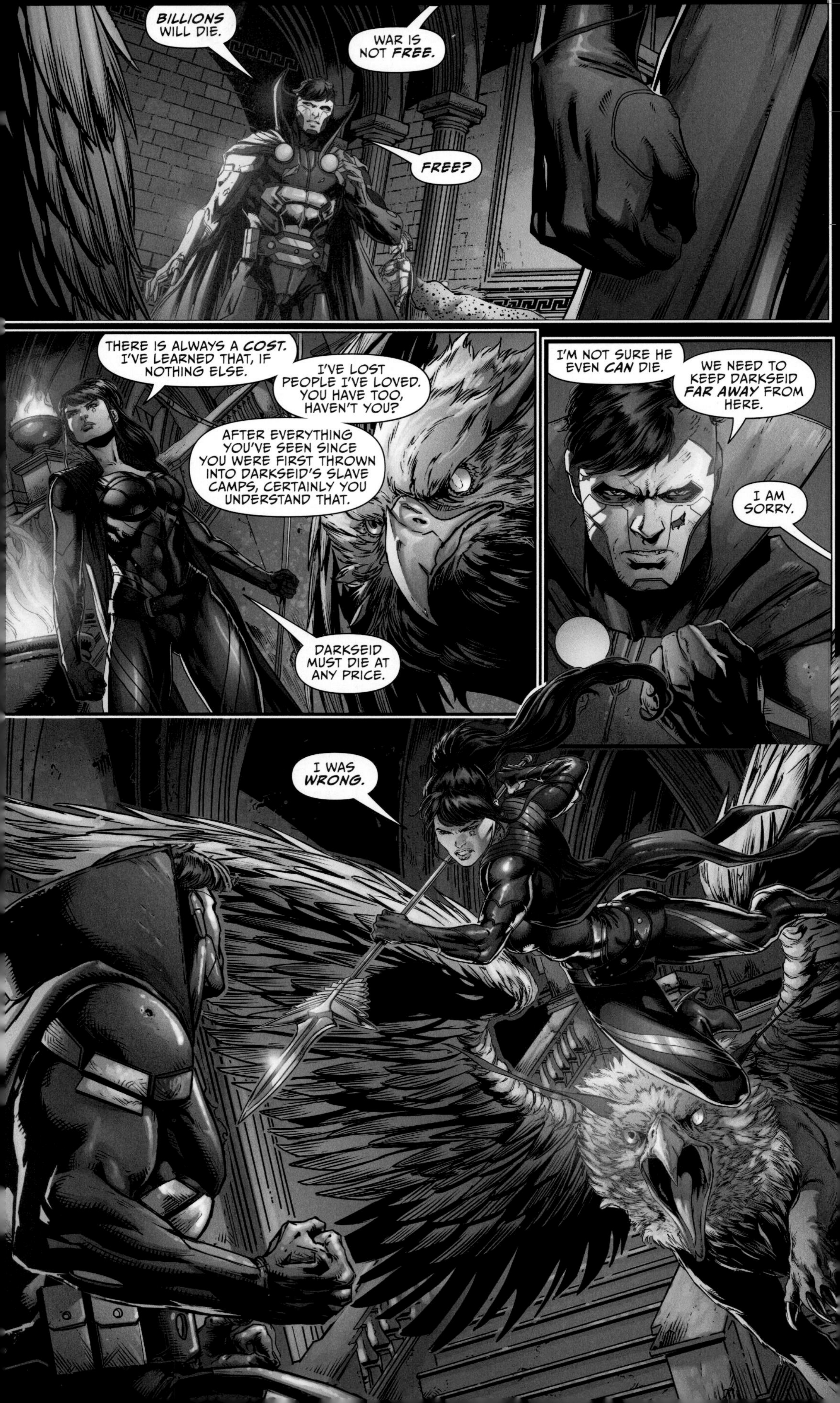
BILLIONS WILL DIE.
WAR IS NOT FREE.
FREE?
THERE IS ALWAYS A COST. I'VE LEARNED THAT, IF NOTHING ELSE.
I'VE LOST PEOPLE I'VE LOVED. YOU HAVE TOO, HAVEN'T YOU?
AFTER EVERYTHING YOU'VE SEEN SINCE YOU WERE FIRST THROWN INTO DARKSEID'S SLAVE CAMPS, CERTAINLY YOU UNDERSTAND THAT.
DARKSEID MUST DIE AT ANY PRICE.
I'M NOT SURE HE EVEN CAN DIE.
WE NEED TO KEEP DARKSEID FAR AWAY FROM HERE.
I AM SORRY.
I WAS WRONG.

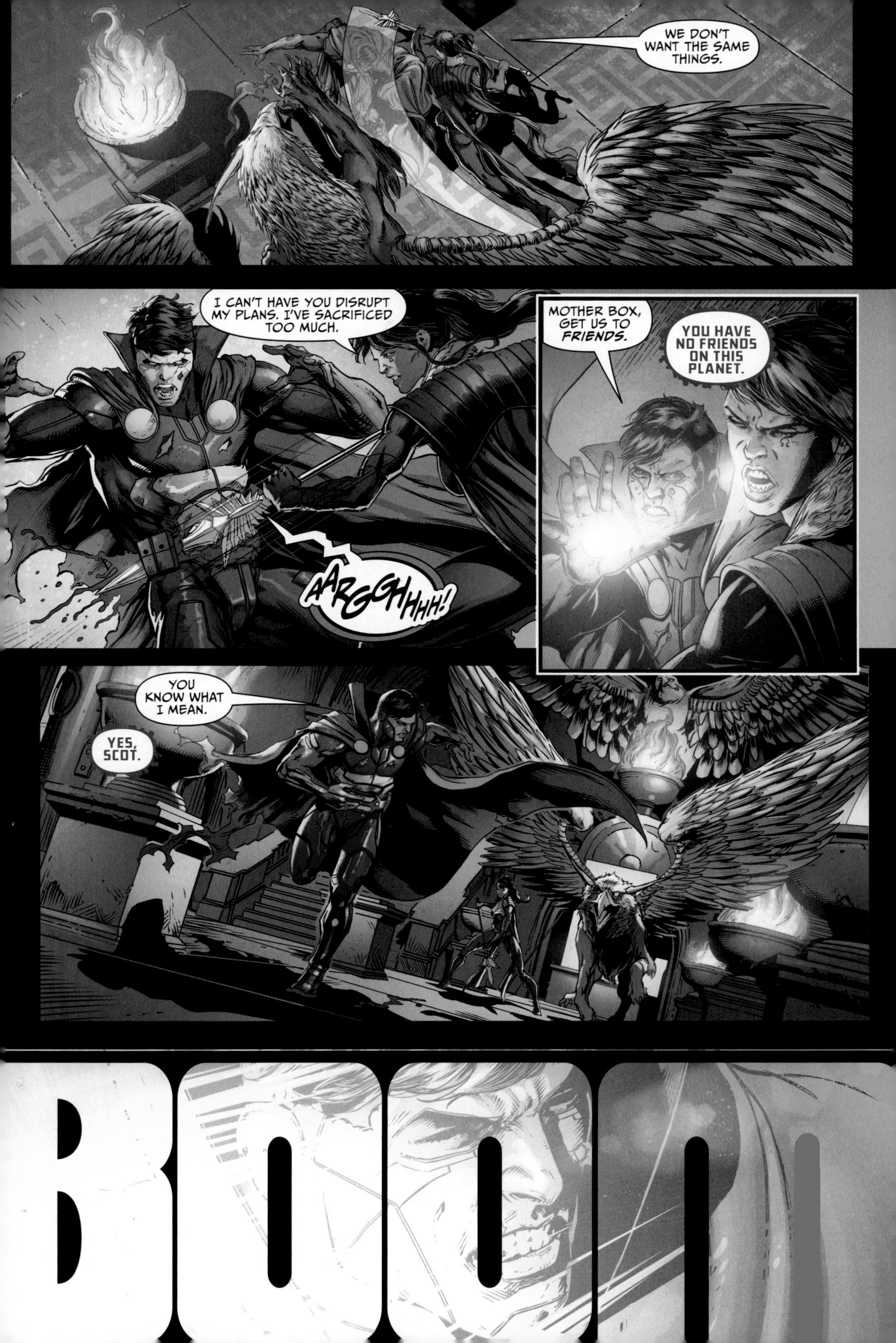
WE DON'T WANT THE SAME THINGS.
I CAN'T HAVE YOU DISRUPT MY PLANS. I'VE SACRIFICED TOO MUCH.
AARGGHHHH!
MOTHER BOX, GET US TO *FRIENDS.*
YOU HAVE NO FRIENDS ON THIS PLANET.
YOU KNOW WHAT I MEAN.
YES, SCOT.
BOOM

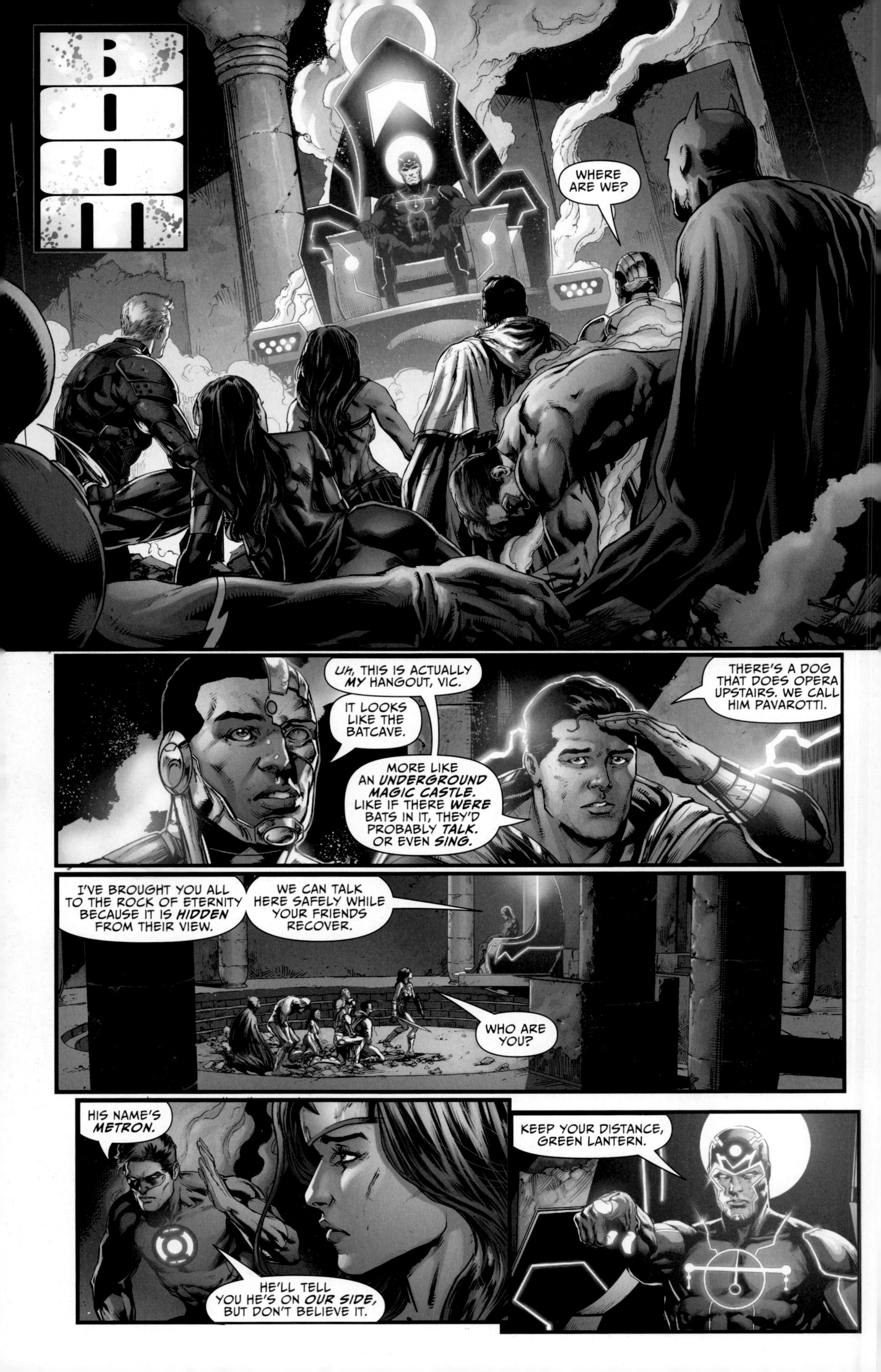
BOOM
WHERE ARE WE?
Uh, THIS IS ACTUALLY MY HANGOUT, VIC.
IT LOOKS LIKE THE BATCAVE.
MORE LIKE AN UNDERGROUND MAGIC CASTLE. LIKE IF THERE WERE BATS IN IT, THEY'D PROBABLY TALK. OR EVEN SING.
THERE'S A DOG THAT DOES OPERA UPSTAIRS. WE CALL HIM PAVAROTTI.
I'VE BROUGHT YOU ALL TO THE ROCK OF ETERNITY BECAUSE IT IS HIDDEN FROM THEIR VIEW.
WE CAN TALK HERE SAFELY WHILE YOUR FRIENDS RECOVER.
WHO ARE YOU?
HIS NAME'S METRON.
HE'LL TELL YOU HE'S ON OUR SIDE, BUT DON'T BELIEVE IT.
KEEP YOUR DISTANCE, GREEN LANTERN.

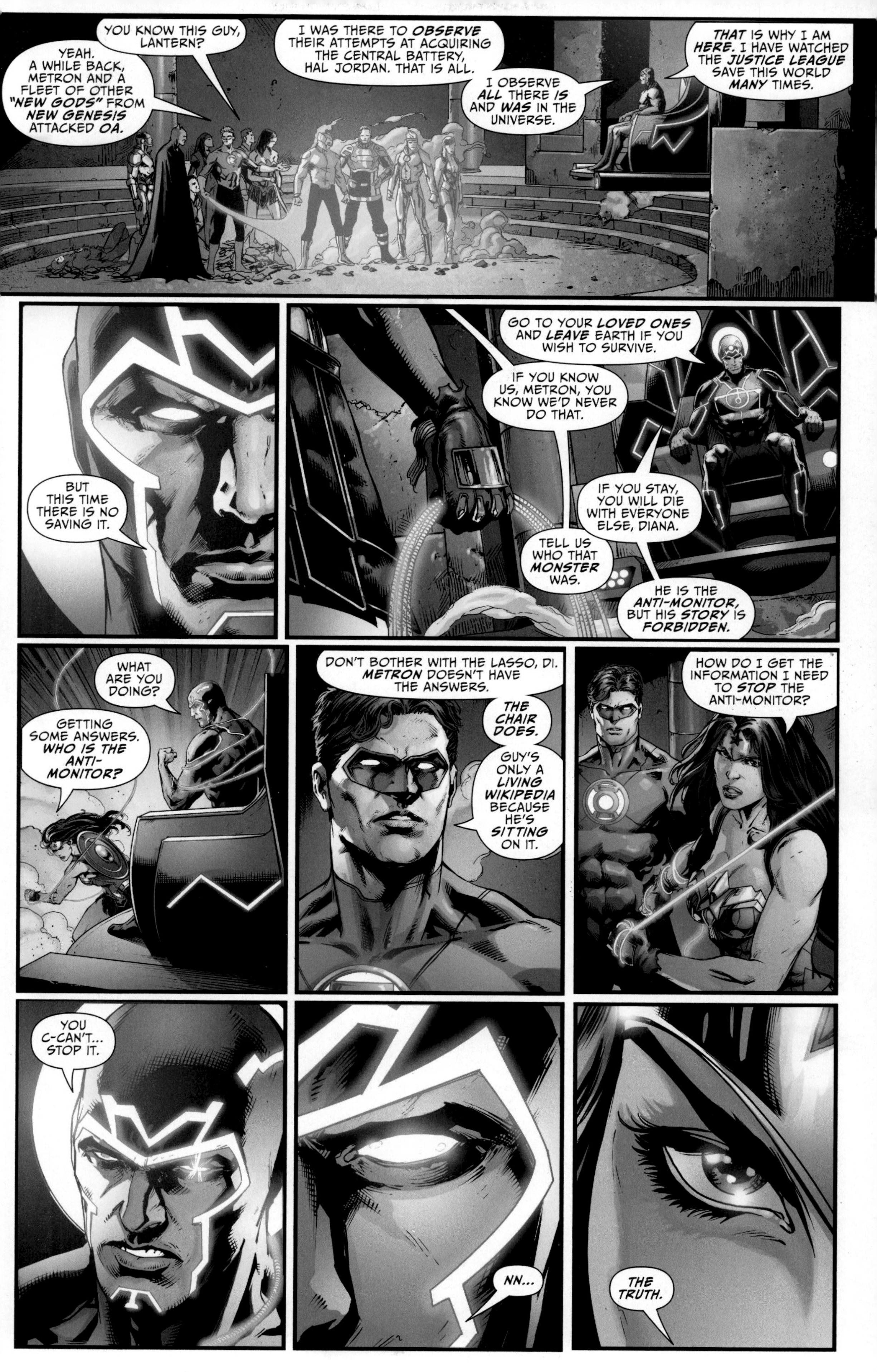

YOU KNOW THIS GUY, LANTERN?
YEAH. A WHILE BACK, METRON AND A FLEET OF OTHER "NEW GODS" FROM NEW GENESIS ATTACKED OA.
I WAS THERE TO OBSERVE THEIR ATTEMPTS AT ACQUIRING THE CENTRAL BATTERY, HAL JORDAN. THAT IS ALL.
I OBSERVE ALL THERE IS AND WAS IN THE UNIVERSE.
THAT IS WHY I AM HERE. I HAVE WATCHED THE JUSTICE LEAGUE SAVE THIS WORLD MANY TIMES.
BUT THIS TIME THERE IS NO SAVING IT.
GO TO YOUR LOVED ONES AND LEAVE EARTH IF YOU WISH TO SURVIVE.
IF YOU KNOW US, METRON, YOU KNOW WE'D NEVER DO THAT.
IF YOU STAY, YOU WILL DIE WITH EVERYONE ELSE, DIANA.
TELL US WHO THAT MONSTER WAS.
HE IS THE ANTI-MONITOR, BUT HIS STORY IS FORBIDDEN.
WHAT ARE YOU DOING?
GETTING SOME ANSWERS. WHO IS THE ANTI-MONITOR?
DON'T BOTHER WITH THE LASSO, DI. METRON DOESN'T HAVE THE ANSWERS.
THE CHAIR DOES.
GUY'S ONLY A LIVING WIKIPEDIA BECAUSE HE'S SITTING ON IT.
HOW DO I GET THE INFORMATION I NEED TO STOP THE ANTI-MONITOR?
YOU C-CAN'T... STOP IT.
NN...
THE TRUTH.

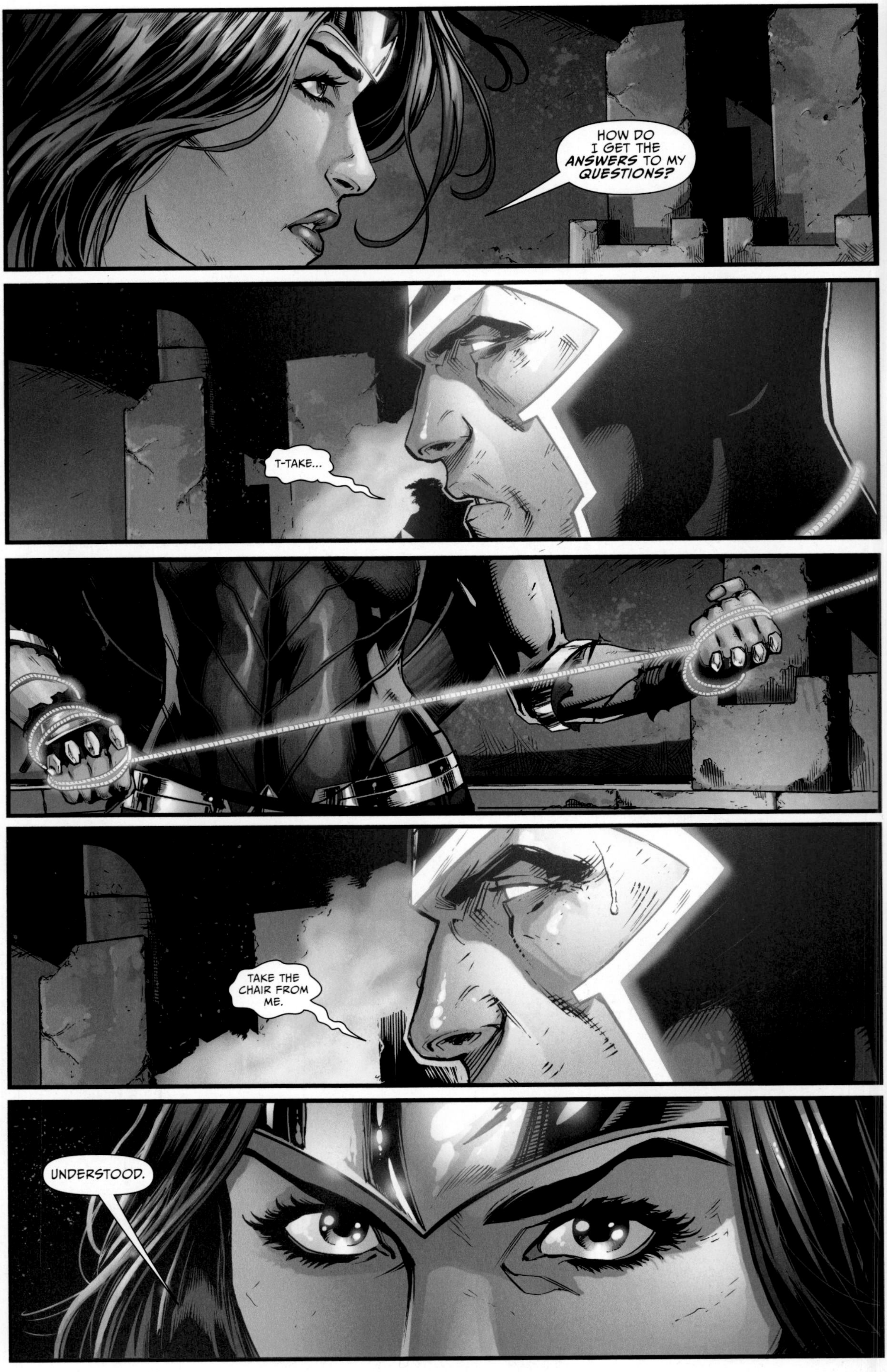
HOW DO I GET THE ANSWERS TO MY QUESTIONS?
T-TAKE...
TAKE THE CHAIR FROM ME.
UNDERSTOOD.

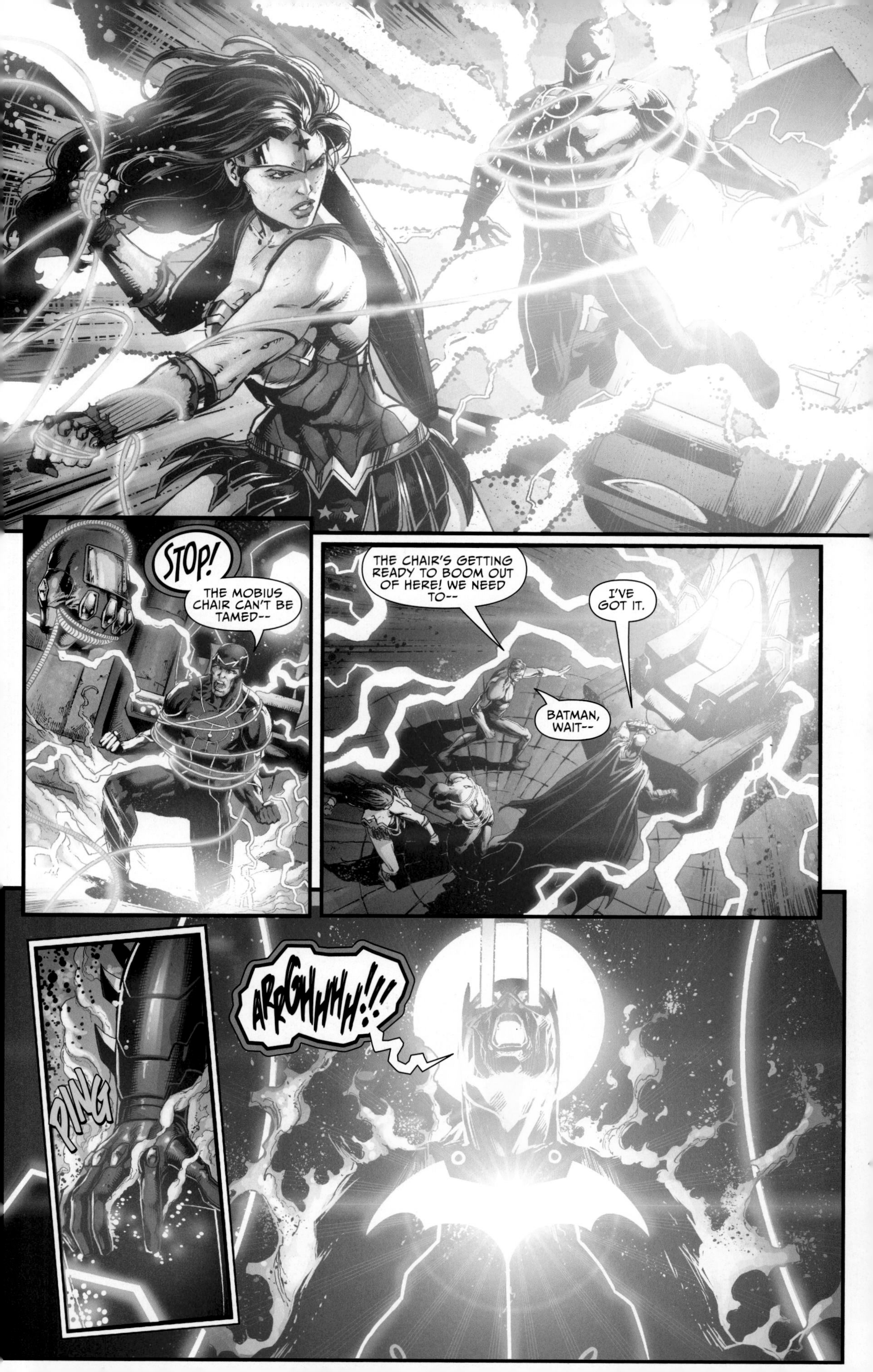
STOP!
THE MOBIUS CHAIR CAN'T BE TAMED--
THE CHAIR'S GETTING READY TO BOOM OUT OF HERE! WE NEED TO--
I'VE GOT IT.
BATMAN, WAIT--
PING
ARRGHHHH!!!

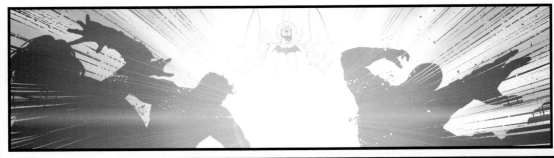

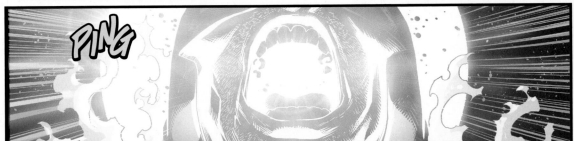

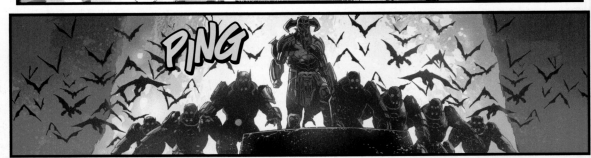

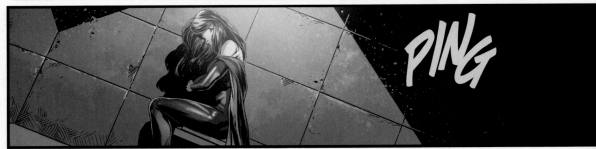

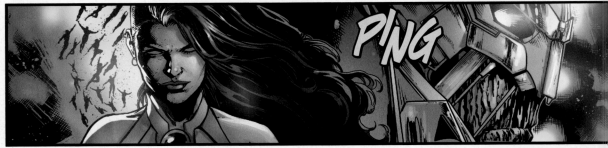

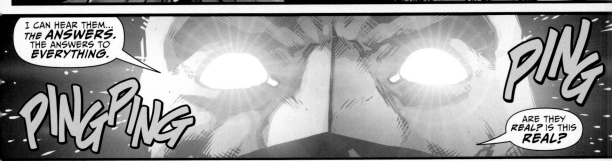

PING
PING
PING
PING
I CAN HEAR THEM... THE ANSWERS. THE ANSWERS TO EVERYTHING.
PING
PINGPING
ARE THEY REAL? IS THIS REAL?

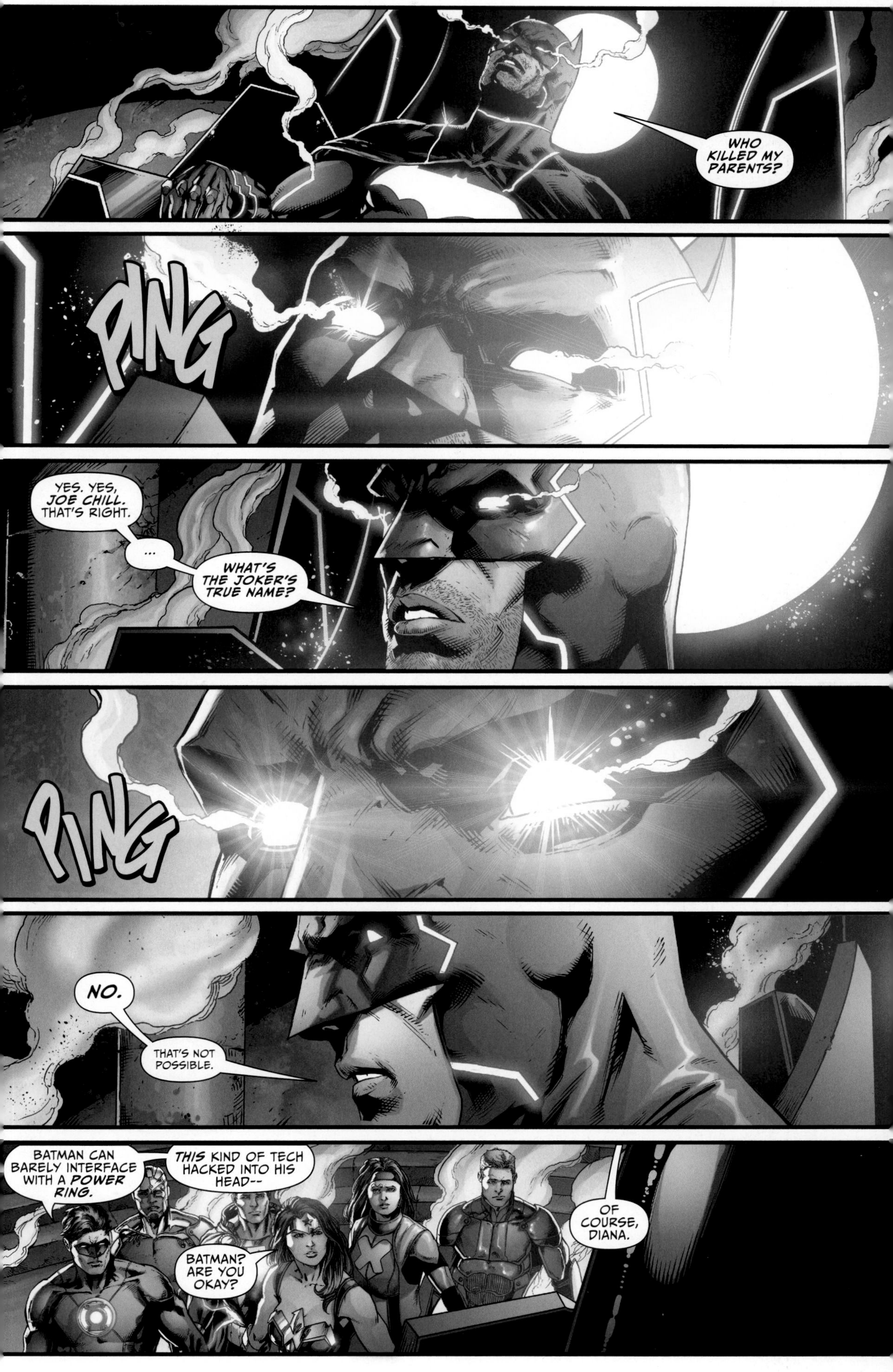
WHO KILLED MY PARENTS?
PING
YES. YES, JOE CHILL. THAT'S RIGHT.
...
WHAT'S THE JOKER'S TRUE NAME?
PING
NO.
THAT'S NOT POSSIBLE.
BATMAN CAN BARELY INTERFACE WITH A POWER RING.
THIS KIND OF TECH HACKED INTO HIS HEAD--
BATMAN? ARE YOU OKAY?
OF COURSE, DIANA.

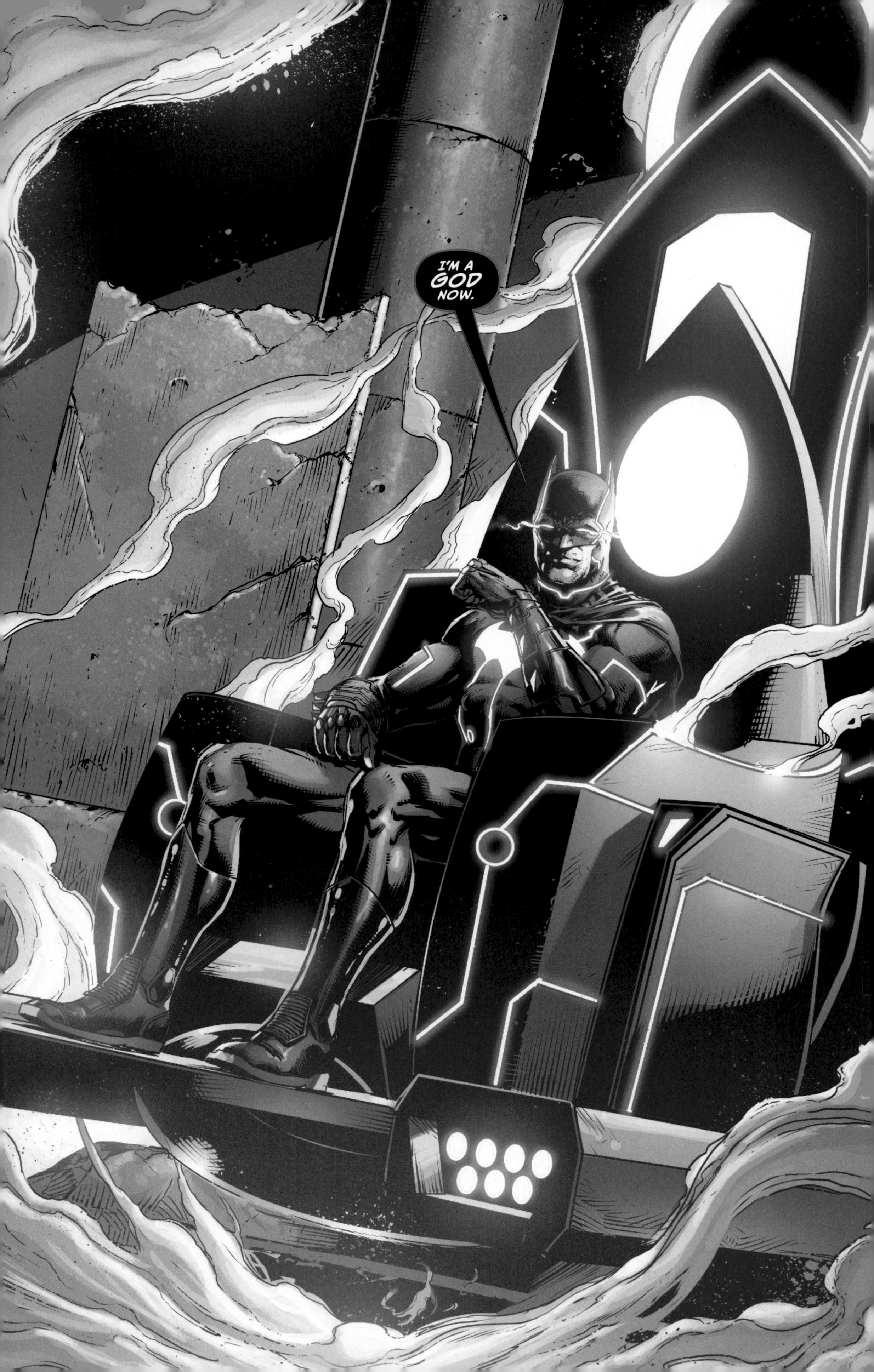
I'M A GOD NOW.

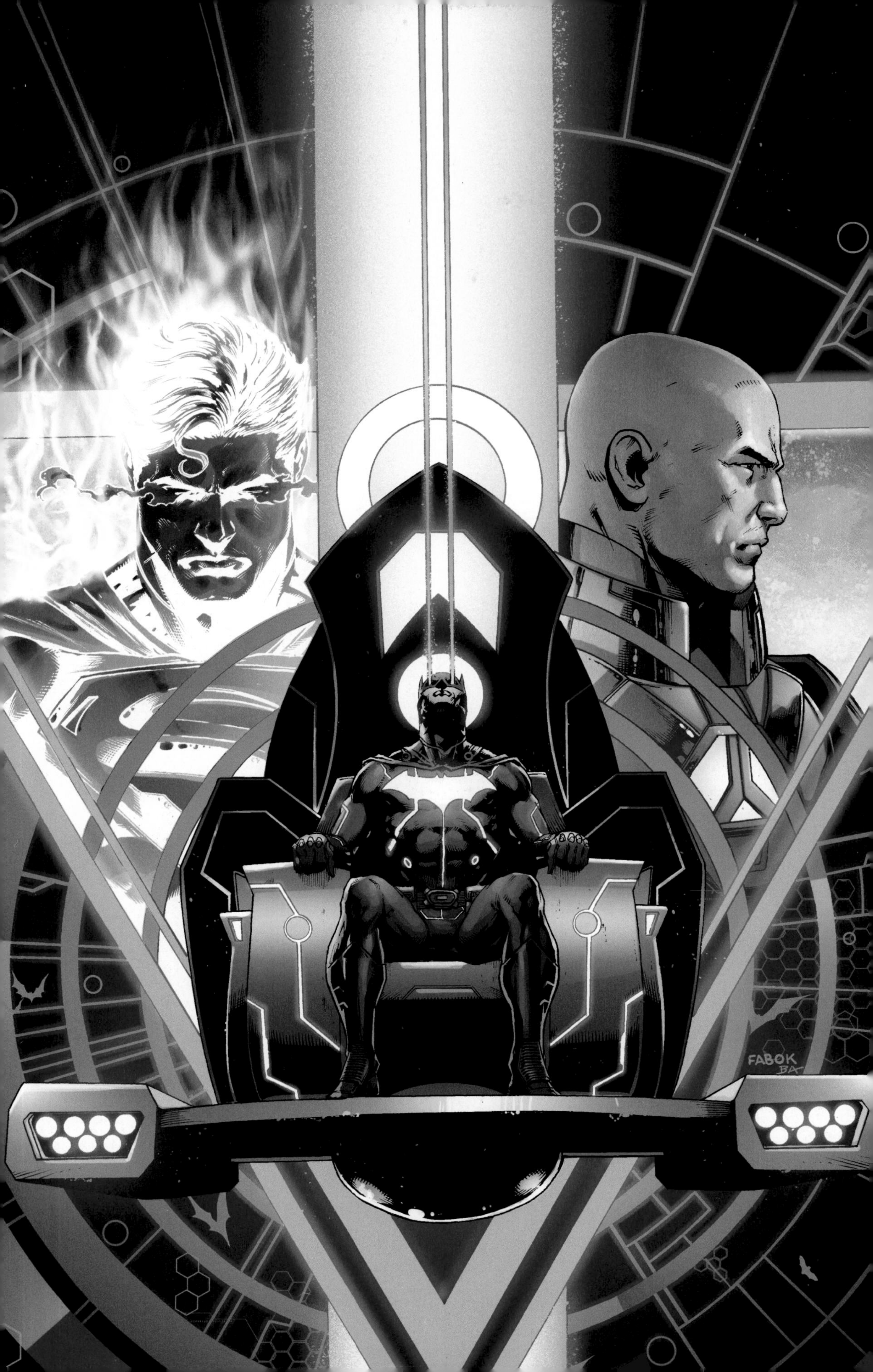
FABOK
BA

DARKSEID WAR CHAPTER THREE: TAKEN

GEOFF JOHNS writer JASON FABOK artist BRAD ANDERSON colorist ROB LEIGH letterer cover by JASON FABOK and BRAD ANDERSON

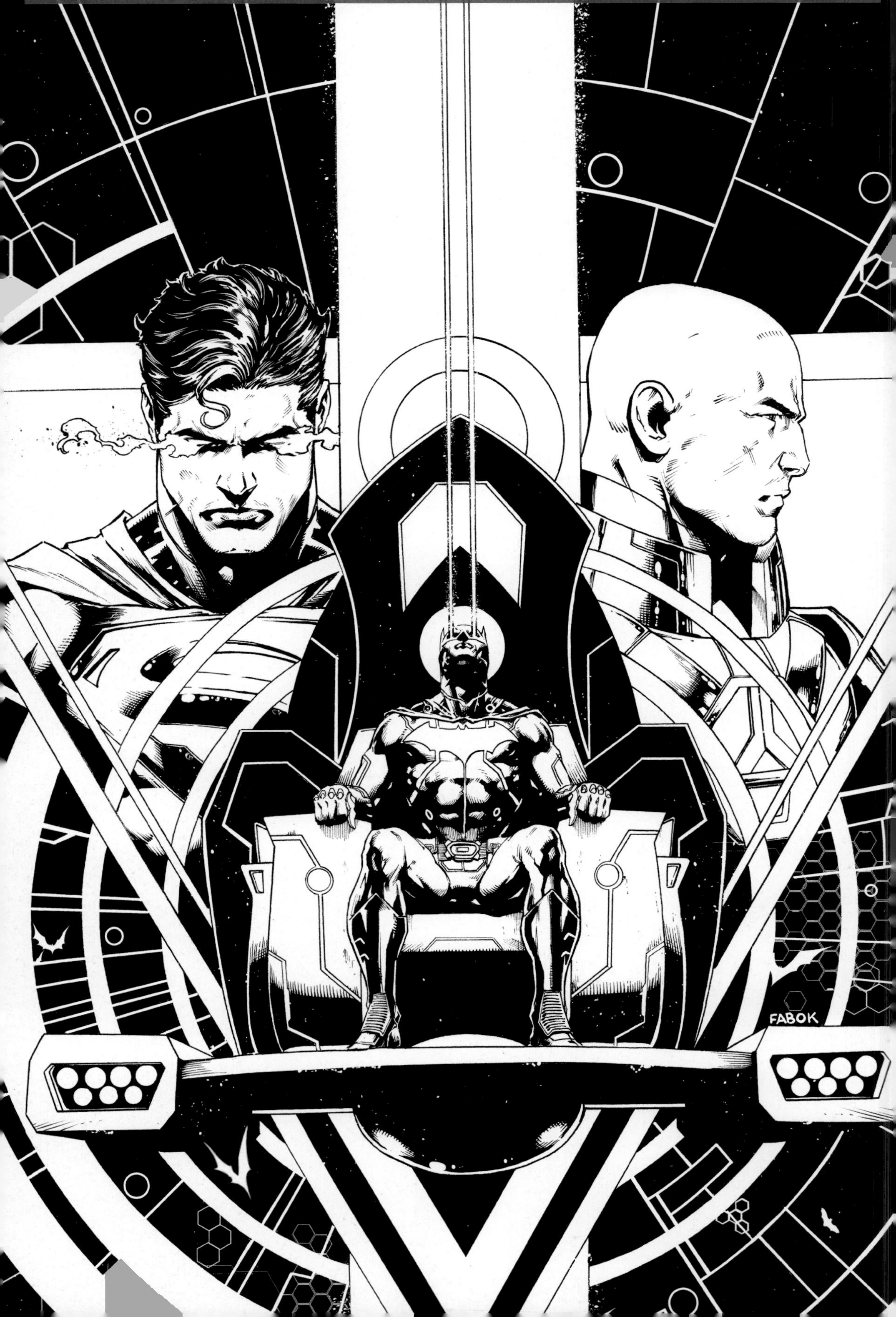
FABOK

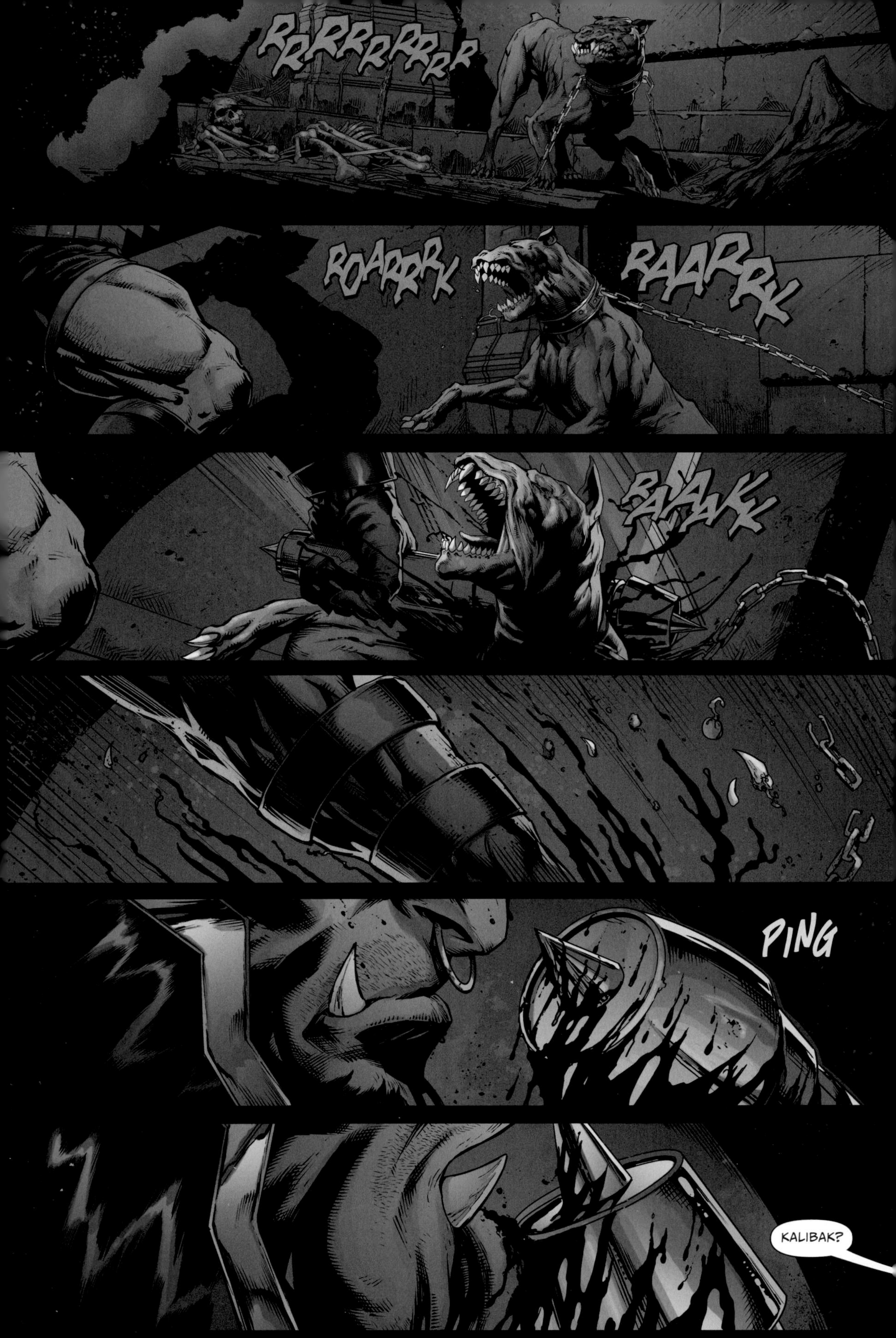
RRRRRRRRR
ROARRRK
RAARRK
RAAK
PING
KALIBAK?

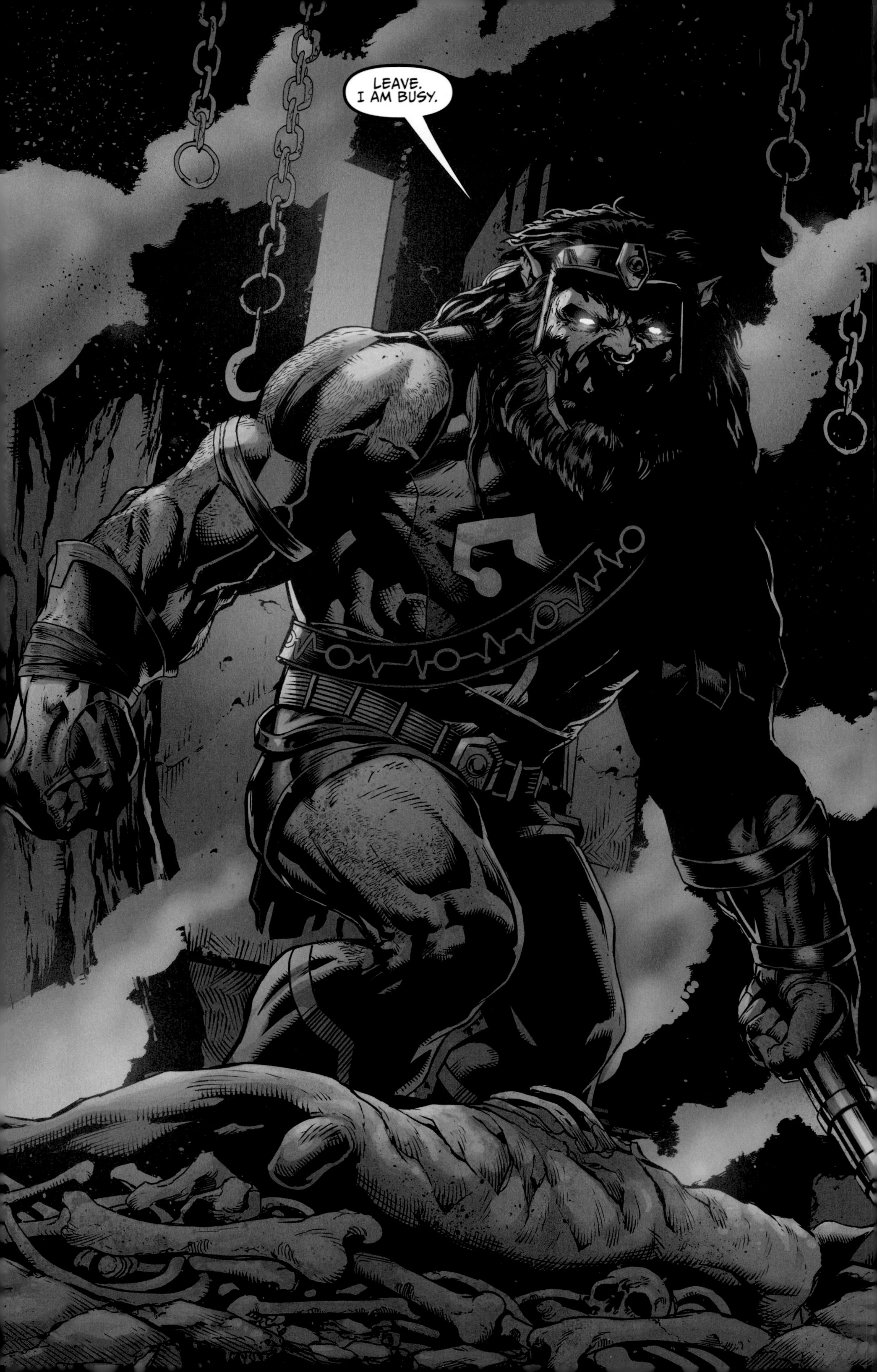
LEAVE. I AM BUSY.

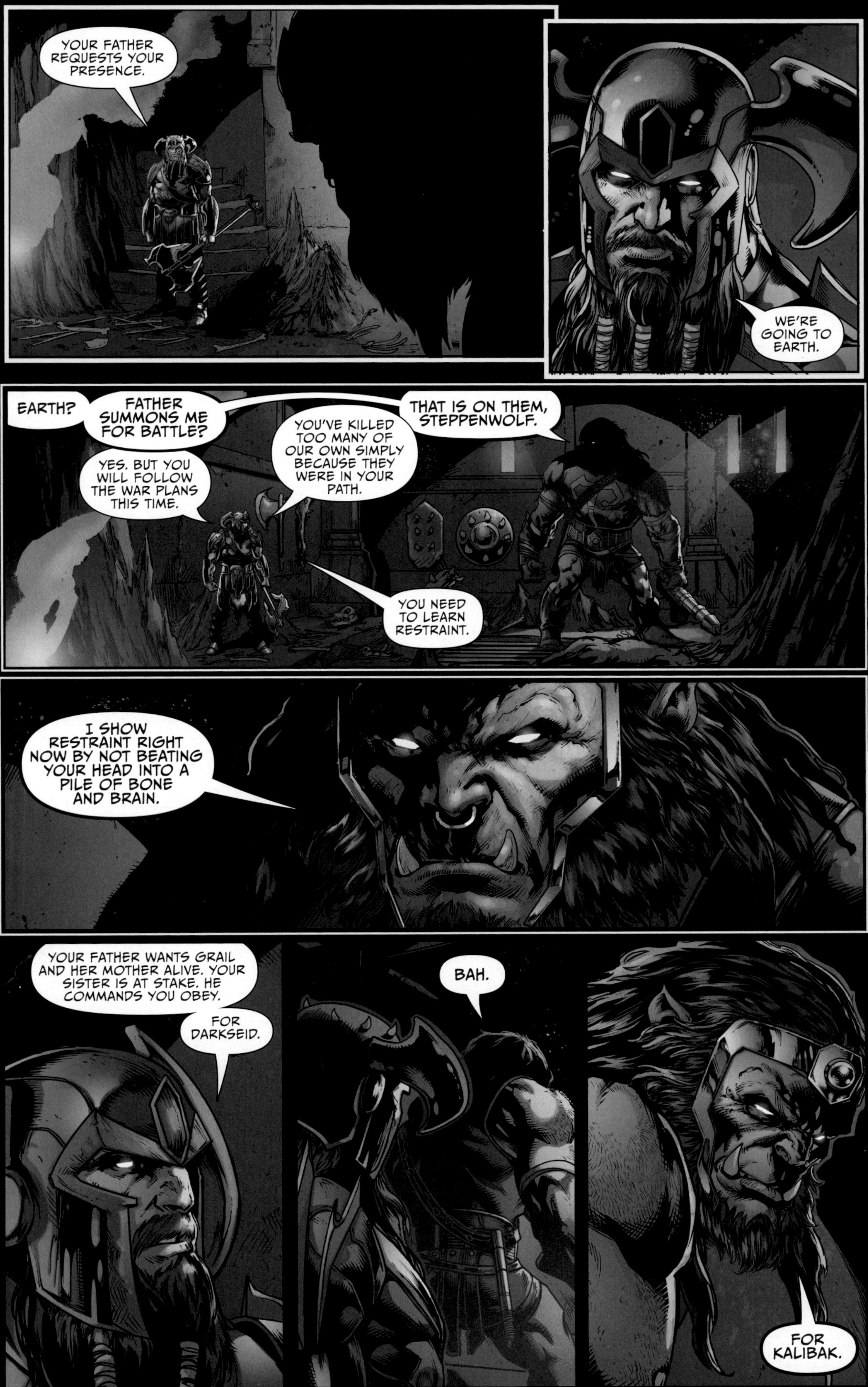
YOUR FATHER REQUESTS YOUR PRESENCE.
WE'RE GOING TO EARTH.
EARTH?
FATHER SUMMONS ME FOR BATTLE?
YES. BUT YOU WILL FOLLOW THE WAR PLANS THIS TIME.
YOU'VE KILLED TOO MANY OF OUR OWN SIMPLY BECAUSE THEY WERE IN YOUR PATH.
THAT IS ON THEM, STEPPENWOLF.
YOU NEED TO LEARN RESTRAINT.
I SHOW RESTRAINT RIGHT NOW BY NOT BEATING YOUR HEAD INTO A PILE OF BONE AND BRAIN.
YOUR FATHER WANTS GRAIL AND HER MOTHER ALIVE. YOUR SISTER IS AT STAKE. HE COMMANDS YOU OBEY.
FOR DARKSEID.
BAH.
FOR KALIBAK.

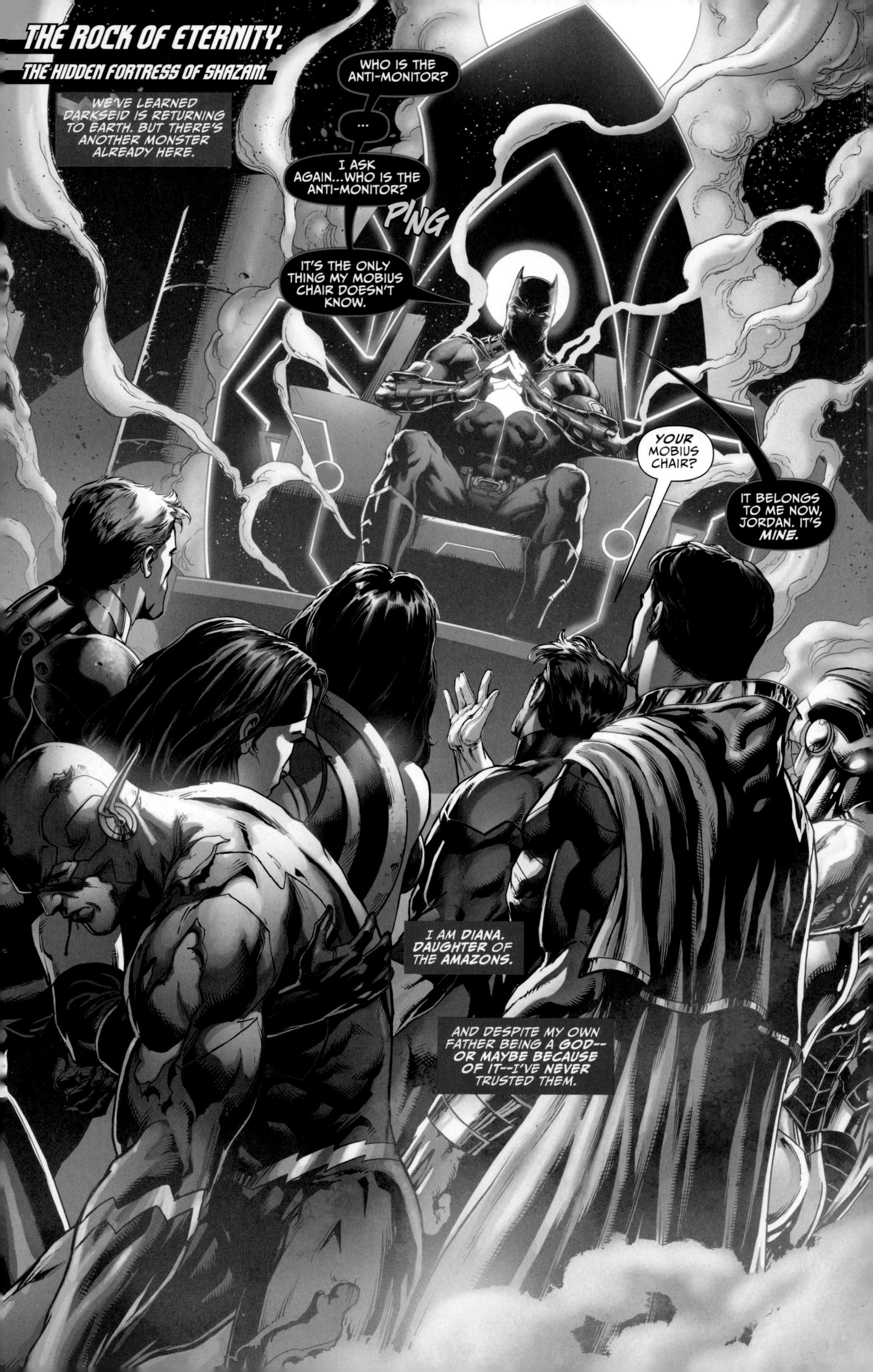
THE ROCK OF ETERNITY.
THE HIDDEN FORTRESS OF SHAZAM.
WE'VE LEARNED DARKSEID IS RETURNING TO EARTH. BUT THERE'S ANOTHER MONSTER ALREADY HERE.
WHO IS THE ANTI-MONITOR?
...
I ASK AGAIN...WHO IS THE ANTI-MONITOR?
PING
IT'S THE ONLY THING MY MOBIUS CHAIR DOESN'T KNOW.
YOUR MOBIUS CHAIR?
IT BELONGS TO ME NOW, JORDAN. IT'S MINE.
I AM DIANA. DAUGHTER OF THE AMAZONS.
AND DESPITE MY OWN FATHER BEING A GOD-- OR MAYBE BECAUSE OF IT--I'VE NEVER TRUSTED THEM.

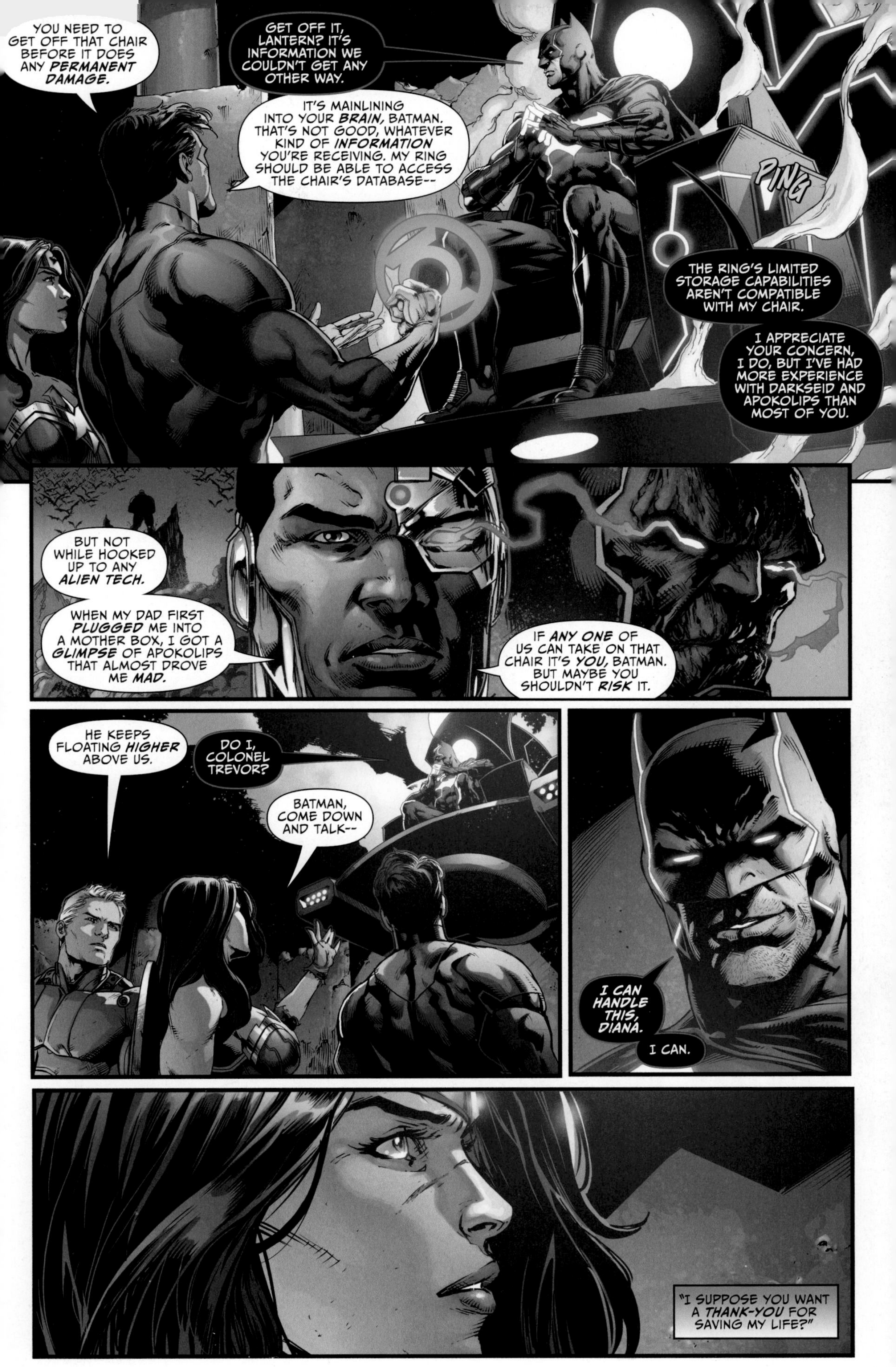
YOU NEED TO GET OFF THAT CHAIR BEFORE IT DOES ANY PERMANENT DAMAGE.
GET OFF IT, LANTERN? IT'S INFORMATION WE COULDN'T GET ANY OTHER WAY.
IT'S MAINLINING INTO YOUR BRAIN, BATMAN. THAT'S NOT GOOD, WHATEVER KIND OF INFORMATION YOU'RE RECEIVING. MY RING SHOULD BE ABLE TO ACCESS THE CHAIR'S DATABASE--
PING
THE RING'S LIMITED STORAGE CAPABILITIES AREN'T COMPATIBLE WITH MY CHAIR.
I APPRECIATE YOUR CONCERN, I DO, BUT I'VE HAD MORE EXPERIENCE WITH DARKSEID AND APOKOLIPS THAN MOST OF YOU.
BUT NOT WHILE HOOKED UP TO ANY ALIEN TECH.
WHEN MY DAD FIRST PLUGGED ME INTO A MOTHER BOX, I GOT A GLIMPSE OF APOKOLIPS THAT ALMOST DROVE ME MAD.
IF ANY ONE OF US CAN TAKE ON THAT CHAIR IT'S YOU, BATMAN. BUT MAYBE YOU SHOULDN'T RISK IT.
HE KEEPS FLOATING HIGHER ABOVE US.
DO I, COLONEL TREVOR?
BATMAN, COME DOWN AND TALK--
I CAN HANDLE THIS, DIANA.
I CAN.
"I SUPPOSE YOU WANT A THANK-YOU FOR SAVING MY LIFE?"

NOT ESPECIALLY, LUTHOR, NO.

MY ARMOR'S *MEDICAL MODE* WOULD'VE KICKED IN ANYWAY.

I'M SURE IT WOULD HAVE. NEXT TIME I'LL REFRAIN FROM TRYING TO HELP.

THIS LOOKS LIKE ONE OF DARKSEID'S SLAVE CAMPS.

LOOKS LIKE? I THOUGHT YOU'D BEEN TO APOKOLIPS BEFORE.

ONLY TO A LIMITED AREA. I HAVE NO IDEA WHERE WE ARE RIGHT NOW. AND THERE'S ONLY ONE WAY BACK TO EARTH.

A *MOTHER BOX.*

I'M BETTING THE SLAVE MASTER OF THIS CAMP HAS ONE. WE NEED TO FIND HIM...

...BUT MY X-RAY VISION ISN'T WORKING. THERE MUST BE *LEAD* IN THE AIR.

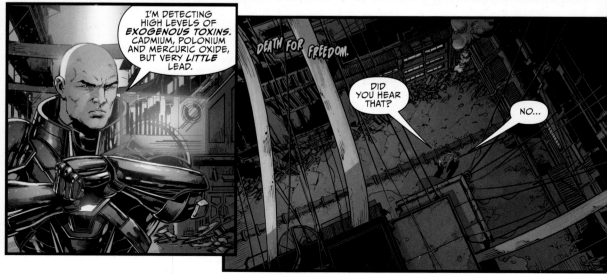

I'M DETECTING HIGH LEVELS OF *EXOGENOUS TOXINS.* CADMIUM, POLONIUM AND MERCURIC OXIDE, BUT VERY *LITTLE* LEAD.

DEATH FOR FREEDOM.

DID YOU HEAR THAT?

NO...

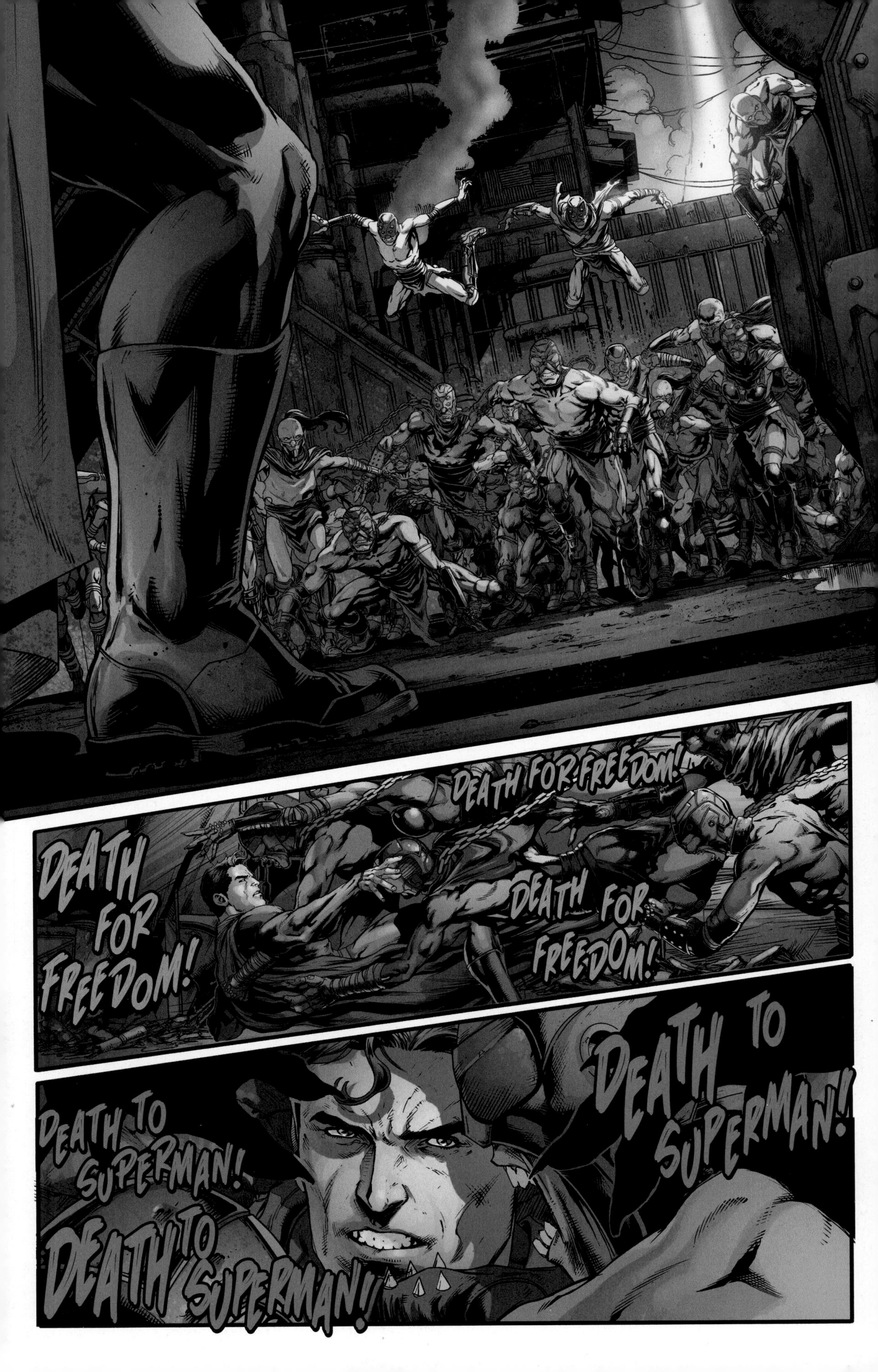
DEATH FOR FREEDOM!
DEATH FOR FREEDOM!
DEATH FOR FREEDOM!
DEATH TO SUPERMAN!
DEATH TO SUPERMAN!
DEATH TO SUPERMAN!

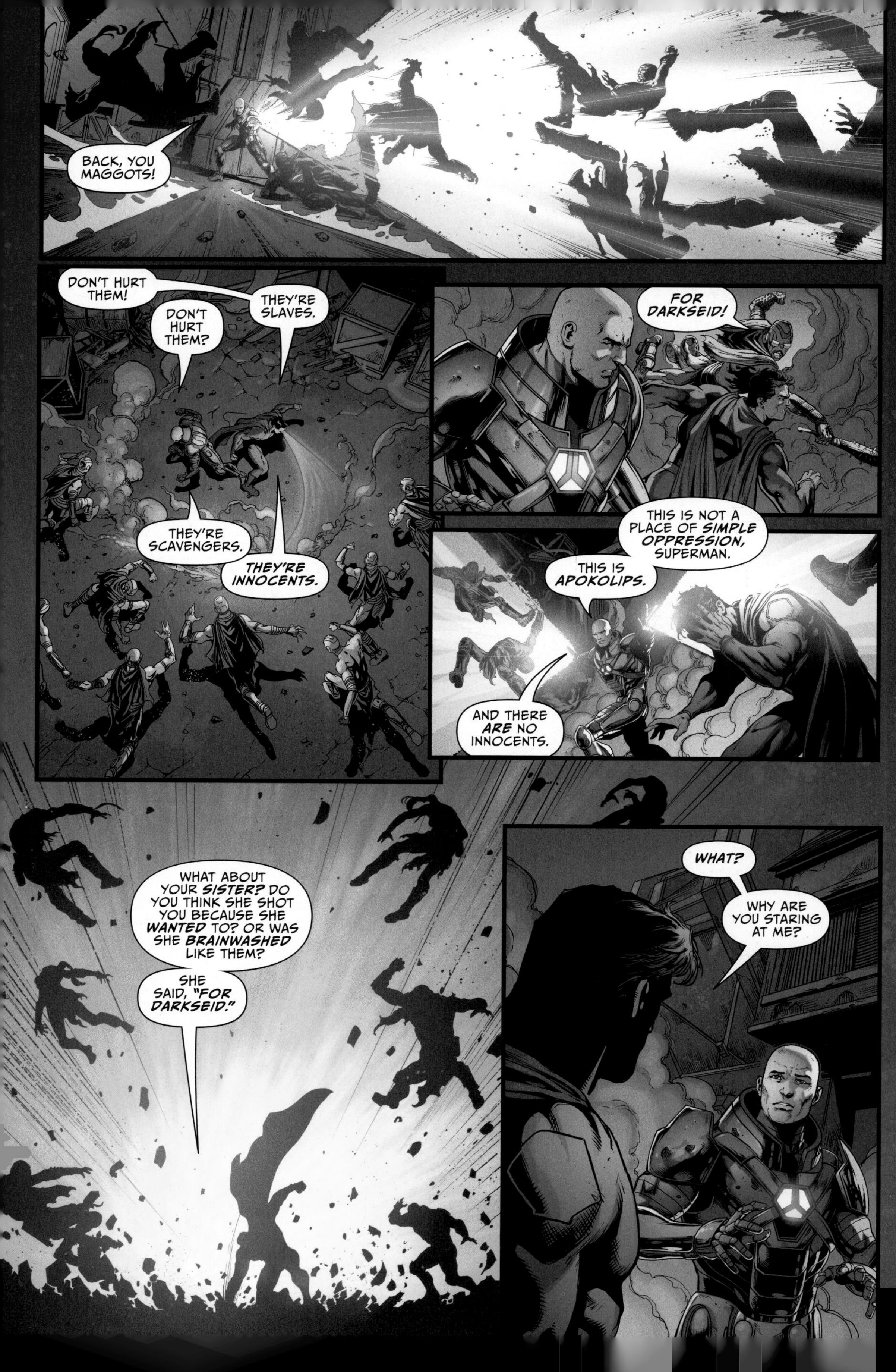
BACK, YOU MAGGOTS!
DON'T HURT THEM!
DON'T HURT THEM?
THEY'RE SLAVES.
THEY'RE SCAVENGERS.
THEY'RE INNOCENTS.
FOR DARKSEID!
THIS IS NOT A PLACE OF SIMPLE OPPRESSION, SUPERMAN.
THIS IS APOKOLIPS.
AND THERE ARE NO INNOCENTS.
WHAT ABOUT YOUR SISTER? DO YOU THINK SHE SHOT YOU BECAUSE SHE WANTED TO? OR WAS SHE BRAINWASHED LIKE THEM?
SHE SAID, "FOR DARKSEID."
WHAT?
WHY ARE YOU STARING AT ME?

IT'S NOT THE LEAD IN THE AIR THAT'S BLOCKING YOUR X-RAY VISION.

THERE'S NO SUNLIGHT.

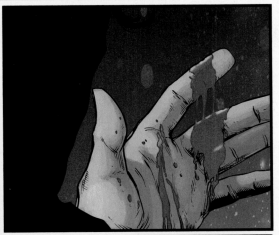

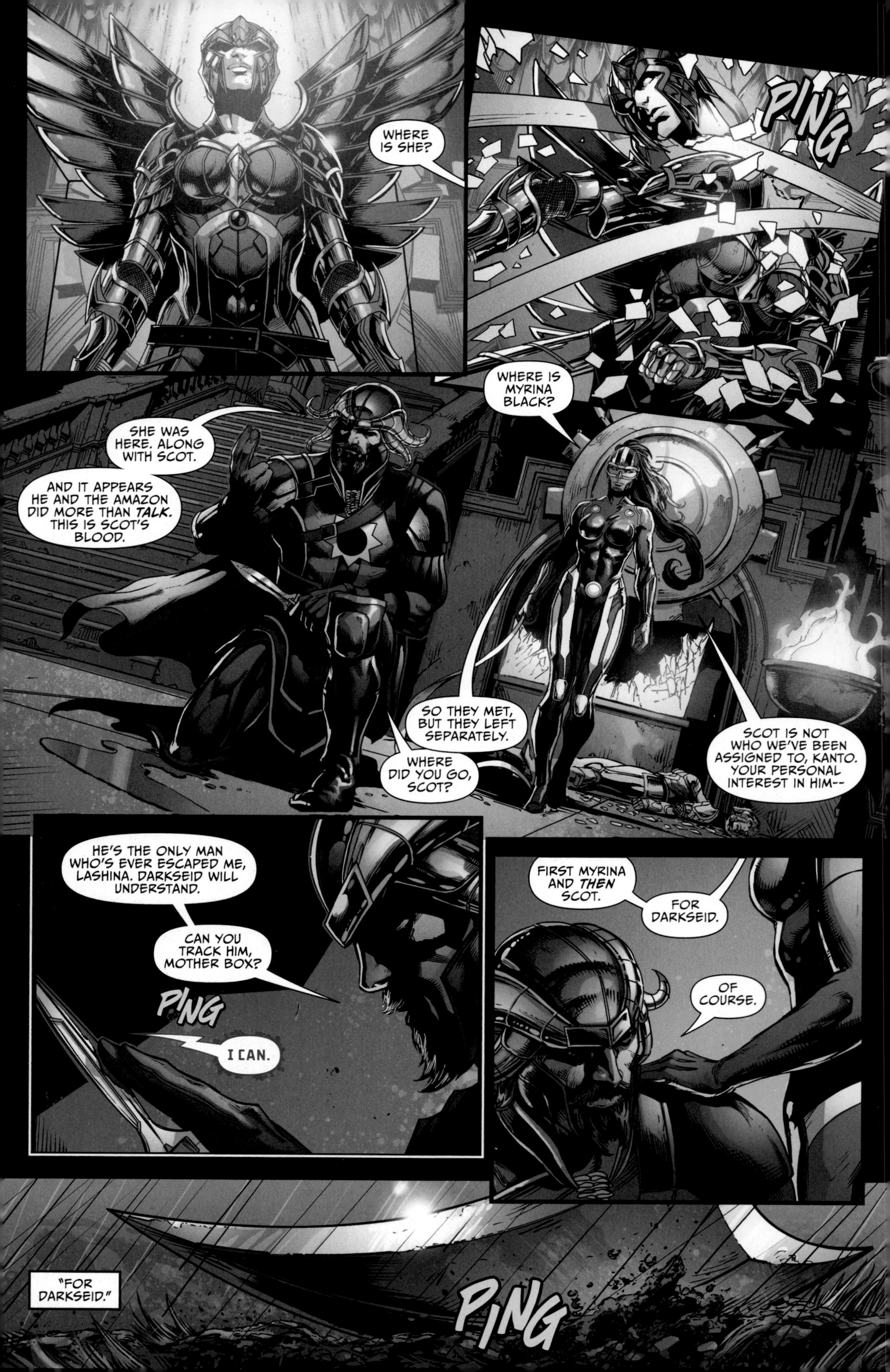
WHERE IS SHE?
PING
WHERE IS MYRINA BLACK?
SHE WAS HERE. ALONG WITH SCOT.
AND IT APPEARS HE AND THE AMAZON DID MORE THAN *TALK.* THIS IS SCOT'S BLOOD.
SO THEY MET, BUT THEY LEFT SEPARATELY.
WHERE DID YOU GO, SCOT?
SCOT IS NOT WHO WE'VE BEEN ASSIGNED TO, KANTO. YOUR PERSONAL INTEREST IN HIM--
HE'S THE ONLY MAN WHO'S EVER ESCAPED ME, LASHINA. DARKSEID WILL UNDERSTAND.
CAN YOU TRACK HIM, MOTHER BOX?
PING
I CAN.
FIRST MYRINA AND *THEN* SCOT.
FOR DARKSEID.
OF COURSE.
"FOR DARKSEID."
PING

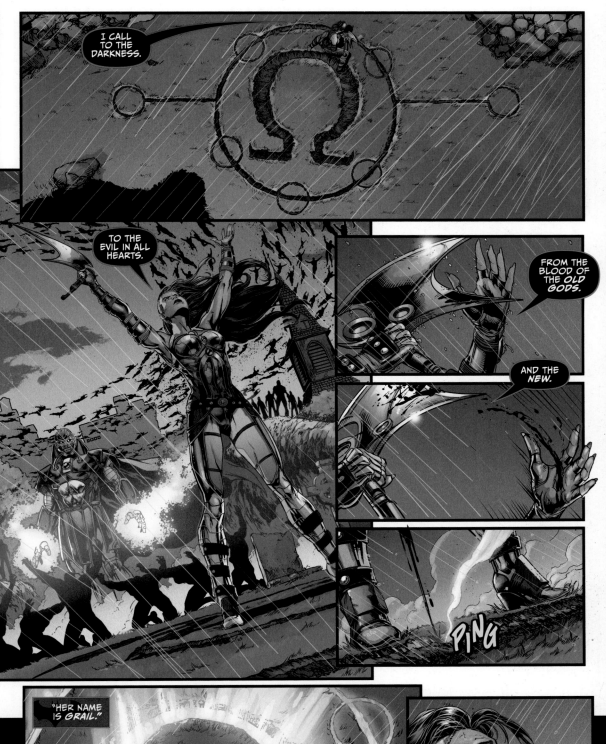

I CALL TO THE DARKNESS.

TO THE EVIL IN ALL HEARTS.

FROM THE BLOOD OF THE OLD GODS.

AND THE NEW.

PING

"HER NAME IS GRAIL."

COME FOR ME, FATHER.

"SHE IS DARKSEID'S DAUGHTER."

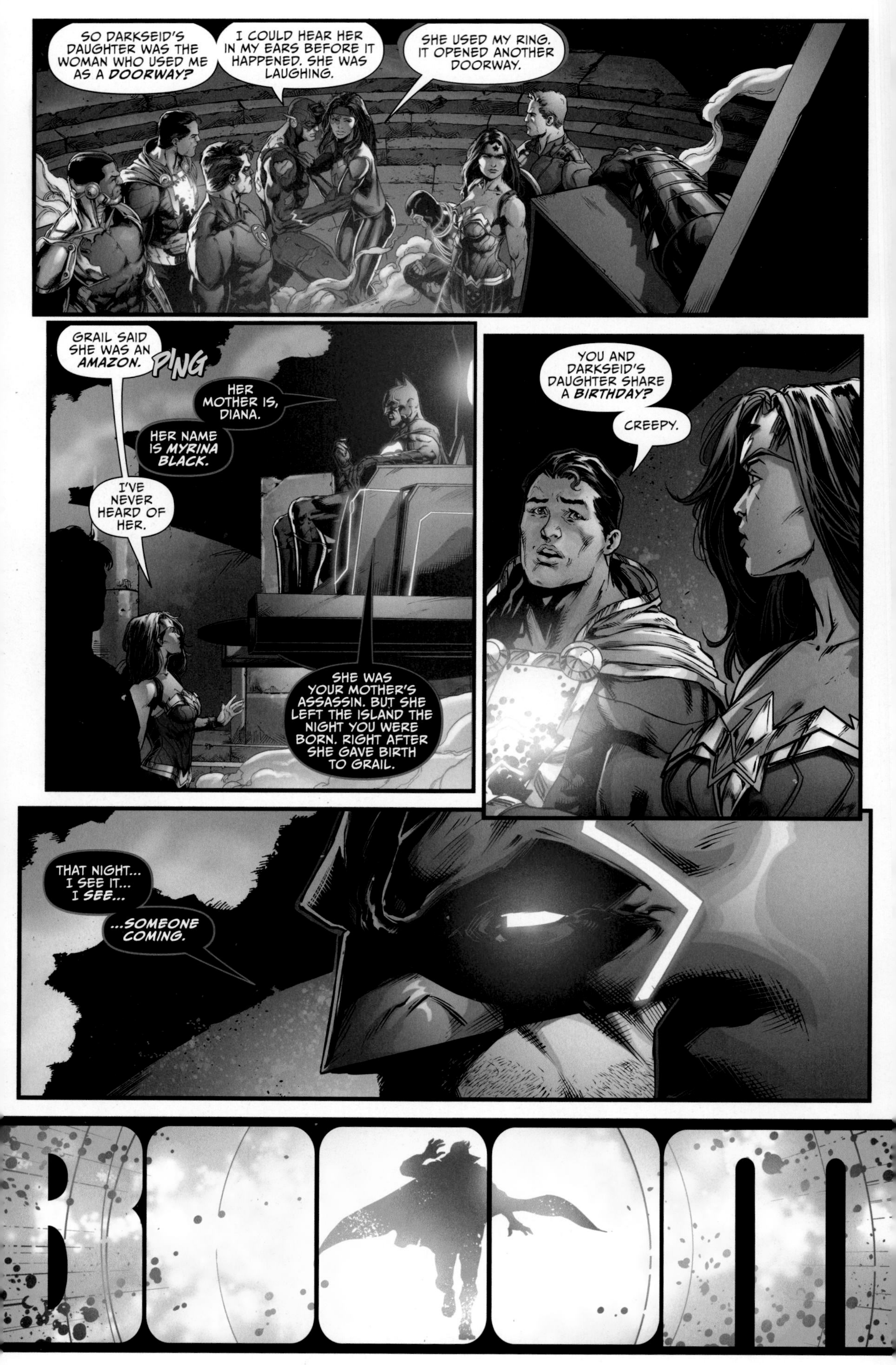

SO DARKSEID'S DAUGHTER WAS THE WOMAN WHO USED ME AS A DOORWAY?
I COULD HEAR HER IN MY EARS BEFORE IT HAPPENED. SHE WAS LAUGHING.
SHE USED MY RING. IT OPENED ANOTHER DOORWAY.
GRAIL SAID SHE WAS AN AMAZON.
PING
HER MOTHER IS, DIANA.
HER NAME IS MYRINA BLACK.
I'VE NEVER HEARD OF HER.
SHE WAS YOUR MOTHER'S ASSASSIN. BUT SHE LEFT THE ISLAND THE NIGHT YOU WERE BORN. RIGHT AFTER SHE GAVE BIRTH TO GRAIL.
YOU AND DARKSEID'S DAUGHTER SHARE A BIRTHDAY?
CREEPY.
THAT NIGHT... I SEE IT... I SEE...
...SOMEONE COMING.

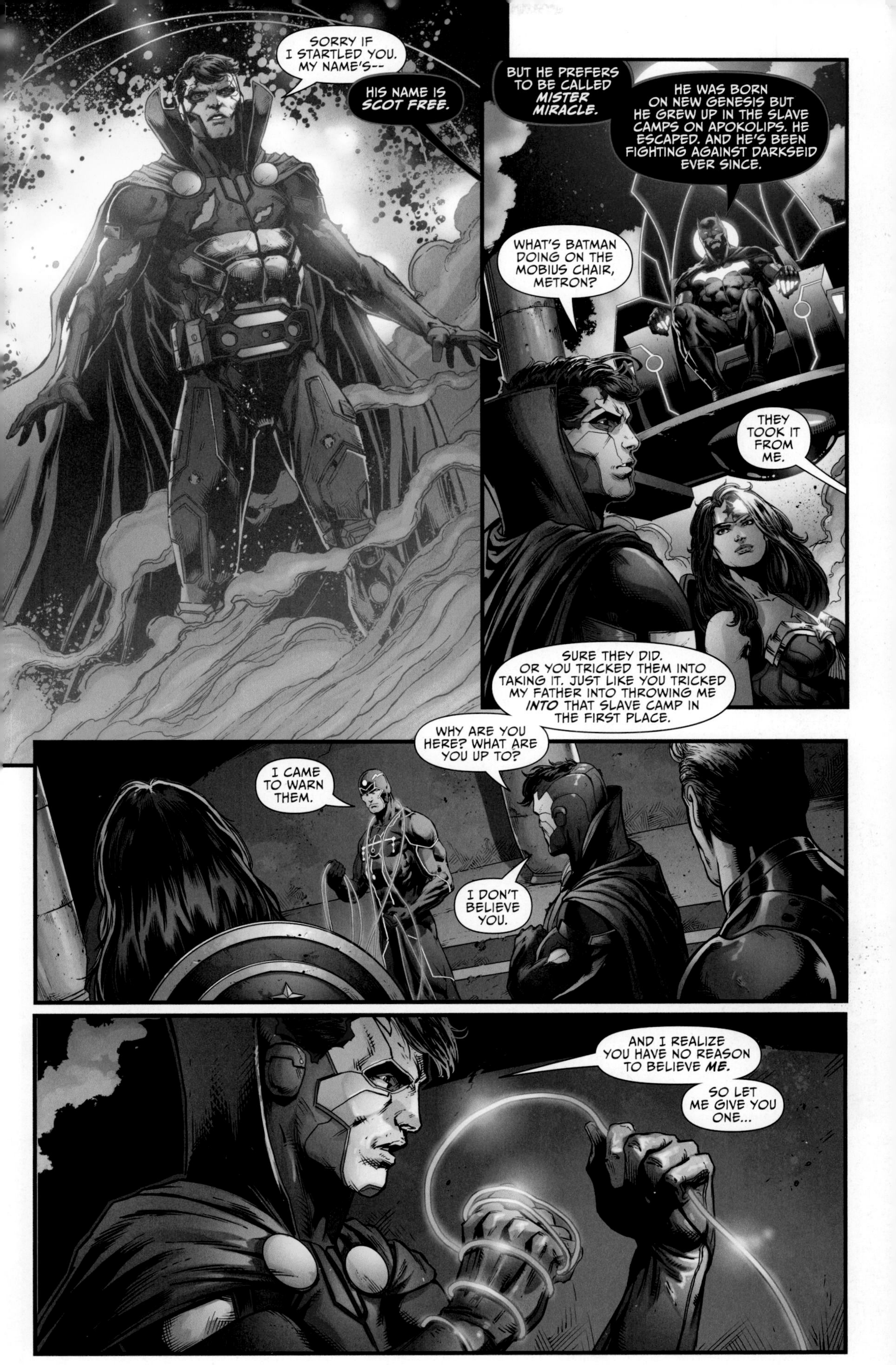
SORRY IF I STARTLED YOU. MY NAME'S--
HIS NAME IS *SCOT FREE.*
BUT HE PREFERS TO BE CALLED *MISTER MIRACLE.*
HE WAS BORN ON NEW GENESIS BUT HE GREW UP IN THE SLAVE CAMPS ON APOKOLIPS. HE ESCAPED. AND HE'S BEEN FIGHTING AGAINST DARKSEID EVER SINCE.
WHAT'S BATMAN DOING ON THE MOBIUS CHAIR, METRON?
THEY TOOK IT FROM ME.
SURE THEY DID. OR YOU TRICKED THEM INTO TAKING IT. JUST LIKE YOU TRICKED MY FATHER INTO THROWING ME *INTO* THAT SLAVE CAMP IN THE FIRST PLACE.
WHY ARE YOU HERE? WHAT ARE YOU UP TO?
I CAME TO WARN THEM.
I DON'T BELIEVE YOU.
AND I REALIZE YOU HAVE NO REASON TO BELIEVE *ME.*
SO LET ME GIVE YOU ONE...

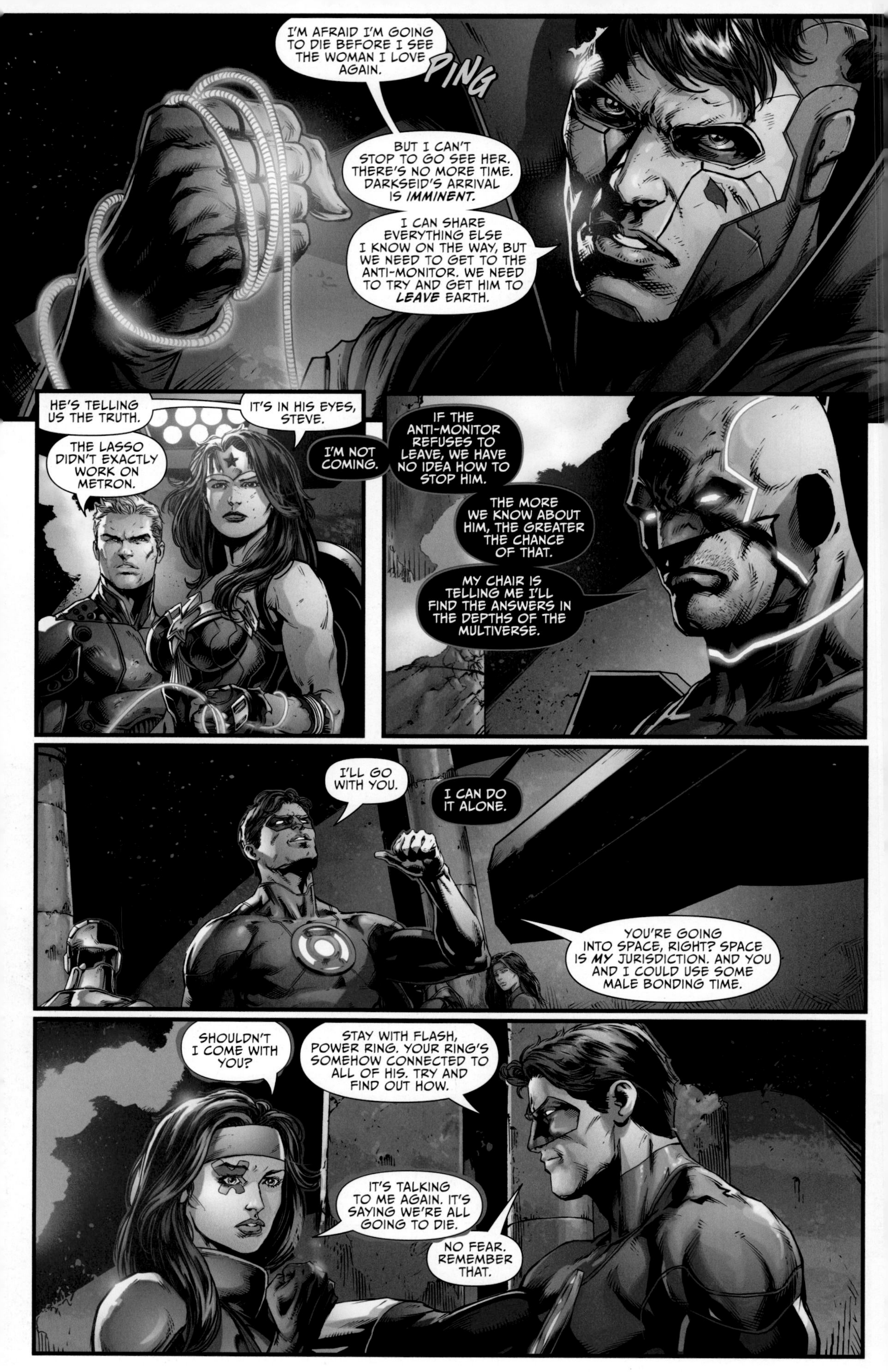
I'M AFRAID I'M GOING TO DIE BEFORE I SEE THE WOMAN I LOVE AGAIN.
PING
BUT I CAN'T STOP TO GO SEE HER. THERE'S NO MORE TIME. DARKSEID'S ARRIVAL IS IMMINENT.
I CAN SHARE EVERYTHING ELSE I KNOW ON THE WAY, BUT WE NEED TO GET TO THE ANTI-MONITOR. WE NEED TO TRY AND GET HIM TO LEAVE EARTH.
HE'S TELLING US THE TRUTH.
IT'S IN HIS EYES, STEVE.
THE LASSO DIDN'T EXACTLY WORK ON METRON.
I'M NOT COMING.
IF THE ANTI-MONITOR REFUSES TO LEAVE, WE HAVE NO IDEA HOW TO STOP HIM.
THE MORE WE KNOW ABOUT HIM, THE GREATER THE CHANCE OF THAT.
MY CHAIR IS TELLING ME I'LL FIND THE ANSWERS IN THE DEPTHS OF THE MULTIVERSE.
I'LL GO WITH YOU.
I CAN DO IT ALONE.
YOU'RE GOING INTO SPACE, RIGHT? SPACE IS MY JURISDICTION. AND YOU AND I COULD USE SOME MALE BONDING TIME.
SHOULDN'T I COME WITH YOU?
STAY WITH FLASH, POWER RING. YOUR RING'S SOMEHOW CONNECTED TO ALL OF HIS. TRY AND FIND OUT HOW.
IT'S TALKING TO ME AGAIN. IT'S SAYING WE'RE ALL GOING TO DIE.
NO FEAR. REMEMBER THAT.

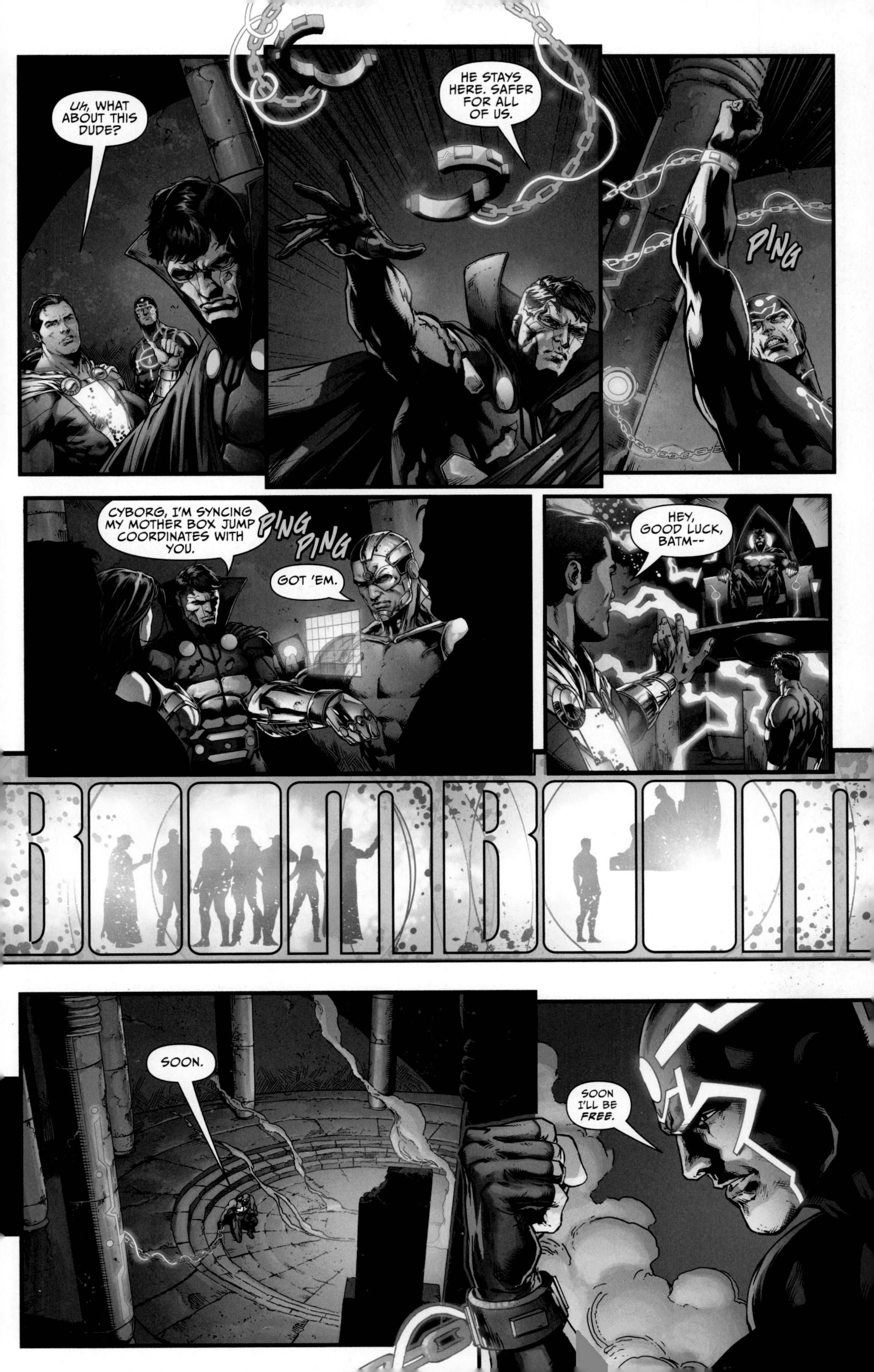

Uh, WHAT ABOUT THIS DUDE?
HE STAYS HERE. SAFER FOR ALL OF US.
PING
CYBORG, I'M SYNCING MY MOTHER BOX JUMP COORDINATES WITH YOU.
PING PING
GOT 'EM.
HEY, GOOD LUCK, BATM--
BOOM BOOM
SOON.
SOON I'LL BE FREE.

THEY'RE COMING FROM ALL DIRECTIONS.

WE NEED TO TALK TO THEM.

AND WHAT IF YOU CAN'T GET THEM ON OUR SIDE, SUPERMAN? WE CAN'T FIGHT THEM ALL, AND IN A MATTER OF HOURS YOU'LL BE--

HUMAN.

YOU'LL BE POWERLESS.

YOU'LL NEVER BE HUMAN.

CAN YOU FLY?

I DON'T THINK SO.

COME ON THEN.

YOU'LL HAVE TO TRUST ME.

DEATH TO SUPERMAN!

DEATH TO SUPERMAN!

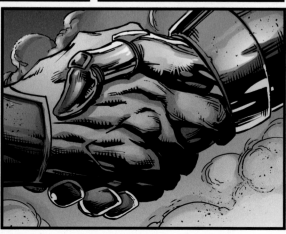

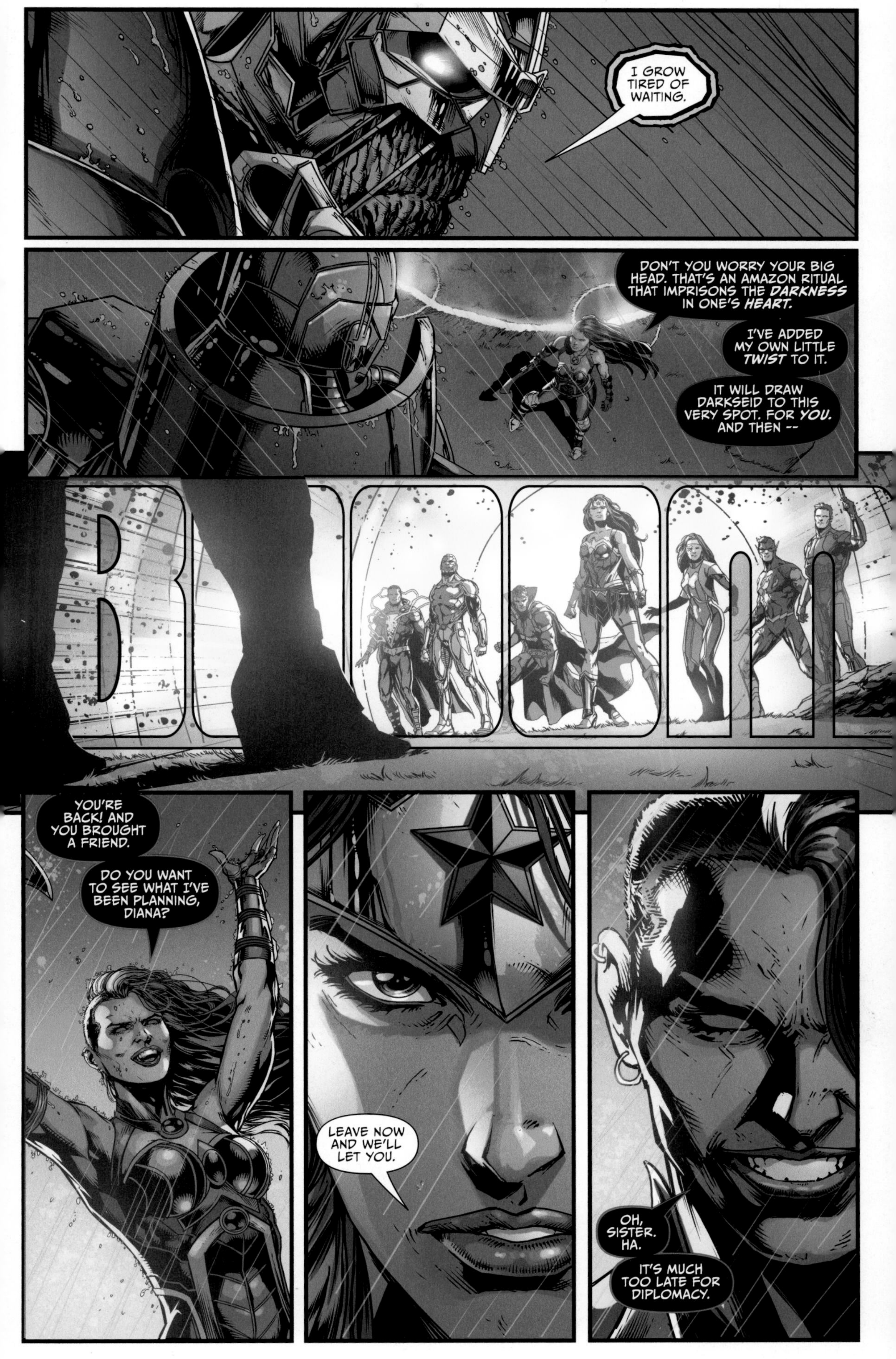
I GROW TIRED OF WAITING.
DON'T YOU WORRY YOUR BIG HEAD. THAT'S AN AMAZON RITUAL THAT IMPRISONS THE *DARKNESS* IN ONE'S *HEART.*
I'VE ADDED MY OWN LITTLE *TWIST* TO IT.
IT WILL DRAW DARKSEID TO THIS VERY SPOT. FOR *YOU.* AND THEN --
BOOOM
YOU'RE BACK! AND YOU BROUGHT A FRIEND.
DO YOU WANT TO SEE WHAT I'VE BEEN PLANNING, DIANA?
LEAVE NOW AND WE'LL LET YOU.
OH, SISTER. HA.
IT'S MUCH TOO LATE FOR DIPLOMACY.

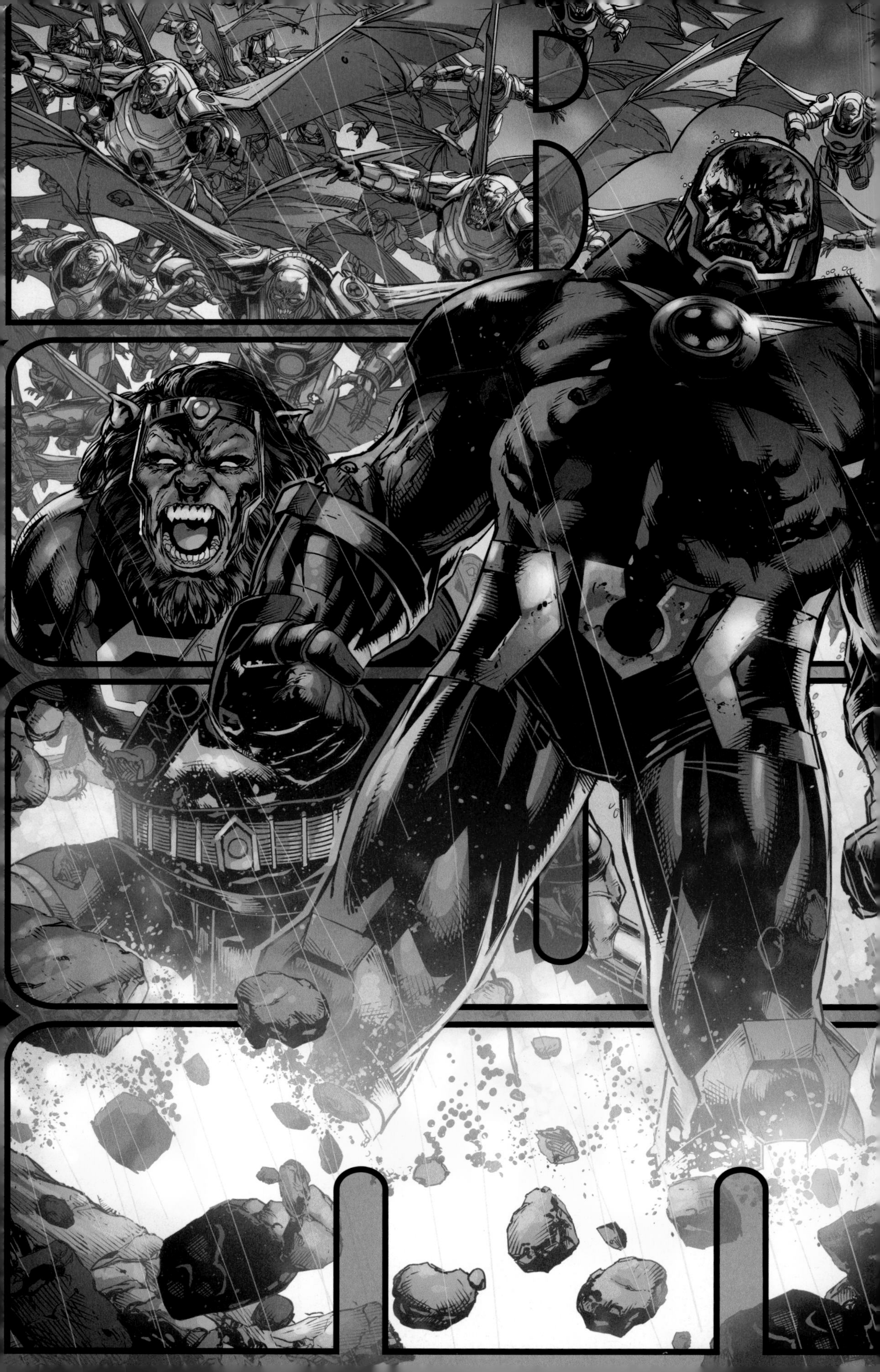

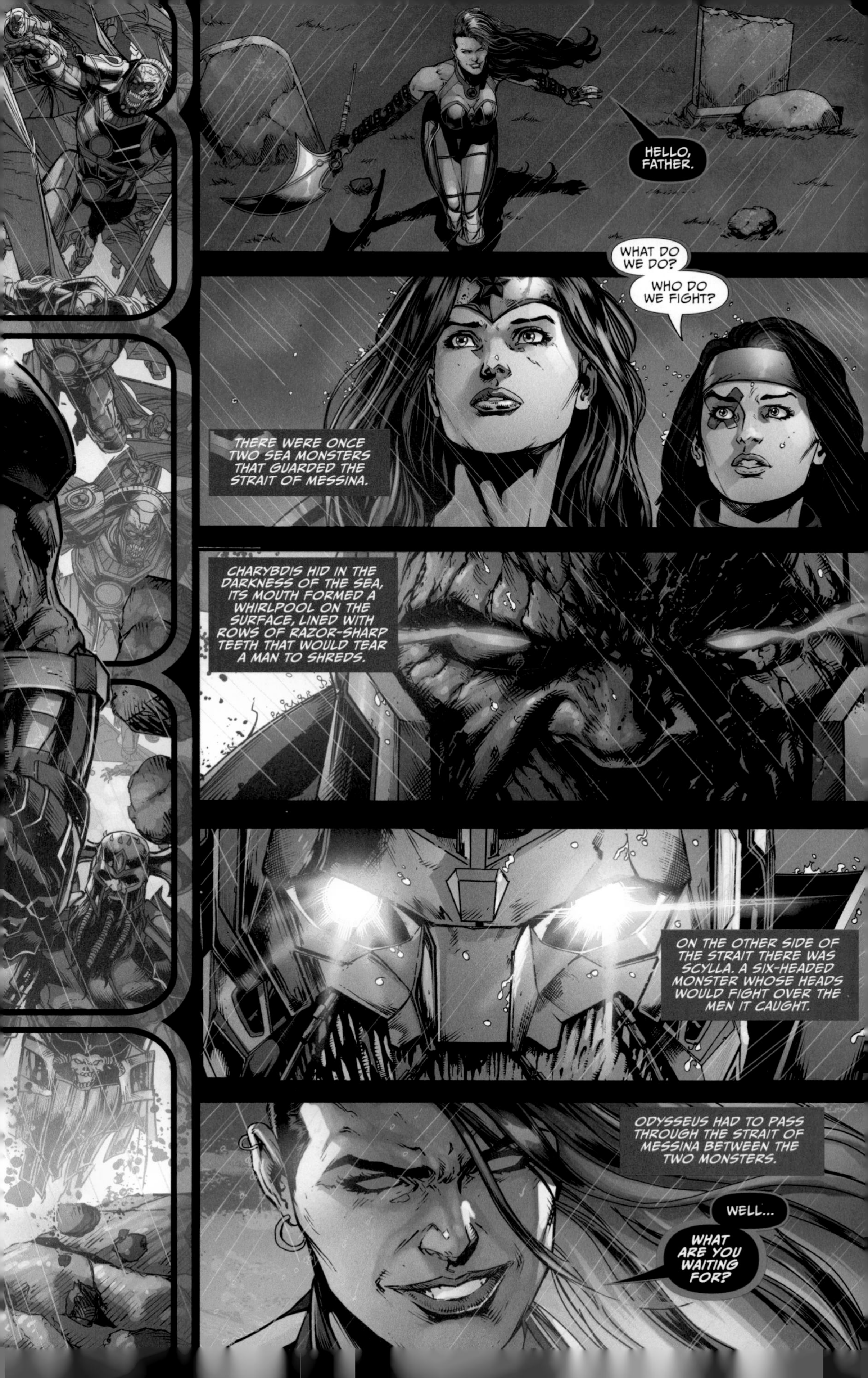
HELLO, FATHER.
WHAT DO WE DO?
WHO DO WE FIGHT?
THERE WERE ONCE TWO SEA MONSTERS THAT GUARDED THE STRAIT OF MESSINA.
CHARYBDIS HID IN THE DARKNESS OF THE SEA, ITS MOUTH FORMED A WHIRLPOOL ON THE SURFACE, LINED WITH ROWS OF RAZOR-SHARP TEETH THAT WOULD TEAR A MAN TO SHREDS.
ON THE OTHER SIDE OF THE STRAIT THERE WAS SCYLLA. A SIX-HEADED MONSTER WHOSE HEADS WOULD FIGHT OVER THE MEN IT CAUGHT.
ODYSSEUS HAD TO PASS THROUGH THE STRAIT OF MESSINA BETWEEN THE TWO MONSTERS.
WELL...
WHAT ARE YOU WAITING FOR?

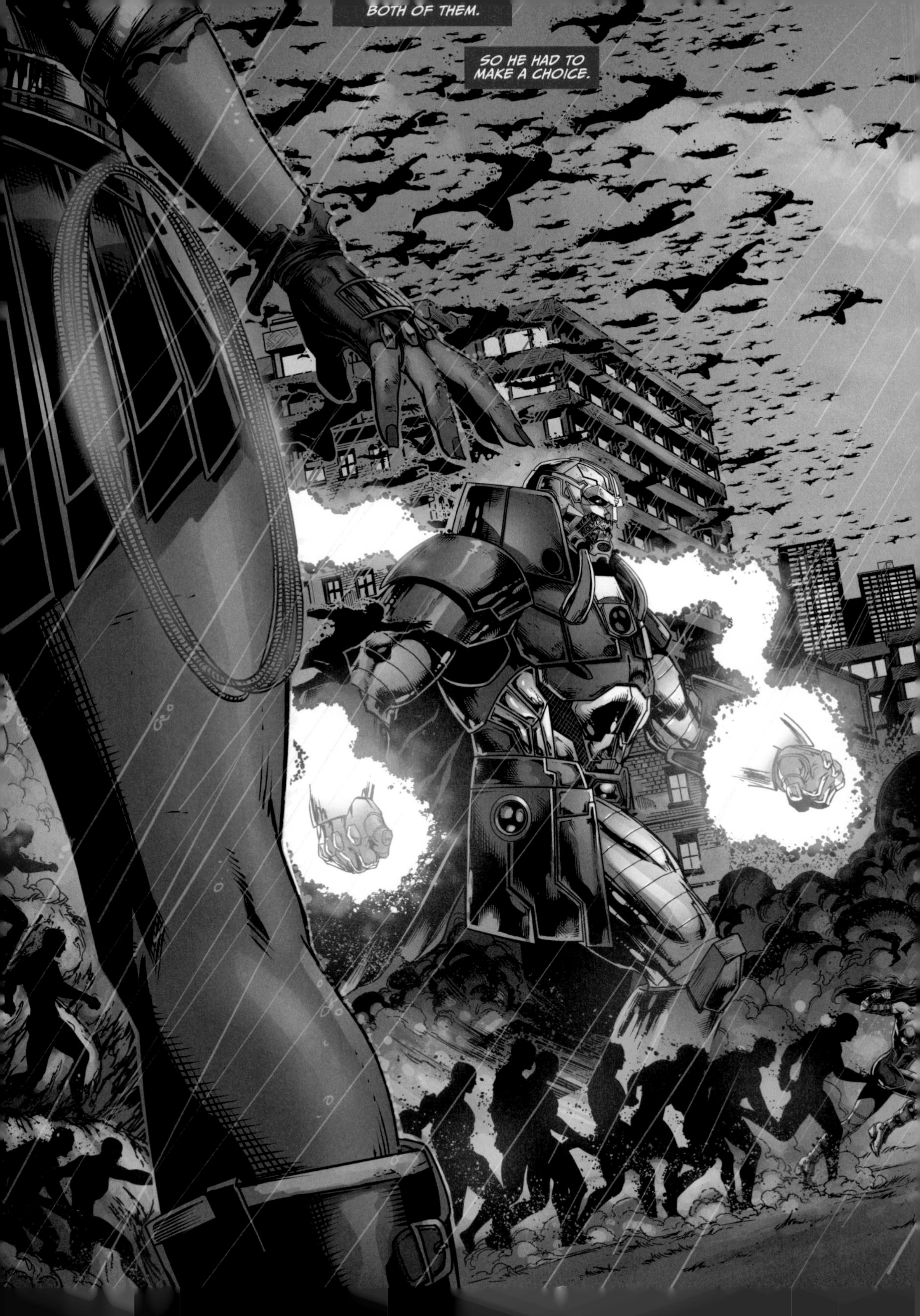
BOTH OF THEM.
SO HE HAD TO MAKE A CHOICE.

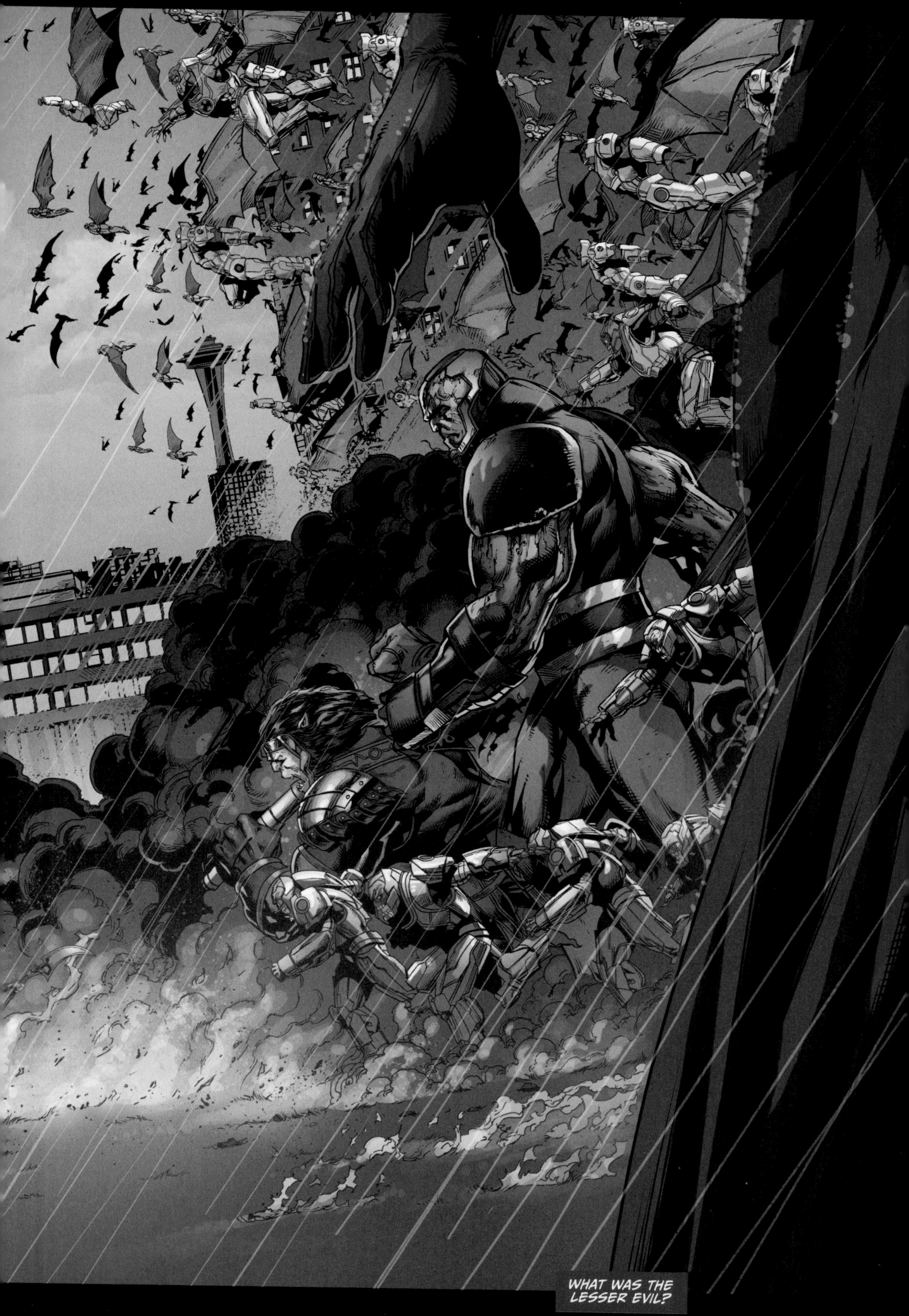
WHAT WAS THE LESSER EVIL?

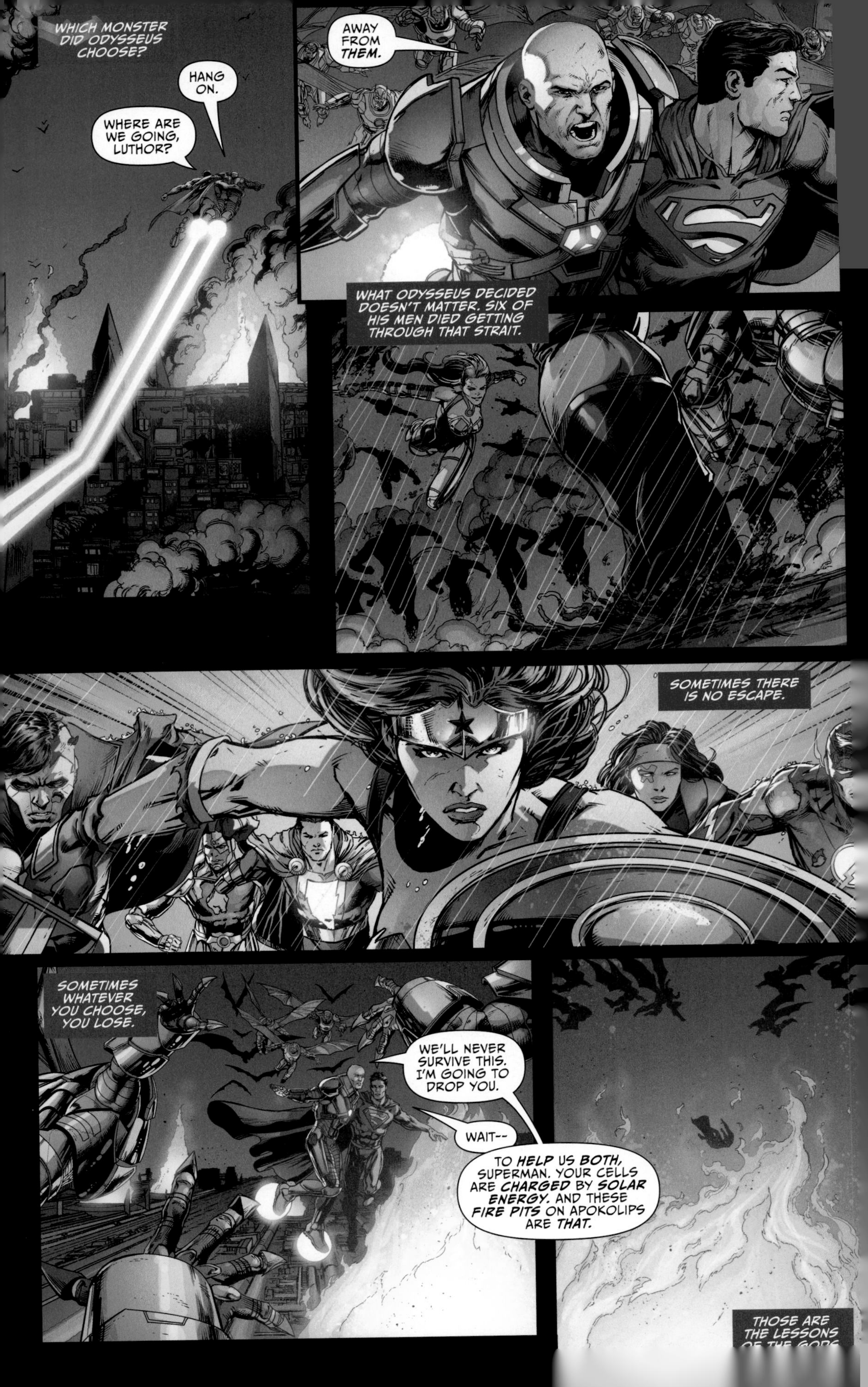
WHICH MONSTER DID ODYSSEUS CHOOSE?
WHERE ARE WE GOING, LUTHOR?
HANG ON.
AWAY FROM *THEM.*
WHAT ODYSSEUS DECIDED DOESN'T MATTER. SIX OF HIS MEN DIED GETTING THROUGH THAT STRAIT.
SOMETIMES THERE IS NO ESCAPE.
SOMETIMES WHATEVER YOU CHOOSE, YOU LOSE.
WE'LL NEVER SURVIVE THIS. I'M GOING TO DROP YOU.
WAIT--
TO *HELP* US *BOTH,* SUPERMAN. YOUR CELLS ARE *CHARGED* BY *SOLAR ENERGY.* AND THESE *FIRE PITS* ON APOKOLIPS ARE *THAT.*
THOSE ARE THE LESSONS

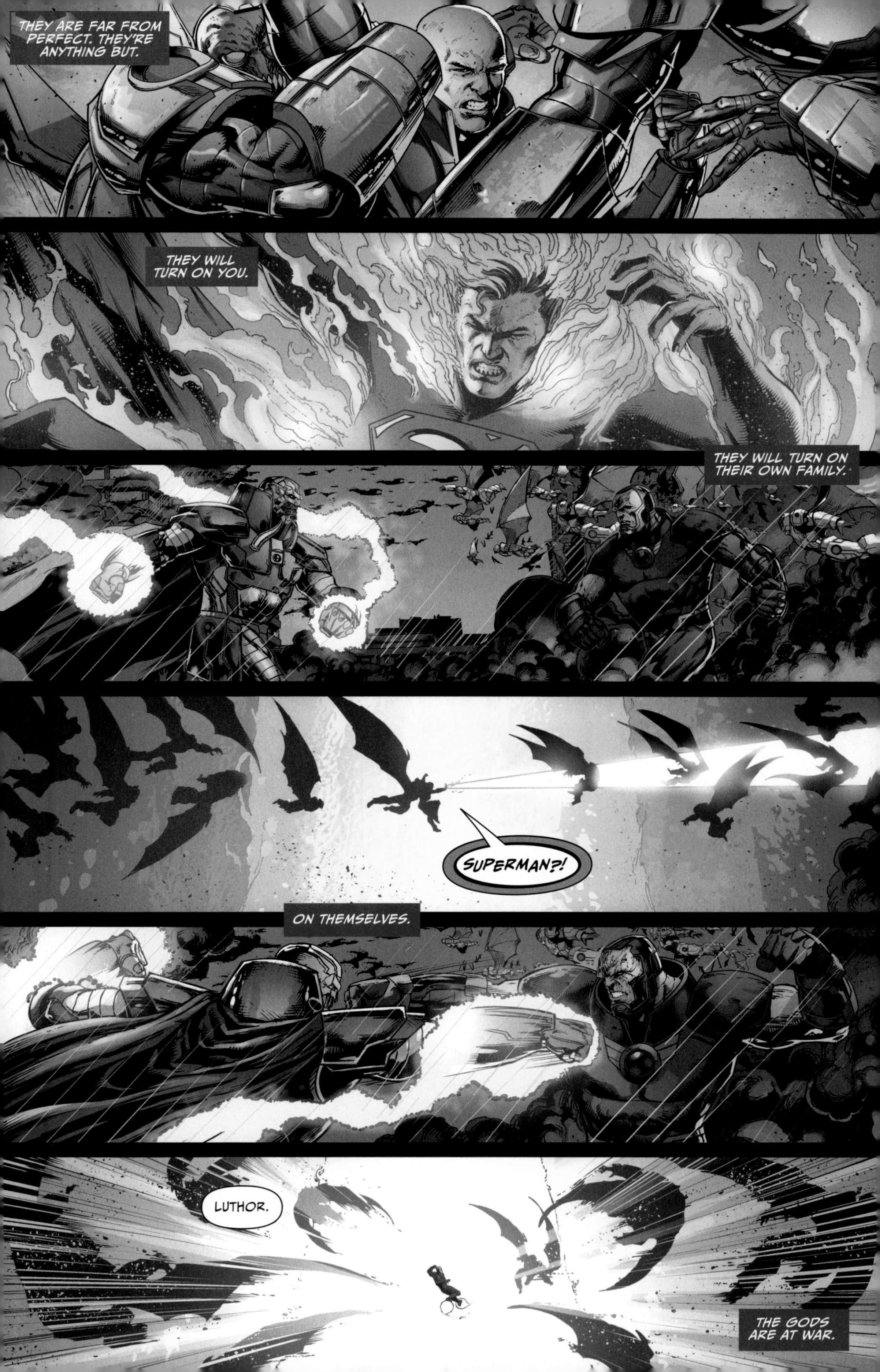
THEY ARE FAR FROM PERFECT. THEY'RE ANYTHING BUT.
THEY WILL TURN ON YOU.
THEY WILL TURN ON THEIR OWN FAMILY.
SUPERMAN?!
ON THEMSELVES.
LUTHOR.
THE GODS ARE AT WAR.

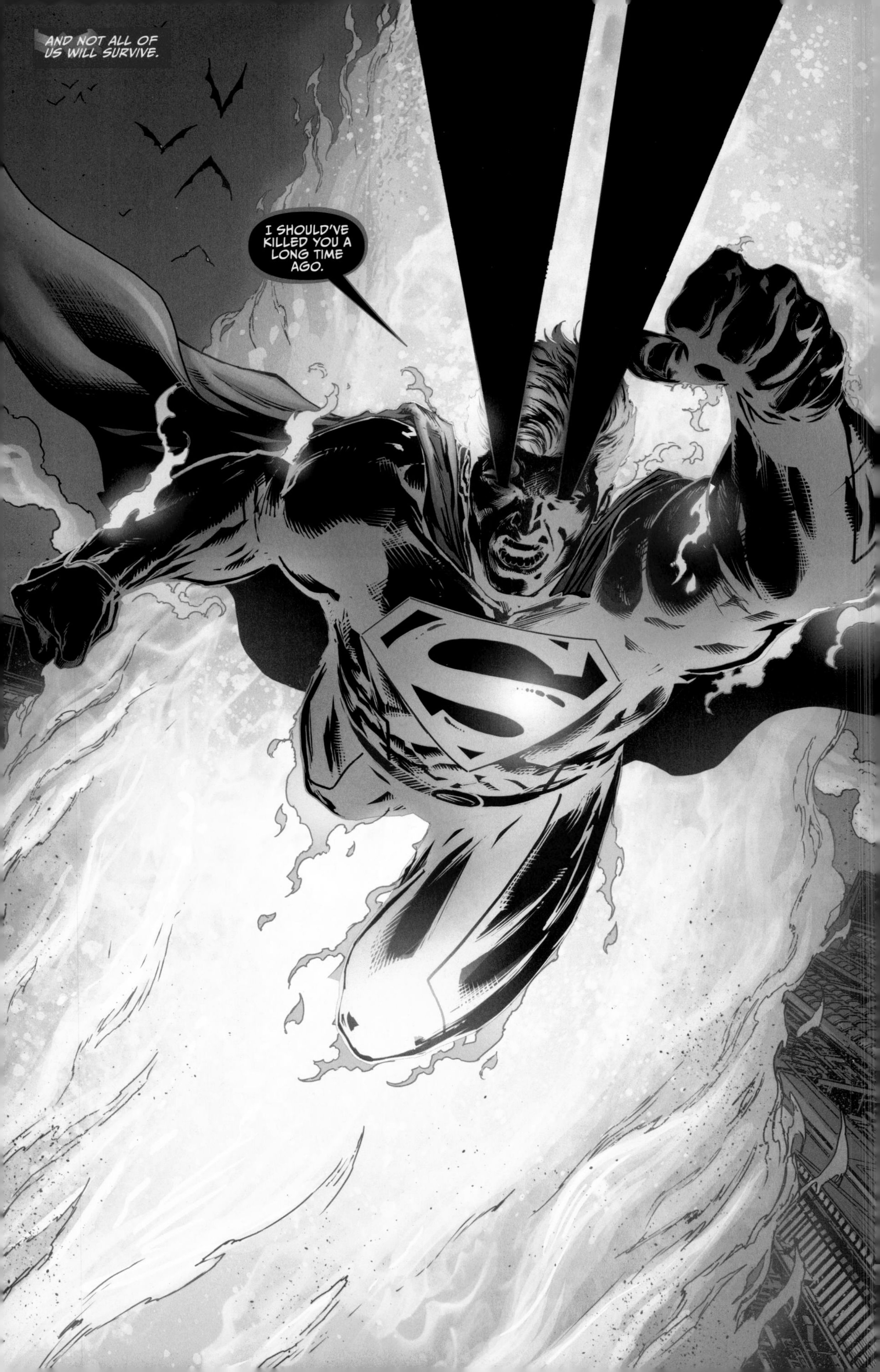
AND NOT ALL OF US WILL SURVIVE.
I SHOULD'VE KILLED YOU A LONG TIME AGO.

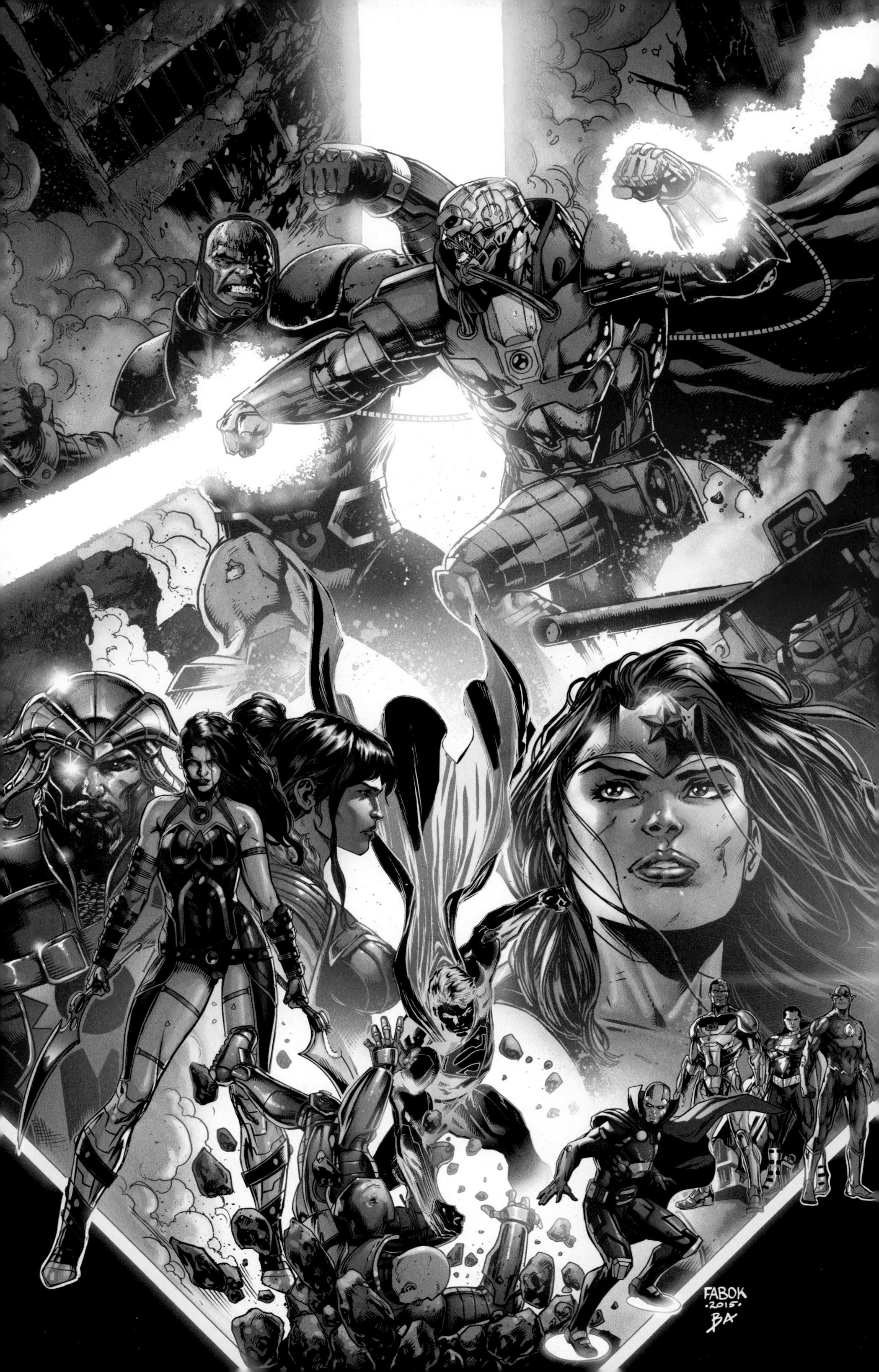
FABOK
2015
BA

DARKSEID WAR CHAPTER FOUR: THE DEATH OF DARKSEID

GEOFF JOHNS writer **JASON FABOK** artist **BRAD ANDERSON** colorist **ROB LEIGH** letterer cover by **JASON FABOK** and **BRAD ANDERSON**

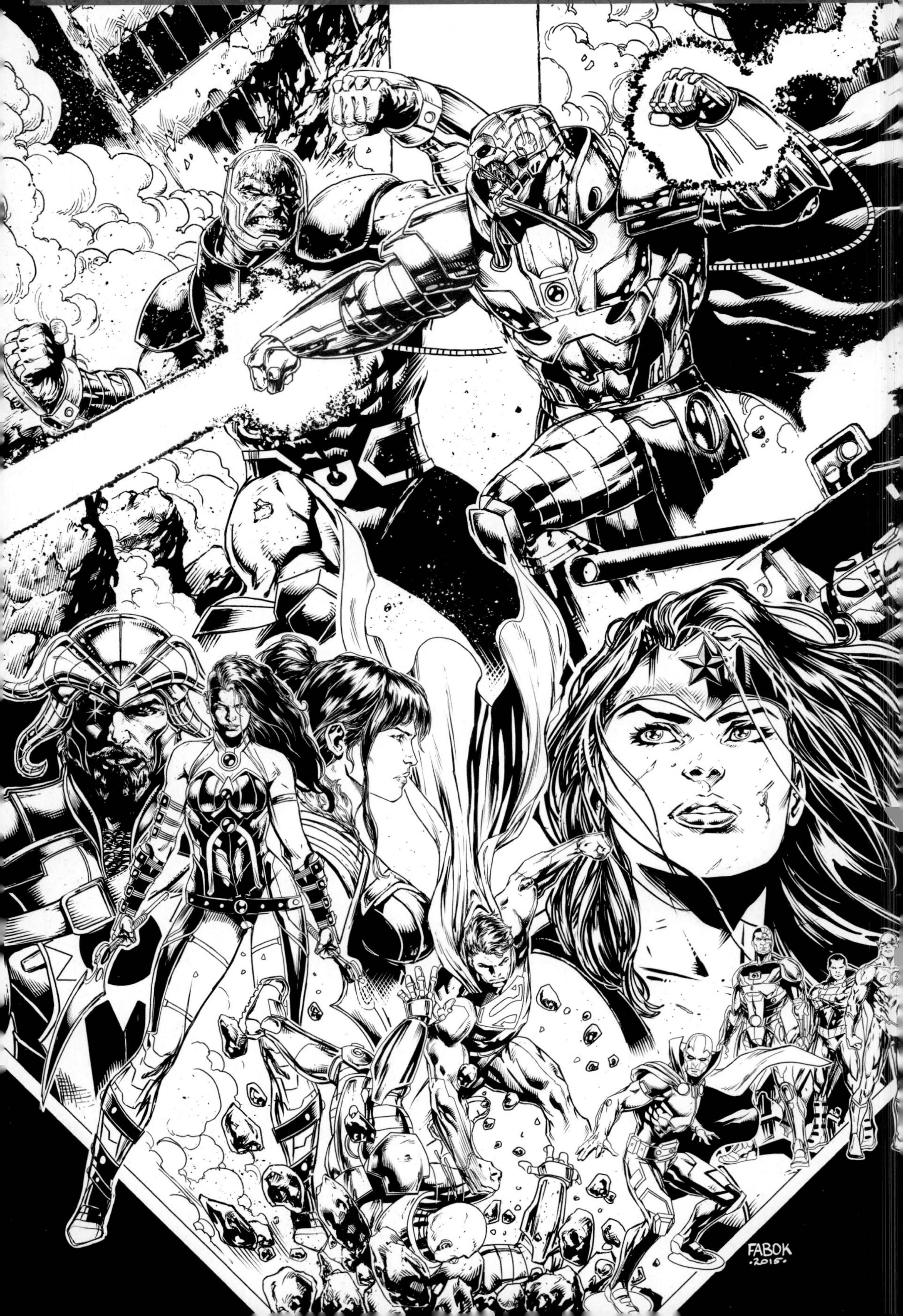
FABOK
2015

THERE WAS ONE GOD MY MOTHER HATED ABOVE ALL OTHERS.

HIS NAME WAS GELOS.

THE GOD OF LAUGHTER.

MY MOTHER DIDN'T DESPISE GELOS BECAUSE THE AMAZONS DON'T BELIEVE IN LAUGHTER.

THEY DO.

IT MIGHT NOT APPEAR EVIDENT AT TIMES, BUT THEY BELIEVE IN JOY, HAPPINESS AND LOVE.

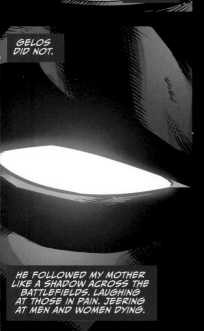

GELOS DID NOT.

HE FOLLOWED MY MOTHER LIKE A SHADOW ACROSS THE BATTLEFIELDS. LAUGHING AT THOSE IN PAIN. JEERING AT MEN AND WOMEN DYING.

HE WAS INVISIBLE TO US, BUT NO MATTER WHERE YOU STOOD, YOU COULD HEAR HIS CACKLING.

IT HAUNTED HER.

BRUCE?

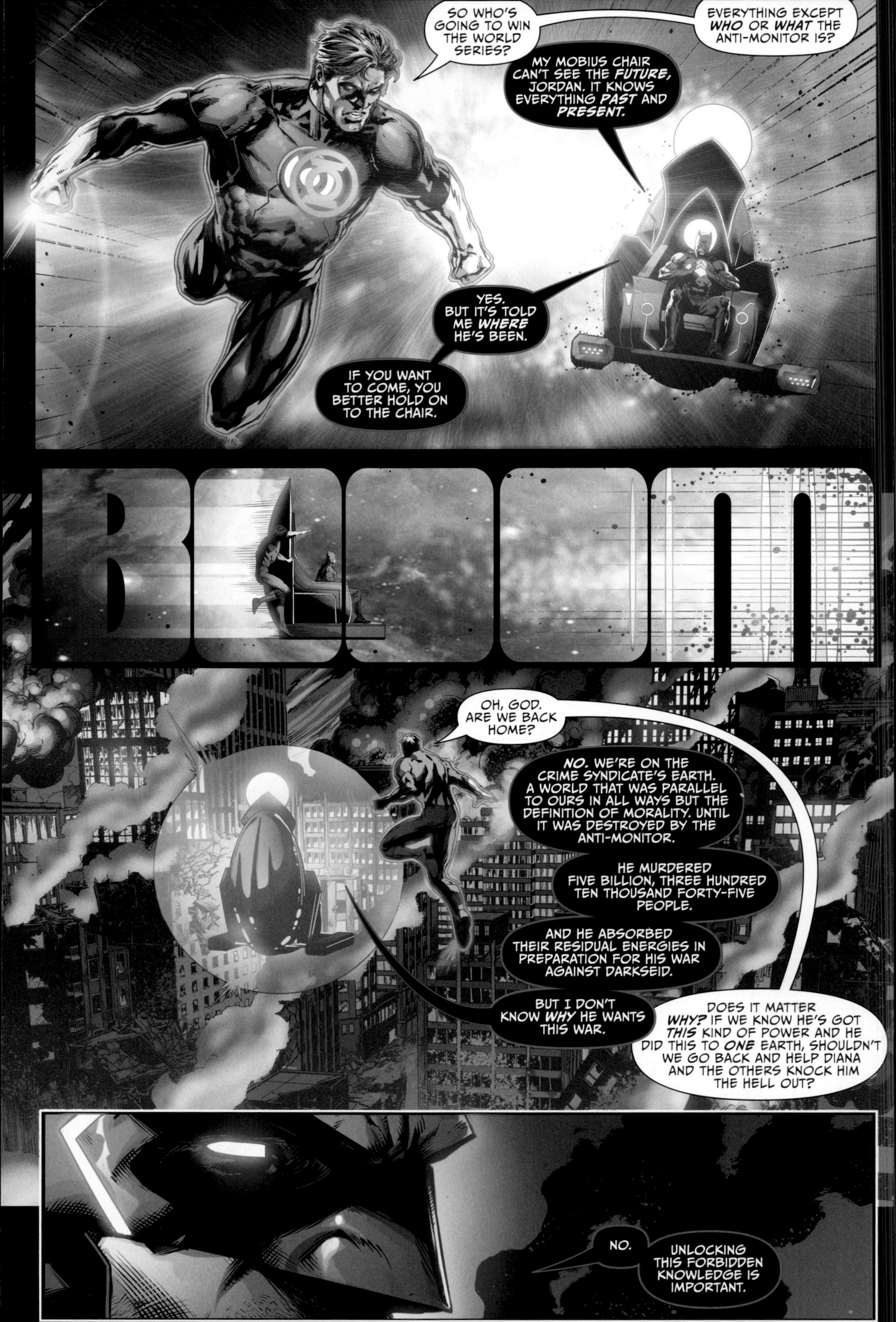
SO WHO'S GOING TO WIN THE WORLD SERIES?
EVERYTHING EXCEPT *WHO* OR *WHAT* THE ANTI-MONITOR IS?
MY MOBIUS CHAIR CAN'T SEE THE *FUTURE*, JORDAN. IT KNOWS EVERYTHING *PAST* AND *PRESENT.*
YES. BUT IT'S TOLD ME *WHERE* HE'S BEEN.
IF YOU WANT TO COME, YOU BETTER HOLD ON TO THE CHAIR.
BOOOM
OH, GOD. ARE WE BACK HOME?
NO. WE'RE ON THE CRIME SYNDICATE'S EARTH. A WORLD THAT WAS PARALLEL TO OURS IN ALL WAYS BUT THE DEFINITION OF MORALITY. UNTIL IT WAS DESTROYED BY THE ANTI-MONITOR.
HE MURDERED FIVE BILLION, THREE HUNDRED TEN THOUSAND FORTY-FIVE PEOPLE.
AND HE ABSORBED THEIR RESIDUAL ENERGIES IN PREPARATION FOR HIS WAR AGAINST DARKSEID.
BUT I DON'T KNOW *WHY* HE WANTS THIS WAR.
DOES IT MATTER *WHY?* IF WE KNOW HE'S GOT *THIS* KIND OF POWER AND HE DID THIS TO *ONE* EARTH, SHOULDN'T WE GO BACK AND HELP DIANA AND THE OTHERS KNOCK HIM THE HELL OUT?
NO.
UNLOCKING THIS FORBIDDEN KNOWLEDGE IS IMPORTANT.

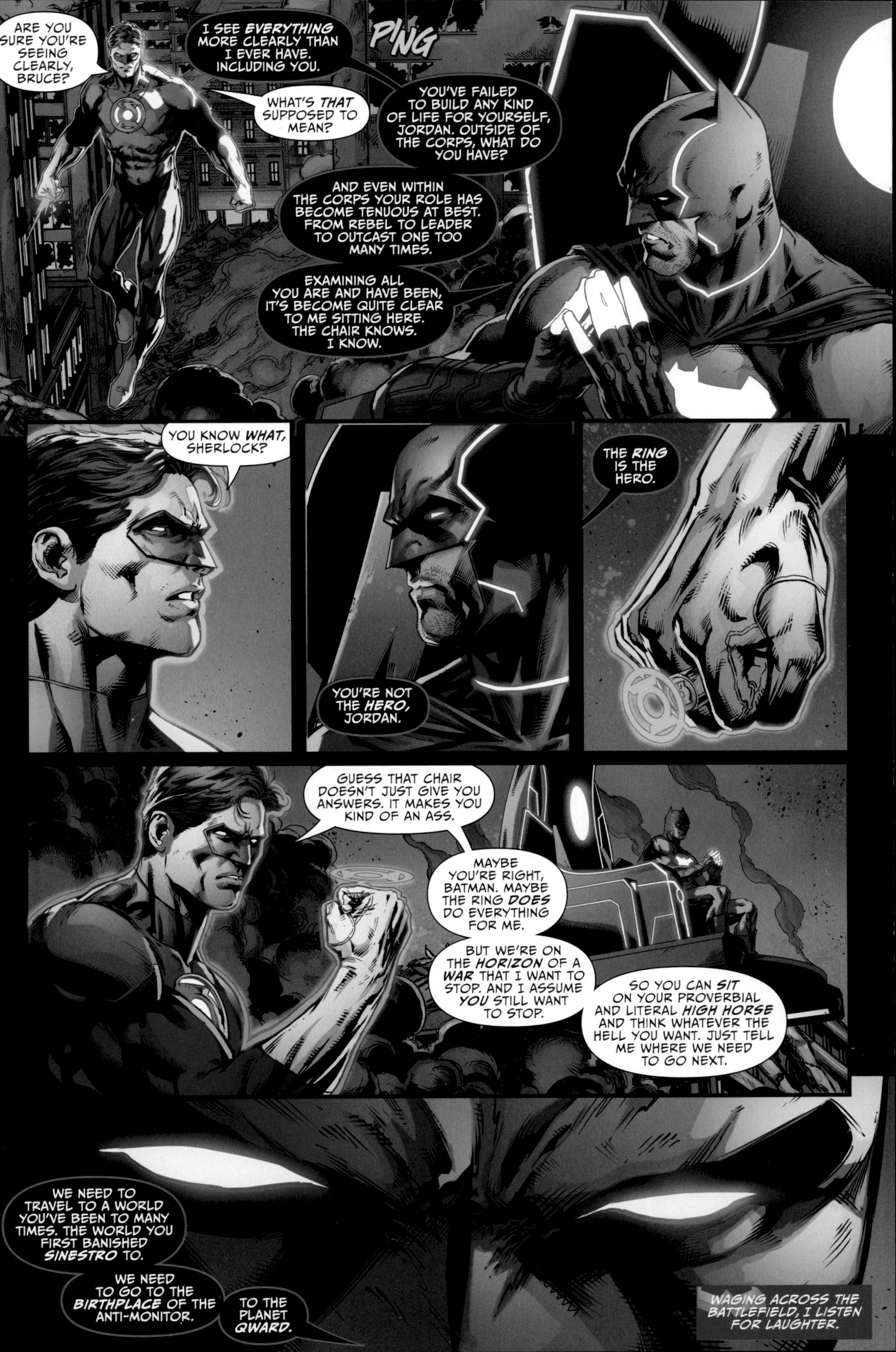
ARE YOU SURE YOU'RE SEEING CLEARLY, BRUCE?
I SEE EVERYTHING MORE CLEARLY THAN I EVER HAVE. INCLUDING YOU.
PING
WHAT'S THAT SUPPOSED TO MEAN?
YOU'VE FAILED TO BUILD ANY KIND OF LIFE FOR YOURSELF, JORDAN. OUTSIDE OF THE CORPS, WHAT DO YOU HAVE?
AND EVEN WITHIN THE CORPS YOUR ROLE HAS BECOME TENUOUS AT BEST. FROM REBEL TO LEADER TO OUTCAST ONE TOO MANY TIMES.
EXAMINING ALL YOU ARE AND HAVE BEEN, IT'S BECOME QUITE CLEAR TO ME SITTING HERE. THE CHAIR KNOWS. I KNOW.
YOU KNOW WHAT, SHERLOCK?
YOU'RE NOT THE HERO, JORDAN.
THE RING IS THE HERO.
GUESS THAT CHAIR DOESN'T JUST GIVE YOU ANSWERS. IT MAKES YOU KIND OF AN ASS.
MAYBE YOU'RE RIGHT, BATMAN. MAYBE THE RING DOES DO EVERYTHING FOR ME.
BUT WE'RE ON THE HORIZON OF A WAR THAT I WANT TO STOP. AND I ASSUME YOU STILL WANT TO STOP.
SO YOU CAN SIT ON YOUR PROVERBIAL AND LITERAL HIGH HORSE AND THINK WHATEVER THE HELL YOU WANT. JUST TELL ME WHERE WE NEED TO GO NEXT.
WE NEED TO TRAVEL TO A WORLD YOU'VE BEEN TO MANY TIMES. THE WORLD YOU FIRST BANISHED SINESTRO TO.
WE NEED TO GO TO THE BIRTHPLACE OF THE ANTI-MONITOR.
TO THE PLANET QWARD.
WAGING ACROSS THE BATTLEFIELD, I LISTEN FOR LAUGHTER.

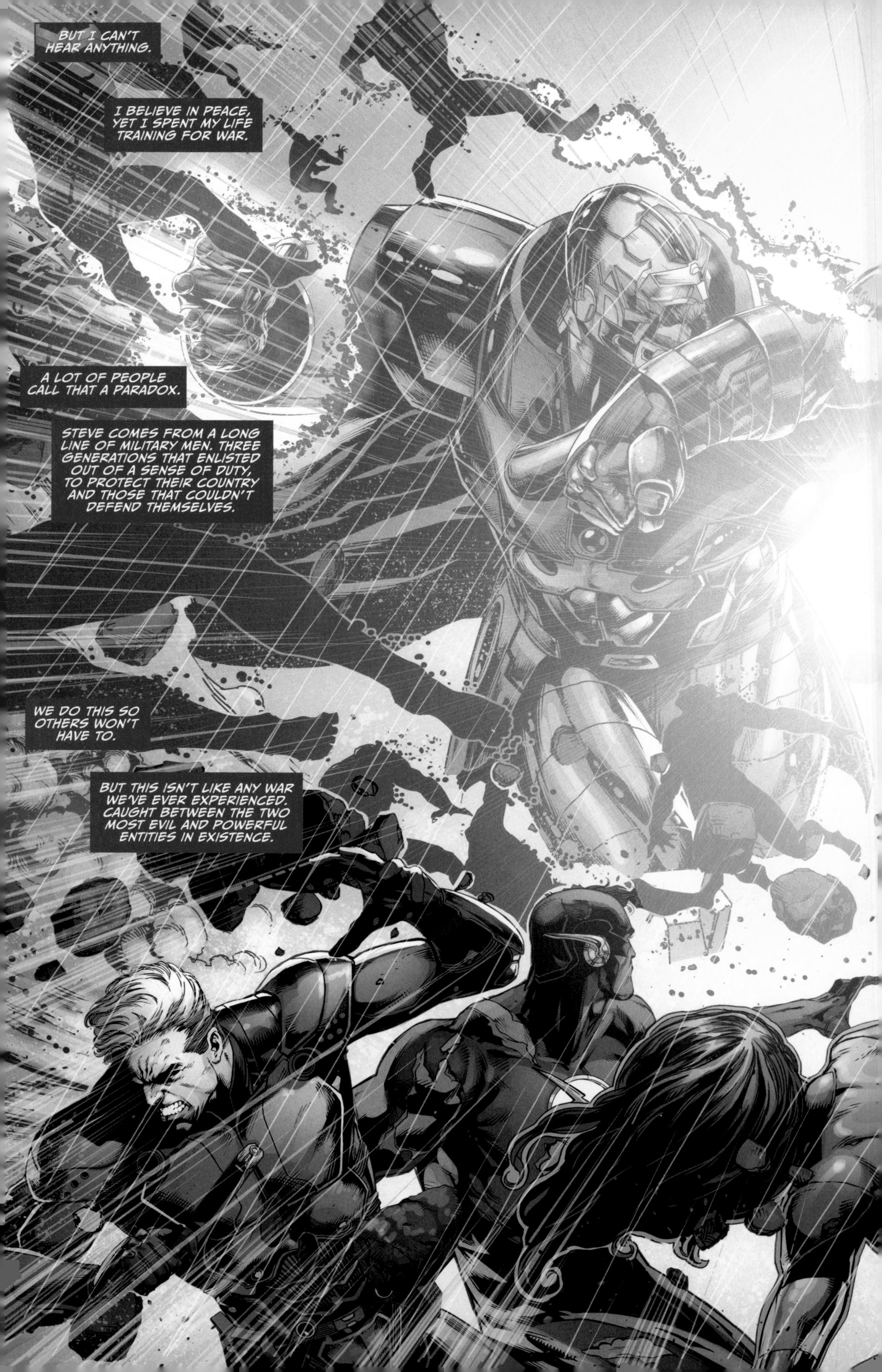
BUT I CAN'T HEAR ANYTHING.
I BELIEVE IN PEACE, YET I SPENT MY LIFE TRAINING FOR WAR.
A LOT OF PEOPLE CALL THAT A PARADOX.
STEVE COMES FROM A LONG LINE OF MILITARY MEN. THREE GENERATIONS THAT ENLISTED OUT OF A SENSE OF DUTY, TO PROTECT THEIR COUNTRY AND THOSE THAT COULDN'T DEFEND THEMSELVES.
WE DO THIS SO OTHERS WON'T HAVE TO.
BUT THIS ISN'T LIKE ANY WAR WE'VE EVER EXPERIENCED. CAUGHT BETWEEN THE TWO MOST EVIL AND POWERFUL ENTITIES IN EXISTENCE.

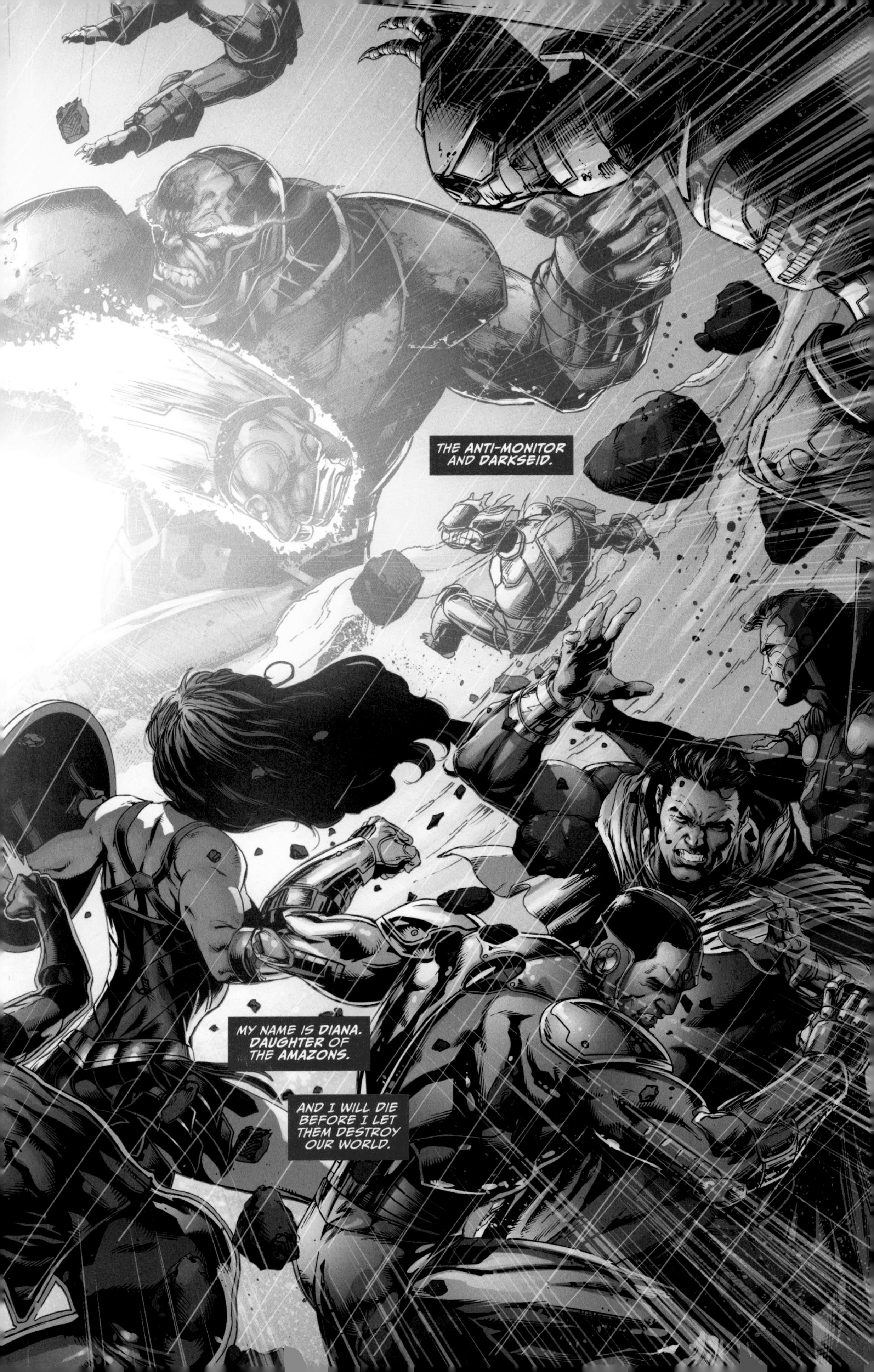
THE ANTI-MONITOR AND DARKSEID.
MY NAME IS DIANA. DAUGHTER OF THE AMAZONS.
AND I WILL DIE BEFORE I LET THEM DESTROY OUR WORLD.

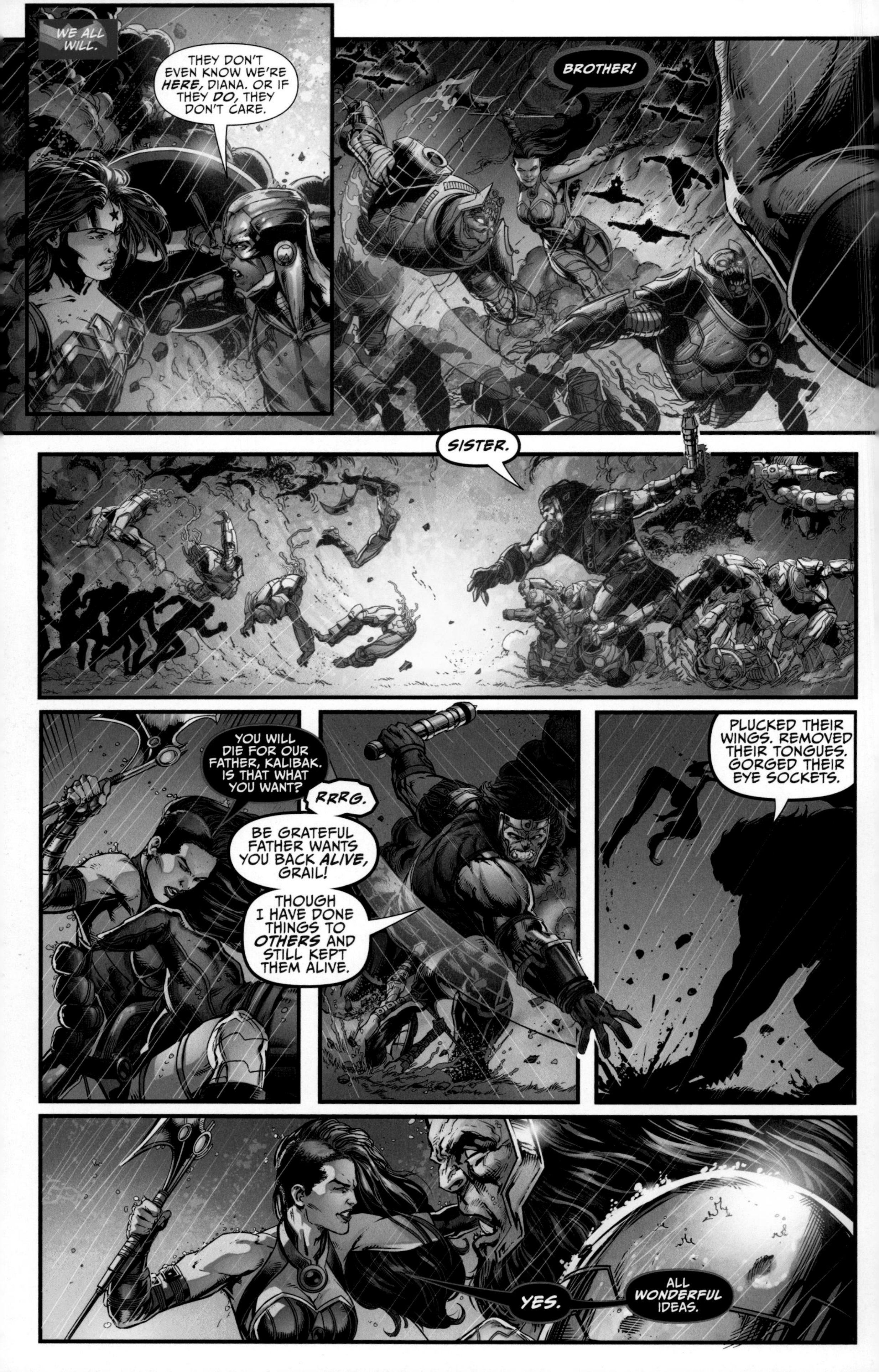
WE ALL WILL.
THEY DON'T EVEN KNOW WE'RE HERE, DIANA. OR IF THEY DO, THEY DON'T CARE.
BROTHER!
SISTER.
YOU WILL DIE FOR OUR FATHER, KALIBAK. IS THAT WHAT YOU WANT?
RRRG.
BE GRATEFUL FATHER WANTS YOU BACK ALIVE, GRAIL!
THOUGH I HAVE DONE THINGS TO OTHERS AND STILL KEPT THEM ALIVE.
PLUCKED THEIR WINGS. REMOVED THEIR TONGUES. GORGED THEIR EYE SOCKETS.
YES.
ALL WONDERFUL IDEAS.

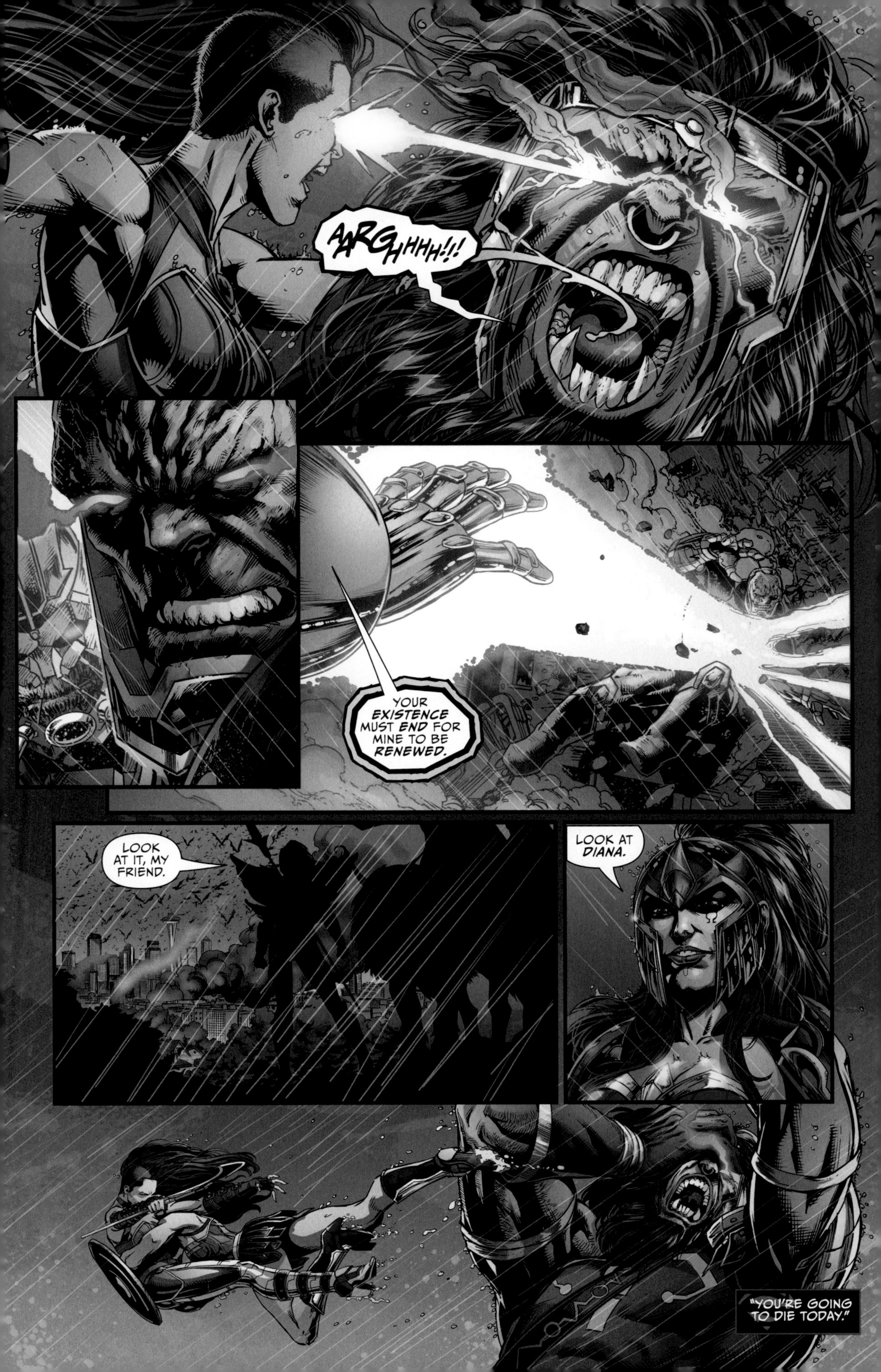
AARGHHHH!!!
YOUR EXISTENCE MUST END FOR MINE TO BE RENEWED.
LOOK AT IT, MY FRIEND.
LOOK AT DIANA.
"YOU'RE GOING TO DIE TODAY."

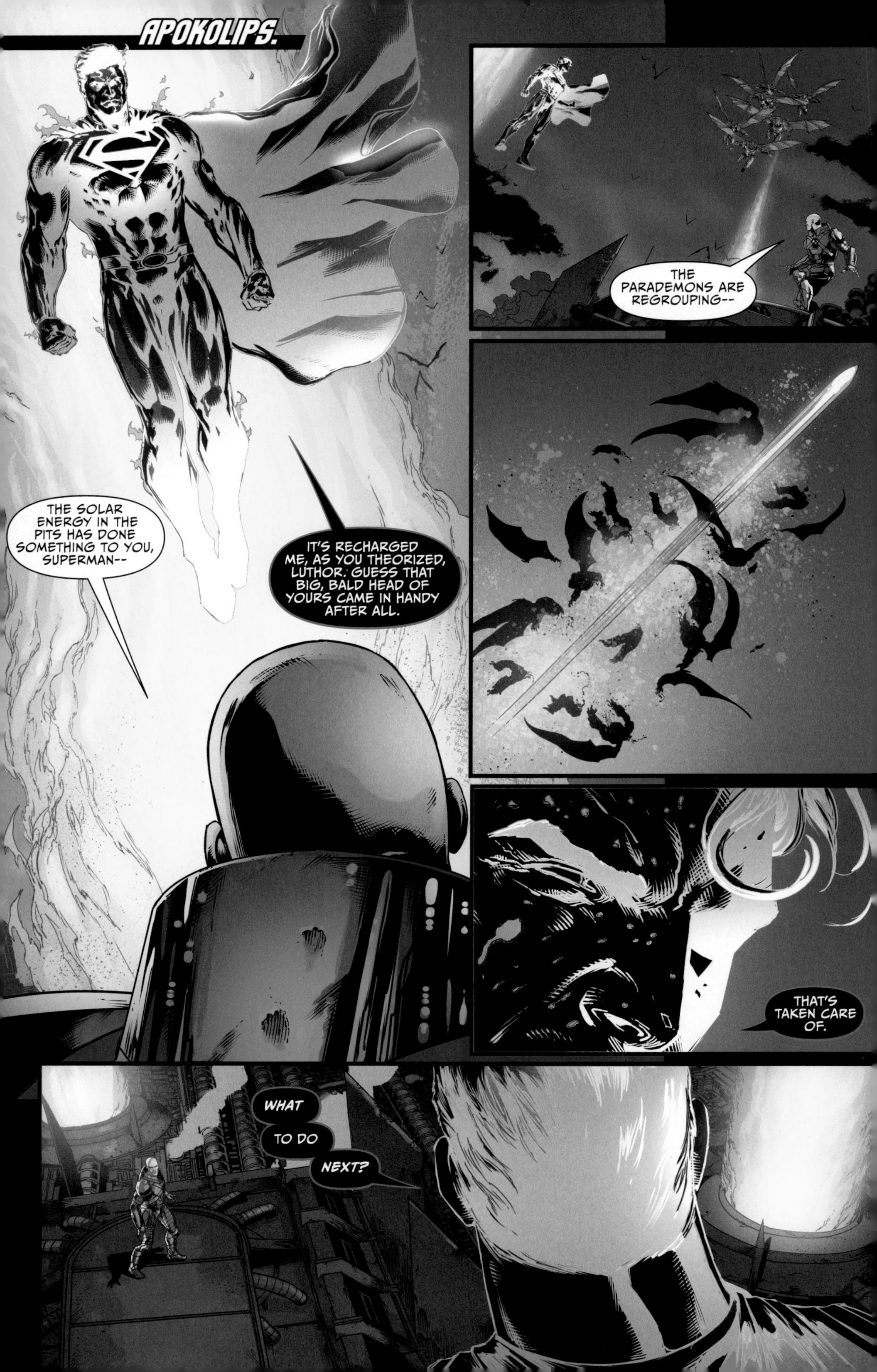
APOKOLIPS.
THE PARADEMONS ARE REGROUPING--
THE SOLAR ENERGY IN THE PITS HAS DONE SOMETHING TO YOU, SUPERMAN--
IT'S RECHARGED ME, AS YOU THEORIZED, LUTHOR. GUESS THAT BIG, BALD HEAD OF YOURS CAME IN HANDY AFTER ALL.
THAT'S TAKEN CARE OF.
WHAT
TO DO
NEXT?

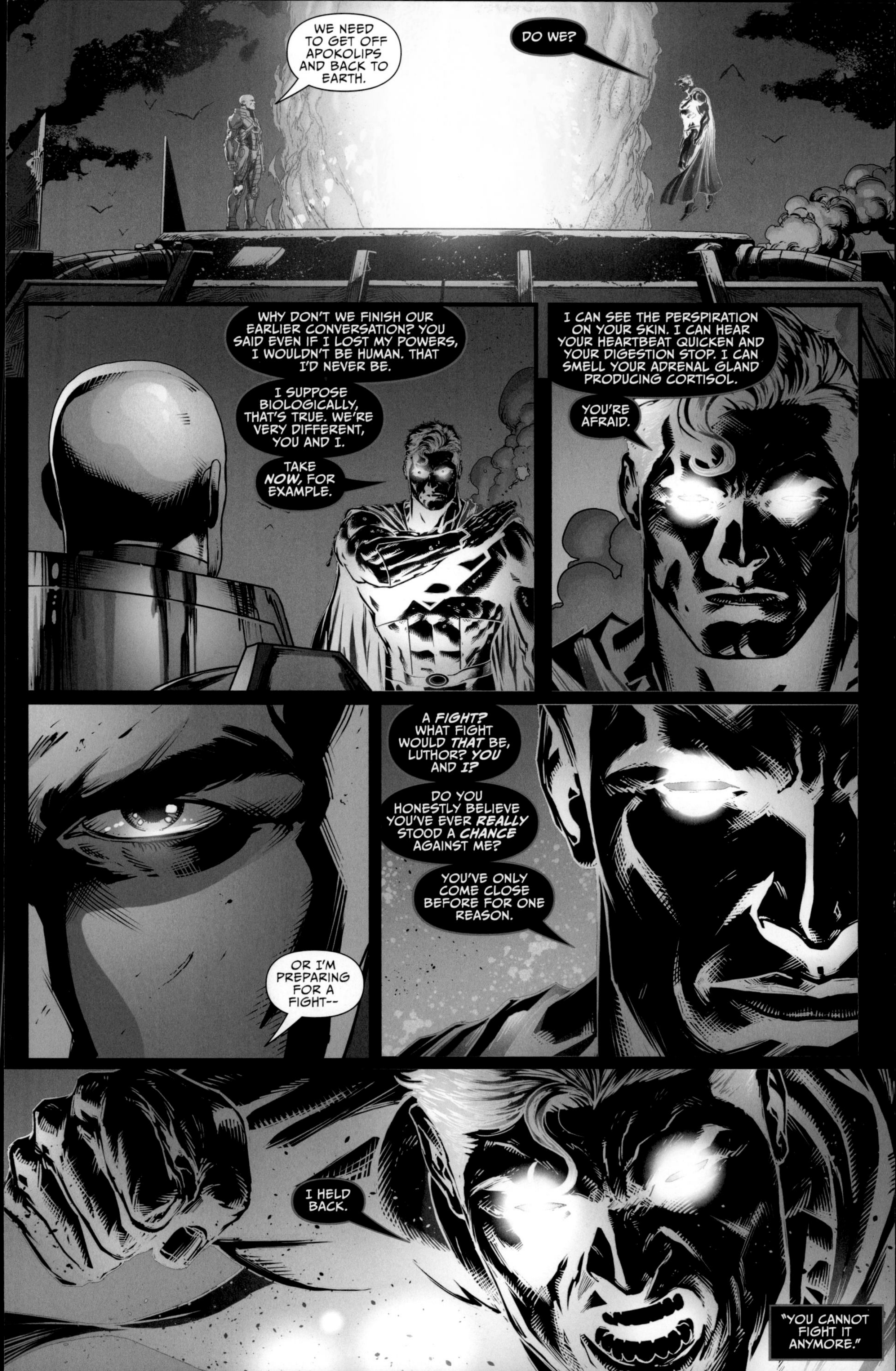
WE NEED TO GET OFF APOKOLIPS AND BACK TO EARTH.
DO WE?
WHY DON'T WE FINISH OUR EARLIER CONVERSATION? YOU SAID EVEN IF I LOST MY POWERS, I WOULDN'T BE HUMAN. THAT I'D NEVER BE.
I SUPPOSE BIOLOGICALLY, THAT'S TRUE. WE'RE VERY DIFFERENT, YOU AND I.
TAKE *NOW*, FOR EXAMPLE.
I CAN SEE THE PERSPIRATION ON YOUR SKIN. I CAN HEAR YOUR HEARTBEAT QUICKEN AND YOUR DIGESTION STOP. I CAN SMELL YOUR ADRENAL GLAND PRODUCING CORTISOL.
YOU'RE AFRAID.
OR I'M PREPARING FOR A FIGHT--
A *FIGHT?* WHAT FIGHT WOULD *THAT* BE, LUTHOR? *YOU* AND *I?*
DO YOU HONESTLY BELIEVE YOU'VE EVER *REALLY* STOOD A *CHANCE* AGAINST ME?
YOU'VE ONLY COME CLOSE BEFORE FOR ONE REASON.
I HELD BACK.
"YOU CANNOT FIGHT IT ANYMORE."

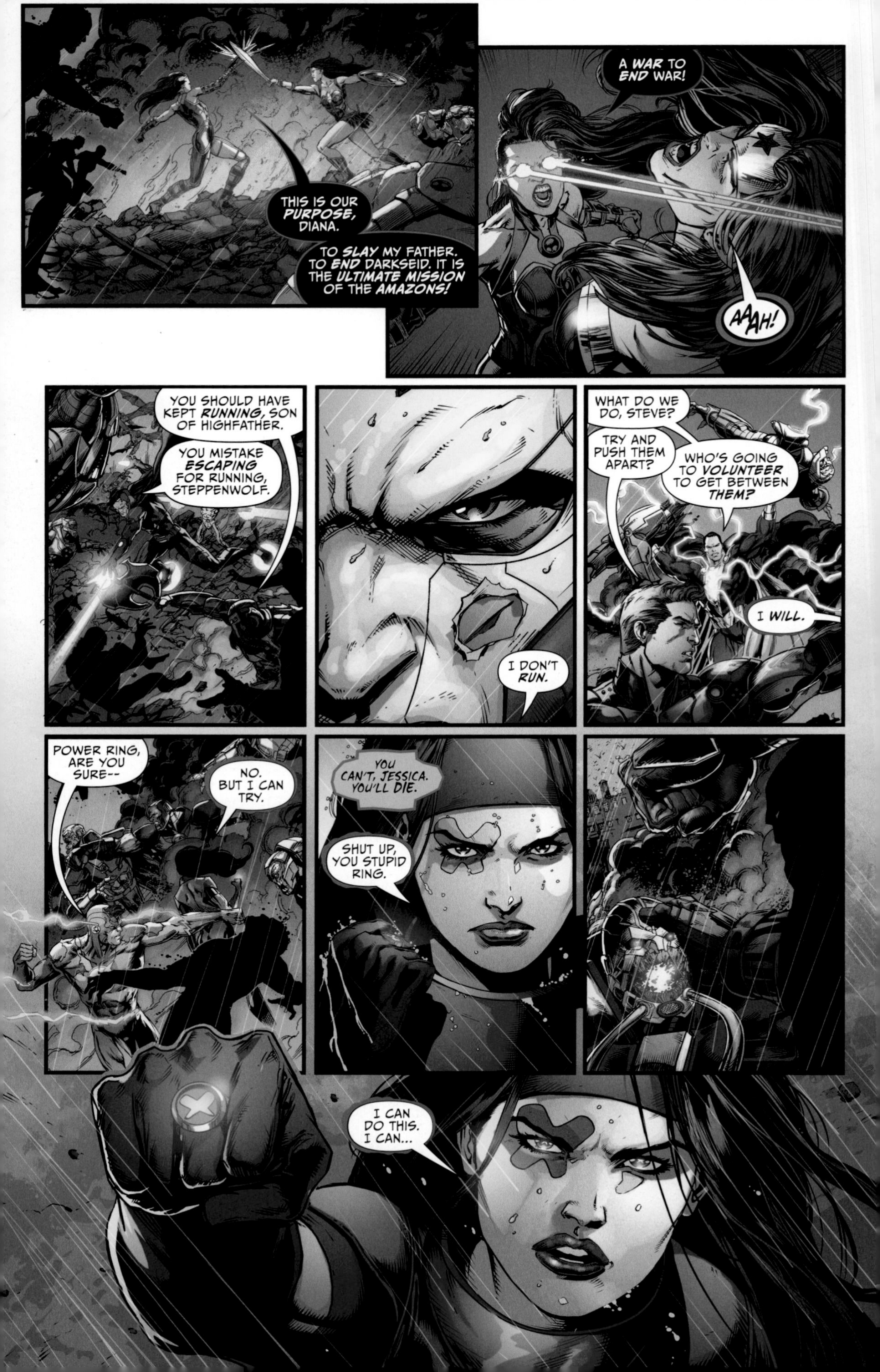
THIS IS OUR PURPOSE, DIANA.
TO SLAY MY FATHER. TO END DARKSEID. IT IS THE ULTIMATE MISSION OF THE AMAZONS!
A WAR TO END WAR!
AAAH!
YOU SHOULD HAVE KEPT RUNNING, SON OF HIGHFATHER.
YOU MISTAKE ESCAPING FOR RUNNING, STEPPENWOLF.
I DON'T RUN.
WHAT DO WE DO, STEVE?
TRY AND PUSH THEM APART?
WHO'S GOING TO VOLUNTEER TO GET BETWEEN THEM?
I WILL.
POWER RING, ARE YOU SURE--
NO. BUT I CAN TRY.
YOU CAN'T, JESSICA. YOU'LL DIE.
SHUT UP, YOU STUPID RING.
I CAN DO THIS. I CAN...

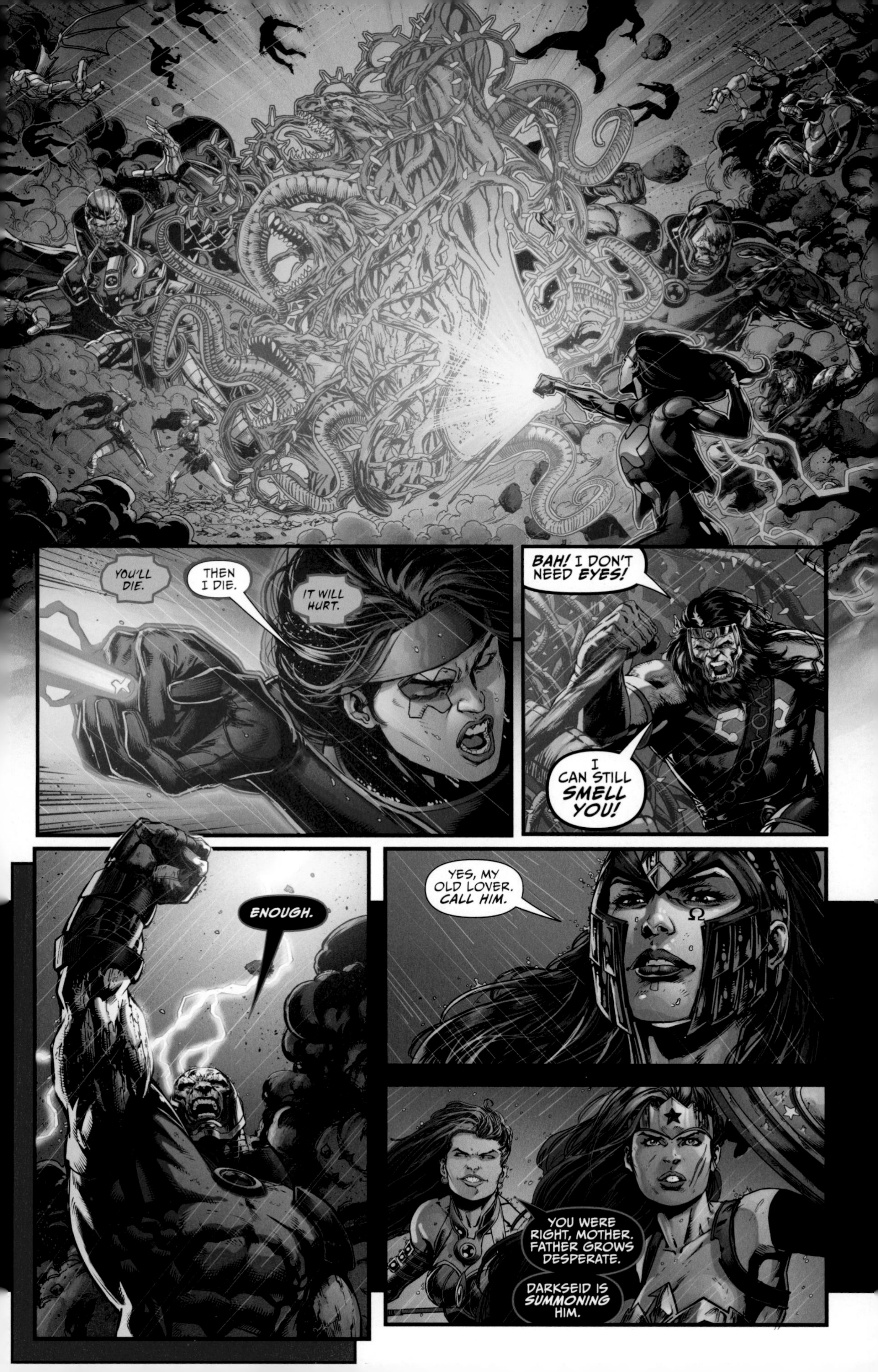
YOU'LL DIE.
THEN I DIE.
IT WILL HURT.
BAH! I DON'T NEED EYES!
I CAN STILL SMELL YOU!
ENOUGH.
YES, MY OLD LOVER. CALL HIM.
YOU WERE RIGHT, MOTHER. FATHER GROWS DESPERATE.
DARKSEID IS SUMMONING HIM.

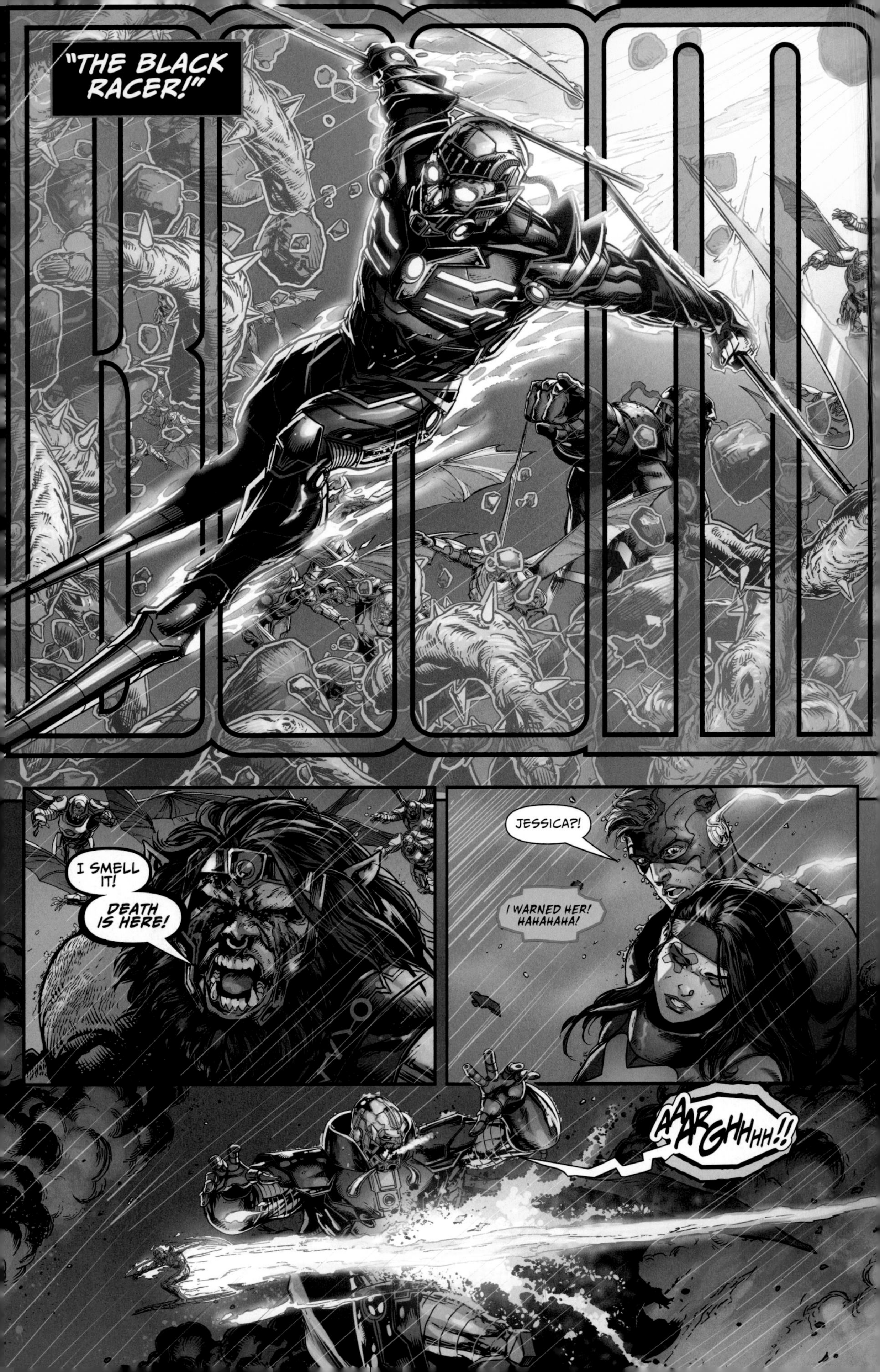
"THE BLACK RACER!"
BOOM
I SMELL IT!
DEATH IS HERE!
JESSICA?!
I WARNED HER! HAHAHAHA!
AAARGHHHH!!

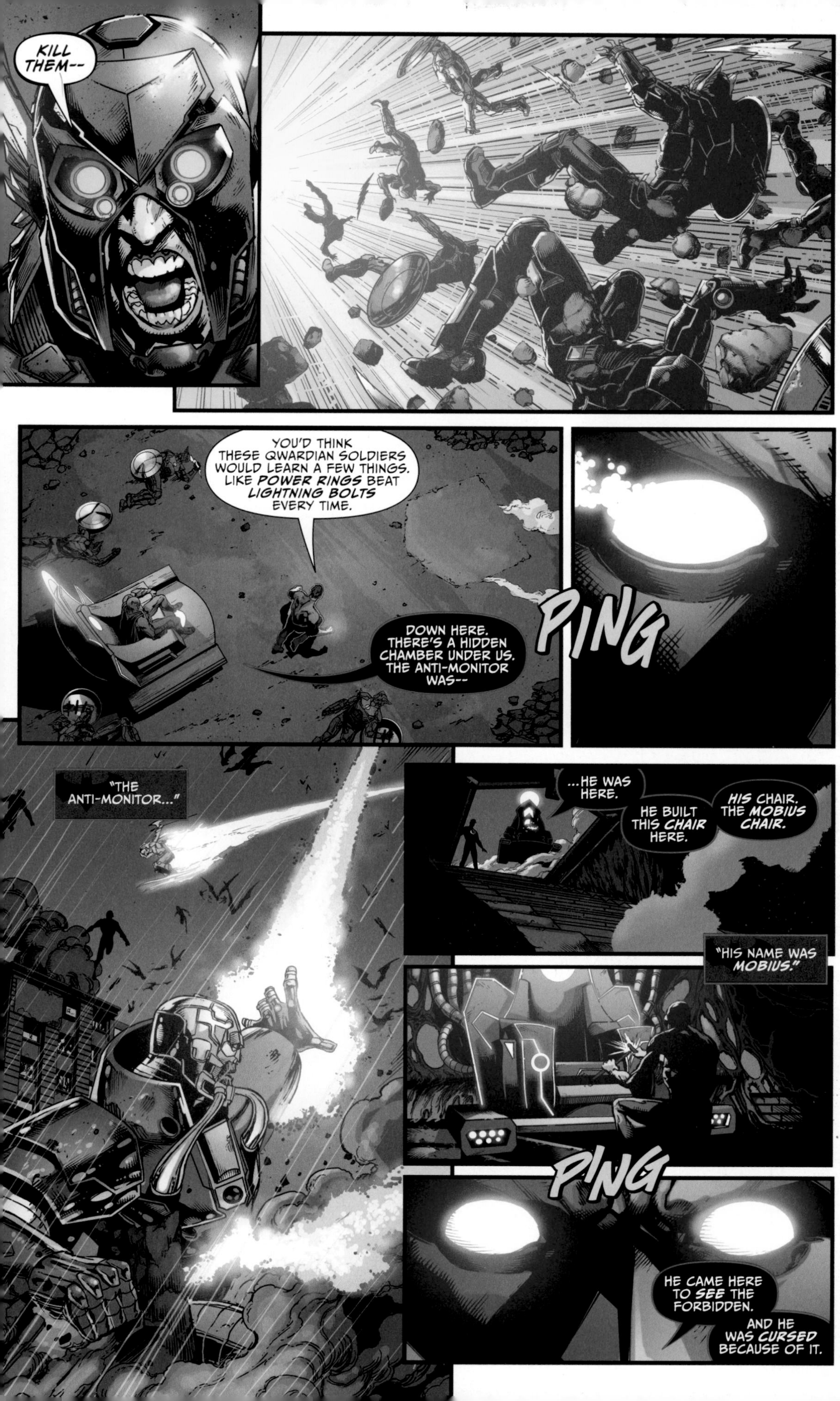
KILL THEM--
YOU'D THINK THESE QWARDIAN SOLDIERS WOULD LEARN A FEW THINGS. LIKE POWER RINGS BEAT LIGHTNING BOLTS EVERY TIME.
DOWN HERE. THERE'S A HIDDEN CHAMBER UNDER US. THE ANTI-MONITOR WAS--
PING
"THE ANTI-MONITOR..."
...HE WAS HERE.
HE BUILT THIS CHAIR HERE.
HIS CHAIR. THE MOBIUS CHAIR.
"HIS NAME WAS MOBIUS."
PING
HE CAME HERE TO SEE THE FORBIDDEN.
AND HE WAS CURSED BECAUSE OF IT.

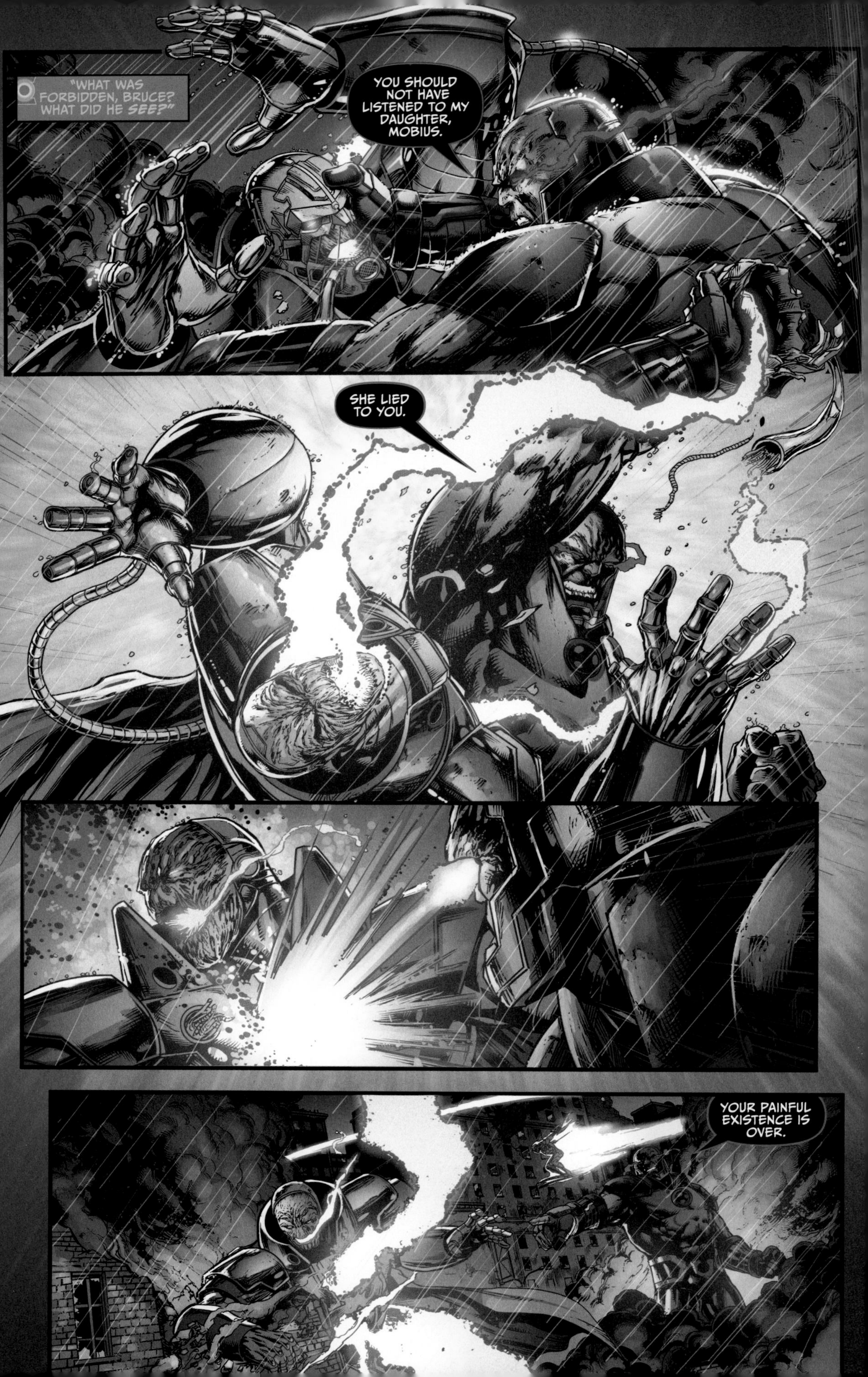
"WHAT WAS FORBIDDEN, BRUCE? WHAT DID HE *SEE*?"
YOU SHOULD NOT HAVE LISTENED TO MY DAUGHTER, MOBIUS.
SHE LIED TO YOU.
YOUR PAINFUL EXISTENCE IS OVER.

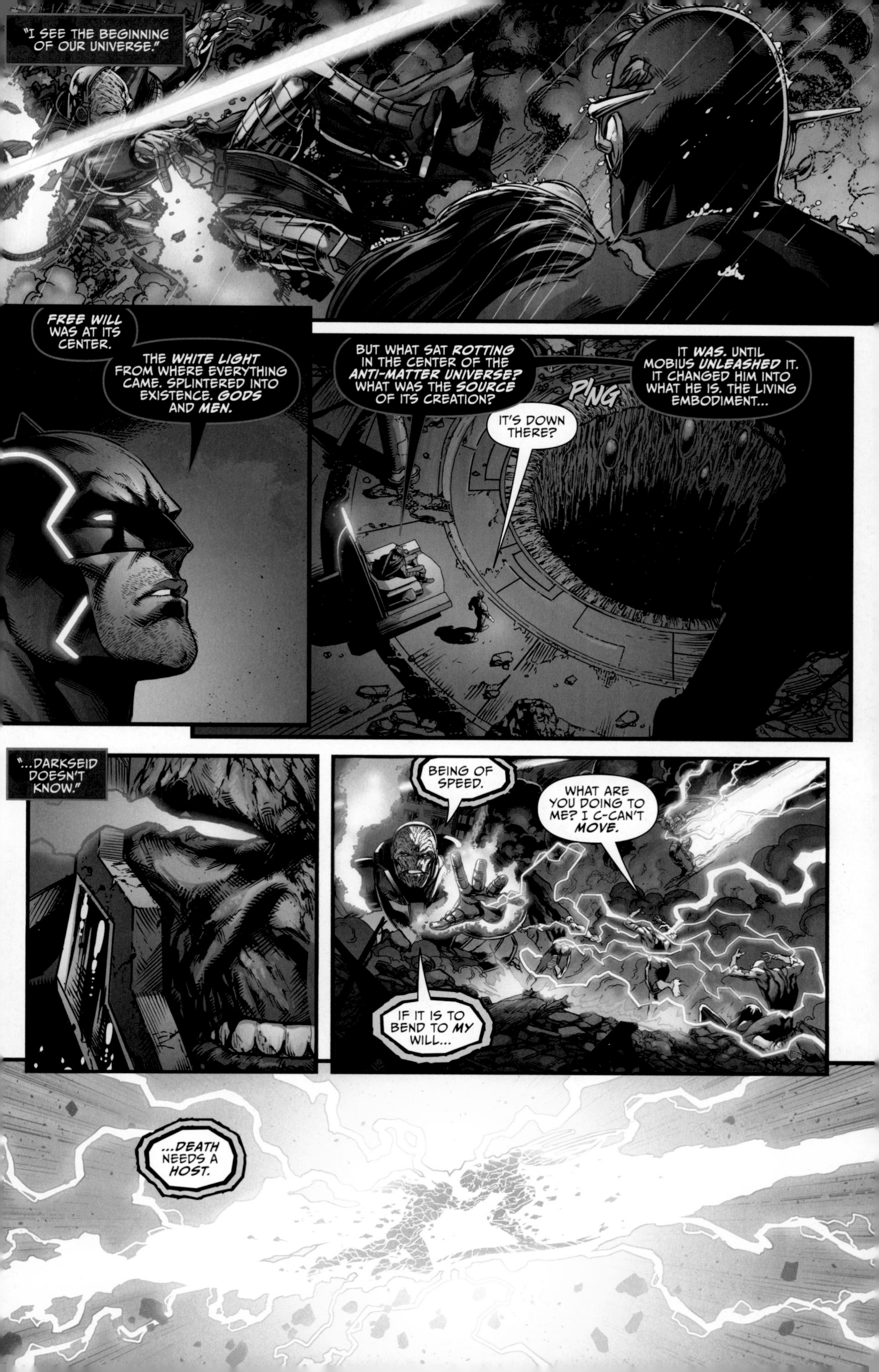
"I SEE THE BEGINNING OF OUR UNIVERSE."
FREE WILL WAS AT ITS CENTER.
THE WHITE LIGHT FROM WHERE EVERYTHING CAME. SPLINTERED INTO EXISTENCE. GODS AND MEN.
BUT WHAT SAT ROTTING IN THE CENTER OF THE ANTI-MATTER UNIVERSE? WHAT WAS THE SOURCE OF ITS CREATION?
PING
IT'S DOWN THERE?
IT WAS. UNTIL MOBIUS UNLEASHED IT. IT CHANGED HIM INTO WHAT HE IS. THE LIVING EMBODIMENT...
"...DARKSEID DOESN'T KNOW."
BEING OF SPEED.
WHAT ARE YOU DOING TO ME? I C-CAN'T MOVE.
IF IT IS TO BEND TO MY WILL...
...DEATH NEEDS A HOST.

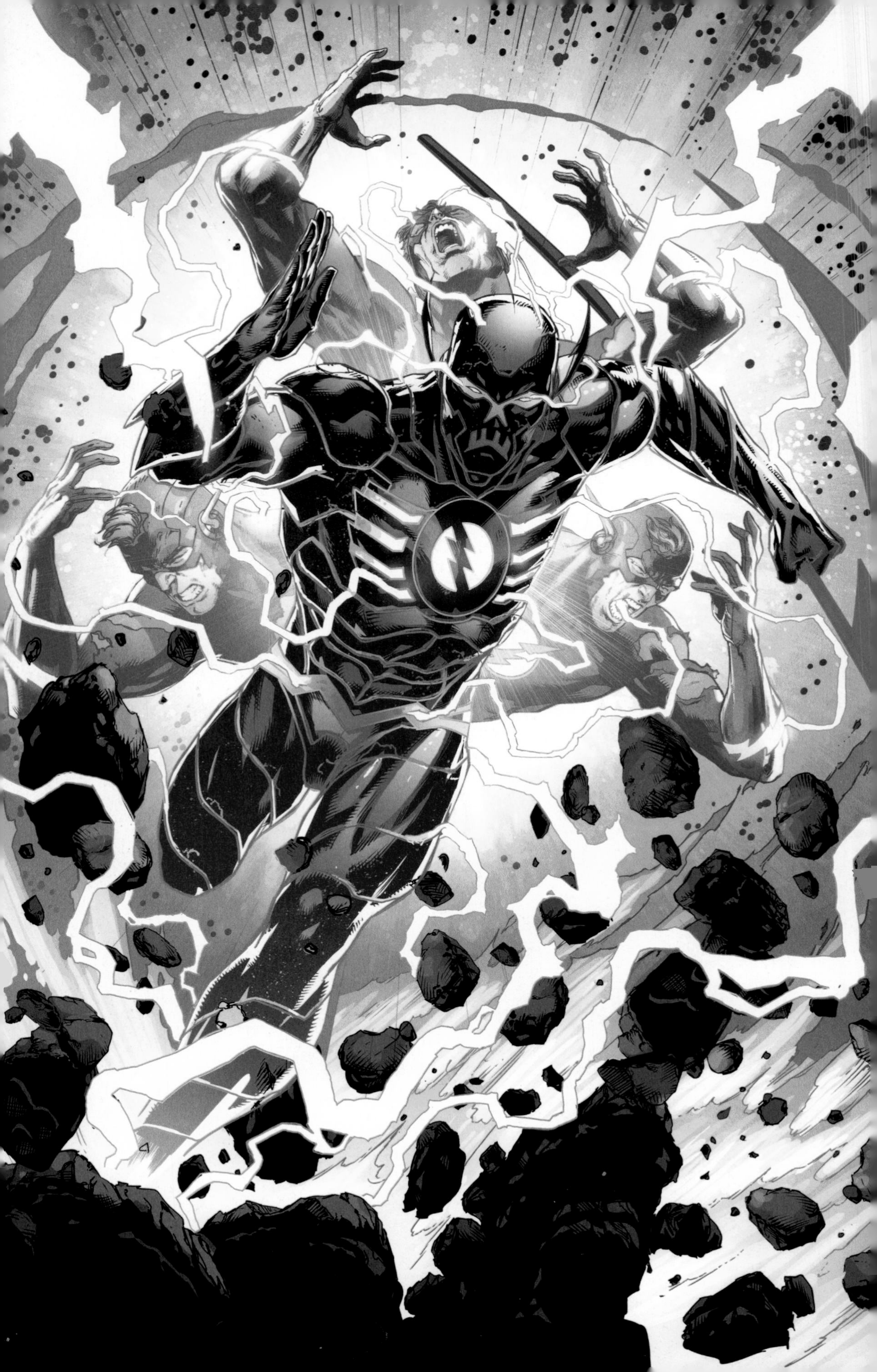

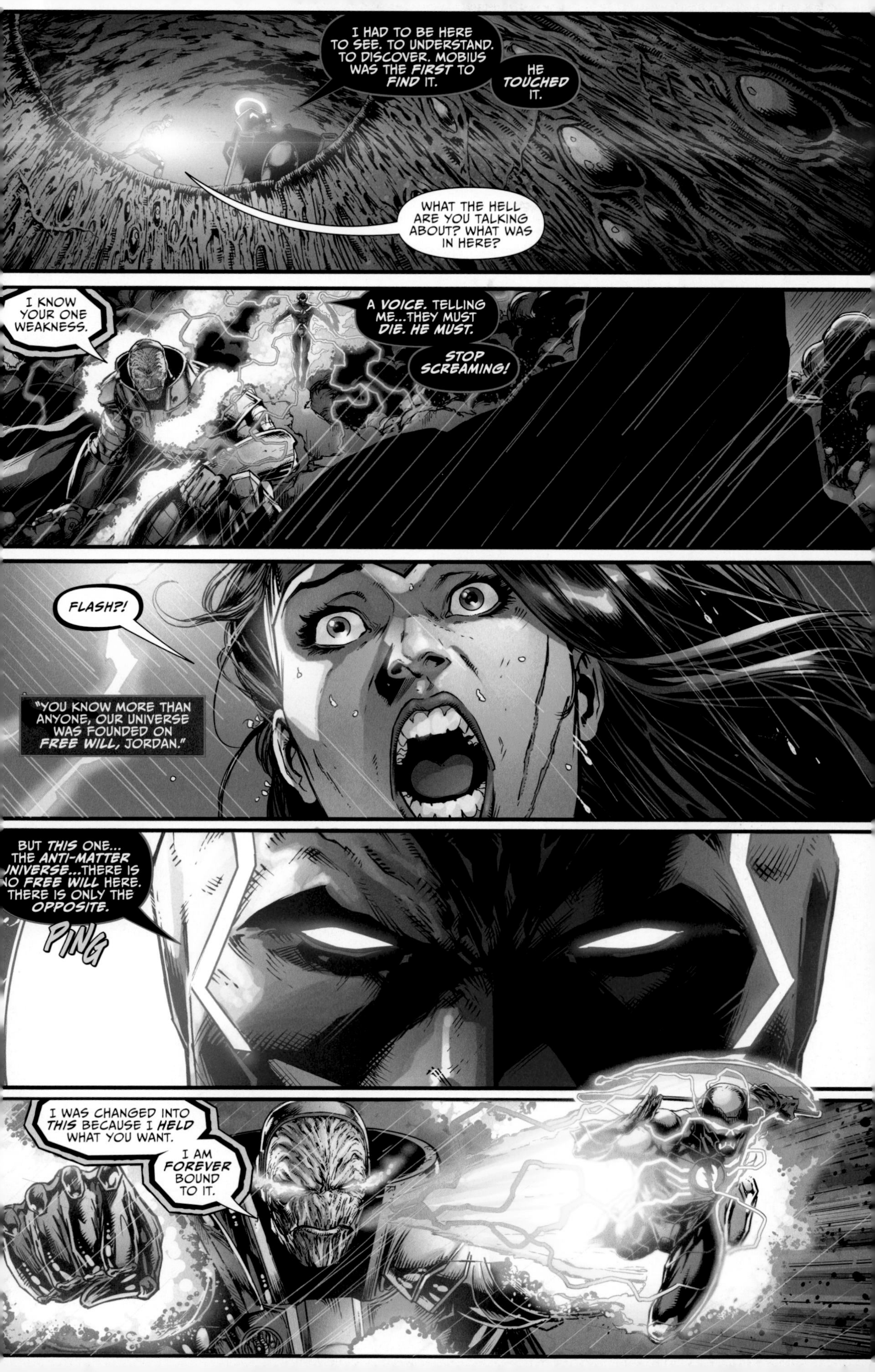
I HAD TO BE HERE TO SEE. TO UNDERSTAND. TO DISCOVER. MOBIUS WAS THE FIRST TO FIND IT.
HE TOUCHED IT.
WHAT THE HELL ARE YOU TALKING ABOUT? WHAT WAS IN HERE?
I KNOW YOUR ONE WEAKNESS.
A VOICE. TELLING ME...THEY MUST DIE. HE MUST.
STOP SCREAMING!
FLASH?!
"YOU KNOW MORE THAN ANYONE, OUR UNIVERSE WAS FOUNDED ON FREE WILL, JORDAN."
BUT THIS ONE... THE ANTI-MATTER UNIVERSE...THERE IS NO FREE WILL HERE. THERE IS ONLY THE OPPOSITE.
PING
I WAS CHANGED INTO THIS BECAUSE I HELD WHAT YOU WANT.
I AM FOREVER BOUND TO IT.

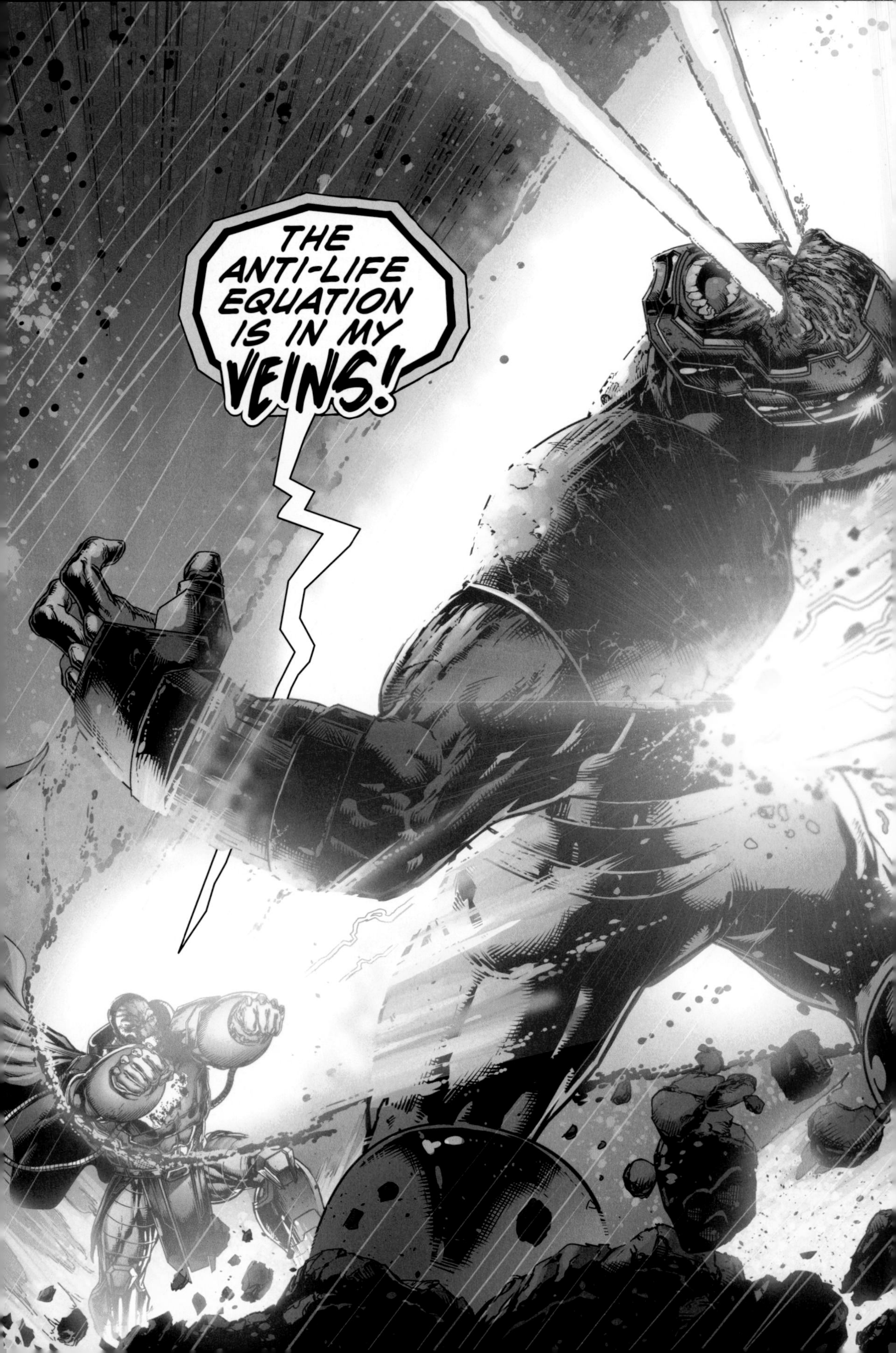
THE ANTI-LIFE EQUATION IS IN MY VEINS!

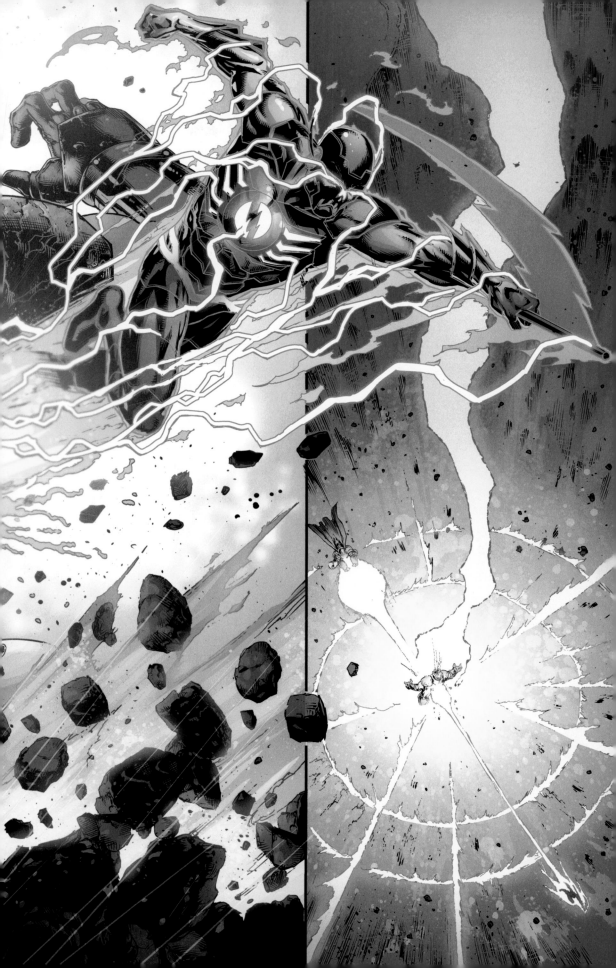

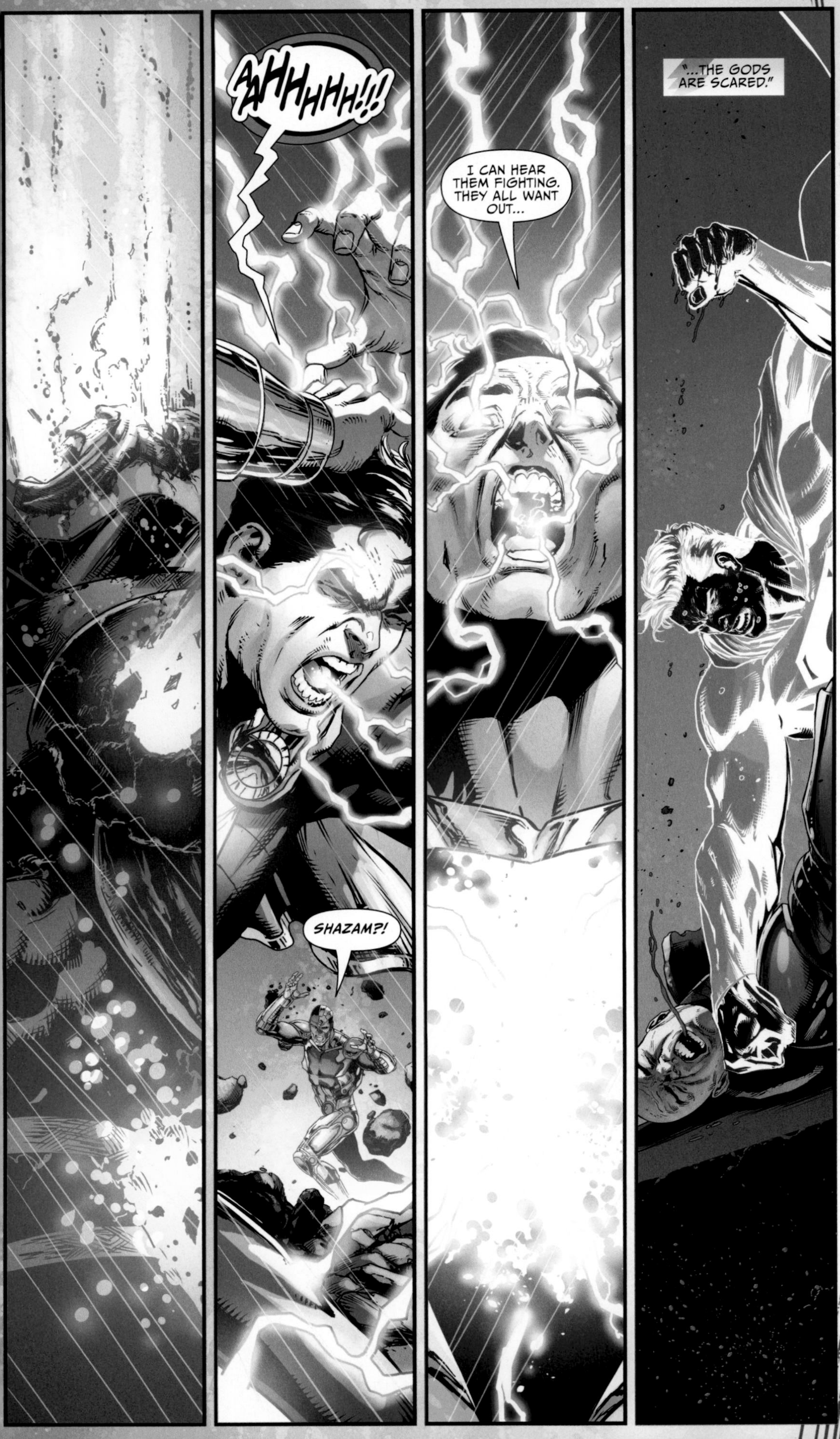
AAHHHHH!!!
SHAZAM?!
I CAN HEAR THEM FIGHTING. THEY ALL WANT OUT...
"...THE GODS ARE SCARED."

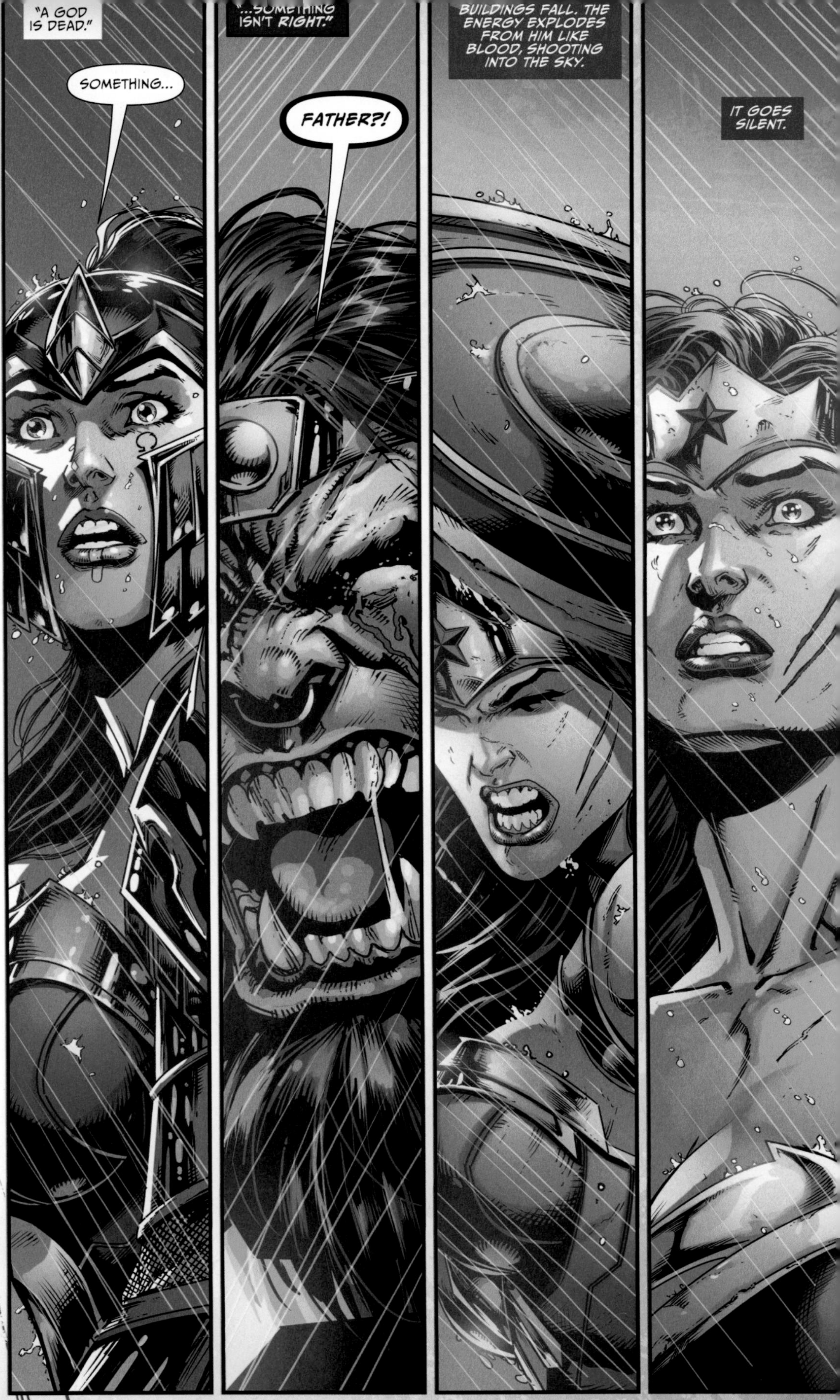
"A GOD IS DEAD."
SOMETHING...
"...SOMETHING ISN'T RIGHT."
FATHER?!
BUILDINGS FALL. THE ENERGY EXPLODES FROM HIM LIKE BLOOD, SHOOTING INTO THE SKY.
IT GOES SILENT.

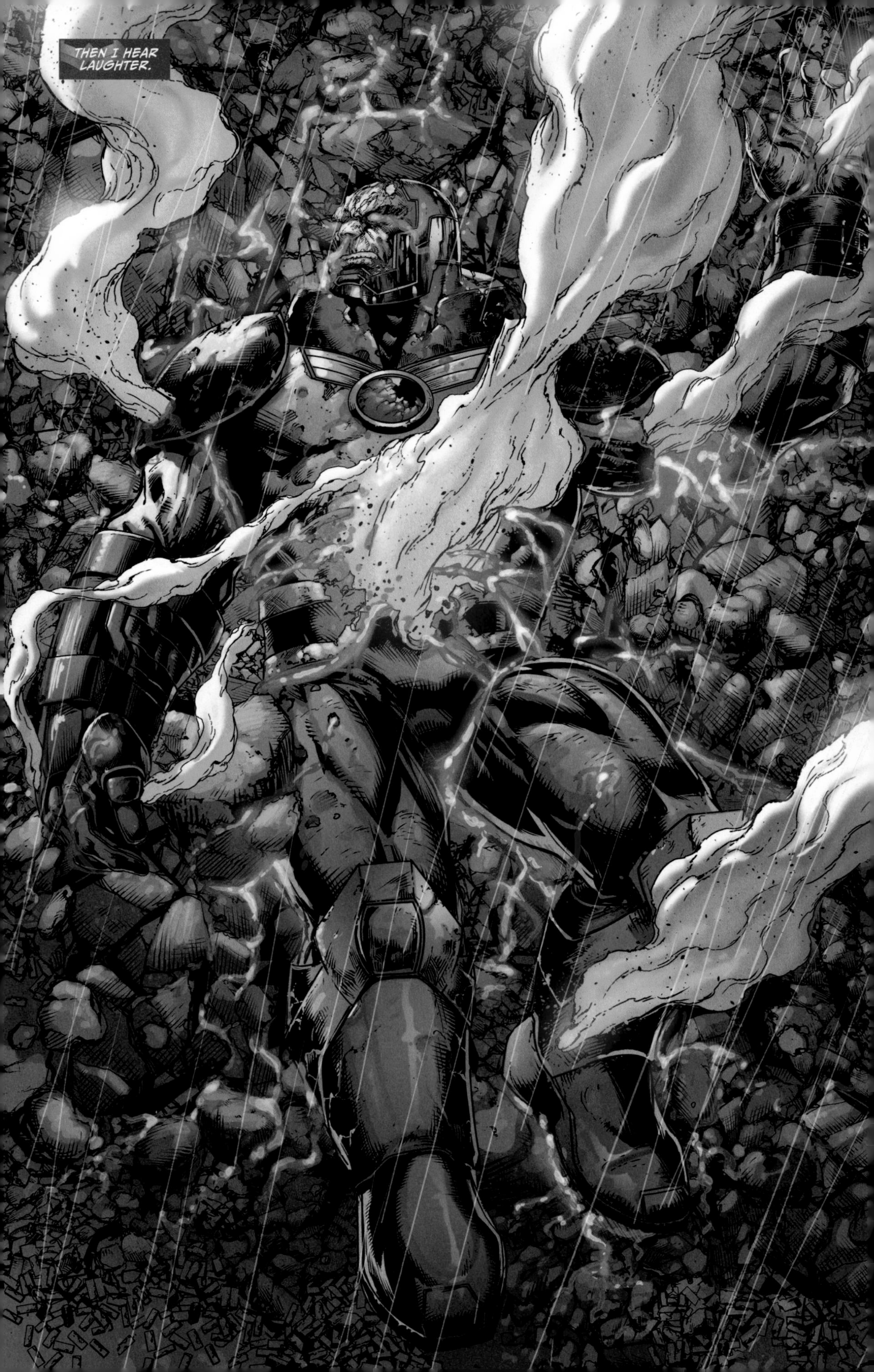
THEN I HEAR LAUGHTER.

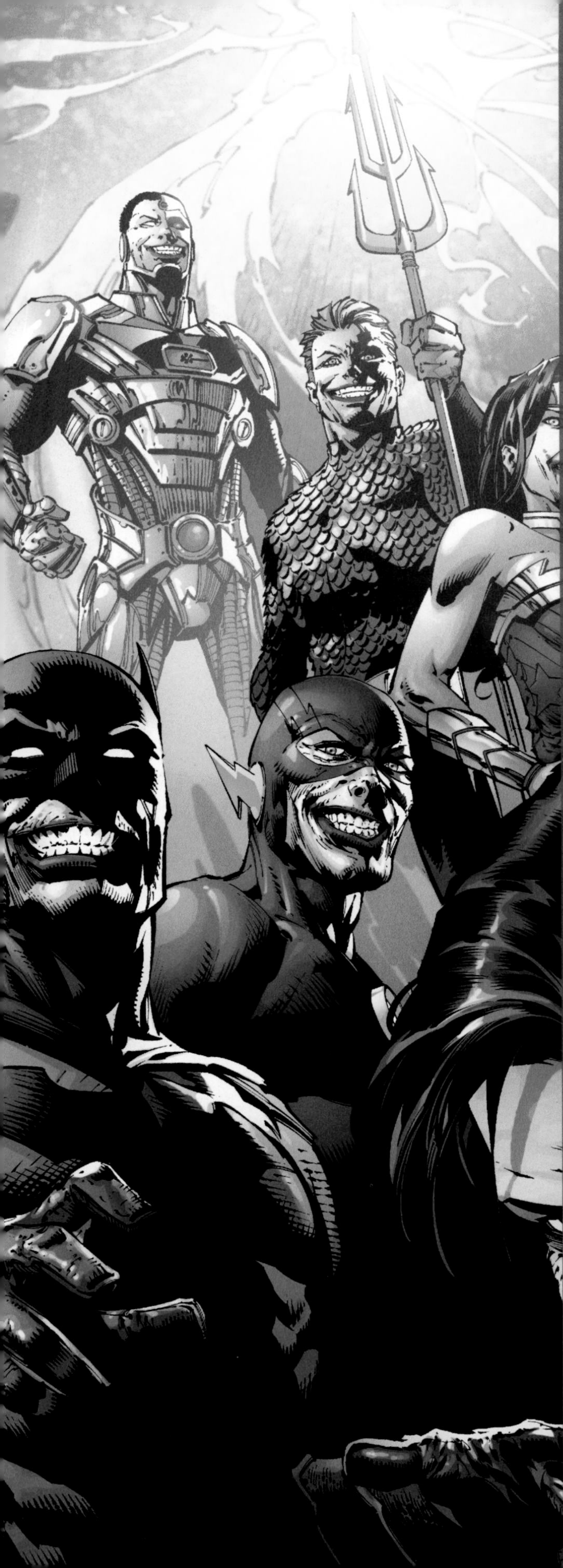

VARIANT COVER GALLERY

JUSTICE LEAGUE #40
VARIANT BY ALEX GARNER

JUSTICE LEAGUE #40
MAGIC MIKE MOVIE POSTER VARIANT BY EMANUELA LUPACCHINO

JUSTICE LEAGUE #41
JOKER 75TH ANNIVERSARY VARIANT BY DAVID FINCH, JONATHAN GLAPION AND BRAD ANDERSON

JUSTICE LEAGUE #41
COMIC-CON INTERNATIONAL SAN DIEGO VARIANT

JUSTICE LEAGUE #42
VARIANT BY JOE QUINONES

JUSTICE LEAGUE #42
TEEN TITANS GO! VARIANT BY DAN HIPP

JUSTICE LEAGUE #43
BOMBSHELLS VARIANT BY EMANUELA LUPACCHINO AND TOMEU MOREY

JUSTICE LEAGUE #44
GREEN LANTERN 75TH ANNIVERSARY VARIANT BY IVAN REIS, JOE PRADO AND ROD REIS

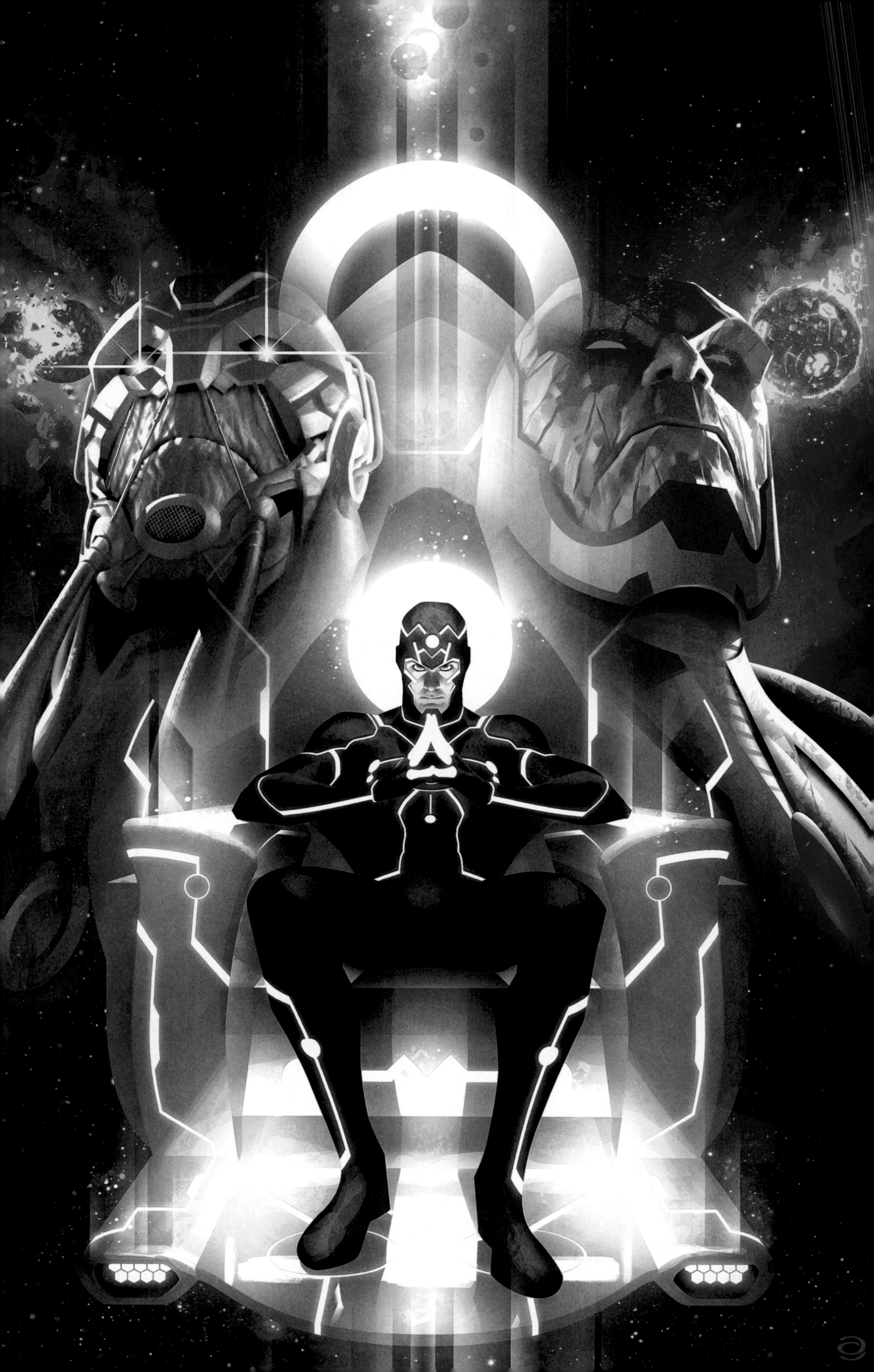

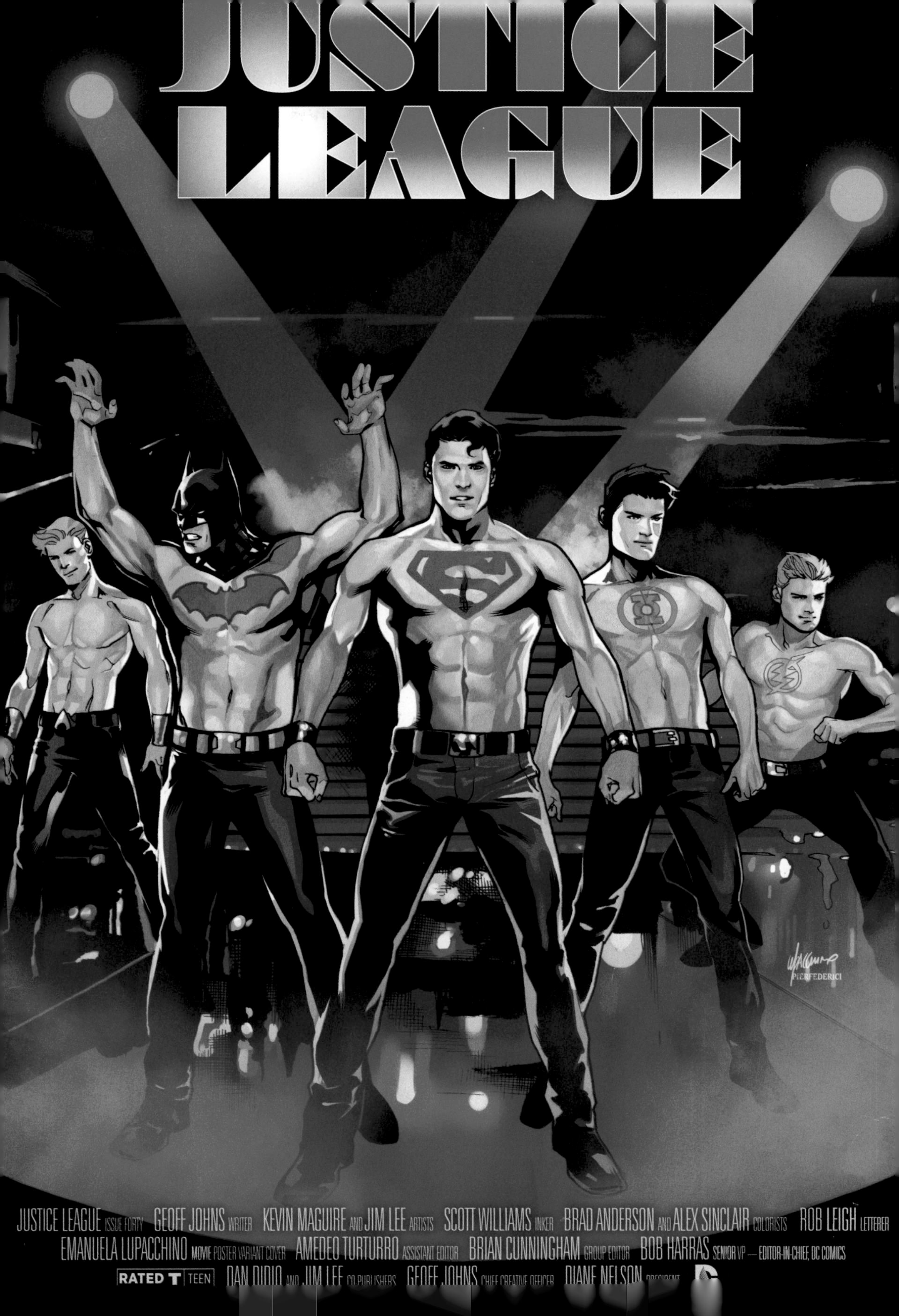
JUSTICE LEAGUE
PIERFEDERICI
JUSTICE LEAGUE ISSUE FORTY GEOFF JOHNS WRITER KEVIN MAGUIRE AND JIM LEE ARTISTS SCOTT WILLIAMS INKER BRAD ANDERSON AND ALEX SINCLAIR COLORISTS ROB LEIGH LETTERER
EMANUELA LUPACCHINO MOVIE POSTER VARIANT COVER AMEDEO TURTURRO ASSISTANT EDITOR BRIAN CUNNINGHAM GROUP EDITOR BOB HARRAS SENIOR VP — EDITOR-IN-CHIEF, DC COMICS
RATED T TEEN DAN DIDIO AND JIM LEE CO-PUBLISHERS GEOFF JOHNS CHIEF CREATIVE OFFICER DIANE NELSON PRESIDENT

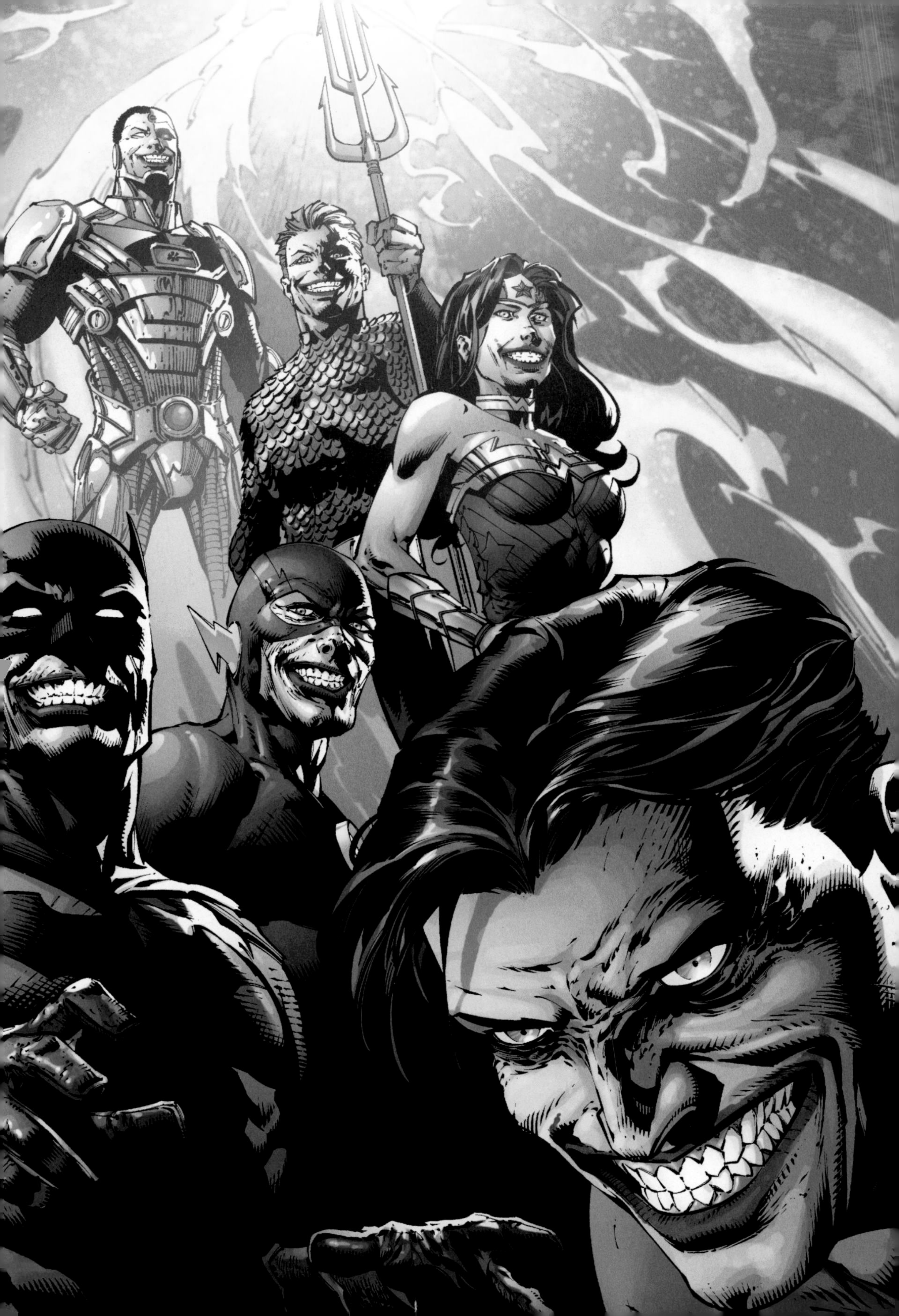

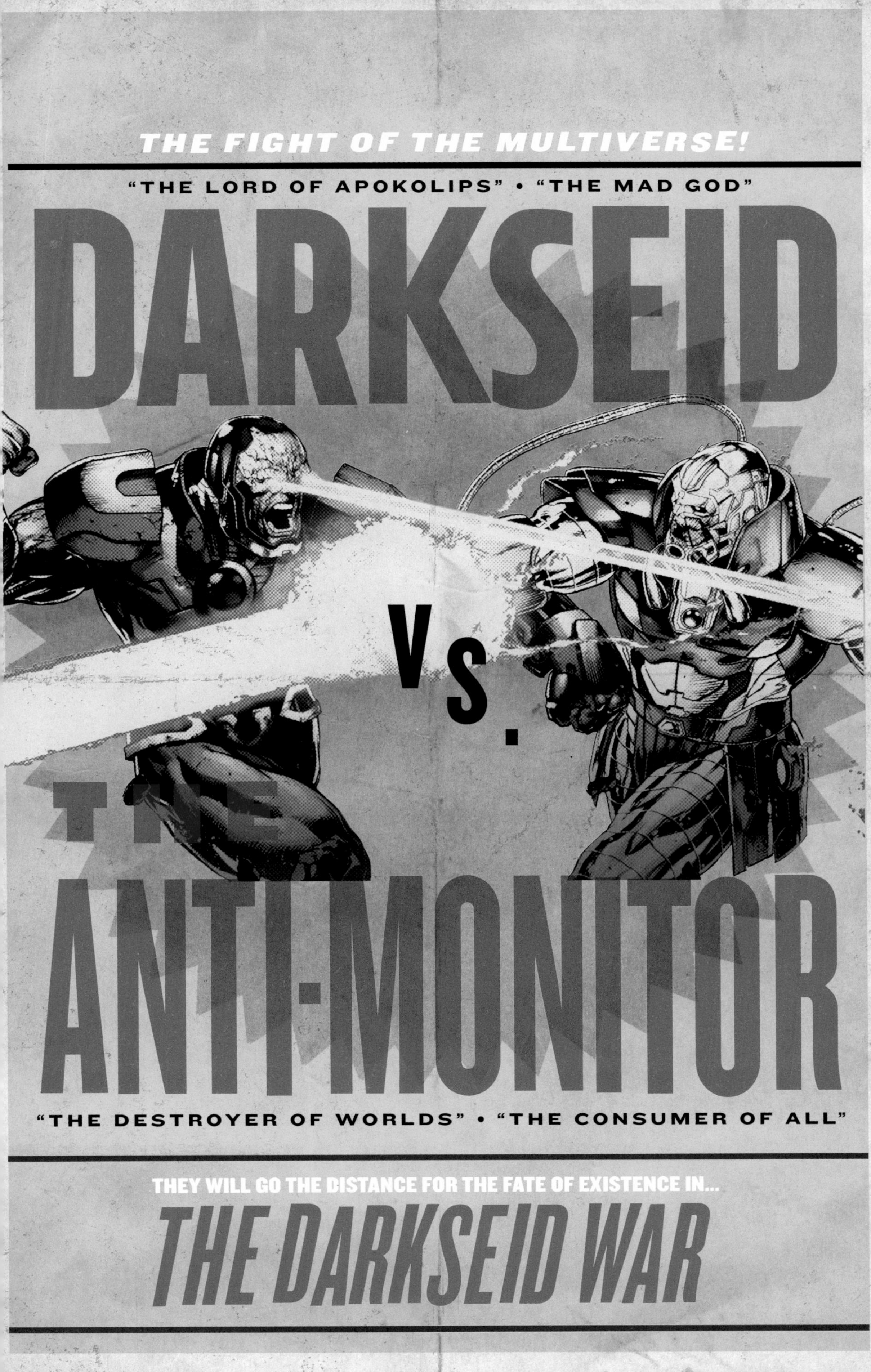
THE FIGHT OF THE MULTIVERSE!
"THE LORD OF APOKOLIPS" • "THE MAD GOD"
DARKSEID
VS.
THE
ANTI-MONITOR
"THE DESTROYER OF WORLDS" • "THE CONSUMER OF ALL"
THEY WILL GO THE DISTANCE FOR THE FATE OF EXISTENCE IN...
THE DARKSEID WAR

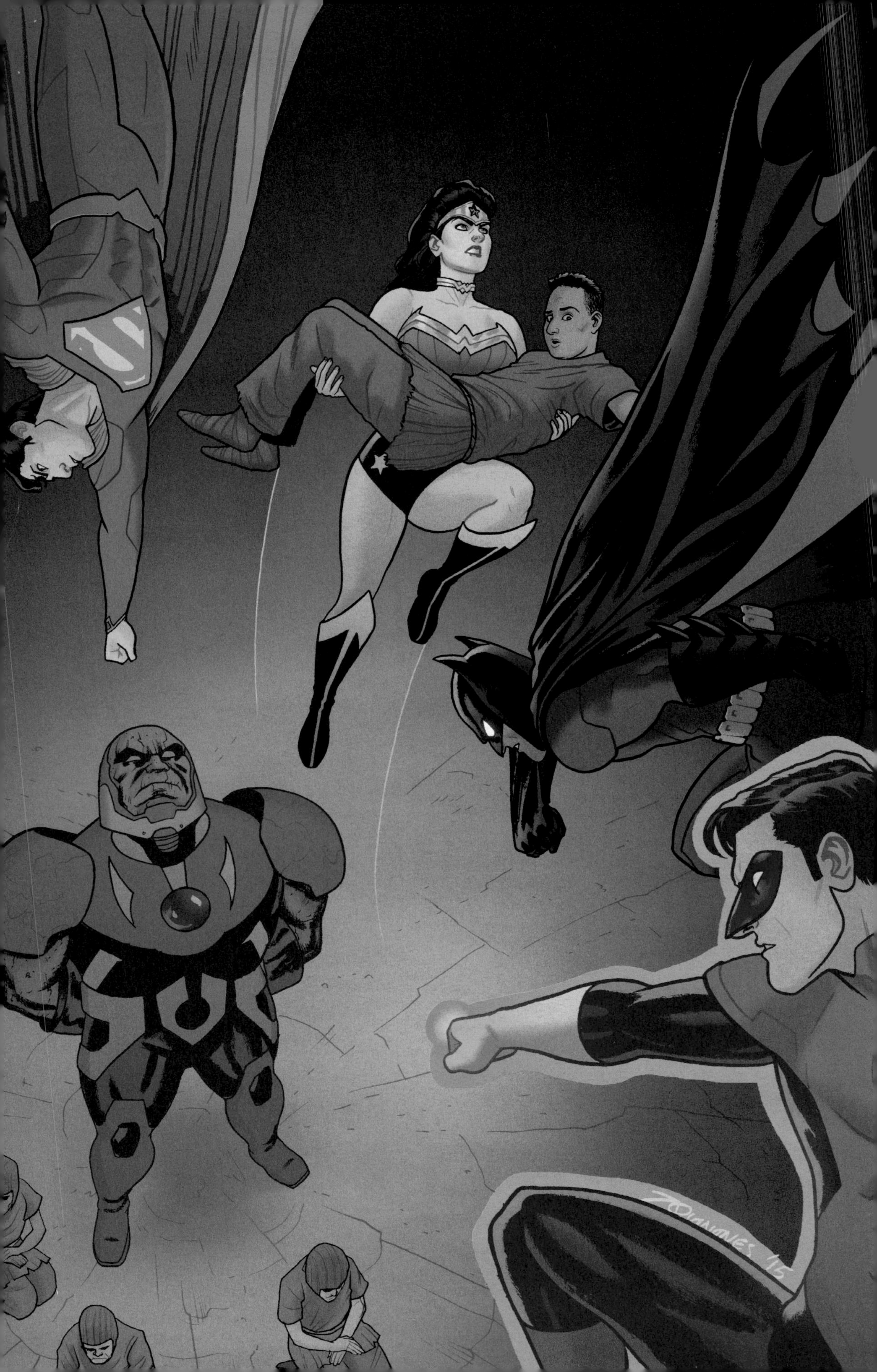

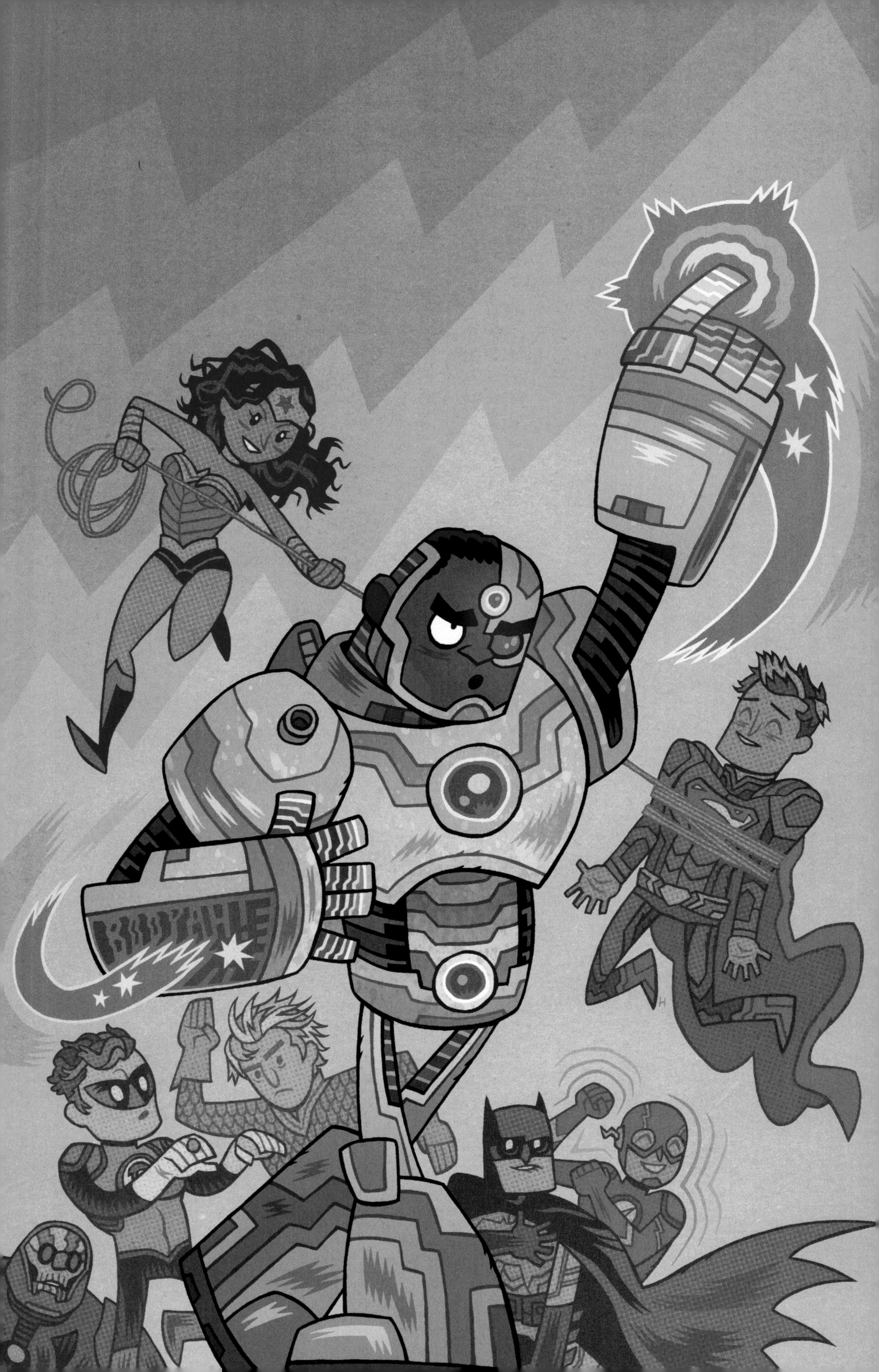

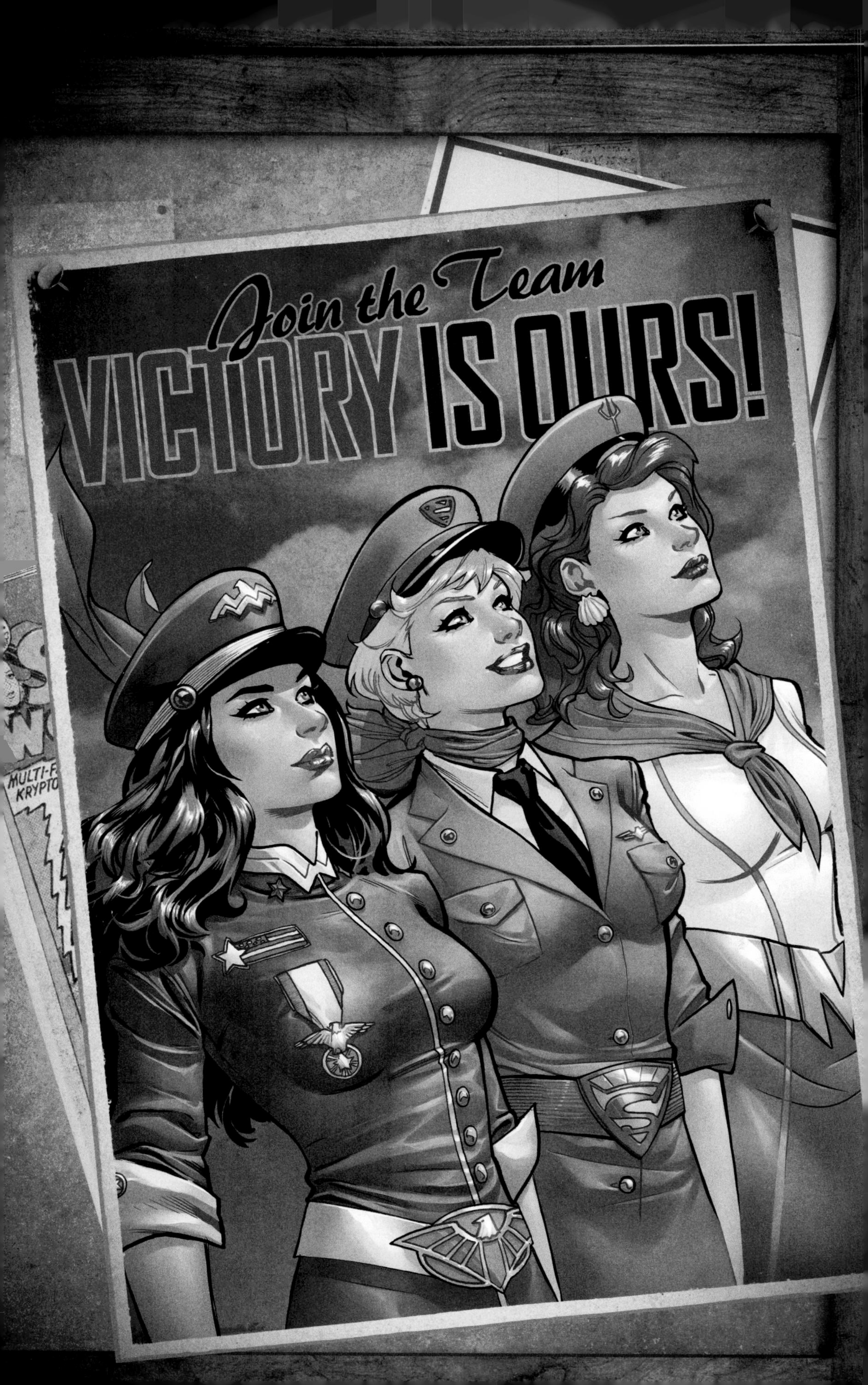
Join the Team
VICTORY IS OURS!

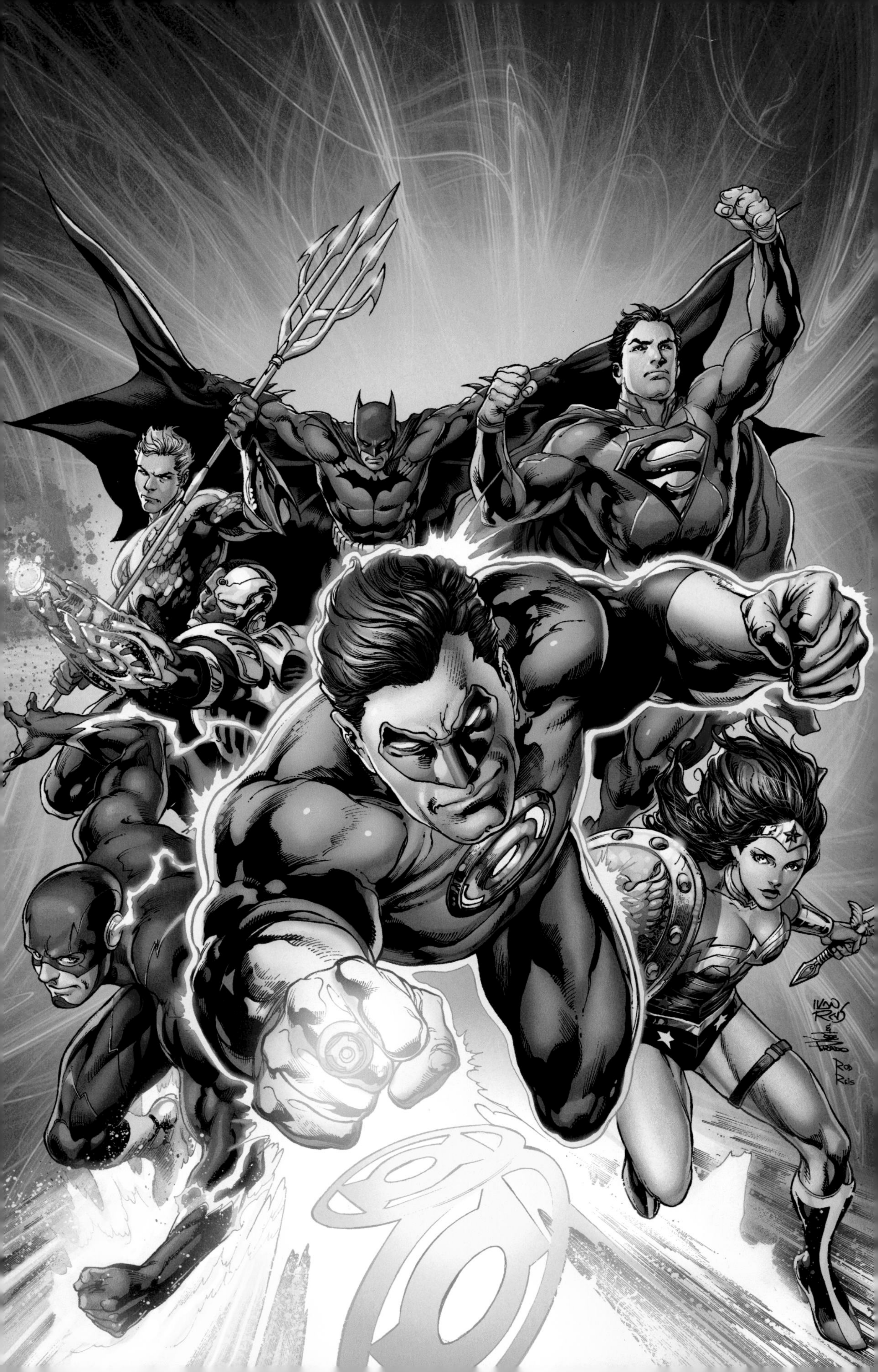

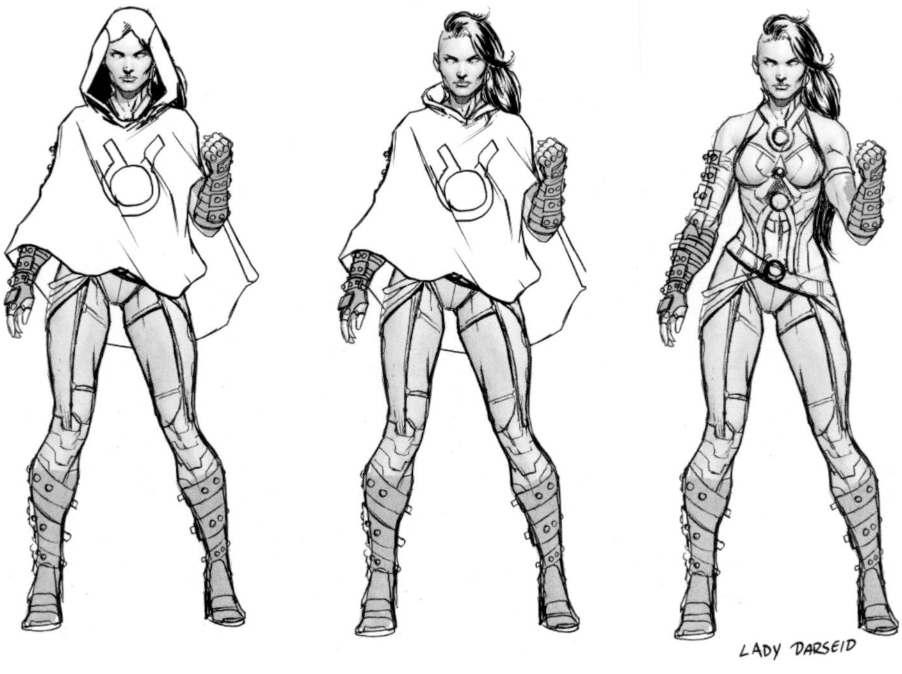
LADY DARSEID

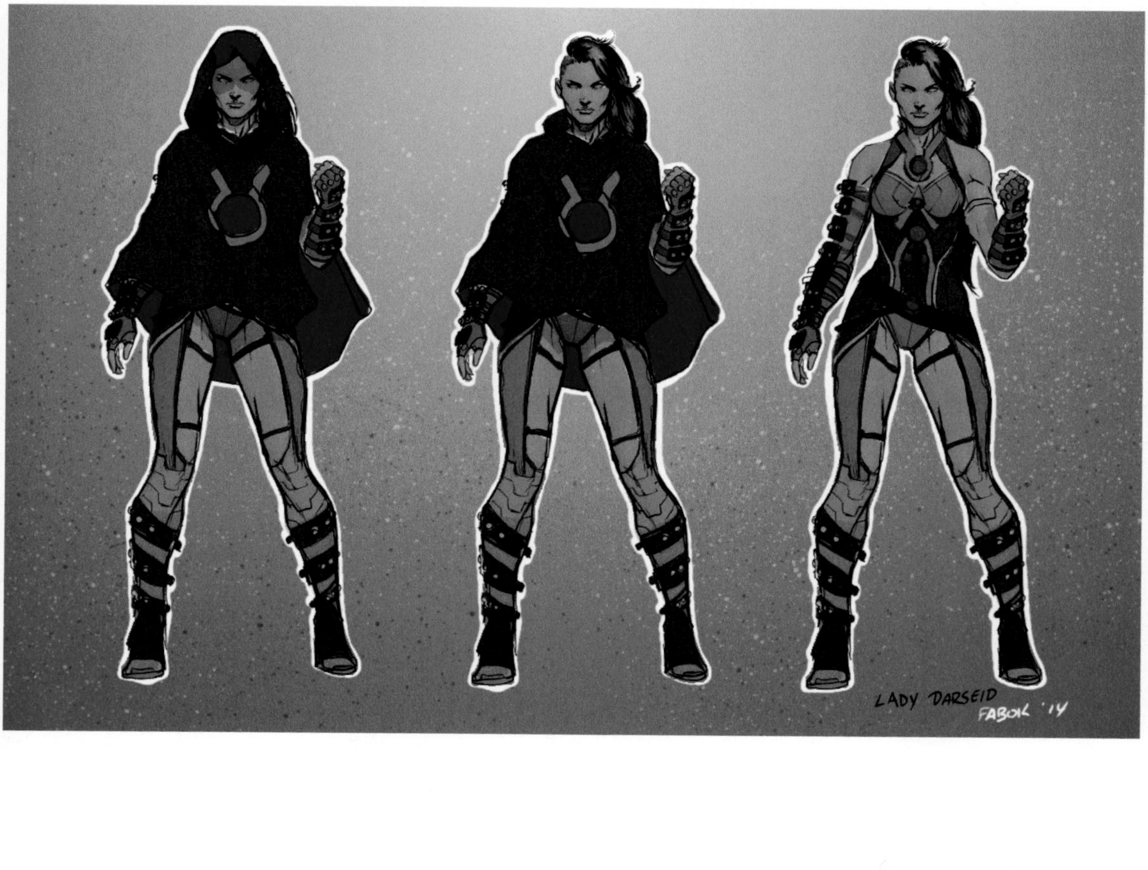
LADY DARSEID
FABOK '14

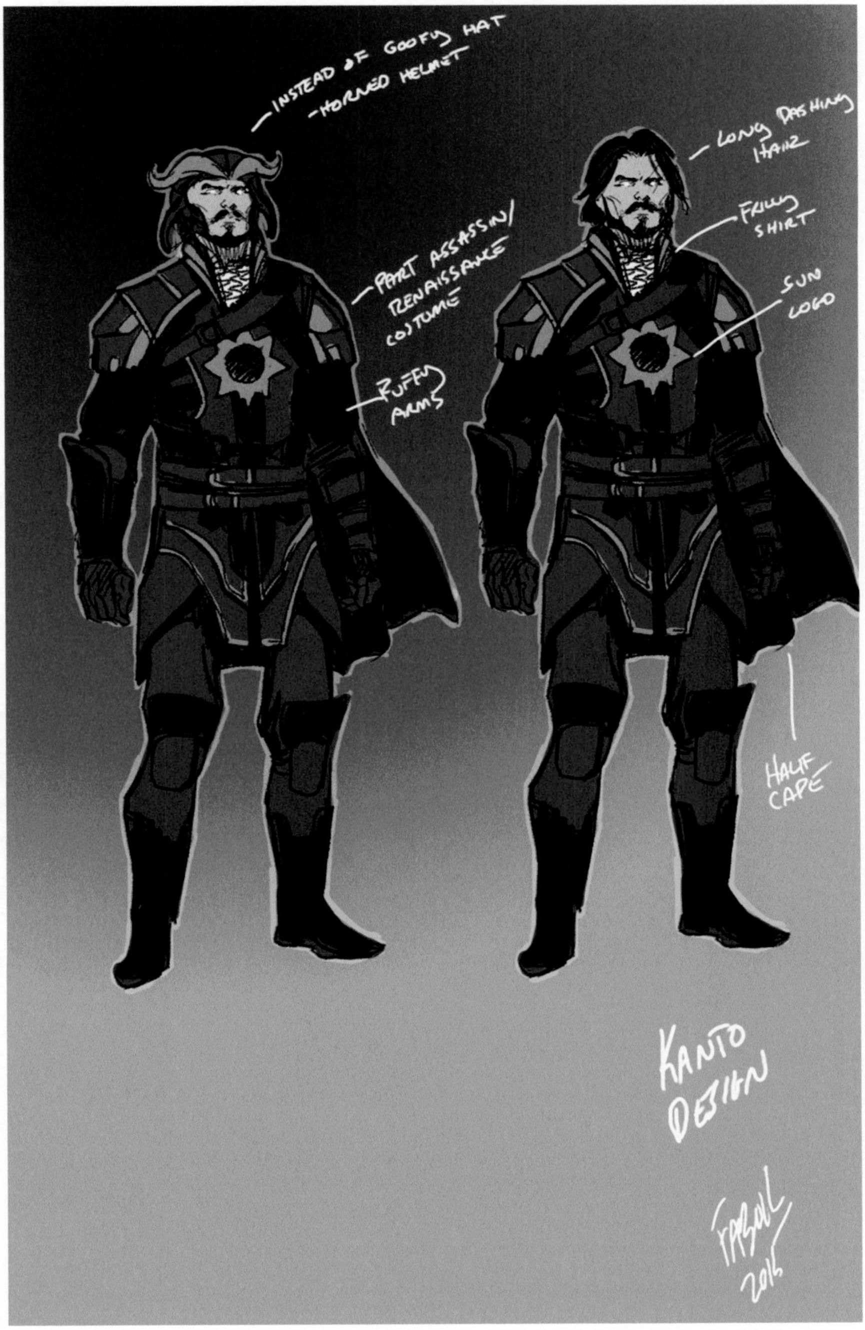

INSTEAD OF GOOFY HAT
HORNED HELMET
PART ASSASSIN/ RENAISSANCE COSTUME
RUFFY ARMS
LONG DASHING HAIR
FRILLY SHIRT
SUN LOGO
HALF CAPE
KANTO DESIGN
2016

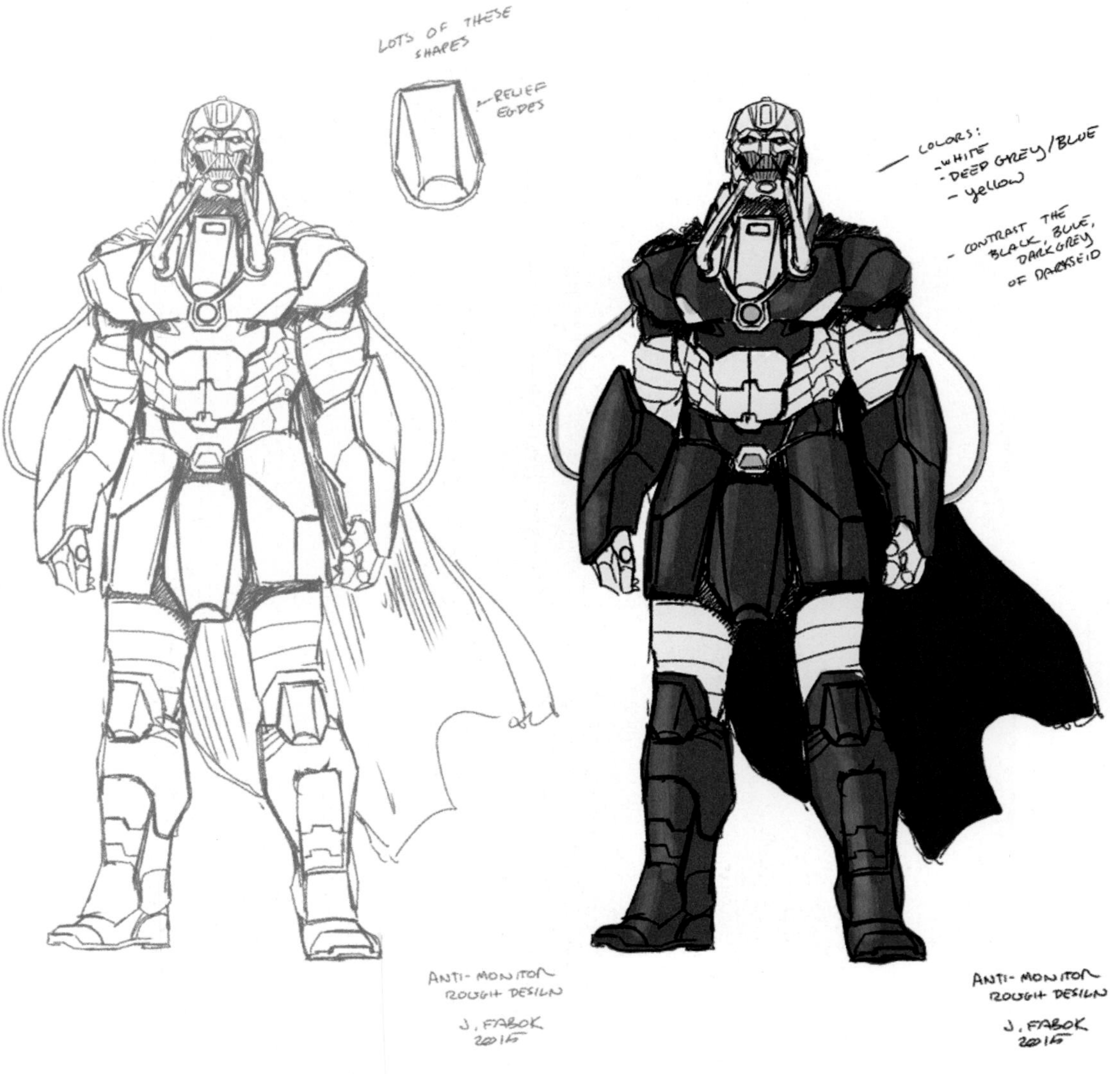
LOTS OF THESE SHAPES
RELIEF EDGES
COLORS:
- WHITE
- DEEP GREY/BLUE
- yellow
- CONTRAST THE BLACK, BLUE, DARKGREY OF DARKSEID
ANTI-MONITOR ROUGH DESIGN
J. FABOK 2015
ANTI-MONITOR ROUGH DESIGN
J. FABOK 2015

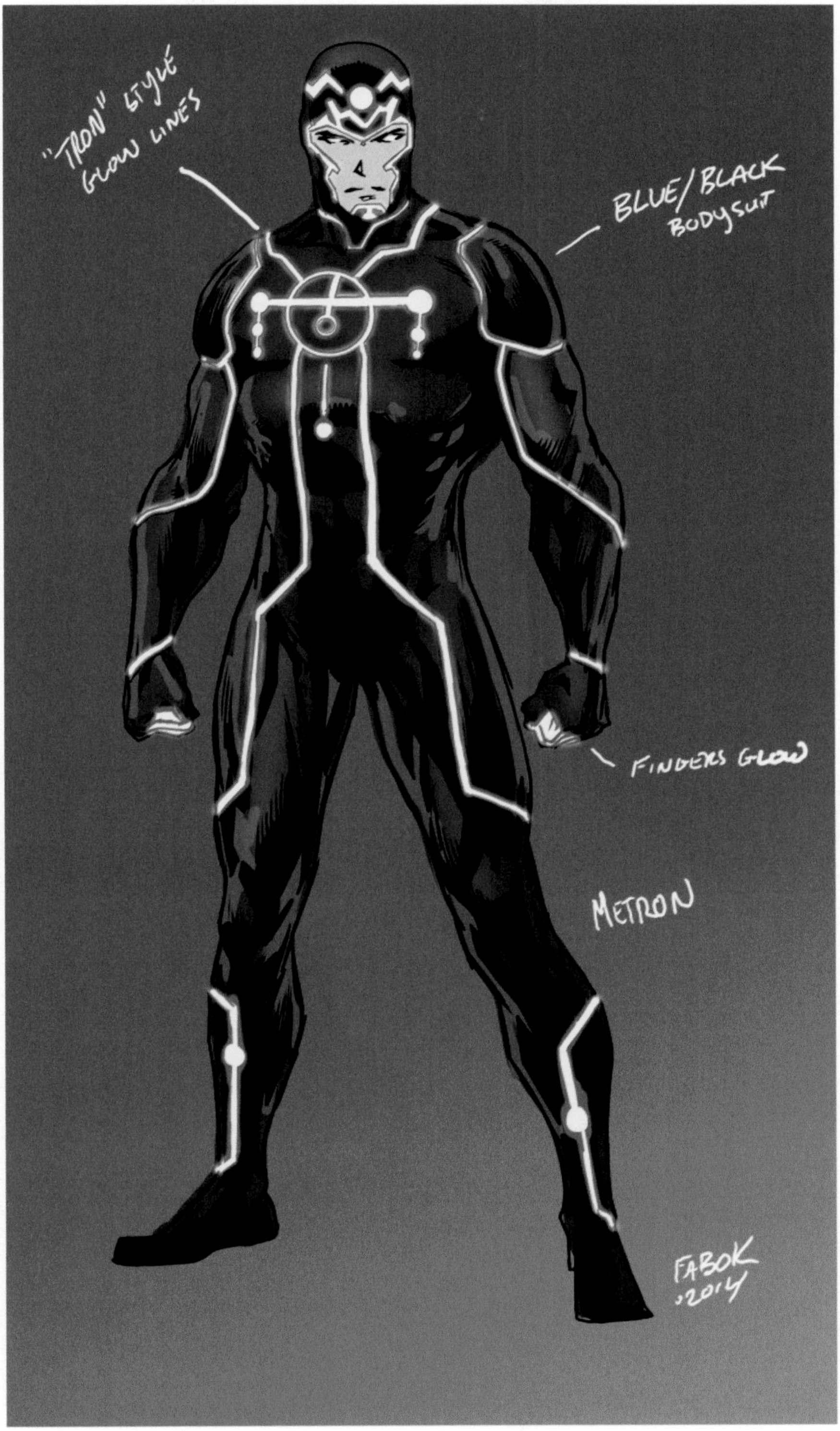
"TRON" STYLE
GLOW LINES
BLUE/BLACK
BODYSUIT
FINGERS GLOW
METRON
FABOK
2014

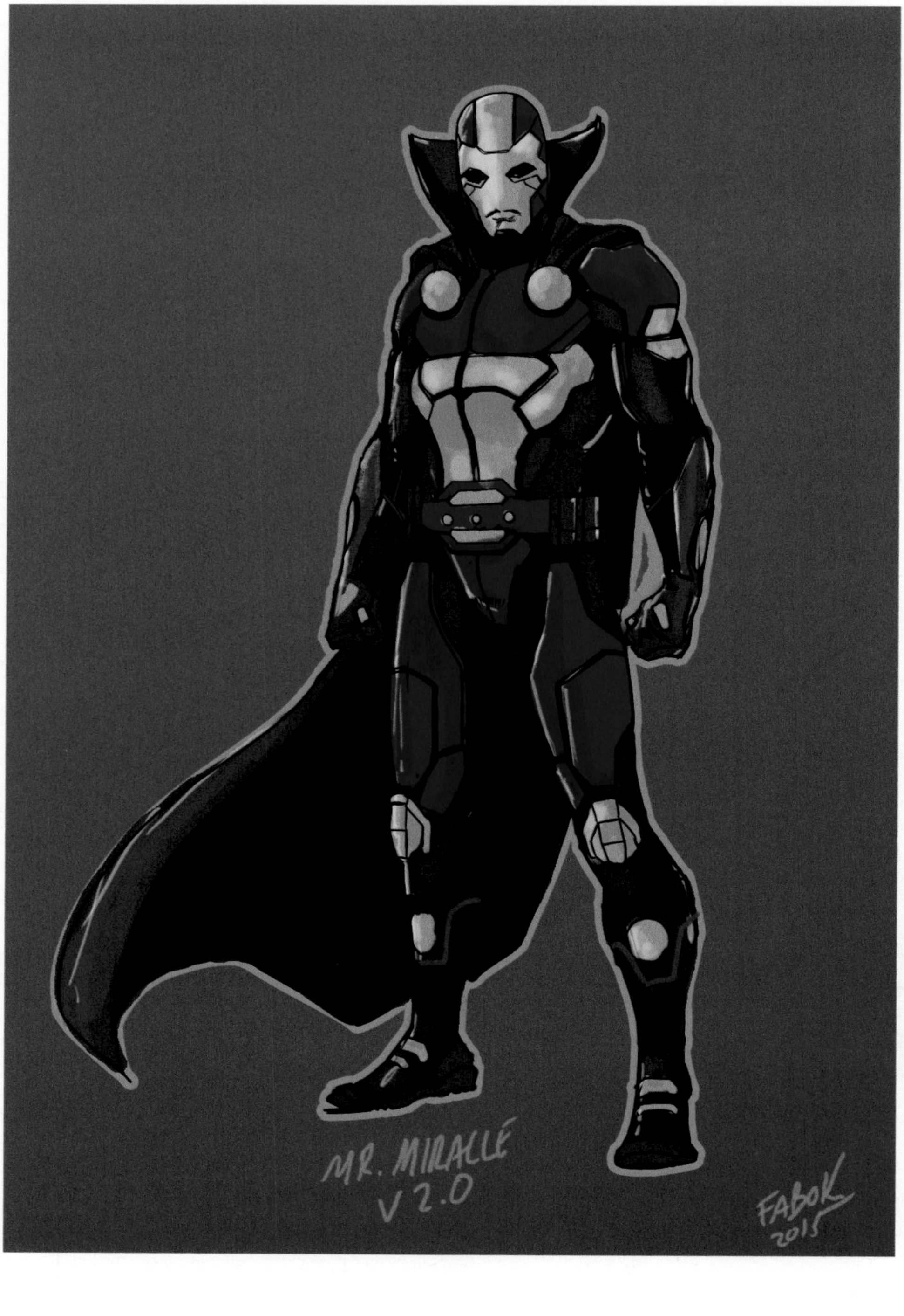
MR. MIRACLE
V 2.0
FABOK
2015

Rough panel layout for the death of Darkseid by Jim Lee, which became the basis for Jason Fabok's spread.

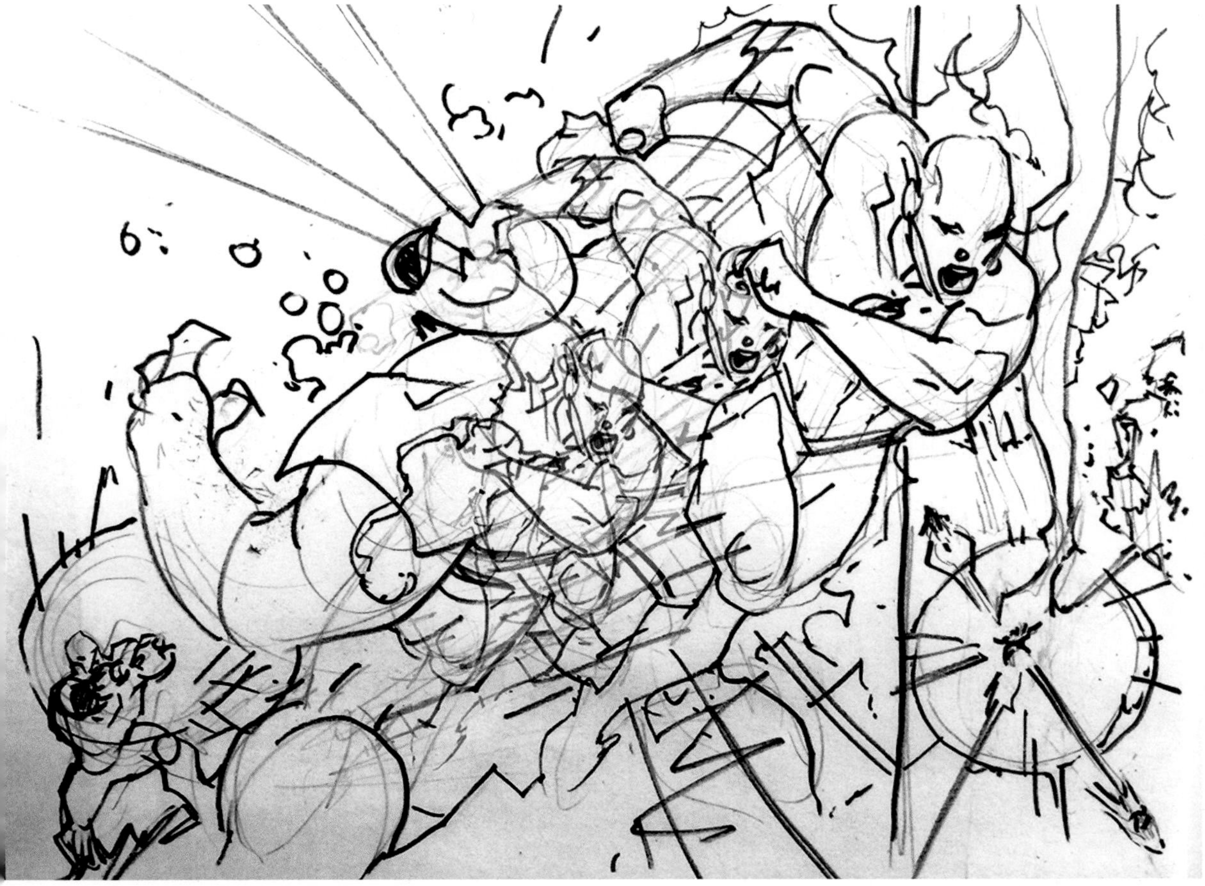

Issue #44 Pages 18-19

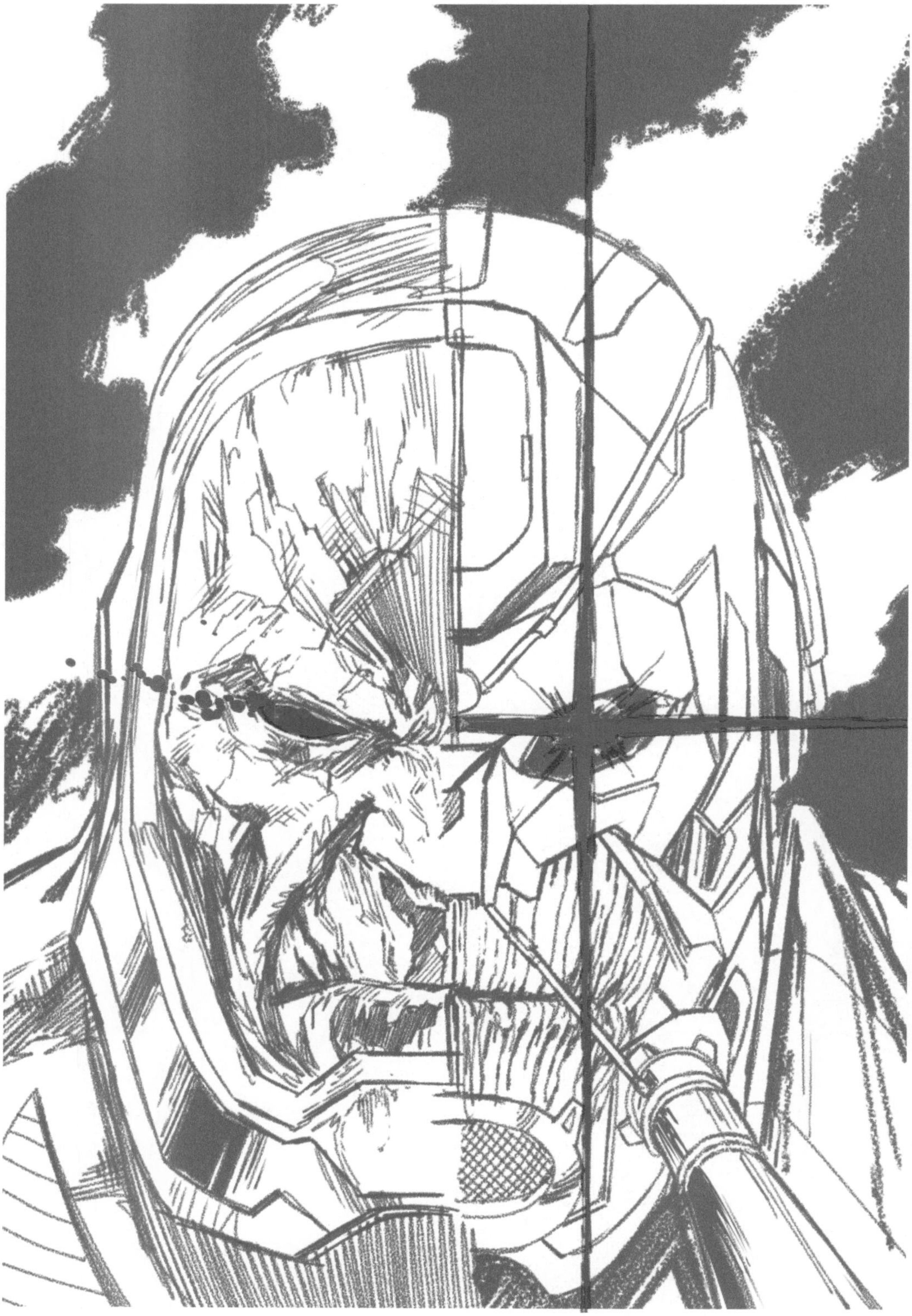

Issue #40 cover sketch

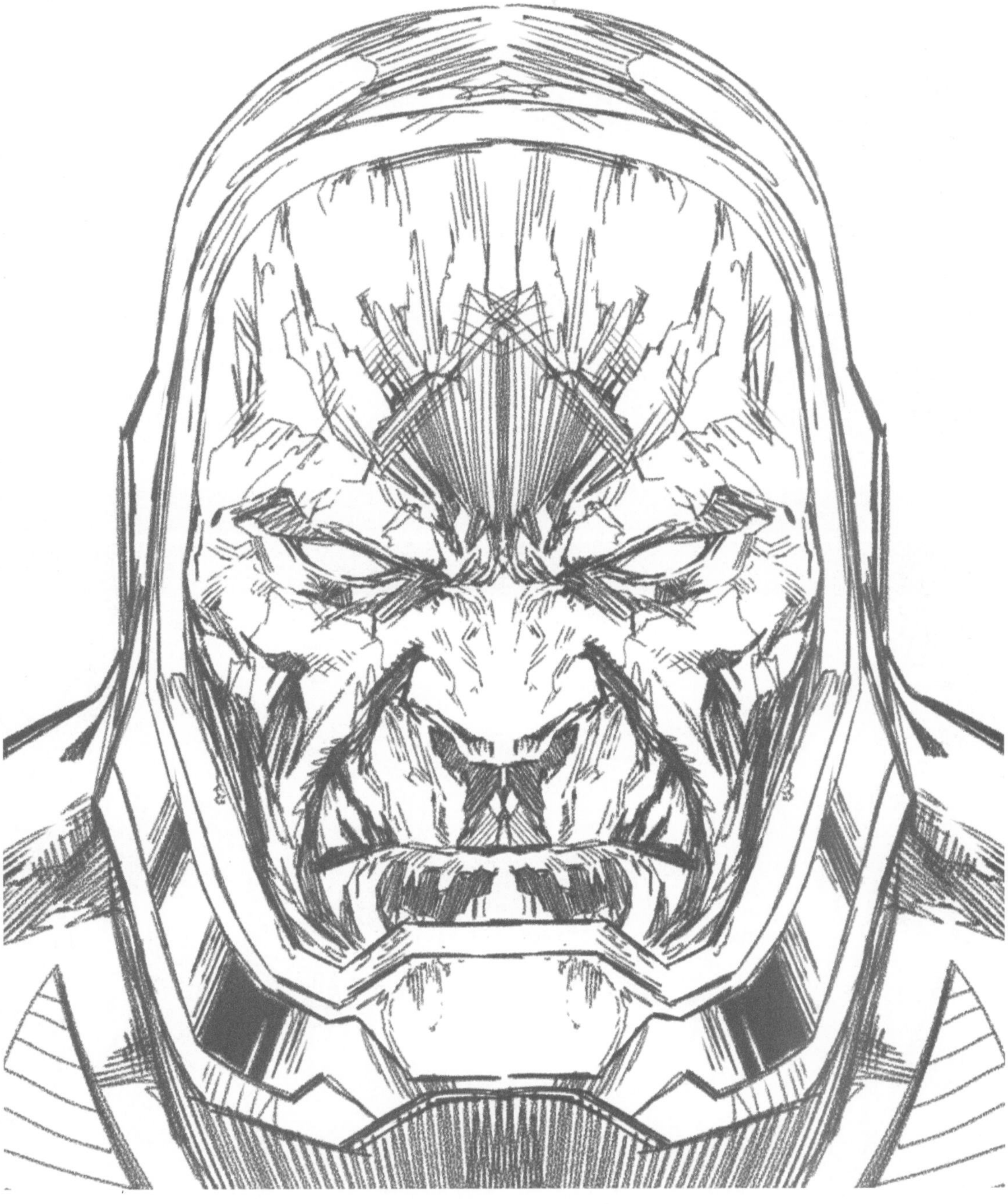

Issue #40 cover sketch

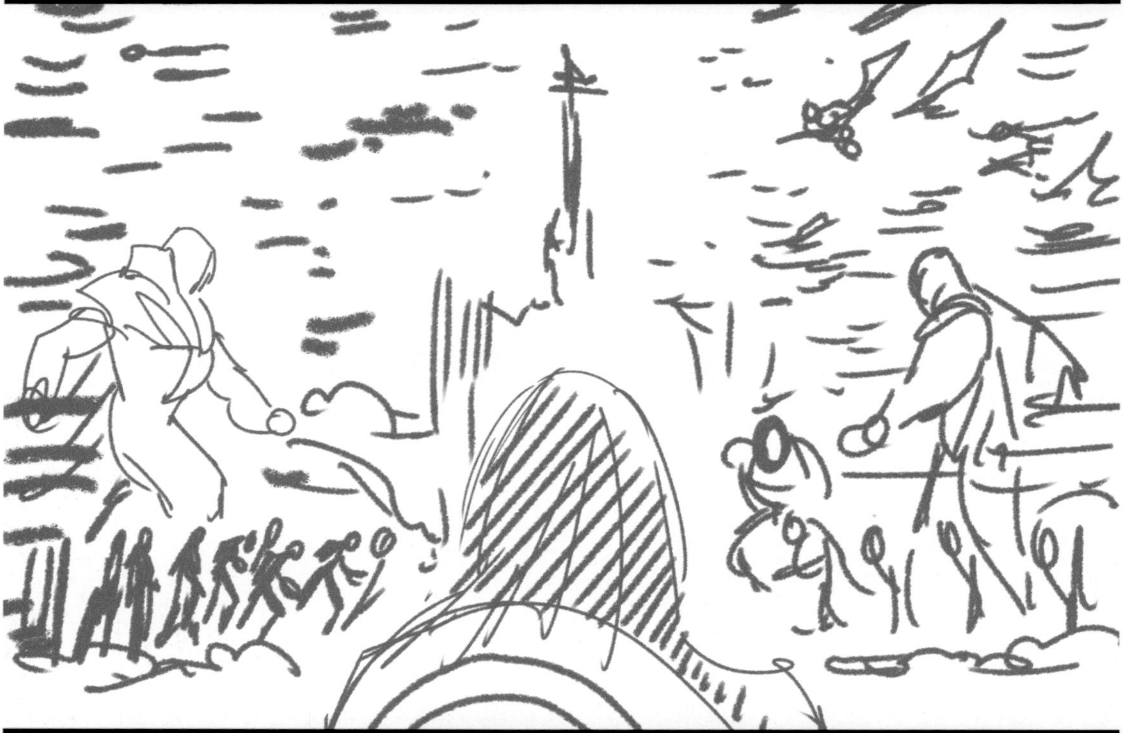

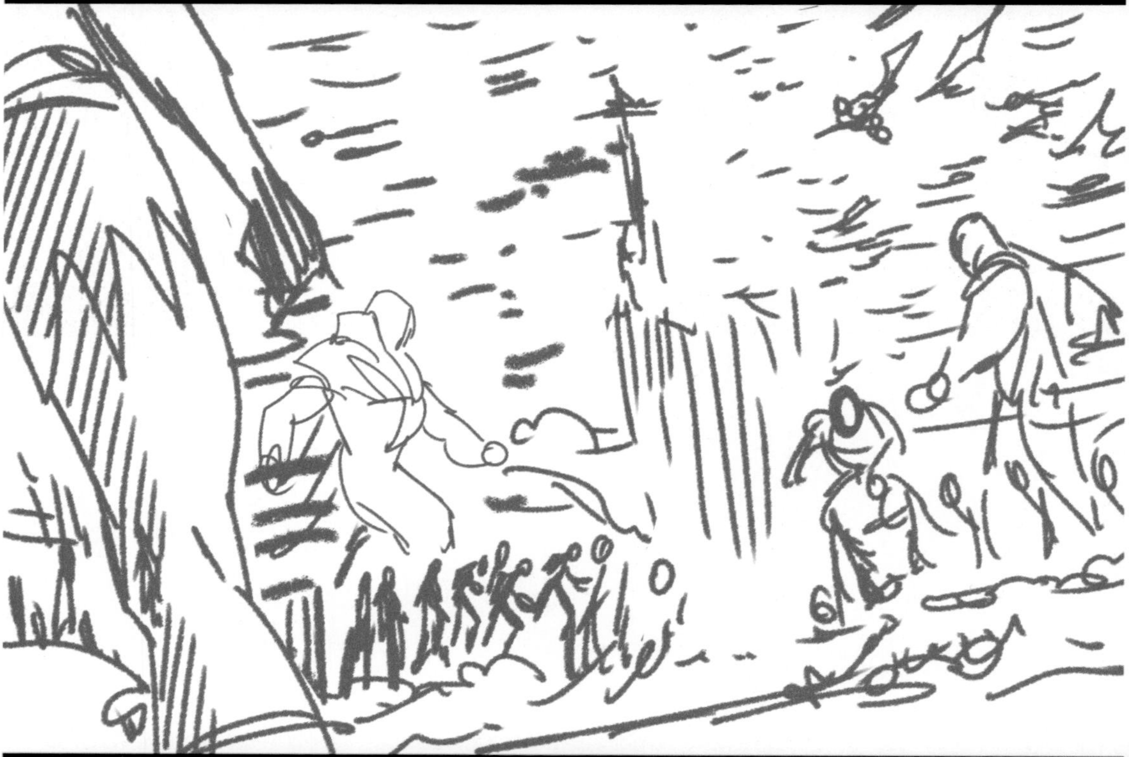

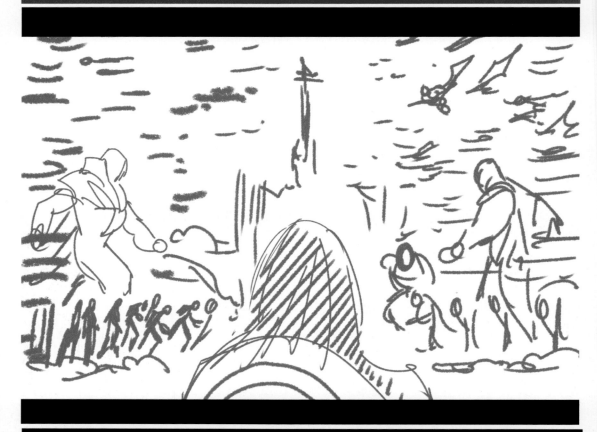

Alternate layouts for issue #43 pages 20-21

STAB!
LOOKS THROUGH TREES

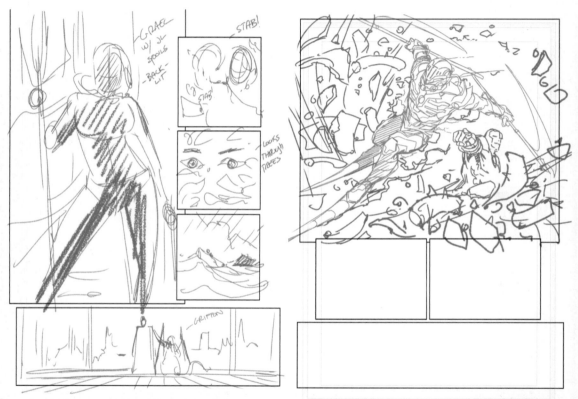

Sketch for page 8 of DC SNEAK PEEK: JUSTICE LEAGUE #1

Issue #44 page 11 sketch

DC COMICS™

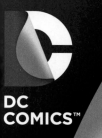

"Writer Geoff Johns and artist Jim Lee toss you–and their heroes–into the action from the very start and don't put on the brakes. DC's über-creative team craft an inviting world for those who are trying out a comic for the first time. Lee's art is stunning."—USA TODAY

"A fun ride."—IGN

START AT THE BEGINNING!

JUSTICE LEAGUE VOLUME 1: ORIGIN

GEOFF JOHNS and JIM LEE

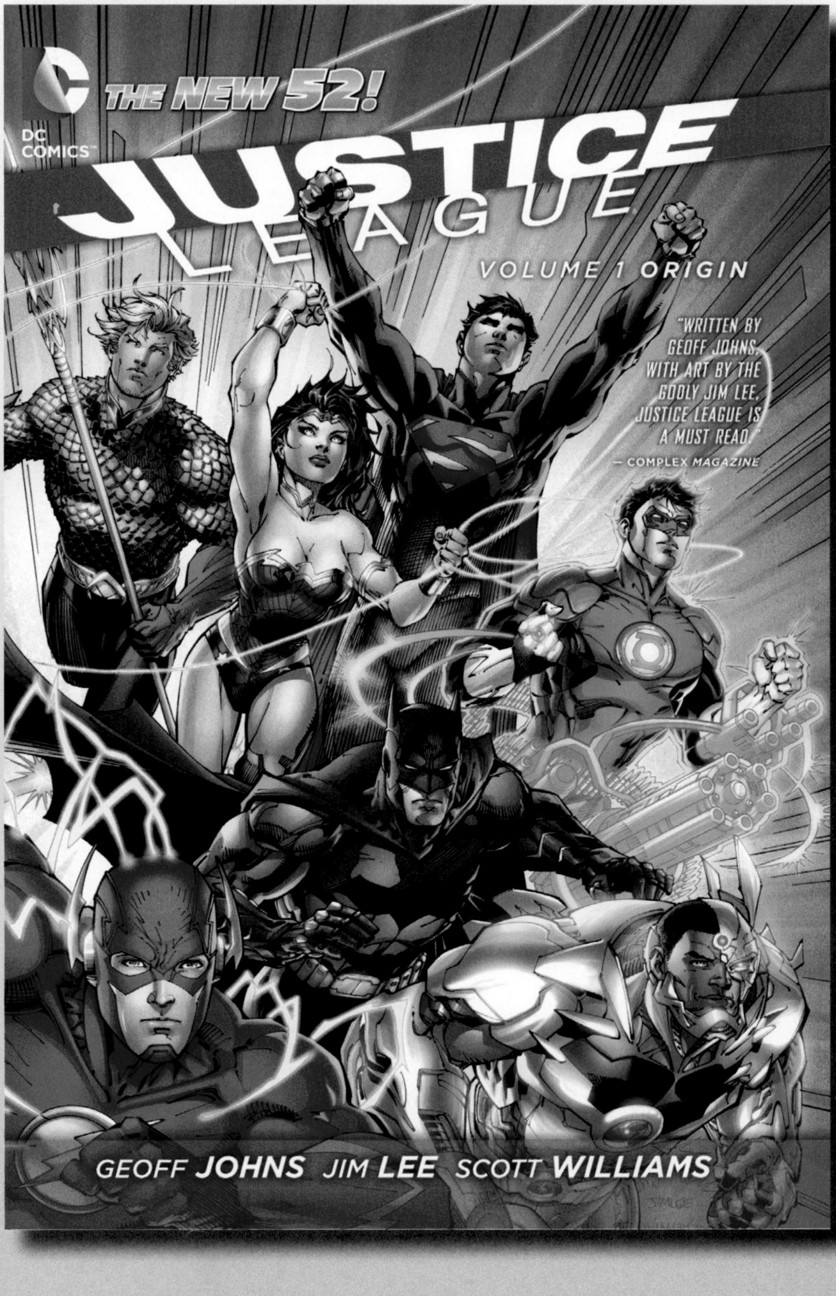
THE NEW 52!
DC COMICS™
JUSTICE LEAGUE
VOLUME 1 ORIGIN
"WRITTEN BY GEOFF JOHNS, WITH ART BY THE GODLY JIM LEE, JUSTICE LEAGUE IS A MUST READ."
— COMPLEX MAGAZINE
GEOFF JOHNS JIM LEE SCOTT WILLIAMS

JUSTICE LEAGUE VOL. 2: THE VILLAIN'S JOURNEY

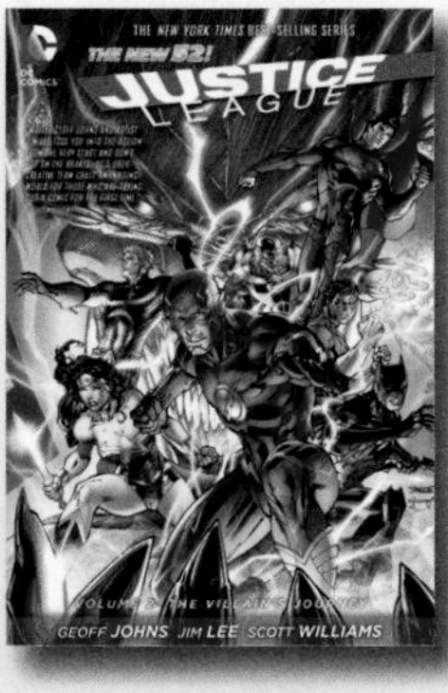
THE NEW 52!
JUSTICE LEAGUE
GEOFF JOHNS JIM LEE SCOTT WILLIAMS

JUSTICE LEAGUE VOL. 3: THRONE OF ATLANTIS

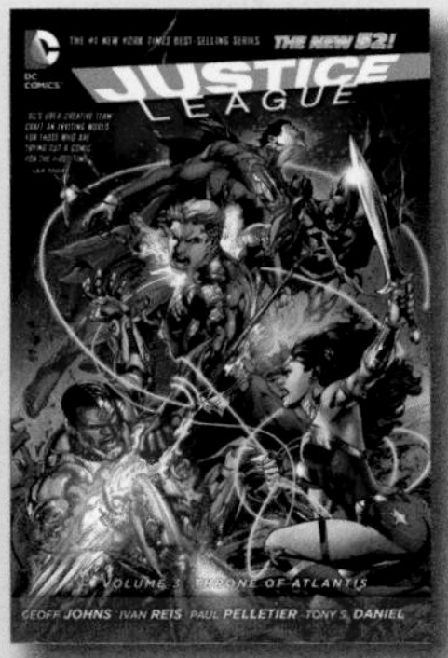
THE NEW 52!
JUSTICE LEAGUE
GEOFF JOHNS IVAN REIS PAUL PELLETIER TONY S. DANIEL

JUSTICE LEAGUE OF AMERICA VOL. 1: WORLD'S MOST DANGEROUS

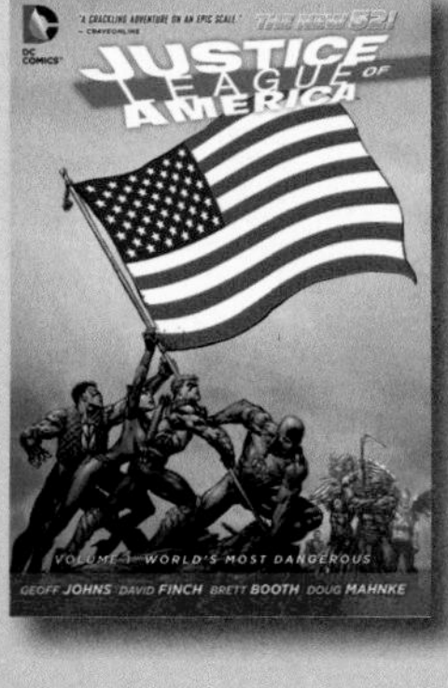
THE NEW 52!
JUSTICE LEAGUE of AMERICA
VOLUME 1 WORLD'S MOST DANGEROUS
GEOFF JOHNS DAVID FINCH BRETT BOOTH DOUG MAHNKE

START AT THE BEGINNING!

WONDER WOMAN VOLUME 1: BLOOD

WONDER WOMAN VOL. 2: GUTS

by BRIAN AZZARELLO and CLIFF CHIANG

WONDER WOMAN VOL. 3: IRON

by BRIAN AZZARELLO and CLIFF CHIANG

SUPERGIRL VOL. 1: LAST DAUGHTER OF KRYPTON

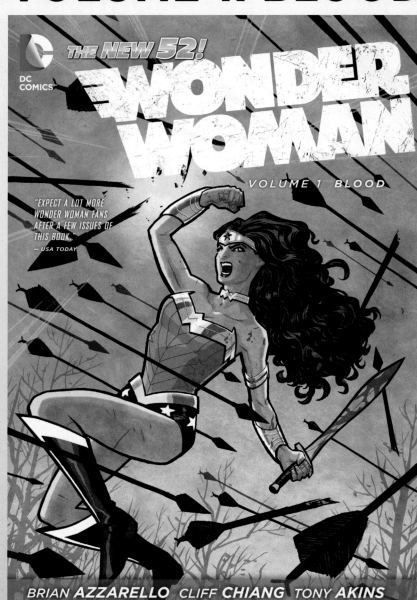